WHAT'S IT WORTH?

An Antiques Collectables **Guide**

Published by
Merricks Media Ltd.,
Units 3-4, Riverside Court,
Lower Bristol Road
Bath BA2 3DZ
www.merricksmedia.co.uk

ALL ENQUIRIES
info@merricksmedia.co.uk
Tel: +44 (0)1225 786800
Fax: +44 (0)1225 786801
www.antiques-collectables.co.uk

MANAGING DIRECTOR
Lisa Doerr
lisa.doerr@merricksmedia.co.uk

GROUP EDITOR
Ali Stewart
ali.stewart@merricksmedia.co.uk

EDITORIAL
Tel: 01225 786818
Managing Editor: Fiona Shoop
Fiona.shoop@merricksmedia.co.uk
Production Editor: Scott Bradbury
Art Editor: Sally Meddings
Art Director: Jon Billington

RESEARCHERS:
Andy Dyer, Louise McCarron,
Kate Ennis, Adam Waring

ADVERTISING
01225 786810
Sales Director: Nick Hemburrow
General Sale Manager: Keith Burnell
Project advertising executive: Peter Sahota
advertising@merricksmedia.co.uk

PRODUCTION
Advert Designer: Becky Hamblin
artwork@merricksmedia.co.uk

SYNDICATION AND LICENSING
Ali Stewart
ali.stewart@merricksmedia.co.uk
BACKSTAMPS
George Perrott's *Pottery and Marks:*
European, Oriental and USA
(Gemini Publications)
COVER PICTURE
David Dickinson by Colin Poole
tel: 020 8347 4348

Merricks Media Ltd

© 2004 Merricks Media Ltd. Printed in
the UK by Polestar. We cannot accept
responsibility for misprints.
Reproduction is prohibited unless
written permission is obtained. Great
care is taken with photographs and
transparencies but we cannot be held responsible for loss or
damage. Unsolicited material cannot be returned. This
version of What's It Worth: An Antiques and Collectables
Guide is exclusive to W.H. Smith.

WELCOME to our first ever *What's It Worth: An Antiques and Collectables Guide*. It's been a fascinating journey through six years of *Antiques and Collectables* magazine and a chance to reflect on the differing trends and prices in that era. As the magazine's latest editor, it's shown me just how much thought has gone behind each issue as we try to predict the next big thing. My top tip? The Aesthetic Movement is in for a huge revival with prices set to escalate. If you don't know what it is yet, why not read the feature on p18? In our Style Series, we've highlighted five different styles from the Gothic Revival to Art Deco with useful information on top names and must-buy goods.

The antiques trade is evolving and we're trying to predict market trends to let you know what's hot and what's not which is what makes this guide so interesting. We give you the current market price but also show you what's changed since the topic was first discussed in the magazine. Mid to low-end furniture prices have been struggling for the last couple of years while modern design has rocketed. Brown goods, as they are known, have given way to brightly coloured plastic and that's why it's a great time to buy wooden furniture – because it's too cheap to resist and so much more exciting than some modern furniture.

Our price guide follows the features and it's handily divided into sections and sub-sections. All of the sub-sections have their own introduction and every page has a factbox providing even more information. You're sure to discover something you didn't know before. I know I did and I've been a dealer for over twenty years, as well as an antiques journalist for over a decade. One thing I've learned in this business is that you never stop learning and that's why we never get bored of the antiques trade. So, whether you're a collector, dealer or just love David Dickinson, you're bound to find something that appeals.

I hope that you enjoy our first ever guide and enjoy reading the features. Don't forget, if you enjoyed this, why not read our magazine, *Antiques and Collectables* which is full of interesting articles every month,

Fiona Shoop

Author of *What's It Worth: An Antiques and Collectables Guide*
Editor, *Antiques and Collectables*

CONTENTS

Contents

FIRST EDITION 2005

12 ART DECO FAVOURITES
Get stylish with our Art Deco feature and collect using our price guide

26 DAMAGED GOODS
Why damaged goods can offer great bargains

30 *DATING It's easy when you know how - an easy guide to reading backstamps and hallmarks*

CONTENTS

205

*PHOTOGRAPHY
This year's must-buy collectable*

211

*ROCK AND POP
7 pages of the hottest collectables including Elvis, The Beatles and Buddy Holly*

■ WHATS IT WORTH

124

*FURNITURE
Turn your home into a comfortable but stunning antiques haven*

■ HOW TO USE THIS GUIDE

- The book is divided into sections with each section divided into sub-sections (eg Clarice Cliff will be found under 'ceramics')
- These all have introductions and all of the guide's pages contain fact files, offering lots of extra information
- The prices shown are the prices listed at the time the pictures were first published with the second price being the current market value.
- The relevant issue of Antiques and Collectables in which the pictures first appeared is listed before the prices.
- The initials by each photograph stand for the auction house or business which supplied the picture and their details are listed on p 301.
- Any photograph without an A&C number has not been used in the magazine but was sourced especially for this publication

Antiques & Collectables issue numbers
1-4 **1998**, 5-9 **1999**, 10-21 **2000**, 22-33 **2001**, 34-44 **2002**, 45-56 **2003**, 57-68 **2004**
Back issues can be ordered by ringing Antiques and Collectables on **01225 786814**

STAR TRADER

It's not often that an antiques expert appears naked in a magazine, with nothing but a Steiff bear for modesty. But it's not often that you meet one as flamboyant as David Dickinson, the bargain-hunting, ballroom-dancing, real-life Lovejoy, also known as 'The Duke'

All pictures courtesy of Colin Poole

LOVE HIM OR NOT, THERE'S NO DENYING THAT David Dickinson has rejuvenated the antiques trade. The success of *Bargain Hunt*, the TV show where two teams spend money buying antiques at fairs and then try to make a profit by selling those goods at auction, is a firm favourite with viewers. So much so that the original daytime series, with new host Tim Wonnacott, an established antiques expert, is going out for forty-five minutes instead of the previous thirty-minute slot. David now presents the prime-time slot proving just how successful he has become since being compared to Lovejoy, the antiques rogue from the Jonathan Gash novels who was portrayed so temptingly by Ian McShane.

David shows how to spot a
bargain by checking for
signatures and any damage

DAVID DICKINSON

The Duke has turned antiques buying into a must-do activity leading to increasing numbers at fairs

That comparison led to a programme about a day in a dealer's life, the dealer in question being David. Although it looks as though his dealing days are over because of his hectic filming schedule, he is still the most famous dealer in the country. If you mention antiques to anyone who isn't in the trade or a collector, they'll name David Dickinson. While most other TV experts have come via the auction houses, The Duke's roots are much more down to earth and he has been a successful dealer for years, running his own shop and stalling at the big fairs such as Olympia, specialising in top quality furniture.

'CHEAP AS CHIPS'

He is probably the most famous of all of the antiques presenters and experts because of his flamboyant style. Quite simply, David is unique. He has a huge personality which comes across in his work and is far removed

from the usual subtly-suited experts from programmes such as *The Antiques Roadshow* his snazzy suits setting him apart from his peers and, unusually, leading to non-antiques shows.

He has succeeded where so few have gone, he is no longer 'just' an antiques expert but an entertainer in his own right and it wouldn't be surprising to see him fronting *The Generation Game* or some similar Saturday night entertainment show. The colourful presenter has made no secret that this is where he wants to go and, with a prime-time show and appearances on non-antiques related programmes such as *The Nation's Favourite Food* and, most famously *Strictly Come Dancing* (where David's early exit from the competition suggested that he had a better eye for antiques than feet for dancing), he is firmly established as a cult figure.

In fact, there was even a cartoon character of the antiques presenter on satirical TV show *2DTV* as well as regular appearances on the popular impersonation programme *Dead Ringers* (on both television and radio) and an appearance on the topical BBC quiz show *Have I Got News for You*. He is such a popular figure that he had a cult rap song written about him, 'Bargain Hunt Booty'.

Interestingly, he doesn't have an agent but is superb at self-marketing, including his infamous 'nude' picture in 'The Radio Times' where his modesty was preserved by the careful positioning of a Steiff bear. The bear-faced cheek of it! His promotional skills were honed through being his wife's manager, the cabaret performer Lorne Lesley who has often been compared to Shirley Bassey, both hailing from Tiger Bay in Wales. Lorne is a very popular figure behind the scenes with more than one crew member talking very fondly of her and her enthusiasm and friendliness endears her to all who meet her. They even worked together on *The Nation's Favourite Food* although, sadly, their choice was not chips despite The Duke's famous 'Cheap as Chips' slogan.

TOP TIPS FOR BARGAIN HUNTING

While not all of the teams featured on the various TV shows set at auction houses make the money they want (let alone pay the auction house's commission), it can be done. Follow these tips to become a successful buyer or seller at auction:

• Mundane pieces of Royal Doulton such as chine (that's where lace was applied to the wet pottery, painted over and then burned off in the kiln during glazing, leaving a textured finish) rarely do well at auction as they are more expensive at fairs – buy at auction, sell at fairs.

• Silver tends to do very well at auction, especially attractive or unusual pieces – don't forget to check the hallmarks when buying or clearing your house – pieces from York are very desirable (see p.32).

• Pretty wooden boxes such as Tunbridge Ware (colourful

decoration made by wooden squares) and Mauchline Ware (Scottish scenic transfers over blond wood) often do very well at auction. I saw one tatty sewing box fetch over £200 when filming *Everything Must Go: Under the Hammer*.

• Jewellery is generally much cheaper to buy at auctions than fairs which is why people wanting to buy special rings (such as engagement, wedding, anniversary or eternity) should check out auction houses first.

• Highly ornate mirrors with ormolu (gilt) surrounds can be costly mistakes to make if you're thinking of buying to sell at auction, these are much better off at fairs where you get the right audience, not at auctions frequented by the trade

• Condition matters. If you are selling scruffy pieces of furniture or grubby crockery, clean them first. Polish furniture until it gleams, it might sound silly but the smell of quality polish can increase your profits.

REMEMBER THE COMMISSION

One of the most frequent complaints we get about the various auction-based TV shows is that they don't talk about commission. Going by my TV experience, some auction houses agree to waive their commissions when being filmed but you need to know the real costs of selling. These will differ between auction houses and be listed on their terms and conditions, normally printed in their catalogues. Always ask about insurance, it might only be around 1% of the hammer price but could save you a great deal money if your goods are accidentally damaged before the auction.

Commission varies hugely from around 8–20%, some auction houses being higher, some lower but the cheapest is not always the best. Do your research first and find out which auction house has the best track record or specialist auctions in your field. Or just watch the various television shows and see which auctioneers you like best – they wouldn't be on TV if they didn't know what they're doing.

If you enjoy *Bargain Hunt*, you might like to know that top auctioneer, Charles Hanson, *Bargain Hunt* and *Flog It!* expert and the Fine Arts Manager at Wintertons in Lichfield is a regular columnist for *Antiques and Collectables*. **WIW**

In his natural setting: David honed his expertise as a furniture dealer at top-quality fairs such as Olympia

WHY COLLECT?

Collecting is not a new concept but has been around for centuries. What did people collect before *The Antiques Roadshow* gave advice? They collected dead people

ABOVE CLOCKWISE FROM TOP LEFT: 1960 Chateau Lafitte Rothschild; Oval stoneware pot by Hans Coper; Dutch walnut longcase clock; The Macallan 50 year old; The Macallan 1950

WHAT IS IT THAT MAKES PERFECTLY normal people get up at 5am to scurry around a field in search of a bargain or drive over 100 miles to an auction to ensure that they don't lose out on a must-have lot? Collecting is a hoarding instinct that probably dates back to cavemen keeping their best bones as proof that they had caught dinner and survived the winter. Sadly, not everyone is a collector and those who prefer minimalism can rarely understand those of us who love clutter or surrounding ourselves with beautiful objects and that's the whole point. Collecting is about beauty. We don't all appreciate the same things and that's just as well because collecting has mass appeal and it's the variety that makes it such an exciting challenge.

HISTORY OF COLLECTING

Collecting is not a new discovery. While the antiques world has changed drastically in the last two decades to incorporate collectables (for which we at *Antiques and Collectables* are very grateful) and kitsch often sells for more than style, the concept is the same – the desire to acquire. And it can become an addiction.

People have collected since ancient times and these collections have preserved creatures which would

otherwise have been forgotten. Strange lizards that were believed to be fearsome dragons were slain and preserved in museums until age turned them to dust. We know what dinosaurs look like because people collected them, whether for private museums or collections. And the last dodo is safe in a museum in Oxford.

There are two main reasons to collect – to acquire goods or to acquire knowledge, sometimes both. Book and ephemera collectors are often collecting attractive objects but it is the words that they contain that generate

Fruitwood pear-shaped caddy, late-eighteenth century

Rare nineteenth–twentieth century Peruvian alabaster chess set, carved as Incas

knowledge and it's a powerful aphrodisiac. Collectors can become obsessive about their need to acquire and their acquisitions, forcing this love affair on their nearest and dearest who might not be quite so besotted.

One avid collector was King Philip II of Spain (reigned 1556–98) who acquired a British wife, Queen Mary, or bloody Mary as the Catholic queen is normally remembered. His various collections provided him with a form of escape, not just from the stresses of politics but of his family. His son and heir, Don Carlos, was dangerously insane and Philip, allegedly, arranged for him to be killed. The loss of his son, wives and lack of immediate male heir, plus the beliefs of the day, made him exceedingly religious, possibly obsessively so. This, in turn, generated a collection of relics. Philip was one of the greatest collectors of these religious body parts amassing 7,000 pieces including 144 heads of saints.

RELICS – THE BIGGEST FAKES OF ALL?

They say that there are so many pieces of the 'genuine' cross on which Christ was crucified that whole forests must have died. All of the pieces, put together, would have built the Ark, let alone a cross. Because, when it comes to religious relics, one of the most powerful forms of collecting, there is a huge trade in forgeries. The debate about whether the Shroud of Turin was actually used to wrap the body of Christ is still very much alive but other

relics are forgotten by those who do not share the beliefs of the Catholic Church, especially in a more cynical age but, at one time, relics, the remains of saints, were revered. They were believed to offer a form of protection and General Franco (1892–1975), the Spanish wartime leader, died clutching the arm of St Theresa of Avila.

Emerald green porcelain bowl by Dame Lucie Rie

MODERN COLLECTING

Today's collections tend to be less gruesome and more hygienic. We live in smaller houses with less space so smalls are a very popular option, especially china. It's traditional to collect one or two makes because the design and quality tally, and the overall effect is appealing. Other collectors colour co-ordinate their collections, especially with blue and white china. Furniture varies from practical chairs to more modern design with Robin Day and Charles Eames changing the shape and style of furniture.

POCKETFUL OF RYE

Studio potteries, such as Rye, are becoming increasingly popular and are priced for all pockets, even the smallest and that's at the heart of collecting and why it has such massive appeal, collecting does not have to be costly. A quick skim through these pages should give you a few ideas of what to collect but no book can cover the entire range of collecting which is what makes it so exciting whether you buy to acquire or have inherited someone else's dream. Collecting is what you make of it. **WIW**

CLOCKWISE FROM BELOW:
French ladies telescopic; A Burgess & Leigh (Burleigh) bowl; Miniature globe, 6.5cm in diameter, on an ebonised stand; A Zeiss Super Ikonta, model B.; Small Russian icon depicting Jesus Christ

ART**DECO**

One of of the most exciting areas for collectors, Art Deco epitomised the period between the two World Wars, a colourful era known as the Jazz Age

A RT DECO IS ALSO KNOWN AS THE JAZZ AGE because of its bright colours and either sharply geometric or flowing lines. The term was coined at the 1925 Paris Exhibition, Exposition Internationale des Artes Décoratifs et Industriels Modernes. It was a new and exciting movement and is still being imitated today with Mock Deco. Officially, the movement finished in 1939 at New York's World Fair, adapting to Moderne in the war years and the rest of the 1940s.

MOTIFS

Art Deco china and glass is instantly recognisable, not just because of the flowing or very angular shapes but because of the motifs. The most common ones being:

- Egyptian motifs inspired by Carter's discovery of Tutankhamen in 1922
- Zig-zags
- Parallel lines
- Chevrons
- Geometric patterns
- Geometric sunrise
- Stylised flowers.

The Scottish terrier, with its angular body, also characterised the era and was a common theme in jewellery, often accompanied by the larger but similarly square-lined Airedale terrier.

COLOURS

Colours provided the movement with energy. Gone were the soft blues, purples, greens and browns of the Art Nouveau. Deco was crude and loud, epitomised by the garish Bizarre range designed by Clarice Cliff. Even the furniture changed colour with pale woods replacing the sombre oaks and mahogany of the previous movements. In china, yellow, orange and red dominated, while blues became brighter and thick black lines accompanied childlike colourful flowers.

TRANSPORT

Lines became sleeker, with furniture and smalls influenced by the flowing lines of the new wave of planes. However, the greatest influence of all was the ocean-going luxury liner, epitomised by the two Cunard ships the Queen Mary and the Queen Elizabeth. Their sleek bows even influenced Art Deco buildings, the BBC's Broadcasting House being based on the ships' design as can be seen in the basement studio used for major radio shows. The liners were reproduced in carpets including one designed for London's Park Lane Hotel, proving how great their influence was as several of the upmarket hotel's guests would have travelled on the vessels. Top designer, Clarice Cliff also brought the concept into her designs with one of her ceramic cruise liners recently selling at auction for £14,950. Travel was exciting, even cars, once big hulking machines, became smoother and more stylish. The Deco period changed everything.

MATERIALS

One of the greatest innovations of the age for jewellery designers, among others, was Bakelite. While purists might argue that Bakelite was only ever black/brown, most people call the thick plastic Bakelite regardless of colour with red being popular, especially the big cherry necklace. It made jewellery bright, cheerful and fun. The plastic could be moulded into shapes and it was affordable. It was also used to make Deco boxes with Scotties on top, napkin ring holders, even cocktail stick tops and handbag clasps. It was part of a party era, the Jazz Age.

CLOCKWISE FROM LEFT: An Art Deco diamond bracelet; Clarice Cliff Bizarre 'Melon' pattern bowl, of octagonal outline, for Newport Pottery. Printed mark, 22cm (8.75in) diameter, (WINT), dressing table set, demi-lune cocktail cabinet

DESIGNER LABELS

Not all Deco is equal, some designers are better than others who simply tried to imitate their success. We'll be covering this in more detail in the Art Deco section of the guide (pages 38–41) and in individual sections but names can make all the difference, especially to the value of a piece. Top designers included:

- Clarice Cliff – brightly coloured china with stylish shapes
- Charlotte Rhead – heavy, tube-line decoration on china
- Susie Cooper – stylish shapes, Deco motifs on china
- Lalique – epitomised Deco glass with stylishly exciting shapes
- Cartier – classic Deco jewellery, watches and compacts
- Eisenberg – top fake diamonds Deco jeweller
- Chanel – couturier whose sleek style epitomised the era
- Schiaparelli – 'shocking' designer of suits, Chanel's rival
- Epstein – Deco designer furniture
- Chiparus – ivory and bronze dancing figurines
- Preiss – ivory (or an imitation ivory) and bronze dancing figures
- Tamara De Lempika – artist with a distinctive style.

Deco is one of the most exciting areas for collectors and can be found at most fairs and auctions. It has never gone out of fashion for collectors – or designers. ***WIW***

STARFISH GIRL A Chiparus bronze, with an ivory face and hands

The elegant style of Art Nouveau has its roots in the Age of Chivalry and is characterised by such leading names as Liberty's and Charles Rennie Mackintosh

ART**NOUVEAU**

ALONG WITH ART DECO, THIS IS ONE OF THE most famous movements of the 20th century. The distinctive style with its long, willowy women, tulips or leaves, has been a mainstay of the antiques world for decades, especially the pieces made for Liberty's, the London shop which dominated the market. Although there

are no official start and end dates for the movement, it is typically deemed to start in around 1884 when the term 'Art Nouveau' was first printed (in reference to the Belgian artists, Sosciété des Vingts or 'Les XX') and finished in 1914 with the start of the First World War. It means 'new art' and was thought to be a brand new style of art covering all forms of art from paintings and sculpture to china, glass and furniture. Some people date it from the 1890s, which is when it is more firmly entrenched.

BACKGROUND

The Art Nouveau period was born out of the Pre-Raphaelites who were influenced by the Age of Chivalry with its tall, languid women with flowing hair. The Art Nouveau period went one stage further – and undressed them. It was an age of the vertical – tall women, tulips and the vertical lines, which epitomised Charles Rennie Mackintosh's work, crossed by shorter horizontal ones.

KEY MOMENTS

- 1892 – Tiffany Glass was established with its much-copied Art Nouveau lights
- 1895 – Samuel Bing opened the influential La Maison de l'Art Nouveau. Tiffany exhibited at the opening of the gallery which was to house some of the best names in the movement
- 1896 – Charles Rennie Mackintosh founded the Glasgow School of Arts (completed in 1909)
- 1900 – Art Nouveau dominated the Universal Exhibition in Paris and Hector Guirnard's famous Art Nouveau entrances were created for the new Paris Metro
- 1900 – Gaudi's famous Art Nouveau architecture in Barcelona was finished with its famous, curving lines
- 1903 – The Wiener Werkstätte was founded and would become famous for its Art Nouveau creations
- 1914 – The First World War led to the end of the creativity of the style which would continue in a less pronounced manner until around 1920.

KEY DESIGNERS

Charles Rennie Mackintosh (1868–1928)

Mackintosh's work dominated the British version of the Art Nouveau style. Unlike Continental versions, it is very masculine with its hard lines. Along with George Walton (with whom he worked on Buchanan's Tearooms in 1899), Ernest Archibald Taylor and other local artists, Mackintosh was part of the Glasgow School. Their work is very architectural as opposed to the almost sensuous, soft lines of the Continental version. As such, it is very distinctive, even though Mackintosh did not sign his work (it is well catalogued). His work is shapelier than the harsher lines of furniture designer and architect, Frank Lloyd Wright. If you want to collect the Scotsman's work, the pre-1912 pieces are viewed as being better than the later, apparently, less creative versions.

Liberty's

In England, the main Art Nouveau retailer was Liberty's, the Regent Street store that commissioned work from designers such as Archibald Knox. Their distinctive style in Pewter (known as Tudric, launched in 1903) or silver (known as Cymric, launched in 1899) is highly collectable but still relatively affordable. Pieces signed by Archibald Knox, one of the few designers allowed to sign his creations, are among the most desirable with clocks a firm favourite with collectors. The goods were not actually made by the store but by W. H. Haseler, the Birmingham silversmiths with whom they formed a partnership in 1901.

A silvered metal table lamp by Orivit, c.1900

WMF

While Liberty's goods were squat and masculine, WMF's (short for Wüttembergische Metallwarenfabrik) were tall and feminine. WMF is the most desirable make of European metalwork. Their claret jugs with the colourful glass being surrounded by the metalwork are highly collectable, although many date from after the period. When buying WMF, look for the famous initials below a stork as these are the earliest pieces, pre-1914. Their Art Deco designs are also very popular but they are best known for the Art Nouveau elongated pewter pieces.

Louis Comfort Tiffany and Other Glassmakers

Tiffany's colourful lamps in his famous favrile (handmade) glass epitomise the Art Nouveau era. Their floral or insect-dominated themes with their heavy black lines are classical examples of the American version of the movement that he led. The work is very distinctive from the European movement, famous for its iridescent designs led by the likes of Austrian firm, Loetz although Tiffany was highly influenced by their wares and sought to emulate them. But it is the French art glass by the likes of Daum and Gallé that most people think of when Art Nouveau glass is mentioned. Their experiments with acid-etched glass and cameo designs created new art – Art Nouveau at its very best and they created some of the most collectable art glass of the twentieth century. *WIW*

Clockwise from below:
Liberty buckle 1903;
Gallé glass vase;
A Liberty & Co silver and ivory four-piece teaset;
Art Nouveau box made of copper and brass.

ARTS&CRAFTS

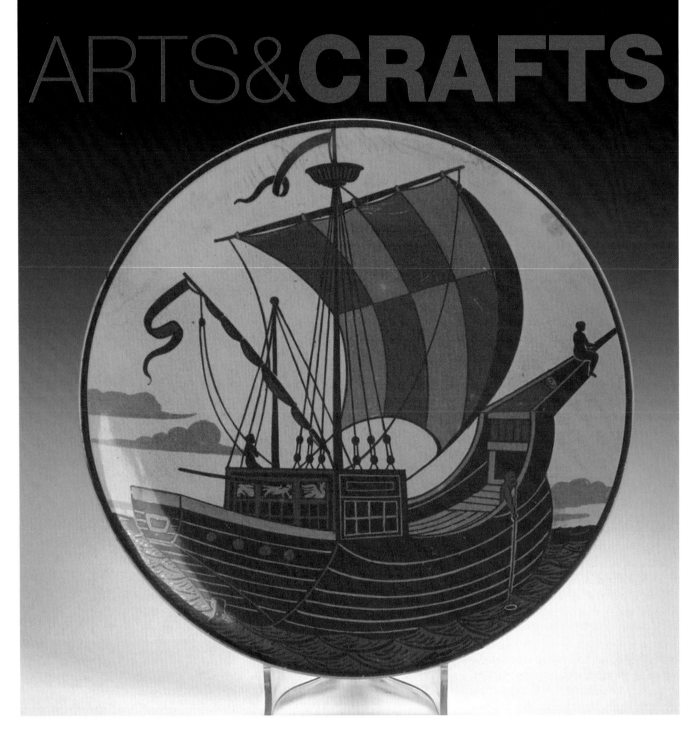

A reaction to the increased industrialisation of the nineteenth century, the Arts and Crafts movement marked a return to handmade craftsmanship for the whole house

THE ARTS AND CRAFTS MOVEMENT WAS BORN out of a fear that the Industrial Age threatened to end craftsmanship with mass-production finally possible at the risk of quality work. Led by William Morris, the artisans formed movements that rejected industrialisation in favour of handmade goods covering everything from furniture (dovetailing hand done, not machined), china and jewellery to metalwork. Movements were set up within movements – The Keswick and Newlyn Schools being two of the most prominent.

COMPLETE DESIGN

The Arts and Crafts movement was the first to be aimed at the entire house from the wallpaper to its furniture.

Everything was to be included in this reworking of the tired old styles which had been in place since the Georgian era. Morris and his colleagues wanted a fresh style and not the continuous repetition of shapes and patterns which had been holding back modern design.

DATES

Unlike the Art Deco movement which began and ended at expositions (Paris in 1925 and New York in 1939), there are no easy dates for the Arts and Crafts style. Most dealers use the 1880–90s as the main era for the movement but it had its roots in Pugin's work in the 1830s and the design for William Morris' South London house, The Red House in 1860 can be seen as its main starting point because the building brought interested parties together. Although Morris' death in 1896 saw the style start to decrease in England, it was at its prime in America, ending in 1915 with the death of Elbert Hubbard, founder of the Roycroft community (one of the most famous names in the American Arts and Crafts movement or the 'Mission Style' as it was known in the USA), who drowned on the Lusitania when it was sunk.

MOTIFS

William Morris' work influenced the other designers of the age, especially when it came to fabric and wallpaper. As can still be seen with the William Morris-style bags sold at Liberty's today, these patterns were to become highly popular. The most common themes were:

- Peacock feathers
- Tulips and other flowers
- Ogee arches (like onion shapes)
- Trees (especially apple trees)
- Plants, mainly with large leaves, eg strawberries
- Birds, especially flying ones.

The patterns were repetitive, aimed at filling the larger rooms of the era. It was to influence the later Art Nouveau era which copied many of the motifs but used them in a more fluid manner.

DESIGNERS AND INFLUENCES

William Morris was the undoubted father of the movement and his work was integral to its style but he, in turn, had been influenced by another of its founding members, John Ruskin and the pre-Raphaelite artists, especially his friends, Edward Burne-Jones and Dante Gabriel Rossetti, despite the latter having a relationship with his wife, the model, Jane Burden. C. R. Ashbee was also a key player and founded the Guild of Handicraft in 1888.

OBJECTIVES OF THE MOVEMENT

The aim of the Arts and Crafts movement was a simple one, they wanted to create handmade goods in an age of

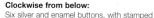

Clockwise from below:
Six silver and enamel buttons, with stamped marks, by William Haseler, 1906; Gold and enamel brooch pendant, by Robert Phillips, 1875; Heal & Son Arts and Crafts chest; William de Morgan ruby lustre dish, possibly painted by Charles Passenger

industrialisation. They rebelled against mass-production and machine-made goods, making everything by hand. Furniture was seen to be handmade with its crude lines and joints made obvious, not subtly concealed as had been done.previously. In an age where machines were creating uniform dovetails to join different pieces of wood together, they embraced these joins and let people see the work that had gone behind making the furniture. They wanted the role of the craftsman to be recognised. Metal was hammered, not machine made and this meant that all of the metalwork is unique whereas machine-made items would have been identical, losing the spirit of the artisan.

MATERIALS

The style was all-embracing, not just restricted to one area of production such as smalls or china but they did have favourite materials and these included:

- Copper
- Stained glass
- Dark woods, especially oak with its Medieval feel
- Wallpaper – like the fabrics, the designs would be hand-printed using wooden blocks
- Woven fabrics, tapestries and carpets
- Heavily-glazed pottery, for example Della Robbia and William De Morgan.

The overall feel was warmth and comfort, the pieces were dark, the furniture sometimes lightened by stained glass detailing and the style distinctive – and collectable. *WIW*

Brannam Pottery vase by John Dewdney, 1905

AESTHETIC MOVEMENT

It was the decadent style of the late-nineteenth century with the motto 'art for art's sake' and it might just be the next big thing for collectors

THE INCREASED INTEREST IN DR CHRISTOPHER Dresser, one of the leading lights of the Aesthetic Movement, has sparked an awareness of this often forgotten artistic ideology. We're tipping it as the next big thing so buy now while you can.

Background

The Movement originated in French literature and spread to all areas of the art world, including furniture design. It started in the 1860s and was to continue until the 1890s, working in parallel with the more famous Arts and Crafts Movement. Its motto was 'art for art's sake' and thrived on decoration and style. The decadent style was championed in literature by Oscar Wilde and his illustrator, the artist Aubrey Beardsley whose work epitomises the era.

Japanese Influence

One of the main influences on the Movement was Japan, especially after the International Exhibition of 1862 which took place in London and where Japanese art was on display. This influence can be seen in the ebonised furniture, the black colouring resembling the black lacquer so popular with Japanese furniture. As well as the distinctive black furniture which epitomised much of the furniture made during this period, bamboo was a popular theme, an almost whimsical notion of Oriental furniture. Designers such as Christopher Dresser, one of the visitors to the 1862 exhibition, used thick layers of lacquer, known as japanning on their furniture. This thick glaze created an almost amber colouring and was ideal for the bamboo or bamboo-shaped designs. Dresser's furniture is hard to find but offers a perfect example of the Japanese influence on the Aesthetic Movement.

Leading Lights

The Movement was dominated by the Aesthetes, the name given to those who led the Movement, some of whom also worked in the Arts and Crafts style. The most famous of the Movement's proponents were:

Right: Aesthetic gilt brass faux bamboo clock
Far Right: Aesthetic movement table clock
Below: Sideboard in the typical ebonised finish

- Dr Christopher Dresser – the most notable Aesthete
- William Morris – who was also the leader of the Arts and Crafts Movement
- Walter Crane – famous for his tile designs and children's book illustrations
- Oscar Wilde – the most decadent of the writers
- Aubrey Beardsley – painted free-flowing, unfettered women who defied Victorian morality
- Charles Eastlake – an artist who wrote books dictating taste in furniture and other items including upholstery. **_WIW_**

GOTHIC **REVIVAL**

Despite a Harry Potter-inspired renewal of interest in the Gothic Revival it remains a buyer's market for those attracted by the movement's decorative feminine style

THE GOTHIC REVIVAL (1830–80) WAS A nostalgic style, looking back to the Middle Ages and the distinctive architecture of the day with its tall spires and trefoils (shamrock-like) decoration. Also known as Neo-gothic, it was the era of the High Church, before the Reformation and the birth of more sedate Protestantism. The main Gothic revival was in the late-nineteenth century and can be seen not just in the furniture of the day but the buildings with St Pancras Station and the fairy-tale Houses of Parliament being prime examples. They were highly decorative buildings, a far cry from the more austere style of Georgian architecture. Gothic Revival is High Victoriana, fanciful decoration breaking free of the stiff moral attitudes of the day. As for the furniture, it was feminine and exciting.

Literature, Art and Music

The furniture and architecture of the age was influenced by the Romantic era, which was dominated by the likes of Keats (1795–1817) who drew on Arthurian legend and the chivalric era with poems such as *La Belle Dame Sans Merci*. This led to some of the most interesting furniture and architecture of the nineteenth century.

Architectural Influence

In America, they refer to the British Gothic Revival movement as the Parish Church movement, believing that it was influenced by the hundreds of small churches that can be found in the country. The original Gothic era (1100–1500) was a period of deep religion and the later, Victorian designers, such as Pugin, believed that it offered the perfect combination of religious and spiritual art.

Far Left: Bookcase with Gothic arches
Above: Feminine dressing table with Gothic features

Augustus Welby Pugin

Pugin was undoubtedly the most important of all Gothic Revival designers. He was an architect and draftsman whose most famous work was the interior of the Palace of Westminster (The Houses of Parliament) and some of the designs for the exterior, although the overall project was designed and managed by the architect, Sir Charles Barry. While most famous for his architecture, Pugin was also a skilled furniture designer and his early Gothic Revival furniture can be seen in Windsor Castle, dating from the 1820s, it actually predates the main period of the style.

Furniture

Walnut and oak were the two most commonly used woods, the dark colours complementing the religious feel of the style. One of the most common examples is a cardinal or bishop's chair, a heavy-set chair on a cross-frame (looks like a large X from the side) and often with trefoil decoration. The church chairs catered for long services for prominent churchmen and, therefore, had to be very comfortable which makes them good buys.

Designers versus Style

Apart from Pugin and the architect and cabinetmaker, Richard Upjohn who took the style to America, the era was not particularly designer-led in the way that later movements, such as Art Deco were to become. The Harry Potter films with their Gothic influence (for example the Hogwarts building) led to increased interest in the movement but prices are still relatively low. ***WIW***

Dark woods created an almost religious feel to the movement

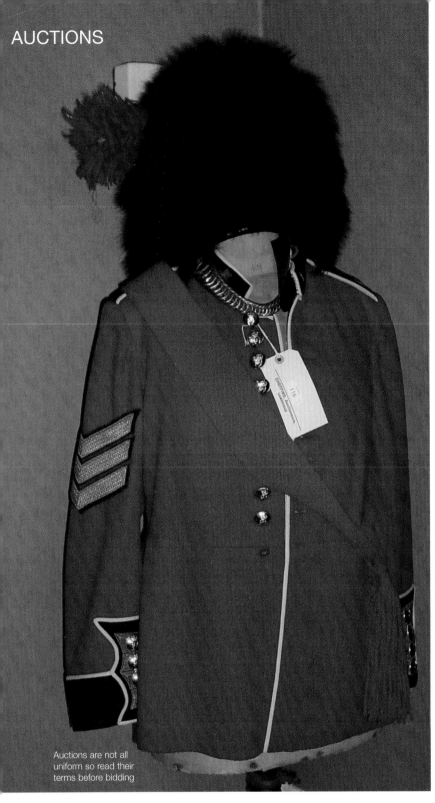

Auctions are not all uniform so read their terms before bidding

Have you ever wondered where to go to get some of the best bargains? General auctions are full of great buys – but be careful not to get carried away

AUCTIONS ARE FANTASTIC PLACES TO PICK UP bargains and they're also a lot of fun but only if you know what you're doing. It can be quite intimidating to go to your first auction and even experienced dealers can feel a sense of trepidation when going to a new auction house because all auctioneers are different and you never know if they'll see your bid or not – unless you bid clearly. A subtle nod or wink is all very well if the auctioneer knows you but don't risk it if not, as you could end up not bidding at all.

HOW TO BID
- Raise your hand clearly
- Raise your bidding paddle in the air if the auction house provides cards (paddles) with your registered bidding number
- Wave your catalogue in the air.

And that's it – not all auctioneers recognise nods from people they don't know – you could just be falling asleep and winks are not well received because there could be something wrong with your eye – stick to clear signals and you can't go wrong. In theory. If your bid is missed (you could be sitting behind a tall person or the auctioneer was just not looking your way) just call out the figure you're bidding – or the one after that if someone else's bid was taken instead of yours. And don't panic, just bid clearly and know your limit.

THE SKY'S THE LIMIT
The problem with auctions is that they are very exciting and it's easy to get carried away, especially if you have not read the small print – we've all done it. You might have bid £100 but that's not what you'll pay – with very few exceptions. Virtually all auction houses will charge a

Bargain Hunting at
AUCTION

buyer's premium and many will charge VAT (17.5%) on top of that. A buyer's premium is generally between 10 and 15% of the hammer price – that's an extra £10–15 on top of your £100, not forgetting the VAT on the premium. It soon adds up and you need to think of that before bidding or you could end up making a costly mistake.

WHAT SHOULD I PAY?

No more than you can afford. You might love an object and want to possess it but you need to know exactly how much you can afford to pay for it, including the extra charges. Even if you can afford it, take care that you're not paying too much – you might not want to sell it on but why overpay? Assuming that this is a proper auction house with expert valuers, find out what the reserve price is and expect to pay around 25% more. Admittedly, as *Antiques and Collectables* regular column What's It Worth shows, there are some huge variations between estimates and hammer prices but, unless what you're buying is rare, most auction houses know their market value – that's why so many of us sell through them. That said, most fair dealers buy at auction because it's a cheap way of buying a lot of stock, especially job lots.

JOB LOTS

One of the most exciting aspects of auctions is the job lots where several goods are sold in one lot, often stored in a box and it's amazing what you can find. I bought one job lot full of china figures for £190 and sold half of it for £2,000, keeping the other pieces for myself.

HOW DO I PAY?

Always telephone and check before travelling as you might only be allowed to pay in cash. A very few auction houses expect you to pay a cash deposit before bidding just to show that you're serious. Some either won't accept cheques from non-regulars or will ensure that the cheque clears before allowing you to collect the goods – which could be inconvenient if you've travelled a distance. And some accept credit or debit cards but ask if there are extra charges for this convenience. Cash is the easiest option, just make sure that you stick to your spending limit.

PACKING IT IN

Not all auctions provide packaging for smalls (china, glass and other small breakables) so take plenty of your own, including bubble wrap and boxes and don't forget to check that you are given

Stand or sit at the back of an auction room to keep an eye on the competition

Auctioneers like George Kidner of Kidner's in Lymington are happy to answer your queries

House auctions, such as this one by Cheffins at Fowlmere House, offer a great variety of goods at good prices

A German silver nef, sold for £4,500 (DR)

everything that you've bought, especially when it comes to job lots. Some people have been known to swap the stickers. Check whether or not your lot has been photographed in the catalogue if this happens, it's the easiest way of proving that you're in the right but ask to speak to the auctioneer or cataloguer if not. This doesn't happen too often but it's best to be aware.

AND FINALLY

As the TV programmes *Cash in the Attic* and *Bargain Hunt* show, auctions are great places for picking up bargains or just having an enjoyable day out. Don't forget to keep your catalogue as it is a useful guide to dates and prices. *WIW*

Attractive display at Brentwood antiques fair

TOP TIPS FOR **FAIRS**

Fairs are great for picking up bargains and getting expert advice from knowledgeable dealers. No matter what the time of day, there are good buys to be had but, for an extra discount, just smile

PEOPLE WHO DON'T KNOW THE ANTIQUES TRADE very well think that there's no point going to an antiques fair unless you can be there early. Okay, so you can get some great buys first thing but many of those pieces will have been left unsold from the last fair that the stallholders did. Most fairs allow early entry for the trade – you can pay a bit more than you would later on (£1-15, depending on the fair) to get in when the trade do. How? Some antiques fairs just take your money without asking any questions whilst others ask for a trade card.

Outside stall at Newmarket

TRADE CARD

Most dealers pay as little as they can for trade cards and you should too. There are two easy ways to get cards, either in person from the machines which you see at larger train stations and some larger shopping centres or via the Internet. One of the most popular sites for these cards is www.vistaprint.co.uk which sells 250 cards for free plus the cost of the postage (£3.08 + VAT), you pay more for faster delivery. These are very attractive cards and the site is easy to use but you do have to wait for them. You might want to order your first 50 from a machine (around £3) and then the rest via the Internet. List your work address if you don't want people to have your home address. Trade cards are also very useful to give dealers if you want them to find goods for you or contact you after a fair – ideal if you've run out of cash or you like their stock. Don't forget to ask for their card and where they'll be stalling next. If you do like their stock, ask if they're in an antiques centre so you can see them or their stock between fairs.

BARGAIN HUNTING

BBC's *Bargain Hunt* changed the way the antiques trade worked. Nowadays, everyone expects a discount but how do you get the best price? Firstly, don't expect the huge discounts you see on TV. Most dealers simply can't afford to give you a reduction of 50%. To get the highest markdown, ask for the trade price and smile nicely. It's amazing what a friendly smile can do, dealers get annoyed by aggressive bargain hunters and can refuse to discount their goods at all, except to fellow dealers. If asked to prove that you're a dealer (even if you're not), simply show your trade card – but most wouldn't dream of asking. By asking for the best or very best price, you're showing that you're a novice and, in all fairness, reductions used to be a courtesy to other dealers so no one has to give you a better price. If you offer to pay a price lower than the marked one (eg £90 for something marked £100), be aware that you could end up paying more than you could have – by asking for the trade price, you should get the best deal immediately without needing to play games. It's simple. When you know how. And don't forget to smile – it could get you an extra 25% off.

AT THE END OF THE DAY

You can still find bargains, no matter what the hour as not everyone will collect the same as you. This is true of larger objects which are heavy to carry or difficult to pack, such as furniture or garden ornaments. It's always worth asking for the trade price – you might be pleasantly surprised at their affordability but always ask if they'll help you to load your car or deliver (often free if local but expect to pay delivery charges if not). You can even find bargains when the dealers are packing up but be extra polite as they tend to be very tired and just want to get home, they won't welcome any hesitation on your behalf. And remember, today's unsold stock is tomorrow's early bargain. ***WIW***

Specialist Clarice Cliff stall at Sandringham antiques fair

Fairs are good for finding what you want from lots of different dealers at good prices. They are usually delighted to share their knowledge with you so you know exactly what you're buying, a very useful advantage

Nostalgic buys at Wood Green Animal Shelter, Godmanchester

Vintage delights at Gray's Antiques Market in London

SUPER MARKETS

Shops and centres offer the comfort of friendliness and knowing where the dealer will be the next day. Unlike auctions, there are set prices and you and can even ask the dealers to source what you're trying to find. Think of centres as antiques supermarkets

ISN'T IT NICE TO WALK INTO AN ANTIQUES CENTRE and be greeted by name? That doesn't happen at fairs and rarely at auctions but it happens every day in the hundred of shops and centres in Britain and elsewhere. These retail outlets have time to build up relationships and they value their customers. They want to see you every day or every week and so ensure that stock is changed regularly, window displays are enticing and, if you're lucky, a hot cup of tea or coffee greets your arrival. It's a very personal way to collect – unless you wish to remain anonymous and then they will let you browse at will. It's not like being at a fair or auction where time is limited and you need to decided immediately. Yes, you can lose out if you hesitate for too long but shops and centres are dependable, you know what to expect.

RELIABILITY

As well as the opportunity to build up a relationship with a dealer, one of the greatest advantages to these premises is that you know where they are. Although some dealers will naturally move on, it's comforting to know that your goods are sold from a set location. A friend of mine once bought something which was not as described. She decided to return it to the centre and succeeded in getting her money back, along with a sincere apology. It would not have been so easy at a fair where you'd have to know the dealer's name to get a refund. Some shops and centres also allow you to buy goods over a period of time, keeping the goods until you have paid in full and it feels much safer to do so when you know where the goods will be, although most fair dealers are also very honest.

Left: Brighton Lanes Antique Centre
Far left: George Bayntun Bookshop in Bath, specialist shops offer expertise as well as quality goods

BETTER SERVICE

When you enter one of these businesses, you are immediately surrounded by expertise. The person behind the counter in shops is often the owner who knows their stock and subject very well. They're always happy to give you advice and take the time to help you to choose the perfect present or piece for your collection. If buying furniture, they generally offer very competitive delivery rates and are very helpful. While you might need to ring the doorbell before being allowed to enter, that's just a sign of the times and shouldn't be off-putting. Once inside, you'll be made welcome and they'll love to talk with you about antiques. It's a great way to find out about local auctions and other shops and they'll know which fairs are worth visiting. They'll also be happy to find goods for you if you become a regular customer.

CENTRE BARGAINS

Centres have changed with the introduction of cabinets allowing dealers to sell through them without having to be there to man the premises (be there to sell). This can work to your advantage as you can take your time to look without feeling pressurised into buying. However, the centre staff can only give you the discount marked on the ticket label (for example 'T10', means £10 discount, 'T' stands for trade). It's always worth asking them to ring the dealer for a better price if buying a costly item or several pieces. They might not be able to help, I always mark my goods for the exact discount I need to cover my overheads (original cost of stock, cabinet rent and the centre's commission) but not everyone does so you might get a bigger reduction if you ask.

SPECIAL EVENTS

Shops and centres love getting regular customers, you pay their rent. As such, you'll get rewarded with invitations to special events such as anniversary or Christmas parties. If you can, take the time to attend – it's a fantastic opportunity to meet the dealers, fellow collectors and catch up on all of the news in the trade. In addition, everyone will make sure that they have extra special stock out to tempt you. *WIW*

Left: Bartlett Street Antiques centre in Bath
Below: Cromwell antiques centre in Sawbridgeworth, one of five centres in the small Hertfordshire town

PERFECTION COSTS

Rare 19th century majolica monkey teapot, missing its lid and with a chip, current value £200–400, perfect with lid £3,000–6,000

Damaged goods will never be perfect but that doesn't mean that they're not worth buying or there is no potential for making a profit

Qianlong dynasty porcelain vase 17th century with some damage, bought for £250 in 1980. Est. £2,000–3,000 (BEAR)

A PERFECT PIECE IS WORTH MORE THAN A damaged one, even a beautifully restored version but that doesn't mean it's not worth buying damaged goods. But why would you want something which is imperfect? There are some very goods reasons for this:

- The piece is so rare you might not find a perfect example
- You can't afford a perfect version
- It's too good a bargain to ignore

- You want to practise restoration
- You're a restorer
- You really like it
- The damage is very limited and can be displayed so that it can't be seen.

WHAT IS DAMAGE?

That's a good question. It should mean anything that is even remotely imperfect, for example anything that is chipped, cracked, has broken limbs, cracked veneer, is not working, has pages ripped or foxed (mouldy marks) or

Book binding and restortion at George Bayntun in Bath

Books need specialist restorers such as the skilled craftsmen at George Bayntun who even mix their own glue from flour and water

is restored is damaged. However, not everyone will tell you so. To some people, a restored item is suddenly perfect again. It isn't, while it's now complete, it is still not perfect.

RESTORATION

Not everyone wants to restore goods. For a start it is costly. Even a small chip in china can cost £20 to repair, with limbs or heads costing around £50 to put on cleanly. As we've all seen, bad repairs (such as supergluing back a head and not cleaning up the glue trails afterwards) can be expensive, not only because it's unattractive but because it's harder to restore a badly mended piece than one left alone. For furniture, dining chairs cost around £60 to have re-caned or re-rushed and that soon adds up.

WHY SHOULD YOU REPAIR GOODS?

There are some very goods reasons for restoring pieces:
- Sentiment, it's a present or an heirloom and deserves to be restored
- It's a beautiful piece, which would look better restored
- You want to use it (for example, furniture)
- You want it to last (such as a book with a tatty spine or foxed pages)
- You broke it and want to make amends.

The last is very common. In the Antiques Advice pages of *Antiques and Collectables* I get asked about restoration more than any other query apart from valuations and my advice is always the same, call in an expert.

WHERE DO YOU FIND AN EXPERT?

Good restorers are always busy but it's worth waiting for them. We advertise restorers as do other specialist publications or you could ask your friendly dealer or auction house for recommendations. It's always worth asking to see examples of their work and, for more costly items, ask to speak to former customers. Most restorers are happy to do so as they are confident in their own

abilities. One small point, it's sensible to be flexible about their estimated time of repair as you don't want them to rush the job and good restoration takes time.

DIY OR NOT?

There are restoration courses all over the country and you might like to learn how to restore furniture or china or reupholster furniture on one of these. DIY restoration if you're unskilled and not steady-handed is not a good idea but lots of people enjoy acquiring the skill to restore goods and it could even lead to a career or a profitable hobby.

Wemyss pig with one ear damaged, chipped snout, body cracked, no tail

KNOCKING SOMETHING OFF THE PRICE

Next time you go to a fair or auction, look at the label or catalogue. Some people will spell it out by writing 'restored' or 'damaged', while others go for the trade term 'a/f' meaning 'all faults' or 'as found'. This means that the item is damaged and should be taken into account with the price but always ask if you're not sure. If, however, you find a piece at a fair or centre that is imperfect when not described as such, ask for a better price because of the damage. If the dealer doesn't take much off or refuses to give you a discount, walk away – don't damage your own profit margin. When you go to fairs, it's always worth remembering that some pieces can get damaged en route and that the dealer might not have noticed, so always check the goods carefully before buying or agreeing a better price.

A WORD TO THE WISE

When is restoration not restoration? When it's a trick to make a piece of furniture seem older or more valuable than it is. Always check under Windsor chairs to see if the cabriole leg (that's the one which goes out at the knee, curves down and then sticks out at the ankle) is attached to the chair – or is a later addition. The original is older and worth much more! **WIW**

BEN NORRIS & Co.
Restorers of Antique Furniture

Before

After

Before

After

We specialise in all aspects of fine period furniture restoration, including marquetry, boulle,
copy chair making, upholstery, carving, gilding, painted and lacquered finishes.

We have extensive experience in restoring architectural fittings — for example panelling and staircases.

We have heated, highly secure storage suitable for disaster management.

We also work in situ and can arrange carriage worldwide.

Established in 1980.

Knowl Hill Farm, Knowl Hill Farm, Kingsclere, Newbury, Berkshire RG20 4NY
Telephone 01635 297950 Facsimile 01635 299851
Colin Bell *Bafra Member/Proprietor*

Inglenook Fine Arts

Your one stop shop for all aspects of Fine Art restoration, cleaning and bespoke picture framing to conservation and museum standards if required (choice of over 800 mouldings).

We have been restoring paintings like the ones shown for over 30 years.

Customers are private owners, public collections, auction houses, dealers, other restorers and insurance companies.

Services we offer including cleaning, lining and relining damaged or torn canvasses, making good paint loss, varnish stripping of oil paintings on canvas and panels, from ancient to modern and also all kinds of frame restoration. We also offer a bespoke swept frame making service from 17mm (0.5inch) to 180mm (7inch) moulding widths.

Picture Sales - We stock a wide range of open and limited edition prints.

Paintings - Commissions taken for landscapes and portraits of your favourite view, person or pet.

Framing - We frame oil paintings, watercolours, prints, tapestries, embroideries, photos, batiks, decoupages, golf clubs, cricket bats, Olympic gold medals, Javan marriage necklaces and just about anything you can think of.

We offer an extensive range of picture mouldings from Nielson and Byron etc.

31 Pillory Street, Nantwich, Cheshire CW5 5BQ
Telephone +44 (0)1270 611188
Email: info@inglenookfinearts.com

38 Green End, Whitchurch, Shropshire SY13 1AA
Telephone & Fax +44 (0)1948 665422
www.inglenookfinearts.com

FREEPHONE 0800 6521071

Period flooring

Reclaimed and new pitch pine, oak, pine

Specialist manufacturers in solid wood period wide flooring

• ideal for new and period homes •

• custom milled •

• excellent quality •

• natural wood flooring at its best •

• skirting and architraves •

• factory outlet - factory prices •

Unit 123, Whitehall Ind. Est, Whitehall Rd, Leeds
Tel: 0113 289 0455
E-mail: leedsreclaimedtimber@yahoo.com

DATING & IDENTIFYING CHINA

When it comes to collecting and valuing china, dating is vital. If you've ever wondered what those strange symbols on the base mean, read on...

The words 'Made in England' on a backstamp, date from post 1891

O f all areas of collectables, china is possibly the easiest to date and value – apart from coins and medals which very kindly have their dates on them. You've probably already noticed that most people in the trade take backstamps for granted but do you know some of the easiest ways to date china?

USA RULES

The USA dictated some of the major changes to imported china by stating that, from 1891, all china imported into America was to include its country of origin on the backstamp. Most china firms made this rule universal.

Made in England appeared on English china after 1891

Nippon was the Japanese word for Japan and the Nippon era was 1891-1921

Made in Japan was used from 1921 after the US decided that Nippon was a Japanese word and that only 'English' words should be used on imported goods

REGISTRATION MARKS

This is one of the most informative marks seen on china. It not only gives the year the pattern or shape was registered but also the day and month and even the parcel number. NB, this is not the date of manufacture but registration

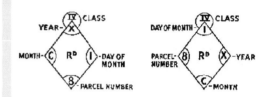

Left hand mark used from 1842-67, right hand version 1868-83, note the different positions for years and the parcel number versus month letter on the bottom

YEAR CYPHERS 1842-67
YEAR LETTER AT THE TOP

A – 1845	J – 1854	S – 1849
B – 1858	K – 1857	T – 1867
C – 1844	L – 1856	U – 1848
D – 1852	M – 1859	V – 1850
E – 1855	N – 1864	W – 1865
F – 1847	O -1862	X – 1842
G – 1863	P – 1851	Y - 1853
H – 1843	Q – 1866	Z – 1860
I – 1846	R – 1861	

1868-83
(YEAR LETTER TO THE RIGHT)

A – 1871	I – 1872	U – 1874
C – 1870	J – 1880	V – 1876
D – 1878	K – 1883	X – 1868
E – 1881	L – 1882	Y – 1879
F – 1873	P – 1877	
H – 1869	S – 1875	

MONTH CODES
FOR BOTH REGISTRATION MARKS

A – December	G – February	M – June
B – October	H – April	R – August (and
C or O –	I – July	1st-19th
January	K – November	September,
D – September	(and December	1857)
E – May	1860)	W – March

Registration numbers were also used to denote the year the design or shape was registered (eg 64520 for the first item registered in January of 1887).

Gemini Publications Ltd

Publishers

bookbasket

30a Monmouth Street, Bath, BA1 2AN, UK

Telephone: 01225 484877
Fax: 01225 334619
Email: sales@bookbasket.co.uk
Web: www.bookbasket.co.uk

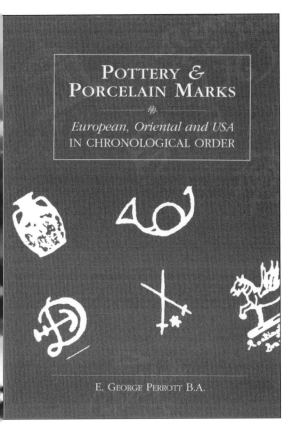

ISBN	**0-9530637-0-4**
Format	**250 x 180mm portrait**
Pages	**667**
Binding	**Hardback**
Cover	**Jacket Art Gloss**
Body	**Black text with illustrations of factory marks**
Price	**£45.00**
Publication	**1st Edition 1997**

SPECIAL OFFER

Until December 2004

£35.00 postage free (UK only)

Contact Gemini Publications Ltd

POTTERY & PORCELAIN MARKS EUROPEAN, ORIENTAL AND USA
By George Perrott

Approximately 10,000 marks and references compiled in date order consisting of marks from the factories of Britain & Europe, USA, Japan & China.

Useful Information for recognising and dating British marks from a few simple tips.

This publication is in fact one of the most original marks books to come onto the market in recent times. It must be the first of its kind that catalogues the factories and potters in date order giving the added perception of their time in history.

The major part of this book concentrates on older marks but a significant effort has been made to include marks from factories and potters that are currently in business and are still producing their wares today.

Information from Ming to Meissen, Wedgwood to Lladro, Vienna to Wade, and every significant pottery and porcelain factory and works in 600 years of ceramic history.

Comprehensive Index covering marks, factories, potters, decorators, etc., in alphabetical order.

If you are a collector or you deal in it as a profession this book is a must for your bookshelf.

Distributed by Gemini Publications Ltd., 30A Monmouth Street, Bath, BA1 2AN, England
Telephone: 01225 484877 Fax: 01225 334619 Email sales@bookbasket.co.uk

DATING GOLD & SILVER

Dating is fun when you know how. No more confusing signs to leave you floundering, with a little know-how, you'll soon distinguish between your castles and pick up some gems - literally

BRITISH GOLD AND SILVER IS VERY EASY TO date once you learn the symbols. There are plenty of pocket-sized hallmark guides on the market for around £5-8 and it's worth investing in one of them. You might also want to buy a loupe (jeweller's magnify glass) which will make it much easier to see the often tiny symbols, even if you think you have perfect sight.

IN THE BEGINNING

Hallmarking started in 1300 when it was declared that no silver was to leave the silversmith until it had been tested (assayed) and then marked with the leopard's head to prove its purity. The standard set was 92.5 per cent, better known as sterling. If you look at silver from the USA or Mexico, it's often just marked 92.5, although the decimal point is hard to spot.

READING THE SIGNS

Hallmarks are generally composed of three symbols, the country of origin, the place of manufacture (or its nearest assay office – that's the place which checks that the gold or silver submitted is pure and set at the correct rate eg 9 carat gold). The first official assay office was opened in London in 1327

COUNTRY OF ORIGIN

English precious metals use a lion as their symbol. Most assay offices use the lion passant which looks like it's walking and looking straight ahead and was first used in 1544. However, Chester, Sheffield and York, use the lion gardant where the lion looks over its shoulder. Ireland uses the harp as its main symbol while Scotland is more confusing, Edinburgh using a castle and Glasgow the lion rampant (standing on its hind legs).

ASSAY OFFICES

Each assay office had its own symbol:

LONDON, the leopard's head (which looks like a lion's head), crowned until 1821 and then with no crown
BIRMINGHAM, the anchor (based on the name of the pub where the symbol was determined, the Crown and Anchor). Used on its side on gold and platinum pieces
SHEFFIELD, a crown until 1975, then a rose
EDINBURGH, the castle. From 1759, a thistle symbol was also used
YORK, five lions passant in a cross formation within a circle. The assay office closed in 1856
NORWICH, lion passant topped by a castle but little silver (if any) produced from 1701
EXETER, round shield with an X until 1701, then a three-towered castle. Assay office closed in 1883
DUBLIN, crowned harp
NEWCASTLE, one castle topped by two castles. Assay office closed in 1884
CHESTER, a sword with three wheat sheaves. Assay office closed in 1962
GLASGOW, tree with a bird, bell and fish. From 1914, the thistle symbol of Scotland was also used. Assay office closed in 1964

YEAR SYMBOLS

What you'll see immediately is that there are several different fonts (writing styles) which give the dates. These can be quite difficult to determine, especially in dirtier or worn pieces or where the script is small. This is when you really need both a loupe and a hallmark book because there are so many variations to learn. If in doubt, ask the dealer for the date or to borrow a hallmark book, most precious metals or jewellery dealers carry them. *WIW*

COMPACTS

Compacts were a popular romantic gift from the 1920s to the 1950s with the more elaborate versions housing lipstick cases, some even being musical. Most simply had a mirror and contained powder. The most desirable are novelty (shaped) compacts by makers such as Pygmalion, with Kigu and Stratton also highly collectable.

KIGU MUSICAL FLYING SAUCER

Kigu's popular flying saucer. This is the rarer two-tone version which is also musical. The one with the butterfly is the rarest (BCCS)

A&C 70, now worth £350-450

SCHUCO BEAR COMPACT

Schuco compact usually made of tin and covered in mohair. The body of each bear opens up to reveal the powder compact hidden inside and one even contains the original powder. Less than 10cm high, also available as perfume bottles (PH ED)

A&C 30, now worth £400-500 each

VOLUPTE LACED HAND

Boxed Volupte hand-shaped compact c 1948. This is the rarer, lace-covered version, also comes as a plain hand (BCCS)

A&C 70, now worth £225-300

Fact File

Compacts were so-called because they were small (or compact) make-up cases, many containing pressed (or 'compacted') powder.

They are believed to have originated in the 17th century from 'patch boxes' when people would stick patches on to their faces to hide the marks of smallpox. For more modern versions check that the mirror is still there and not broken as this will affect their value and is hard to replace.

Stick to novelty, stylish or signed examples for best buys and be prepared to pay for better examples. Although plainer ones tend to sell for around £8-12, novelty versions, such as the Pygmalion piano, can fetch around £150-200 but the very best are the jewelled Art Deco examples by Cartier worth several thousand pounds.

THE ENVELOPE

Coty's Envelope compact was famously used in Hitchcock's classic film, *Marnie* and is signed on the inside (BCCS)

A&C 70, now worth £75-125

COTY FLYING COLOURS

Coty's patriotic Flying Colours, a triple vanity (lipstick, powder and cigarettes) based on eagle's wings with red, white and blue (BCCS)

A&C 67, now worth £150-200

PYGMALION GLOBE

Pygmalion globe, 1951. The firm was famous for its novelty compacts, although Pygmalion did not make them themselves, relying on firms such as Kigu (BCCS)

A&C 70, now worth £125-150

JINGLE BELLS

Boxed Coty Jingle Bells compact with six bells at the top of the compact (BCCS)

A&C 70, now worth £100-150

THE DIAL

Compact resembling an old telephone dial, 1954. Originally sold for $2. As with all compacts, try to avoid any with scratched surfaces which devalues them (BCCS)

A&C 70, now worth £175-225

ACCESSORIES

HANDBAGS

This essential bag is as much a status symbol as a practical method of carrying day-to-day necessities, with some more practical than others. The most collectable versions are designer (for example Chanel) or 1950s versions made of perspex, which are transparent but stylishly retro.

1950S HANDBAGS

Two 1950s handbags, valued at around £10–15 each

A&C 39, est £10-15, now worth £40-60 each

CHANEL

Three Chanel handbags sold in separate lots. For many, the Chanel bag is still the ultimate status symbol, including vintage ones

A&C, now worth £200-300 each

WEIGHING UP THE MOTIFS

Handbag with motifs including warriors and animals in a Bakelite frame

A&C, now worth £100-150

CHANEL

Pair of Chanel belts with miniature pendant handbags, sold as a pair (CHRIS)

A&C 39, sold for £322, now worth £300-500

VALENTINO

Collection of handbags by Valentino (CHRIS)

A&C 39, est £200-400 each, now worth £250-500

Fact File

Plastic handbags from the 1950s have a great sense of fun which would have been missing in the war years. They were predominantly American with the most sought after being made by Llewellyn. Of these, the most desirable is the beehive bag, made of honey-coloured plastic in 1951. It was much copied by other designers, with the original costing £200–300.

Handbags came in different shapes with the bucket-style bag of Enid Collins of Texas (£45-90, depending on shape, pattern and condition) being very popular – as well as practical.

Many of the bags bought now will not just be for collecting but using so choose with care.

WALDYBAG

The British 'Waldybag', a luxury evening bag with purse. By Wald & Co, in cream silk, with beaded flower motif and label, 1950-54. (V&A Picture Library)

A&C 39, now worth £200-400

KITSCH COLLECTABLES

Pair of 1950s kitsch handbags. Poodles were a popular symbol of the era. This bag is made of plasticised raffia. The apple-topped bag is now worth £120-150

A&C 23, est £65-85, now worth £80-100

BLACK AND WHITE BUYS

Chanel handbag, with a pair of unworn matching shoes (CHRIS)

A&C 39, sold for £402, now worth £400-600

WALKING STICKS

The supporting sticks were made from a variety of materials other than wood including whalebone, minerals (including malachite, a rich green colour) and even glass. What makes the sticks so attractive tends not to be the stick itself but its handle with carved ivory, colourful enamel and decorative silver being the most appealing.

ALBATROSS STICK

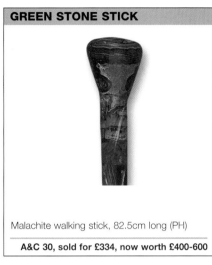

Bone-mounted albatross walking stick with exaggerated beak creating a handle (PH)

A&C 30, sold for £173, now worth £200-400

GREEN STONE STICK

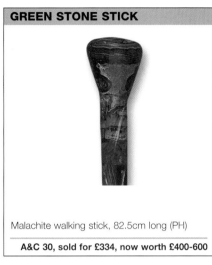

Malachite walking stick, 82.5cm long (PH)

A&C 30, sold for £334, now worth £400-600

HOUNDY SUPPORT

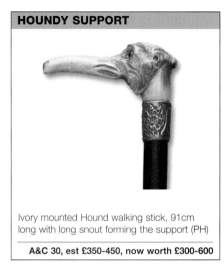

Ivory mounted Hound walking stick, 91cm long with long snout forming the support (PH)

A&C 30, est £350-450, now worth £300-600

Fact File

It is illegal to sell swordsticks (walking sticks with swords inside) to anyone, no matter what their age so we recommend that you do not buy these sticks, no matter how attractive. Ask if the tip or top of the stick unscrews before buying to save you from a costly purchase – you won't be able to sell it on if it is a swordstick.

If you need a stick for walking, it is worth being aware that many of the older walking sticks, such as the Regency ones, were not intended to offer support but merely as an effect and were popular with the Dandies of the day. Some even contained pomanders to ward off the evil smells of the street in an unhygienic age.

BALL TOP STYLE

Late-19th century ivory and hardstone mounted lady's cane with frog carving, 88cm long (PH)

A&C 30, sold for £299, now worth £500-600

STARRY STICK

Late-19th century Austrian silver and jewel mounted walking cane, 85cm long (PH)

A&C 30, sold for £265, now worth £400-600

LADY'S CANE

Late-19th century ivory and enamel mounted lady's cane, 91cm long (PH)

A&C 30, sold for £322, now worth £400-600

BEAR STICK STAND

A carved wooden bear acts as a stick stand. The late-19th century, Black Forest stand has a detachable drip tray (CHEF)

A&C 28, sold for £2,800 now worth £2,500-4,000

PORCELAIN TOP

Porcelain and silver mounted lady's cane, c 1904, 89cm long. Estimate £300-400

A&C 30, sold for £437, now worth £500-700

Bagham Barn Antiques
Chilham, Kent

- Over 4,500 sq. ft of High Quality Antiques
- For the Specialist, Collector & Enthusiast
- Close to Channel Tunnel & M20
- Shipping can be arranged
- Restoration services available
- Minutes from Historic Canterbury
- Open Tues - Sun 10 am - 5pm

- Large Cabinets filled with collectables
- Courier Service to Mainline Stations
- Adjacent to Chilham Railway Station
- Euro's & Cedit Cards accepted
- 14th Century B&B, perfect for weekends
- Cafe & Large Car Park
- Open Bank Holiday Mondays

Collectively over 200 years experience in the trade makes us your first port of call

For further information contact:
Peggy Boyd on 01227 732 522 or 07780 675201
Baghan Barn, Canterbury Road, Chilham, Kent CT4 8DU
www.baghambarn.com

ADVERTISING

This area has mass appeal whether you wish to concentrate on one make (eg Guinness), a subject (eg chocolate) or a type of advertising such as signs. These goods were created to attract business, encourage loyalty and raise awareness of a brand or new product, which makes many of them innovative. It's an exciting area to collect.

CAMEL PAPERWEIGHT

Cammell Laird shipbuilders paperweight from 1920. ship-related goods are popular (MILL)

A&C 56, sold for £75–£85, now worth £80–90

HAIR RESTORER

Elaborate 19th century ceramic figure promoting Mrs S A Allen's hair restorer (MILL)

A&C 56, worth £3,000, now worth £3,200

OXO DISPENSER

Brass OXO dispenser, 1910. OXO tins are very collectable with their distinctive letters (MILL)

A&C 56, worth £150–75, now worth £160-180

SHOP DISPLAY

Three early shop advertising tins from 1880. Tea goods are very popular (MILL)

A&C 56, worth £400–500, now worth £450–500

Fact File

Sadly, there are thousands of fake advertising goods on the market. However, such forgeries are usually quite easy to spot as they exhibit no real signs of age.

The metal boards were generally designed for displaying outside shops but many of the modern versions are just too clean – rust is a good sign of age as is genuine cracking of the enamelling, not regular cracking which will have been faked. Look for hammer marks around the holes.

Beware of Guinness fakes which proliferate the market – the supposed Carlton Ware figures are too brightly coloured, the weight is wrong (unbalanced or too light) and the moulding crude.

MIRROR

Palethorpes Sausages mirror, from 1920, popular with interior designers (MILL)

A&C 56, worth £250–300, now worth £250–300

ENAMEL SIGN

Selo Film enamel cut out sign, dated 1920 appealing to camera collectors (MILL)

A&C 56, worth £200–250, now worth £250–300

MENU HOLDER

Perrier metal menu holder (1925–1935). Bottle-shaped goods are very popular (MILL)

A&C 56, worth £25–30, now worth £30–50

CHIQUITA BANANA

'Naked Girl in a Banana', Mel Ramos (b.1935) and Pietro Psaier (b.1939), acrylic and silk screen on canvas (CHEF)

A&C 63, sold for £550, now worth £600–700

ART DECO

CHINA AND DESIGNS

Art Deco china is always popular whether you have the funds to collect top quality makes such as Clarice Cliff or Charlotte Rhead or wish to buy at the more affordable end of the market, collecting makes such as Myott and Grindley. It's easy to spot, just look for brightly coloured, stylish pieces, especially in yellow and orange patterns.

CLARICE CLIFF TREES

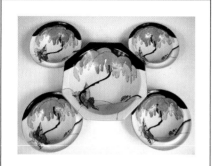

Clarice Cliff 'Woodland' pattern, factory painted and impressed marks. She used tree patterns quite often (SWORD)

A&C 65, sold for £400, now worth £400–600

BIZARRE PATTERN

Clarice Cliff Bizarre 'Melon' pattern bowl, of octagonal outline, for Newport Pottery. A less renowned pattern (WINT)

A&C 34, sold for £290, now worth £200–400

Fact File

Clarice Cliff and Charlotte Rhead might be the top makes in terms of quality and design but some of the more affordable Deco such as Myott and Grindley are great to collect now because prices are so reasonable – but not for long.

Now is the best time to buy the less popular/renowned makes because Clarice is peaking and buyers are looking for the next big thing. You might also want to think about concentrating on a certain type of Deco china such as jugs or figures. Goldscheider figures are probably the best but makes such as Wade do some stunning versions which are surprisingly affordable – not to mention stylish.

SUSIE COOPER

Four-piece Moons and Mountains Susie Cooper part teaset with worn enamel, teapot, teacup, plate and cream jug (GORR)

A&C 43, sold for £650, now worth £XX

BRIGHTLY COLOURED DECO

Susie Cooper silver lustre floral plate with wide green borders, 27.5cm (GORR)

A&C 43, sold for £120, now worth £100–200

DOTTY DECO

Susie Cooper egg set, produced by the Crown Works, Burslem. Susie Cooper's designs are highly sought after (SHREW)

A&C 6, for sale, £44, now worth £60–100

CLASSIC CLARICE

Clarice's Bizarre conical coffee set in 'Applique Orange Lucerne'

A&C 38, sold £10,350, now worth £10–15,000

SUSIE COOPER JUG

A large Susie Cooper jug painted with stylised foliage in muted colours

A&C 43, sold for £100, now worth £100-150

GEOMETRIC DESIGNS

Susie Cooper jugs and charger, typical colours and designs of the era with the geometric style very collectable (BON)

A&C 43, jugs now worth £100–200 each

DECO FLOWERS

Latona Bouquet Lotus jug by Clarice Cliff, from around 1930, painted with stylised flowers and leaves (SOTH)

A&C 66, sold £1,920, now worth £1,500–2,500

GERMAN DECO

Bock-Walllendorf, German Art Deco figure, an exotic female dancer (DAH)

A&C 16, sold for £140, now worth £250–350

SCHNEIDER GLASS VASE

Schneider glass vase from 1925, Art Deco with Art Nouveau lines (SOTH)

A&C 51, sold for £1,680, now worth £1,500–2,500

PAUL PHILIPPE

Paul Philippe cold painted bronze and ivory figure of *Girl with Parrot*, c.1930, typical Deco movement (SOTH)

A&C 51, sold £12,600, now worth £10–15,000

FERDINAND PREISS

Autumn Dancer, bronze and ivory figures cast and carved from a model by Ferdinand Preiss, 37cm high (CHRIS)

A&C 57, sold £21,150, now worth £20–25,000

CHIPARUS

Starfish Girl, signed Chiparus bronze, with ivory face and hands, wearing a green cold painted costume (GORR)

A&C 45, sold £11,800, now worth £10–20,000

Fact File

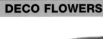

Clarice Cliff's colourful, often bizarre work influenced much of British Deco china but it almost never happened. The pottery's salesmen laughed at her outrageous designs – but sold out in two days, launching one of the most popular movements of all time.

Where Art Nouveau had looked backwards to medieval times, Deco celebrated life and the cheerful colours and garish flowers – not real flowers but free-flowing versions – make this one of the happiest movements of all time, one of the reasons why it is so popular. It's strange to think that highly sought after pieces such as those by Clarice Cliff were actually made for the masses and sold at Woolworths.

SUSIE COOPER STYLE

Homage to the past, 'Recumbent Deer' set, limited edition of 500, 1997. Picture courtesy of Josiah Wedgwood & Sons Ltd.

A&C 43, now worth £20–30

BRUNO ZACH

Bronze and ivory scuplture by Bruno Zach, modelled as a classical female warrior riding a horse, 46cm (FELL)

A&C 57, sold for £5,800, now worth £5–7,000

ART DECO

FURNITURE

For the first time in years, furniture took on a very different style. Deco changed the shape of furniture. Sweeping lines were created, the circle dominated and light coloured wood replaced the austerity of mahogany. Deco furniture dared to defy convention, but despite this, much of it is surprisingly affordable and very stylish.

COCKTAIL CABINET

Fluted demi-lune (semi-circular) cocktail cabinet, the upper section opens to reveal a pink mirrored interior (SWORD)

A&C 56, sold for £1,900, now worth £2–4,000

SMOKER'S COMPANION

Walnut veneered smoker's companion, with two cross banded tiers, and cantilever support, classic curves (MALL)

A&C 50, sold for £360, now worth £300–500

CLASSIC DECO ARMCHAIR

English lounge chair, classic Deco shape but of superior quality (CHRIS)

A&C 38, est. £700–900, now worth £700–900

DESIGNER DECO

Walnut armchair, attributed to Pierre Patout, one of the best Deco designers

A&C 38, est £3–4,000, now worth £3–5,000

Fact File

Deco bedroom furniture is surprisingly cheap to buy at auction – around £500 for a non-designer set, including a dressing table with that all-important circular mirror.

Names to look out for include Epstein (the family of Beatles' manager, Brian Epstein), Sue et Mare, Heal and Son (famous London furniture shop) and Jean Dunand. However, Deco furniture does not have to be designer to be desirable and is easily found at fairs, centres and auctions, as well as on the Internet so it's worth shopping around, especially for the ubiquitous cocktail cabinet.

As with all older goods, change all old electrical cords before use – some cocktail cabinets can be lethal, otherwise. Expect to pay over £100 for even the most basic Deco cocktail cabinet.

EGYPTIAN INFLUENCE

Pair of macassar ebony side chairs by Emile-Jacques Ruhlmann showing an Egyptian influence, a popular theme (SOTH)

A&C 14, sold for £27,600, now worth £20–35,000

CHROME AND BAKELITE

An Art Deco chrome and bakelite coffee table, typical materials of the era and popular with designers, 60cm in diameter (PH)

A&C 5, sold for £42, now worth £150–250

JEWELLERY AND FIGURES

The Art Deco period produced fantastic vintage jewellery from the glamour of Cartier's real jewellery to Eisenberg's ice range – fake diamonds which are worth hundreds of pounds. Women were important to the success of the style, not just as buyers but their naked form, seen typically in figures and on clocks.

DECO DIAMONDS

Art Deco diamond plaque brooch, the buckle centre with mille-grain set diamond cluster (CHRIS)

A&C 28, sold for £3,525, now worth £5–7,000

JOSEF LORENZI CLOCK

Art Deco figural clock by Josef Lorenzi, from around 1930, the crouching nude modelled holding a circular dial (SOTH)

A&C 65, sold £8,400, now worth £8–10,000

RECLINING NUDE

'The Hunter', a gilt bronze and marble figural clock, cast from a model by Georges Lavroff, 1920s. Geometric dial and panels cast with leaping gazelles, colourful marble base, surmounted by figure of Diana the Huntress (CHRIS)

A&C 28, sold for £1,762, now worth £2–4,000

THE BIRTH OF DECO

A French Art Deco bronze octagonal plaque 'Exposition Internationale Des Arts Décoratifs et Industriels Modernes', Paris 1925, signed P. Turin (ACAD)

A&C 7, sold for £100, now worth £300-500

DECO DANCER

Josef Lorenzi Art Deco silvered bronze dancer on an onyx plinth (GORR)

A&C 53, sold £1,100, now worth £1,500–2,500

Fact File

When it came to jewellery, green or red, teamed with black, dominated the era. It was an age influenced by Egypt, especially the discovery of Tutankhamen in 1922, three years before Deco offically started and this influenced some of the styles of the day, including designers such as Chanel, with colourful scarabs (Egyptian-style beetles) a popular theme.

While Cartier dominated real jewellery, combining quality with innovative designs, costume jewellery thrived and produced collectable styles from Trifari's 'jelly bellies' (Lucite-centred brooches which looked like jelly – but beware of fakes) to Bakelite jewellery and accessories – the thick plastic enduringly popular, especially the brilliant red (not really Bakelite according to purists but termed as such by the costume jewellery world).

COCKTAIL RING

Cocktail ring, Art Deco, diamonds and sapphire, a popular pairing (CLEV)

A&C 36, sold £4,000, now worth £4,500–6,000

WALLMASK

Face mask probably by Colcough & Co, featuring a typical hairstyle of the era (FELL)

A&C 43, sold for £95, now worth £80–120

CARTIER

A Cartier gold and platinum mounted pendant inset with a mother of pearl plaque carved with a study of The Ascension and set with pearls and diamonds with an enamel border (GORR)

A&C 56, sold £1,300, now worth £1,500–2,000

ART NOUVEAU

GLASS

The Art Nouveau period produced some of the best studio glass ever with French designers, Daum and Gallé dominating the market along with American Louis Comfort Tiffany, famous for his Tiffany lamps. The period also inspired iridescent glass with its oil-like colouring in greens, pinks and purples.

LOETZ GLASS

Silver-mounted large Loetz vase, after 1905, top Art Nouveau glass (SOTH)

A&C 58, sold for £5,400, now worth £6-7,000

IRIDESCENT GLASS

Large Loetz iridescent glass bowl, 18.5cm with pewter surround (DREW)

A&C 38, est £200-250, now worth £800-1,200

DRAMATIC TABLE LAMP

Iridescent glass and bronze table lamp c 1910, by Gustav Gurschner (SOTH)

A&C 51, sold for £5,400, now worth £6-7,500

WMF METAL WITH GLASS BOWL

WMF Art Nouveau silvered metal and green glass bowl centrepiece with scroll handles. The German firm often used glass to complement their metal (GORR)

A&C 61, sold for £400, now worth £400-600

WINE JUG

Art Nouveau wine jug, the silver-plated mount moulded with intertwined irises and leaves, the bulbous body etched with a stylised foliage design (DAH)

A&C 8, sold for £220, now worth £400-600

Fact File

Louis Comfort Tiffany was the son of esteemed jeweller, Charles Lewis Tiffany. He was originally a painter and trained in the USA and France before deciding to become a glassmaker.

He coined the term 'favrile' for his work basing it on the Latin word, *faber*, meaning 'craftsman' because his colourful glass was handmade.

It is much copied, allowing everyone to own a piece of Tiffany's legacy, even if real pieces are beyond the pockets of most people with the record price at auction being set in 1997 when prices were at their highest and a Tiffany lotus lamp sold at Christie's for $1.2 million (around £750,000 at the current exchange rate).

GALLE CAMEO VASE

Acid-etched cameo glass vase by Gallé, one of the most distinctive styles of the movement and highly collectable (CHRIS)

A&C 53, sold for £3,290, now worth £3-4,000

GALLÉ FLUID GLASS

Gallé vase, one of the best known of the Art Nouveau glassmakers (CHRIS)

A&C 53, sold for £3,290, now worth £3,500

DAUM GLASS

Acid-etched glass with crocus design by Daum, another of the top makers of French Art Nouveau glass (CHRIS)

A&C 17, sold £7,050, now worth £6-8,000

JEWELLERY

Art Nouveau jewellery is beautiful and surprisingly subtle, relying on predominantly green and blue enamels for its appeal. Two names dominated the era – Charles Horner and Liberty & Co, the London shop, whose jewellery designers included Jessie M. King, Fred Partridge and Archibald Knox.

LALIQUE BROOCH

An enamel, diamond and baroque pearl brooch, c 1890, by Lalique (CHRIS)

A&C 12, sold £47,700, now worth £50-70,000

GEORGES FOUQUET

A gold and enamel Hornet brooch made in 1901 by Georges Fouquet, one of France's top designers (© Mucha Trust/ADAGP, Paris and DACS, London)

Estimated value £10-15,000

Fact File

The jewellery often explored nature, with insects such as dragonflies and flowers such as lilies and irises being especially popular.

When looking at enamel jewellery from this era, always look for the initials 'C. H.' – Charles Horner, whose work epitomised the jewellery of the era with its enamelled designs. The blue-green enamelling pays a homage to the Arts and Crafts era, especially Ruskin's work

Although Archibald Knox was allowed to add his name to Liberty & Co pieces, other designers such as Jessie M. King and Frank Partridge were not but King's examples are more feminine than her male counterparts and she was particularly notable for using enamel flowers, especially rosebuds, on her jewellery.

ENAMEL BROOCH

Charles Horner blue enamel brooch with two paste stones, 1908, scratched (ACC)

A&C 58, now worth £100-150

HAIR ORNAMENT

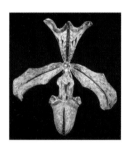

Orchid hair ornament made from gold, enamel, diamonds and rubies, designed by Philippe Wolfers in 1902 (Copyright DACS)

A&C 12, now worth £20-40,000

DIAMOND PENDANT

Art Nouveau diamond, enamel and chased gold heart shaped pendant with Baroque pearl and flower detail, made in 1905 (BON)

A&C 41, est £700, now worth £800-1,000

PENDANT NECKLACE

Philippe Wolfers enamel, diamond and pearl pendant necklace c 1900. Only 139 Art Nouveau pieces were made, of which 109 were jewels, crafted by Wolfers rather than a production piece by Wolfers Freres (CHRIS)

A&C 12, sold £23,000, now worth £30-40,000

DRAGONFLY WOMAN

René Lalique Dragonfly Woman using gold, enamel, chrysoprase, moonstones and diamonds, c 1897-98. The wings feature plique à jour enamel. (Copyright Calouste Gulbenkian Museum, Lisbon)

A&C 12, now worth £50-80,000

HAIR COMB

A rare Art Nouveau horn and enamel hair comb by Philippe Wolfers c 1895 (CHRIS)

A&C 12, sold £10,350, now worth £12-18,000

ART NOUVEAU

METALWORK

Art Nouveau metalwork is very distinctive with its elongated look – willowy women and stretched plants, especially tulips and lilies. Firms such as WMF and Liberty created the distinctive, almost feminine style with silver and pewter being the most popular of the metals, closely followed by copper.

LIBERTY TUDRIC BOWL

Liberty Tudric pewter bowl with Clutha liner, Archibald Knox design (CHRIS)

A&C 23, sold for £3,525, now worth £4-5,000

ENAMEL RELIEF

Art Nouveau box made of copper and brass, the lid decorated with an inset enamel panel adding interest (GORR)

A&C 64, sold for £240, now worth £200-300

PICTURE FRAME

Art Nouveau pewter picture frame with symmetrical design (The Antique Trader)

A&C 16, sold £1,200, now worth £1,500-1,800

SILVER BUCKLE

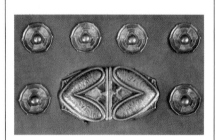

Silver Liberty buckle with six hexagonal green and blue enamel buttons, marked 'L & Co., Cymric', Birmingham, 1903. From their popular silver range (SWORD)

A&C 56, sold for £1,150, now worth £1,000-1,600

LIBERTY TEASET

A Liberty & Co silver and ivory four-piece teaset, designed by Archibald Knox, 1905, their top designer (CHRIS)

A&C 23, sold £7,050, now worth £8-12,000

Fact File

Liberty & Co is a famous retail store in London's Regent Street and they set the trend for the movement in Britain. Their most famous metalwork designer was Archibald Knox whose heavy-set pieces are very distinctive and do extremely well at auction – expect to pay around £300 for a small, fairly standard clock, over £1,000 for a more unusual version and several thousand for teasets.

You'll hear two words mentioned when it comes to Liberty's – Cymric and Tudric. The former was the name for their silver range, the latter pewter. Liberty's work was actually inspired by the German firm, WMF (*Württemembergische Metallwarenfabrik*) but is bulkier, almost more masculine than the German make and tends to command higher prices in the British market.

CANDELABRUM

A pewter candelabrum, c 1900 with the typical Art Nouveau willowy figure inspired by the Age of Chivalry (CHRIS)

A&C 16, sold for £3,525, now worth £4-6,000

CHRISTENING CUP

An Omar Ramsden and Alwyn Carr christening cup, London, 1906 (CHRIS)

A&C 23, sold for £1,645, now worth £2-4,000

ORIVIT LAMP

A silvered metal table lamp with naked lady, made by Orivit, c 1900 (CHRIS)

A&C 16, sold for £2,232, now worth £3-5,000

FURNITURE

Arts and Crafts furniture was made to be used, it's sturdy and was designed to show its workmanship, you're meant to see its lines. It's a very distinctive style, much heavier than the later Art Nouveau movement, with tulips a popular theme and dark wood the preferred option. Tables are chunky but stylish and prices are rising fast.

MAHOGANY CHAIR

Arts and Crafts-style mahogany chair, early-twentieth century (AMER)

A&C 30, sold for £190, now worth £350-500

HEAL'S AND SON OAK CHEST

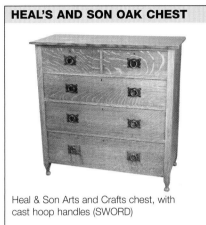

Heal & Son Arts and Crafts chest, with cast hoop handles (SWORD)

A&C 53, sold for £800, now worth £800-1,000

RENNIE MACKINTOSH

Two low-backed armchairs designed by Charles Rennie Mackintosh.(BON)

A&C 11, sold for £41,100, now worth £30-60,000

HEAL & SON CHEST

A Heal & Son oak chest of drawers, c.1904. The Tottenham Court Road shop was famous for the quality of its designs and work (CHRIS)

A&C 20, est £600-800, now worth £800-1,000

Fact File

What sets Arts and Crafts furniture apart from other styles is the workmanship – not only is it good but it's meant to be seen. It's a celebration of the art of furniture making. Table legs became an important part of the decoration, not there simply to hold up a table.

Some of the best examples were sold at Liberty's with top designers including Charles Voysey, a famous architect, as well as a designer. Liberty's furniture was typically British Arts and Crafts with its emphasis on the symmetrical.

One of the most famous names of the movement was William Morris whose company, Morris & Co made highly desirable furniture including the famous Sussex chair, famous for its rustic simplicity.

SIDE TABLE

A rare side table by Charles Rennie Mackintosh (BON)

A&C 11, sold for £42,000, now worth £30-50,000

PANNELLED SETTLE

Arts and Crafts settle, with panelled back and circular embossed plaques above solid seat, on shaped stretcher supports (CRIT)

A&C 13, sold for £1,700, now worth £1,500-3,000

VOYSEY REPRODUCTION

A replica of a Voysey high back chair. It retails for £750, while an original Voysey piece would be valued at around £50,000. (The Arts & Crafts Home)

A&C 20, sold for £750, now worth £750

SIDEBOARD

Sideboard, cornice with protruding angles above an arched mirror plate, flanked by typical Arts and Crafts leaded glass and panel doors. (PH ED)

A&C 28, sold for £2,990, now worth £2,000-4,000

ARTS & CRAFTS

JEWELLERY

The whole ethos of the Arts and Crafts movement was to show the craftsmanship behind the work and this can be seen with the stunning jewellery which was produced during this late Victorian era. The green-blue enamelling for which the movement was renowned was typified in the work of Ruskin and his imitators including Kensington.

LIBERTY BELT BUCKLE

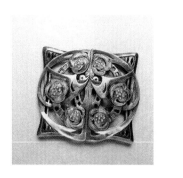

Silver and enamel belt buckle for Liberty (BON)

A&C 60, sold for £2,000, now worth £1,800-2,000

Fact File

Some jewellery experts suggest that the movement was hindered by its refusal to use machinery and the lack of training in goldsmithery, claiming that the work is amateurish when compared with later movements but others disagree, valuing the freshness of the designs and their use of colour.

Although the designs were original, they also owed much to the Renaissance, especially the looped necklaces and large crosses.

The most famous jewellery designer of the movement was C. R. (Charles Robert) Ashbee who established the Guild of Handicraft in 1888 with many of his pieces signed 'G of H Ltd' or, less often, 'C.R.A.'. Because it was handmade, all of his work is unique which is what makes the movement so desirable.

BROOCH PENDANT

Gold and enamel brooch pendant, by Robert Phillips, 1875 (SOTH)

A&C 60, sold for £900, now worth £800-1,000

LIBERTY NECKLACE

Enamel, opal and pearl necklace from 1900, in a fitted case by Liberty & Co Ltd (SOTH)

A&C 60, est £4,000-6,000, now worth £4,000-6,000

LIBERTY'S PARTNER

Set of six silver and enamel buttons, with stamped marks, by William Haseler of Birmingham, 1906 (BON)

A&C 60, sold for £940, now worth £800-1,200

BERNARD CUZNER

Arts and Crafts gold pendant in the style of Bernard Cuzner, a baroque pearl drop suspended below (GORR)

A&C 60, sold for £2,000, now worth £2,000-2,500

SIBYL DUNLOP

Gem-set cross by Sibyl Dunlop with enamel floral design on the back (SOTH)

A&C 60, est £3,000-4,000, now worth £3-4,000

COMPARE TO ART NOUVEAU

A pair of Charles Horner Art Nouveau enamelled brooches, one openwork kidney shaped, the other winged shape, the designs simpler than Arts and Crafts (BON)

A&C 60, sold for £180, now worth £150-250

CHINA & METALWORK

Copper came into its own with the Arts and Crafts movement, the metal becoming almost fluid under the master craftsmen who handcrafted the wares. The Guild of Handicraft excelled during this period, turning metal into artwork. They were highly influenced by Medieval times which, in turn, would influence the Art Nouveau era.

RED LUSTRE PLATE

William de Morgan circular red lustre plate, painted with a galleon weighing anchor.(BON)

A&C 59, sold for £850, now worth £800-1,200

Fact File

Some of the greatest names in metalwork of this genre were The Roycrofters, a community in East Aurora, America which was started by Elbert Hubbard with similar ideals to the Guild of Handicraft. Although influenced by the English Arts and Crafts movement, they were distinctly American and are highly collectable, especially their hammered metalwork and furniture which is known as Aurora Colonial furniture or Mission Style.

In England, one of the greatest exponents of the art was John Pearson who honed his skills while working for William de Morgan and whose copper charges with their stylised birds, snakes and other motifs greatly influenced the Newlyn School, another collectable area in this genre based around the community of artists in Cornwall.

WILLIAM DE MORGAN

William de Morgan ruby lustre dish, possibly painted by Charles Passenger, and impressed J. H. Davis (DREW)

A&C 59, sold for £720, now worth £800-1,200

NEWLYN COPPER

A large Newlyn copper bowl with a frieze of fish. Newlyn copper is very collectable and commands premium prices (WO WA)

A&C, est £700-900, now worth £700-1,00

BRANNAM VASE

Early-twentieth century Brannam Pottery vase, by John Dewdney. Decorated with scraffito Arts & Crafts inspired floral motifs. Incised signature and dated 1905, 42.5cm high (AMER)

A&C 35, sold for £290, now worth £300-450

NEWLYN TEASET

Newlyn copper three-piece teaset stamped Newlyn, som damage (WO WA)

A&C, est £200-300, now worth £500-600

KESWICK SCHOOL

Rare charger depicting stags and the Tudor rose, made by the Keswick School of Industrial Arts, one of the most collectable makes of Arts and Crafts metalwork (WO WA)

A&C, est £2,200-2,800 now worth £2,000-4,000

GUILD OF HANDICRAFT

A Birmingham Guild of Handicraft copper lamp, the conical hammered shade on a waisted cylindrical stem with four arched feet, 57cm high (WO WA)

A&C, sold for £1,500, now worth £1,500-2,500

JOHN PEARSON

Large copper charger signed JPEARSON, 1896. John Pearson was one of the best metalwork designers of the movement and his work is highly sought after (WO WA)

A&C, sold for £2,000, now worth £2,000-3,000

AUTOGRAPHS & LETTERS

SCRIPOLOGY

This is a very exciting area to collect, which falls under two headings – ephemera (paper goods) or scripology (the love of writing) and has many sub-divisions, for example political and entertainment or you might want to collect letters covering certain areas such as love letters, social history or exploration.

MARILYN MONROE

1950s autographed photograph of the screen star, Marilyn Monroe (SOTH)

A&C 46, est £3–5,000, now worth £6–8,000

AUDREY HEPBURN

The elegant actress, Audrey Hepburn in checked hat and overcoat (FRAS)

A&C 48, sold £975, now worth £1,000–1,200

ELVIS, THE KING

Souvenir menu for a Summer Festival at the International Hotel, Las Vegas signed on the cover by Elvis (CO OW)

A&C 46, est. £250–300, now worth £350–450

THE COMPLETE BEATLES

Autographs on a scrap of notepaper signed by all four Beatles (CO OW)

A&C 42, sold for £1,400, now worth £7–8,000

Fact File

Not all letters are equal and the same goes for autographs. A letter from Nelson discussing a famous battle (such as Trafalgar) or historical event is of far more value than a more mundane version to a friend or family member.

The content is vital for maximising profits although autographs by themselves are highly desirable if for the right person.

It's worth remembering that James Dean died young so had less time to sign than the long-lived Joan Crawford who spent the last few decades of her life signing autographs, including all of her fan mail, so his signature is worth far more than hers (£3,000–3,500 compared to around £15–30). The same is true of Marilyn Monroe and Diana, Princess of Wales.

ROB ROY

A rare signed letter from Scotland's Rob Roy about his agreement with the Duke of Montrose requesting payment (LY TU)

A&C 21, sold for £14,000, now worth £12–16,000

CHRISTOPHER LEE

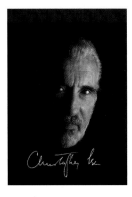

Christopher Lee is said to be one of the most prolific film actors and his filmography includes some cult films, especially horror classics

A&C 57, est £100, now worth £100–150

ON THE ROAD

Signed photograph of popular comedy duo, Bob Hope and Bing Crosby (CO OW)

A&C 56, sold for £110, now worth £150–180

MARGARET THATCHER

As Britain's only female PM and because of her strong personality, Margaret Thatcher's autograph's is a good buy

A&C 57, sold for £150, now worth £400–500

WALT DISNEY

An autograph book with Walt Disney's signature, dated 1935 (SOTH)

A&C 47, est. £350–450, now worth £400–500

OL' BLUE EYES

Frank Sinatra still has a huge following and, despite his longevity, his signed photo can sell for more than that of Elvis (CO OW)

A&C 56, sold for £620, now worth £600–700

PADDINGTON BEAR

Paddington's creator Michael Bond is popular with all ages, ask him to sign your children's books – his crime books for adults are not as good investments

A&C 57, est. £50–70, now worth £60–80

RECORD PRICE

'Love Me Do', signed by Paul McCartney, one of the Fab Four. John Lennon still manages to outsell his fellow band members however (BON)

A&C 57, sold for £13,513, now worth £12–15,000

J. K. ROWLING

J. K. Rowling rarely signs anything so her autograph is at a premium (FRAS)

A&C 57, est £1,000, now worth £1,000–1,250

Fact File

Collecting signatures from living people is not only free but enjoyable – if you do it in person. One of the easiest ways to do this is to hang outside the stadium or theatre where they are performing or playing – or the TV or radio station for other types of 'celebrities', including politicians.

When thinking about collecting politician's signatures, you should be aware that some of them rarely reply themselves, relying on their PAs or researchers to answer their post for them. The busier the person, the more likely you are to be sent a facsimile signature – that's when a signature pen or computer signature is used – and it's not worth anything. It's advisable only to buy from established businesses when buying autographs as there are so many fakes around, especially of elusive stars such as the late Marlon Brando. Autograph books are more reliable as they were collected in person.

The *Autograph* Shop

www.autograph-shop.co.uk
Tel: 01869 320494

BOOKS

BOOK collecting has changed hugely over the last twenty years. Antiquarian books with their exquisite bindings have been overtaken by modern first editions where the emphasis is placed on the condition of the dust jacket. Certain genres sell better than others – crime and sci-fi top the league while illustrated books are always good buys and children's books cater to the nostalgia field, especially highly illustrated versions or modern favourites.

NORTHERN LIGHTS

Philip Pullman, 'Northern Lights', first edition, very light marking to extreme edges of some pages, original boards, dust-jacket, 1995

A&C 59, sold for £3,400 now worth £3–3,500

THE LORD OF THE RINGS

Tolkien's 'The Lord of the Rings', three vol., first edition, bookplate on verso of front cover, original cloth, tatty condition, 1954–55

A&C 59, sold for £4,000 now worth £4–4,500

HARRY POTTER

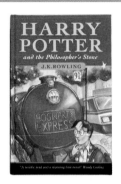

J. K. Rowling, 'Harry Potter and the Philosopher's Stone', first edition, (one of just 500 copies), original pictorial boards, very slight discolouring to top- and fore-edge, otherwise a fine copy, 1997

A&C 59, sold for £12,500 now worth £12–15,000

BIRDSONG

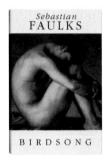

'Birdsong' by Sebastian Faulks, first edition, very slightly creased along top edge, otherwise a fine copy from 1993 (BLOOM)

A&C 59, sold for £400, now worth £300–400

KNOTS & CROSSES

Ian Rankin, 'Knots & Crosses', first edition, original boards, dust-jacket, 1987 (BLOOM)

A&C 59, sold for £650, now worth £600–700

Fact File

Illustrated children's books are always popular which is why we have a series on them in *Antiques and Collectables* with top names to spot including Kate Greenaway and Arthur Rackham whose popular work included 'Peter Pan' and 'Mother Goose'.

Books are often overlooked at general auctions and it's always worth taking the time to look through the job lots – it's possible to get around three boxes full of books for around £5 at the smaller, local auctions. What the dealers do is take out any books of interest and leave the rest there to sell at the next auction so they don't even have to worry about storage. It's the perfect way to pick up bargains.

FLAUBERT'S PARROT

Julian Barnes's 'Flaubert's Parrot', first edition with original boards and dust-jacket, from 1984

A&C 59, sold for £260, now worth £250–300

THE LETTER OF MARQUE

Patrick O'Brian, 'The Letter of Marque', first edition, original boards, dust-jacket, 1988

A&C 59, sold for £160, now worth £200–250

HOUND OF THE BASKERVILLES

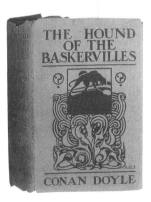

An original immaculate copy of Sir Arthur Conan Doyle's 'The Hound of the Baskervilles'

A&C 52, est. £100,000, now worth £80–100,000

Potteries Antique Centre

- Over 50 display cabinets filled with Royal Doulton, Beswick, Moorcroft, Wedgwood, Minton, Wade, Coalport, Royal Worcester, Charlotte Rhead, Clarice Cliff, Carltonware, Paragon, Pendelfin, Crown Derby and lots more...
- Figurines, Animals, Birds, Vases, Character & Toby Jugs, Limited and Special Editions, Rare and Discontinued.
- A huge selection of Antique and Reproduction Furniture, Mirrors, Pictures, Statuary & Jewellery.
- Over 8000 items to purchase on our website.
- Specialists in worldwide mail order.
- Computer 'Wants' service – for that hard to find piece.

271 Waterloo Road
Cobridge
Stoke on Trent
ST6 3HR
Tel: 01782 201 455
Fax: 01782 201 518
Email: sales@potteriesantiquecentre.com

Open Monday to Saturday 9am til 5.30pm

www.potteriesantiquecentre.com

The Brighton Lanes Antique Centre

Situated in the heart of the historic Lanes, offering a fine selection of furniture, clocks, silver, glass, lighting, ceramics, jewellery, Art Nouveau/Deco, decorative antiques, memorabilia, pens, watches and much more . . .

New stock arriving daily

Car access/loading bay

Open 7 days a week

All types of antiques purchased for cash

12 Meeting House Lane
Brighton, Sussex BN1 1HB
Tel: 01273 823121 Fax: 01273 726328
Email: contact@brightonlanes-antiquecentre.co.uk
www.brightonlanes-antiquecentre.co.uk

THE ANTIQUARIAN BOOKSELLERS' ASSOCIATION

2005 FAIRS

The Antiquarian Booksellers' Association
Sackville House, 40 Piccadilly
London W1J 0DR
Telephone 00 44 20 7439 3118
Email: admin@aba.org.uk
www.abainternational.com

ABA/PBFA Antiquarian Book Fair

25 and 26 March 2005
The Assembly Rooms
George Street, Edinburgh, Scotland
www.abainternational.com

The Antiquarian Book Fair

9 to 12 June 2005
Olympia Exhibition Centre
Hammersmith Road, London W14
www.olympiabookfair.com

The Chelsea Book Fair

4 and 5 November 2005
The Chelsea Old Town Hall
Kings Road, London
www.chelseabookfair.com

BOXES

BOXES

These are practical but beautiful collectables from a more elegant era. Writing boxes were ideal for transportation when their literate owners moved between the town and country, while sewing and jewellery boxes offered feminine storage. When looking at boxes, always check whether they have secret drawers.

POLITICAL APPEAL

From the estate of the late J. Marshall esq. A 20ct gold Irish Freedom Box presented by the city of Cork, Dublin, 1882, Carden Terry and Jane Williams of Cork (SO STH)

A&C 25, sold for £40,250, now £45–50,000

DRINK STORAGE

Regency flame mahogany cellarette, of sarcophagus shape, with raised hinged lid (ROSE)

A&C 63, sold for £1,300, now worth £1,400

IMPERIAL SEAL BOX

Eighteenth century imperial presentation box, made from carved zitan wood and silk brocade. It would have originally contained a very fine seal and a stand for use in the Imperial court (NICHOLAS S PITCHER)

A&C 62, worth £3–4,000, now worth £4,000

TABLE CABINET

Rosewood and brass-inlaid table cabinet combining spaces for writing and jewellery. The fine work and 'monumental form' are typical of the English Regency period (Joseph O'Kelly and Antigone Clarke)

A&C 56, sold for £4,000, now worth £4,200

Fact File

Some of the most popular boxes date from the Regency period and have a lion's head handle. The ring through its mouth was ideal for lifting the box, but you should avoid doing this.

When handling boxes, always lift from underneath to avoid breakage. Some boxes have been adapted for modern use, turned into decanter storage or for stationery, the original dividers removed and sometimes replaced by crude new ones.

While this might make them more practical for some people, it also devalues them. It's also worth checking that the veneer is intact and that marquetry (decoration created by using thin strips of wood) is in perfect condition – they can lift over time if not properly polished – wax polish is the best for old wood.

OAK BOX

A fine oak box with attractive painted detail, c.1630 (HAMP)

A&C 11, sold for £3,700, now worth £5–6,000

LETTER BOX

Victorian oak letter box with brass plaque and metal insignia, panelled door and rectangular base (MALL)

A&C 58, sold for £850, now worth £800–900

BELL-SHAPED CASE

A Shibayama single case gold lacquer inro (box) of bell form, signed Shibayama, Meiji period (1868–1912) (SO STH)

A&C 25, sold for £16,100, now worth £12–15,000

NOVELTY BOX

Jewellery box in the form of a Georgian house with painted ivy and two dormer windows, 13cm wide by 10cm high (SWORD)

A&C 58, sold for £850, now worth £1,200

TEA CADDIES

Some of the most attractive boxes are tea caddies, often coffer-shaped and sometimes decorated with ivory. Tea was the rich man's drink, used to denote status and the caddies reflect this, storing the tea leaves in a suitably lavish container. They were originally lead-lined to keep the contents dry but this is not safe for modern use.

REGENCY TORTOISESHELL

Regency tortoiseshell tea caddy with unusual octagonal pagoda shape and dark tortoiseshell on its embossed sides (Phillips, Edinburgh)

A&C 11, sold for £8,050, now worth £10–12,000

GEORGIAN SATINWOOD

George III satinwood and mother of pearl, the interior fitted with a mixing bowl and twin compartments (MALL)

A&C 60, sold for £400, now worth £400–600

GEORGIAN TORTOISESHELL

A fine pressed tortoiseshell tea caddy, c.1830, with oriental influence (HAMP)

A&C 7, sold for £5,200, now worth £7–9,000

GEORGE IV

George IV tortoiseshell, the domed cover with silver wire inlay on ball feet (GORR)

A&C 60, sold for £1,000, now worth £1,200

Fact File

Tea as a social nicety was at its peak in the mid-nineteenth century, which is when many of the most lavish tea caddies were produced.

The word caddy (formerly 'catty') originated from the Malayan word, *kati,* and dates from 1792. It was actually a form of measure (about a pound and a half), the weight in which tea was ordered and its meaning changed to incorporate the tea's container.

Although we usually think of tea caddies as being made of wood, there are also silver versions and an oval brass caddy with a lion symbol was created to celebrate the 1924 British Empire Exhibition at Wembley and is still easy to find today (worth around £20–30).

HORN & IVORY

A rare nineteenth century Anglo-Indian antler horn and ivory tea caddy, Vizagapatam, c.1800. (HAMP)

A&C 23, est £800–1,000, now worth £1,500–2,000

FRUITWOOD NOVELTY CADDY

Fruitwood Caddy Late-eighteenth century, pear-shaped, 18cm high (AMER)

A&C 31, sold for £3,300, now worth £5–7,000

HOUSE OF TEA

Novelty painted wood cottage with arched roof, door and windows (GORR)

A&C 56, sold for £500, now worth £500–600

VICTORIAN CADDIES

A pair of Victorian mother-of-pearl and painted tea canisters, mid-nineteenth century (SOTH)

A&C 63, sold for £1,200, now worth £1,200

BUSTS

HEAD AND SHOULDERS

It is believed that busts were based on the word *bustum*, an Etruscan custom that used a figural representation of a dead person for their ashes. Modern busts retain this desire to recreate people's images, whether famous or artists' models, and reproduce their heads, necks and shoulders, often including a hint of cleavage.

ITALIAN MARBLE BUST

Gilt bronze and marble bust of a woman with delicate features, made by Italian artist, Affortunato Gory (1895–1925) (GORR)

A&C 51, sold for £5,000, now worth £4–6,000

PARIAN WARE

A Copeland Parian Ware bust, *Hop Queen* by J. Durham, A.R.A.C. 1873 (HAMP)

A&C 8, sold for £1,500, now worth £2–3,000

PASTORAL PLEASURES

Lead bust of an eighteenth-century pastoral figure, on fluted base (DREW)

A&C 40, sold for £400, now worth £400–600

PRESERVED FOR POSTERITY

Plaster bust of William Chambers, an Edinburgh publisher and author, brother of Robert Chambers, 75cm high (PH ED)

A&C 34, sold for £300, now worth £400–600

Fact File

You might see the words 'Parian Ware' listed in an auction's catalogue when describing busts or figures. This is not a maker's name but it's actually a type of porcelain which is semi-matt so has a slight sheen to it, almost like skin. The porcelain's raw materials were mixed with the mineral feldspar so it did not need a glaze to protect it. Its name originated because of its similarity to the white marble from the Greek island. That's why it's always spelt with a capital P.

Take care when packing Parian ware because it can get stained by newspaper print – use tissue paper or bubble wrap instead and never soak in water, just clean with a cloth and avoid too much handling.

The best busts are the most detailed ones with distinct features. Female busts are generally more popular than their male counterparts because they tend to be more attractive and decorative.

ALABASTER BUST WITH BRONZE LAUREL

An alabaster bust with head to one side wearing a bronze laurel wreath signed by Professor Antonio Garella (1864–1919) (SOTH)

A&C 25, sold for £4,715, now worth £6,000–8,000

SIXTEENTH CENTURY MAN

Chalk bust of a sixteenth century male with inscription 'Antonio Pollaiolo Museo N Florence'. Probably a reproduction

A&C 1, estimated value £75–100, now worth £250–350

Ceramics

China, pottery, porcelain, call it what you will – we call it ceramics – is still the most collectable area of all and it covers a vast area. That's why we have forty pages dedicated to this exciting field, complete with essential backstamps

WHAT

Ceramics remain the most popular area of collecting, possibly because of the sheer versatility under the same banner. Ceramics is the all-encompassing term for china, porcelain, pottery and bone china although the word itself has only been in use since 1850 and comes from the Greek, *keramos* meaning 'pottery' or 'potter's clay'.

WHERE

Potters need the raw materials used to create pottery – clay, water and wood (for fire) – to survive which is why they tended to be located in areas rich with those natural substances – Limoges in France and Staffordshire and its Potteries in England. Although, as you will see from our list, there are other heartlands of potteries including Derby and Worcester, The Potteries is the location for most of Britain's most collectable makes of ceramics including Royal Doulton, Clarice Cliff and Spode, the oldest of the English potteries which has been operating on the same site since 1770.

WHY

But why should ceramics have such a mass appeal? One of the main reasons is practical, unlike furniture, ceramics fit into most homes, for this reason, it is often referred to as 'smalls', along with glass and other smaller collectables. There is something very tactile about ceramics, even the 'eggshell' thin china produced in Japan. Above all, it is beautiful, whether you're looking at the rich colours of Charlotte Rhead with its tubular designs or the brown colours of studio potters such as Bernard Leach, china draws you in. Earlier works such as blue and white and Flight and Barr's fantastically painted plates continue to appeal to collectors because of the quality of the work. In these days of mass-production and transfers, we've lost some of the beauty of earlier wares, handmade pots, hand-painted designs but some modern china is very collectable – makes such as Dennis Chinaworks with their brilliant designs pay homage to the old-fashioned ways while Wade's smaller, collectable figures continue to create a new generation of collectors.

HOW

How should you collect? Some people stick to one make – Wedgwood or Meissen are very popular. Others go for themes such as jugs or animals, some for colours – blue and white has always been popular – and others for era – Art Deco china is always a big draw. But what if your eyes are bigger than your pockets? One of the greatest appeals of china is that it appeals to all ages and purses – you don't have to have a fortune to collect – unless you're only attracted to work by the big names, the Clarice Cliffs and William de Morgans of the world. But if you do like Deco and just can't afford or justify spending money on Clarice or Charlotte Rhead, why not go for a more practical make such as Myott or Grindley? If you love china, the next few pages should whet your appetite and, as you'll see at all but the specialist fairs and auctions, ceramics are everywhere. They dominate the market which is why *Antiques and Collectables* ensures that we write about them most issues and let you know what the next must-buy areas will be.

CERAMICS

BELLEEK

The creamy porcelain is one of Ireland's most important potteries, the pearly porcelain instantly recognisable after you've seen it once. It was founded in Belleek, Co. Fermanagh in 1863 and was also known briefly as Fermanagh Pottery. The goods are sometimes referred to as 'cabinet objects', intended for admiration, not use.

OYSTER DISHES

Pair of first period Belleek oyster dishes, on nautilus shell feet (GORR)

A&C 64, sold for £230, now worth £200–300

SHAMROCK DESIGN

Nineteenth century three-piece teaset with basket bodies painted with three leaf clovers for which they, in Ireland, are famous (GORR)

A&C 64, sold for £130, now worth £150–250

FILIGREE WORK

Belleek oval covered basket, 1865–1889, in typical creamy glaze (SOTH)

A&C 64, sold for £660, now worth £600–800

SPIDER DESIGN

Belleek first period tray, 1875 of rectangular form with scalloped edges and moulded prunus, the centre moulded and painted with a spider, 24.8cm (SWORD)

A&C 64, sold for £340, now worth £300–450

SCENT BOTTLE

A very rare scent bottle. The centre is pierced while the scent is held in the wheel around the bottle (The National Museum of Ireland)

A&C 23, est. £3,000, now worth £3,000–5,000

Fact File

The most common backstamp for Belleek is the Irish wolfhound with a harp, a tower and Irish shamrocks over a banner saying Belleek. The tower is believed to be Devenish Round Tower, which is on Devenish Island in Lower Lough Erne, the Belleek pottery located by the River Erne, downstream from Lough Erne.

The word Belleek comes from its location where the river flowed over a waterfall to form a calm pool, known as Beal Leice in Gaelic, meaning 'the ford mouth of the flagstone'.

Seventh Mark, April 1, 1980–December 22, 1992

GOTHIC REVIVAL

Pair of Belleek 'Gothic' candlesticks, second period (1891–1926) (SOTH)

A&C 64, sold for £960, now worth £1,000–1,200

BIRD SPOUT

First Period Belleek teapot moulded and painted with leaves and ribbon-tassled handle, spout in the form of a bird, cover with printed instructions within (GORR)

A&C 64, sold for £240, now worth £250–400

TURNIP DESIGN

Rare 'Turnip' vase, first period (1863–1890), unusually earthy design (SOTH)

A&C 64, sold for £1,200, now worth £1,000–1,800

BESWICK

The Staffordshire-based pottery which closed in 2003 is famous for its animals and characters such as Winnie the Pooh, Alice in Wonderland and Snow White. Founded in 1894, it was bought by Royal Doulton in 1969 and appeals to their collectors as well, having the same quality and attention to detail as the famous make.

TOAD OF TOAD HALL

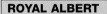

Beswick Toad of 'Wind in the Willows' fame

A&C 65, est. £60–80, now worth £60–80

ROYAL ALBERT

A rare Royal Albert Old Mr Pricklepin figure. Take care not to confuse the two makes, both owned by Doulton, both made Beatrix Potter figures, check the backstamps (POT SPEC)

A&C 11, sold for £400, now worth £400–600

JEMIMA PUDDLEDUCK

Jemima Puddleduck, the first of Beswick's Beatrix Potter figures, this is a later model

A&C 65, est. £50–70, now worth £60–70

Fact File

Beswick is pronounced Bez-ick, the 'w' being silent. If you're thinking of collecting the pottery, you might want to concentrate on one particular theme or designer (for example David Hands, Kitty McBride or Thelwell).

They are famous for their horses, some of them selling for several hundred pounds – look for grey-muzzles on brown horses, which is a sign of early versions and the rocking-horse grey is rarer than brown with Thelwell's designs always being a good buy for around £150 or less if you can.

RARE HORSE

Rare, right-facing brown chestnut mare, always check that legs, ears and tails are perfect before buying as they can get broken

A&C 65, sold for £600, now worth £600–700

FLOPSY, MOPSY & COTTONTAIL

2002 Beatrix Potter tableau of Flopsy, Mopsy and Cottontail, one of their last designs

A&C 65, est. £300, now worth £250–300

GUINEA PIG

Beswick's The Amiable Guinea Pig, from Beatrix Potter's Appley Dapply's Nursery Rhymes, produced between 1967–1983 (CHRIS)

A&C 11, sold for £460, now worth £600–800

PETER RABBIT PLAQUE

A Beswick Peter Rabbit Wall plaque with figures in relief (stick out slightly) (POT SPEC)

A&C 11, est. £50–70, now worth £100–150

RARE DUCHESS

Duchess with Flowers, from The Pie and the Patty Pan, produced between 1955–1967. This figure is the rarest of all the Beatrix Potter figures; it was the first to be withdrawn as it was thought to be too dull (CHRIS)

A&C 11, sold for £1,265, now worth £1,500–2,000

BLUE AND WHITE

Blue and white ceramics originated in China where the colouring was a popular theme in the seventeenth century. Spode was the first potter to create blue and white patterns in the late-eighteenth century and transfer prints allowed for extensive designs at affordable prices. But blue and white is so much more than simple colouring.

RUINED CASTLE

A 'Ruined Castle' tureen from 1815–1825, attributed to Robert Hamilton, the foreground shows cows wading (BON)

A&C 49, sold for £1,586, now worth £1,400–1,800

INDIAN SPORTING SERIES

A Spode blue and white 'Indian Sporting' Series, earthenware lozenge-shaped dish, c.1820, very collectable pattern (BOO)

A&C 13, sold for £520, now worth £800–1,000

GIANT SPODE TOWER

An enormous Spode 'tower' teapot of the 'Bridge of Salaro near Porta Salara' from 1820–1830 (BON)

A&C 49, sold for £763, now worth £750–1,000

STEVENSON AND WILLIAMS

A Stevenson and Williams earthenware part dinner service from around 1825 (SOTH)

A&C 49, sold for £1,175, now worth £1,000–1,500

HUNTING DESIGN

Spode meat platter 'Shooting a Leopard' pattern, cracked. Est. £800–1,000 (SWORD)

A&C 45, sold for £800, now worth £800–1,200

Fact File

Flow blue was an ingenious invention in which a chemical was added to the blue paint. This allowed it to 'run' which made transfer-printed goods look hand-painted and, as such, more valuable. It initially started as an accident when the paint ran during the glazing process and the heated colour ran over the edge of the design.

This proved to be so popular that, in late Victorian times, this was created artificially by adding chemicals to the glaze just before it was fired. Some people just collect flow blue, appreciating the richness of the colouring (often a darker blue than normal blue and white) and the hand-painted effect.

LONG SPOUTED COFFEE POT

A William Smith & Co 'tea party' pattern coffee pot from 1825–1835 (DREW)

A&C 49, sold for £580, now worth £600–800

WORCESTER WINE FUNNEL

A rare Worcester large wine funnel, c.1770, the exterior printed in underglaze blue with butterflies and sprays of flowers and leaves. The interior is decorated with roses, flowers and a butterfly (DREW)

A&C 8, sold for £4,000, now worth £5,000–7,000

GREEK SERIES

Greek series potted meat dish together with sauce tureen, attributed to Spode from around 1810 (DREW)

A&C 49, sold for £260, now worth £300–400

OSTERLEY PARK PATTERN

Osterley Park pattern washbowl, c.1815–1825, architecture was a popular theme (DREW)

A&C 49, sold for £120, now worth £100–200

FOREST LANDSCAPE I

Two Spode 'Forest Landscape I' supper set tureens and three crescent form dishes from 1810–20, one cover reveals an egg frame with two egg cups and a condiment well (BON)

A&C 49, sold for £446, now worth £500–700

DRUG JAR

Drug jar, Delft blue and white, probably Bristol, 9cm high (WINT)

A&C 38, sold for £2,200, now worth £2,500–3,000

IT'S ALL GREEK TO ME

One of a pair of Greek series dessert dishes attributed to Spode from around 1810 (DREW)

A&C 49, sold for £170, now worth £200–300

CHINESE INSPIRATION

A Spode 'Gothic Castle' supper set from 1810–1815 with a European style fortress in a Chinoiserie setting (BON)

A&C 49, sold for £305, now worth £300–450

PIERCED BASKETS

Pair of pierced baskets and stands in the Greek series attributed to Spode from around 1810 (DREW)

A&C 49, sold for £720, now worth £700–1,000

Fact File

Some blue and white collectors opt for themes, including sport. The most sought after of these is Spode's Indian Sporting range which was created in 1820. Hunting themes are also very popular, especially ones with horses, appealing to non-hunters as well as hunters because of the quality of the design and rich colouring. However, some of the themes can be deemed too gruesome to appeal to a wide range of collectors, including badger baiting and hare coursing.

Many collectors will start with established favourites such as Asiatic pheasants, the Italian pattern (first introduced by Spode in 1816) and the Willow pattern. People often mistake the Broseley and Willow patterns as they are very similar but Broseley is in a paler blue than Willow, has two ornate temples and there are only two figures on the bridge, instead of Willow's three.

LIVERPOOL

A small Christian's Liverpool blue and white slender baluster vase from around 1770 with floral decoration (SOTH)

A&C 49, sold for £611, now worth £600–800

BRISTOL BLUE

A large Delftware dish, probably Bristol, from around 1710, (SOTH)

A&C 49, sold for £2,115, now worth £2,000–3,000

CERAMICS

THE COWMAN

This Cowman pattern oval drainer from 1820–1830, an idyllic rural scene (DREW)

A&C 49, sold for £230, now worth £250–450

SAUCEBOAT

A dark blue sauceboat with a small group of butterflies on flowers, from around 1780–1790 with delicate handle (DREW)

A&C 49, sold for £60, now worth £80–120

HICKS AND MEIGH

Hicks and Meigh stone china part dinner service with exotic birds among foliage, from between 1815–1822. Birds are a popular theme of blue and white (DREW)

A&C 49, sold for £1,700, now worth £2,000–2500

POSSET POT

Delftware posset (hot milk and alcohol) pot, probably London, late-seventeenth century. Delftware uses a very white base with less blue than traditional blue and white (SOTH)

A&C 49, sold for £998, now worth £1,200–1,500

ICE PAILS

A pair of Chinese blue and white Fitzhugh pattern ice pails and covers, c.1800 (WO WA)

A&C 18, sold for £5,000, now worth £6,000–8,000

DUTCH DELFT

A late-seventeenth, early-eighteenth century Dutch Delft blue and white wall plaque. The self framed baroque panel incorporating shells about a scene of a Chinese soldier and his acolyte (minor chips) (RT)

A&C 13, sold for £1,750, now worth £2,500–3,000

MASONS DRAGON EWER

1920s Masons octagonal Dragon pattern jug with hydra (snake) handle, 27.5cm high (Picture by Lovers of Blue & White)

A&C 49, est. £295, now worth £300–500

LOWESTOFT BOWL

Rare Lowestoft blue and white bowl with ship design from around 1770 (SOTH)

A&C 61, sold for £9,360, now worth £9,000–12,000

Fact File

There is a story behind the Willow pattern, possibly the most famous of all blue and white designs. It was based on pieces of Chinese porcelain but was actually created by Spode in 1780 where the story was woven around it.

It tells the story of a rich girl who falls in love with her father's secretary – much to her father's disgust. He arranges a more suitable marriage for her and she runs away with her lover but, when they are caught, they are killed and reunite in death in the form of two lovebirds – portrayed at the top of the pattern.

WWW.ANTIQUES-OF-BRITAIN.CO.UK

The Antiques Centre at Olney

13 OSBORNS COURT, off HIGH STREET SOUTH,
OLNEY, BUCKINGHAMSHIRE MK46 4LA
Tel. 01234 710942

This charming village is located midway between Northampton, Wellingborough, Bedford and Milton Keynes.

Open: Tuesday–Saturday
10.00–5.00,
Sunday 12.00–5.00,
Closed Monday

100 Showcases and Units Selling Antique Furniture, Quality Silver, Porcelain, Clocks, Watches, Teddy Bears, Fine Jewellery and Much More

The Herts & Essex Antiques Centre

The Maltings, Station Road, Sawbridgeworth, Hertfordshire. Tel. 01279 722044

Situated opposite Sawbridgeworth railway station · Easy access from M11 Junctions 7 or 8

OVER 30 ANTIQUES SHOPS
AND 120 SHOWCASES UNDER ONE ROOF

The quality stock of more than one hundred professional dealers displayed on four floors

Monday to Friday 10am to 5pm
Saturday and Sunday 10.30am to 5.30pm

COFFEE SHOP ON SITE

LEICESTER ANTIQUES WAREHOUSE

Clarkes Road, Wigston,
Leicester LE18 2BG Tel: 0116 2881315

The 80 dealers in the Centre offer an enormous stock of quality antiques. In 16,000 Square Feet of space the Centre has a huge selection of antique furniture as well as showcases displaying quality silverware, china and jewellery. A full furniture restoration service is also available on site.

Antique Furniture	Jewellery	Old Pine Furniture	Porcelain
Architectural Items	Glassware	China	Watches
Garden Ornaments and	Antiques Restorers	Ephemera	Dolls & Bears
Tools	Fireplaces	Clocks	Silverware

Free Parking – Coffee Shop On Site

Open: Tuesday–Saturday 10.00–5.00, Sunday 12.00–5.00, Closed Monday

To Rent Floor Units, Showcases or Racking at any of our Centres please call
Michael Hall on 07778 171915

CERAMICS

CARLTON WARE

Founded in 1890, Carlton Ware is one of the most versatile of the potteries from its costly jazz-aged Deco designs to its more affordable novelty range, including walking ware with feet supporting the crockery. Carlton was made to be used and, until it closed in 1989, the novelty ranges combined style with comedy.

Fact File

Some of Carlton's most popular designs are also its most copied – Guinness Wares. Based on the designs of John Gilroy, the toucans were moulded to create lamps and flying birds. Their success led to other animals being produced including a kangaroo, seal and, most desirable of all, a horse and cart. Their popularity led to fakes but the crudely moulded pieces are easy to spot.

MARTELL BRANDY

Carlton Ware ceramic Martell Brandy advertising figure, 20cm high (GARD)

A&C 8, sold for £80, now worth £150–180

MY GOODNESS

Guiness Carlton Ware lamp base in form of a sea lion. 'Guiness is Good For You' inscription. Factory mark on base. 9cm high. Ideally, try to find ones with matching lampshades (PH)

A&C 5, sold for £180, now worth £300–400

LUSTROUS PARROT

A Carlton Ware footed ovoid vase with everted rim printed and painted in colours and gilt on a dark blue background, decorated with parrots, impressed and painted marks (ACAD)

A&C 7, sold for £210, now worth £300–600

UNUSUAL COLOURING

Fantastically coloured, hand-painted jug, unusual yellow colouring for Carlton Ware whose hand-painted range tended more to blues and soft purples (CLEV)

A&C 33, sold for £560, now worth £500–800

FLYING BIRD

A baluster vase decorated with an exotic bird flying through willow trees, 17.5cm. Carlton Ware and Crown Devon are often mistaken for each other because the painters and designers worked at both potteries (FELL)

A&C 16, sold for £340, now worth £500–700

THE QUEEN

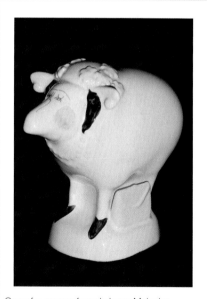

One of a range of royal sheep Malcolm Gooding designed in the 1980s. The queen, recognisable by her famous handbag, is the most common – look for the bare-breasted Koo Stark or pink-hatted Princess Diana

A&C, now worth £50–70

ANTIQUES

Open 7 days 10.00am–5.00pm
Easy Parking

Eversley Barn Antiques is situated on the A327 to Reading, just two miles from Hartley Wintney. In our 16th Century barn you will find a large and varied selection of quality antique and later furniture. We also stock porcelain, silver, glass, linen, books, mirrors, rugs, jewellery, clocks, lighting and collectables etc.

Please enquire if you wish to sell or part exchange any antiques, we will be happy to advise you. We occasionally have space to rent.

Church Lane, Eversley, Hampshire RG27 0PX   Telephone: 0118 932 8518
Email: eversleybarn@hotmail.com   Website: www.eversleybarnantiques.co.uk

HEATHERLEY'S

SCHOOL OF FINE ART, CHELSEA   Est. 1845

FULL TIME
DIPLOMAS IN PORTRAITURE & SCULPTURE
FOUNDATION & PORTFOLIO COURSE
CONTINUING STUDIES

PART TIME
OPEN STUDIO
DAY & EVENING CLASSES
SUMMER COURSES

80 UPCERNE ROAD, CHELSEA, LONDON SW10 0SH
TELEPHONE 0207 351 4190 FAX: 0207 351 6945
www.heatherleys.org

The Thomas Heatherley Educational Trust Ltd. exists to provide education in the Arts, and administers the Heatherley School of Fine Art.
Registered Company No. 977615   Registered Charity No. 312872

CERAMICS

FLORAL DESIGNS – CHINTZ

Chintz is the all-encompassing term for goods decorated all over with flowers. From 1851, the word chintzy referred to common (in a disparaging sense) fabric but chintz, while not to everybody's taste, is a popular form of decoration led by Royal Winton, part of Grimwade, who have started reproducing their 1920–30s wares.

ROYAL WINTON

This Royal Winton Somerset teapot, together with another piece (CHRIS)

A&C 28, sold for £235, now worth £250–350

SUMMERTIME

Summertime was the second chintz pattern to be introduced by Royal Winton. This teapot was sold with another item (CHRIS)

A&C 28, sold for £305, now worth £300–450

Fact File

The word 'chintz' originates from the Hindi word *chint*, meaning 'bright' and the brightly coloured chintz brought freshness into English homes, although the flowery fabrics originally came from India. Chintz brought the country into cities and, while the shapes were modern, the flowers were old-fashioned England at its best.

The transfer sheets bearing the decoration needed great skill to be used to ensure that the patterns fitted exactly. The patterns had names, usually those of women such as Julia and Hazel, two of Royal Winton's most sought-after patterns, while firms such as Crown Ducal stuck to floral names like Peony.

Royal Winton's first pattern was Marguerite in 1928 and they produced eighty patterns in all, including Petunia.

ENGLISH ROSE

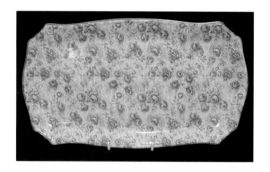

Royal Winton English Rose, £75 (Picture by Rick Hubbard Art Deco)

A&C 52, est. £75, now worth £70–90

FLORAL PLATE

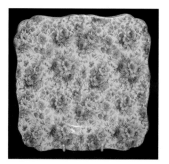

Royal Winton Summertime plate (Picture by Rick Hubbard Art Deco)

A&C 53, est. £65, now worth £50–75

OLD COTTAGE COFFEE POT

Royal Winton coffee pot, Old Cottage Chintz pattern (Picture by Bath Antiques Online)

A&C 52, est. £225, now worth £200–275

SUGAR SHAKER

1930s sugar shaker by A. J. Wilkinson Ltd (Picture by Bath Antiques Online)

A&C 52, est. £145, now worth £180–220

BLUSHWARE, PRE-CHINTZ

Royal Worcester blushware ewer (jug) showing the simple use of flowers even a decade pre-chintz, date code 19 (LOCK)

A&C 60, sold for £220, now worth £250–350

ROYAL WINTON BREAKFAST SET

Six-piece Royal Winton, Evesham 'Countess' breakfast set (CHRIS)

A&C 28, sold for £646, now worth £400–700

ROYAL WINTON JULIA

One of Royal Winton's most popular patterns, Julia, in a six-piece breakfast set. The springtime flowers are highly sought after (CHRIS)

A&C 28, sold for £352, now worth £400–600

Fact File

As well as some patterns being more desirable than others, so some shapes are more collectable. Toastracks were particularly difficult to decorate all over and, therefore, those versions are more sought after than ones where the divisions are left plain.

Chintz was made to be used so plates are often found with scratch marks. These, understandably, devalue the crockery so check carefully before buying as some of the scratches are hard to distinguish among the heavily flowered ware. Most desirable are teapots, biscuit barrels and the all-over toastracks with breakfast sets on trays very collectable – but always check for damage before buying.

FIRST MODERN CHINTZ

A 'Grafton' shape milk jug in the Royal Winton Marguerite pattern. Marguerite is considered to be the first 'modern' chintz, and was produced from 1928, 15cm high (Courtesy of Ken Glibbery, Chintzworld International)

A&C 13, est. £175–200, now worth £150–250

ROYAL WINTON SUGAR BOWL

A sugar bowl in Marguerite chintz (Courtesy of Royal Winton Porcelain, by Eileen Busby)

A&C 28, est. £60 now worth £40–60

ROYAL WINTON SWEET PEA

A Royal Winton 'Sweet Pea' pattern plate, 30cm diameter (FEL)

A&C 16, sold for £110, now worth £80–120

ROYAL WINTON PRESERVE POT

Preserve pot and cover (lid) in Sweet Pea which was sold with two jugs. As with all lidded items, check for damage around the rim (CHRIS)

A&C 28, sold for £293, now worth £200–300

CERAMICS

CLARICE CLIFF

When it comes to Art Deco ceramics, one name stands above all others – Clarice Cliff, the acclaimed designer whose work dominated the market and influenced other designers. Her most famous work was the brightly-coloured Bizarre Ware range with its fantastic shapes, which she created for Newport Pottery.

CLARICE BROTH

Clarice Cliff Fantasque 'Broth' pattern vase, painted with brown bubbles above horizontal rib moulding, 20.5cm high (CHEF)

A&C 63, sold for £300, now worth £300–500

BIZARRE TEA FOR TWO

'Rudyard' tea for two set in the classic Art Deco Stamford shape (CHRIS)

A&C 38, sold for £6,900, now worth £8–10,000

Fact File

While an acclaimed designer herself, designing around 2,000 patterns and 500 shapes in all, Clarice also worked as a supervisor for the very collectable 1933–34 Circus range which was designed by famed painter, Dame Laura Knight.

This included the rare circus lamp which portrayed clowns forming a human pyramid and supporting five female acrobats as well as matching glassware. Confusingly, the china range is signed Clarice Cliff Bizarre Ware.

One of the first buyers of the series was the film star and singer, Gracie Fields who used to go on signings with Clarice and Sir Malcolm Campbell. These appearances helped to establish Clarice's reputation in the public eye. She was the first female Art Director in the Potteries.

CANDLESTICKS AND BOWL

Coral Firs Bizarre cube 658 candlesticks, 6cm high, and a bowl. (CHRIS)

A&C 44, sold for £881, now worth £800–1,200

NO PLACE LIKE HOME

Three Fantasque Bizarre coffee cups, sold for between £517 and £747 each. They were based on Clarice's own home (CHRIS)

A&C 38, sold for £517–747, now worth £600–900

LATONA RED ROSES

Latona Red Roses by Clarice Cliff, with red and black decoration, 45.5cm high, marked 'Latona' with Bizarre mark. Very unusual style, shape and pattern for Clarice (BON)

A&C 49, sold for £4,465, now worth £5,000–6,000

SUGAR SIFTER

Conical 'Red Tulip' sugar sifter in her famous, much imitated conical shape (CHRIS)

A&C 45, sold for £1,997, now worth £2,500–3,000

THAT'S A RELIEF

Clarice Cliff Bizarre wall plaque, moulded in relief with flowers, printed mark, 42cm high, much cheaper than the Bizarre ware (SWORD)

A&C 45, sold for £220, now worth £200–400

LAUGHING WALL MASK

Clarice Cliff didn't just design plates and vases, as this unusual mask shows (Courtesy of www.claricecliff.com)

A&C 38, now worth £2,000–4,000

BON JOUR TEAPOT

Green Chintz: a Fantasque Bizarre Bon Jour teapot and cover (CHRIS)

A&C 53, sold for £940, now worth £1,000–1,500

RED AUTUMN

'Red Autumn' (Balloon Trees): a Clarice Cliff Isis vase, c.1930–1934 (SOTH)

A&C 23, sold for £6,210, now worth £6,000–8,000

CASTELLATED CIRCLE

A Clarice Cliff 'Castellated' circle Bizarre plate, 23cm diameter (CHRIS)

A&C 15, sold for £1,150, now worth £1,000–2,000

RARE MAJOLICA CLARICE CLIFF TEAPOT

Clarice Cliff Majolica teapot with mouse finial and mice in relief (CHRIS)

A&C 58, sold for £67,550, now worth £60,000–80,000

Fact File

Although Clarice's designs are still influencing modern potters such as Lorna Bailey, in their day they were seen as outrageous and even crude. When she showed her first designs, the sales reps laughed at her, only to return two days later having completely sold out. Before Clarice, china was sedate, flowers recognisable and not stylised while colours were demure. Clarice changed that with her vivid imagination and use of colours and design. She is also famous for falling in love with the pottery's owner, Colley Shorter, whom she married after the death of his invalid wife in 1940. On his death, she sold the two potteries (Wilkinson and Newport) to Midwinter but her legacy lives on.

LIDO LADY

Rare Clarice Cliff figure of a Lido Lady. Estimate £1,000–1,500 (CHRIS)

A&C 15, sold for £7,475, now worth £8,000–12,000

DEVON SHAPE

Devon pattern vase, shape no. 358 (CHRIS)

A&C 15, sold for £2,990, now worth £4,000–6,000

UkArtPottery.com

SUPPORTING THE FULL DENNIS CHINAWORKS FROM CURRENT RANGE

- The largest display of Sally Tuffin works in the country, including Limited Editions, Commissions and Retired pieces.

- Request the latest catalogue from our website or by phoning us on 01706 830803

- Order securely online with all major credit cards or visit us at Holden Wood Antiques (10.00–5.30pm, 7 days)

- No question return policy.

- Items usually despatched within 48 hours.

- Free delivery throughout the UK.

Holden Wood Antiques, Grane Road,
Haslingden, Lancashire
Tel. 01706 830803

'Magnolia'
— just one of the magnificent series of the current range

Keep up-to-date with all the news about the new ranges and join our mailing list

www.ukartpottery.com

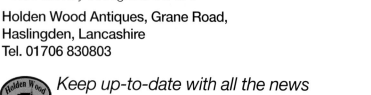

TALENTS OF WINDSOR
Stockists of Fine Luxury Gifts & Collectables

    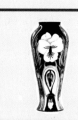 

Daum LOET VANDERVEEN   Steiff BUTTON IN EAR HAZLE CERAMICS JAY STRONGWATER MOORCROFT

TALENTS OF WINDSOR
12 Church Street, Windsor,
Berkshire, SL4 1PE.

Tel. 01753 831 459
Email: shop@talentsofwindsor.com
www.etalents.com

OPENING HOURS
Monday – Saturday 10.00am – 5.30pm
Sunday 11.30am – 5.30pm

LOCATION
Adjacent to Windsor Castle
(behind the Guildhall and Crooked House)

COALPORT

Founded in 1795, Coalport Porcelain Works started life in Coalport, Shropshire before being moved to the Cauldon Works in Stoke-on-Trent in 1926 after years of different owners and its failure to recover after the harsh war years. The pottery, renowned for its pastille burners and figures, is now part of the Wedgwood group.

RARE MINIATURES

A rare miniature jewelled Coalport gold ground part tea service. Early-twentieth century (WO WA)

A&C 18, sold for £2,500, now worth £3,000–4,000

Fact File

Coalport bought the famous Caughley pottery in 1799, which greatly enhanced its reputation. Despite being founded in 1795, later pieces bear the date 1750 which has caused confusion among collectors with some books claiming that this is simply a mistake and others stating that this dates from their acquisition of Caughley which stood on the site of an earlier pottery founded in 1750. Coalport are famous for their pastille (scent) burners which were generally made in the shape of cottages and were traditionally used to disguise unpleasant odours.

TEA SET

Five-piece Coalport porcelain, jewelled, pattern no. T2334, tea set from late-nineteenth/early-twentieth century (SWORD)

A&C 50, sold for £980, now worth £1,000–1,500

IMARI-STYLE

Anstice Horton & Thomas Rose Coalport dish, c.1812. Hand decorated with Imari-style pattern, no.1272

A&C 8, on sale £75, now worth £100–200

TEAPOT ON FEET

Coalport organic moulded teapot and cover, reg. design 197455, 1890s. No vent hole in lid. On sale for £55 SHREWSBURY

A&C 8, on sale for £55, now worth £150–200

POT POURRI VASE

Coalport pot pourri two-handled vase, painted with oval reserves of Loch Katrine (LOCK)

A&C 60, sold for £95, now worth £100–200

TWO-HANDLED VASE

Coalport International Exhibition two-handled vase and cover from around 1862. The event, also known as the Great London Exposition was set in South Kensington (SOTH)

A&C 46, sold for £3,525, now worth £4,000–5,000

HAND-PAINTED SCENE

A Coalport yellow, ground baluster lidded vase, decorated with bejewelling and Continental lakeside scene, c.1900s (FELL)

A&C 16, sold for £380, now worth £500–800

JEWELLED VASE

Pair of Coalport 'jewelled' vases and covers, c.1900, decorated with faux fire opals and rubies within gilt ground. Domed covers (both restored), 26cm high (HAMP)

A&C 34, sold for £650, now worth £800–1,500

CERAMICS

CONTINENTAL CERAMICS

One of the first things that you'll notice when you go to an antiques market in France is how few pieces of china there are in comparison to Britain. While china dominates the UK market, in France, furniture does but we get a large amount of imported ceramics from the Continent and it's often undervalued by general dealers.

FRENCH SPILL VASES

French porcelain spill vases modelled with a gentleman and companion, nineteenth century, 42cm high (ROSE)

A&C 62, sold for £400, now worth £500–700

LIMOGES

Renaissance style Limoges chargers, enamel, one after Pierre Reymond, c.1870 (CHRIS)

A&C 45, sold for £18,025, now worth £18–24,000

DOCCIA PORCELAIN

Urn-shaped vases by Italian make Doccia porcelain, modelled with four white figures and gilt floral swags (GORR)

A&C 51, sold for £1,200, now worth £1,200–1,800

HAVILAND LIMOGES

Haviland Limoges dessert service with hunting theme, comprising eleven plates, two square dishes and one large tray (BON ED)

A&C 40, sold for £600, now worth £600–1,000

LIMOGES VASES

Pair of Limoges Sèvres-style vases, with pierced gilt metal feet (DREW)

A&C 40, sold for £400, now worth £400–600

Fact File

Some British auctioneers are not always as informed as they should be when it comes to Continental china which is why it's well worth learning as much as you can to take advantage of the lack of knowledge in this market.

Although they know the larger potteries such as Meissen and Sévres they tend to overlook other potteries, simply listing them by country or even 'continental' and that's where you can profit.

George Perrott's book *Pottery and Porcelain Marks: European, Oriental and USA* (Gemini Publications, ISBN 0 9530 6370 4, £35) is very helpful in helping to identify backstamps.

LLADRO

Jose Javier Malavia's evocative 'Hopes and Dreams', retired in 2002 (picture courtesy of Attenborough Associates)

A&C 54, est. £425, now worth £300–500

ROYAL BONN

Two-handled Royal Bonn vases with stylised cherry blossom and sparrow decoration, influenced by Japanese designs (MALL)

A&C 51, sold for £200, now worth £400–600

LLADRO BALLERINAS

'Merry Ballet'. This beautiful bisque-finish piece was sculpted by Salvador Debón and stands 54cm high, retired in 1991 (picture courtesy of Attenborough Associates)

A&C 54, est. £775, now worth £600–900

ROYAL DUX MIRROR

Art Nouveau mirror by Royal Dux, the bevelled plate flanked by a lady in flowing gilt dress over a tray base, surmounted by water lilies, No. 1097, 59cm (GORR)

A&C 45, sold for £600, now worth £600–800

ROYAL DUX FIGURE

Early Royal Dux figurine of a semi clad female, seated on a rockwork base, drying her feet, 54cm high. Typical Dux colouring (SWORD)

A&C 54, sold for £940, now worth £900–1,200

LIMOGES BOX

Early-twentieth century Limoges circular box and cover, painted in coloured enamels, 21cm diameter, signed 'Mala' (DREW)

A&C 40, sold for £200, now worth £200–300

FIGURAL CRUET

Three-piece condiment set, comprising a sugar shaker and salt and pepper pots with silver-gilt footrims (DREW)

A&C 40, sold for £300, now worth £300–500

MEISSEN-STYLE PARROT

A Meissen-style porcelain box in the form of a parrot head with gilt metal mounts, 7cm high (SWORD)

A&C 52, sold for £300, now worth £300–400

VIENNESE PORCELAIN

A silver-mounted enamel bowl and cover, Ludwig Pollitzer, Vienna, from around 1900 with chicken finial (SOTH)

A&C 62, sold for £800, now worth £800–1,200

Fact File

A common mistake is to assume that Limoges is a make of pottery. Actually, there are lots of different potteries who carry the Limoges name because it's an area of France, not the name of an individual pottery. The same is true of Delft. They're just like the Potteries where the raw materials are so good that different potteries have sprung up in the same area. Of the Limoges firms, one of the most famous is Charles de Havilland but always check which de Havilland you're buying as the family owned several different potteries using the de Havilland surname but different first names or initials just read the small print – the backstamp.

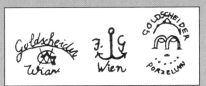

SEAU (WINE COOLER)

Sévres porcelain ormolu mounted seau, with Bacchus handles and dolphin supports, marked Henry IV chez Michau (MALL)

A&C 58, sold for £880, now worth £800–1,200

PARISIAN FIGURES

Paris porcelain figures, a pair, nineteenth century. Blue crossed swords mark (a popular device copied) and letters 'EC' (FELL)

A&C 39, sold for £500, now worth £600–800

CERAMICS

SOUVENIR OR CRESTED WARE

Crested ware is also known as souvenir ware. It was designed for the tourist market from the late 19th century and the crests commemorated the towns or cities which were visited. The best known make is W H Goss but other firms also created the popular white ware including Carlton China (part of what we know as Carlton Ware).

MOTORBIKE

Vehicles are always good collectables and crested ware is good (DREW)

A&C 39, now worth £60-80

VINTAGE CAR

Check that the tyres are not broken when buying cars (DREW)

A&C 39, now worth £50-80

SIDECAR

The arms on this unusual crested ware figure are prone to damage (DREW)

A&C 39, now worth £80-120

GOSS PEACE PLATE

Goos commemorative plate, one of the few pieces of their crockery worth buying (DREW)

A&C 39, now worth £60-120

Fact File

The most popular resorts tended to be coastal eg Blackpool, Brighton and Southend-on-Sea and, therefore, produced the most crested ware, catering to the tourists. Unless you have a particular affiliation with any of these places, it's best to stick to more unusual towns which were less touristy in their day eg Northampton. Whilst some collectors opt for towns, others go for designs with the Louis Wain-inspired designs, featuring his famous cats, always popular. The First World War led to commemoration pieces including tanks, the Cenotaph and cannons.

W. H. G.
W. H. GOSS

ARCADIAN
ARCADIAN CHINA

ROYAL CRESTED WARE

Collection of Goss depicting coats-of-arms, predominantly royal ones, showing the range of crested china (Goss Collectors' Club)

A&C 39, Queen Victoria jug (centre back) now worth £50-80

FIRST WORLD WAR GUNNER

World War I pieces command top money, such as this gunner (DREW)

A&C 39, now worth £100-150

THE DERBY POTTERIES

Derby, established in 1748 merged with Chelsea porcelain in 1770 to produce one of the finest firms in England, its proud owner calling it 'the second Dresden'. It acquired a crown in its backstamp after George III showed approval in 1775 and then became Royal Crown Derby in 1890 under Queen Victoria but is still the same make.

ROYAL CROWN DERBY

Royal Crown Derby, Imari-style six setting (forty-two pieces) with post war marks. Look for the cypher (eg L) to date this make (SWORD)

A&C 61, sold for £580, now worth £800–1,000

ICE PAIL

Derby porcelain ice pail, with cover and liner, c.1815. Paintings of exotic birds. Two slight stress cracks, 25.5cm (WINT)

A&C 39, sold for £1,500, now worth £1,500–2,500

LAZY SUSAN

'Lazy Susan' Derby Imari palette, plus other late-nineteenth/early-twentieth century Derby Imari porcelain (DREW)

A&C 62, sold for £1,050, now worth £1,000–2,000

ROBERT BLOOR

Three Derby (Robert Bloor) bough pots, with pierced liners and gilt leaf-scroll handles. Estimated value £1,500–2,500 (DREW)

A&C 50, sold for £3,900, now worth £2,500–5,000

DERBY VASES

Derby porcelain twin-handled pair of vases, of compressed circular shape with domed cover, from around 1884 (SWORD)

A&C 66, sold for £220, now worth £200–400

Fact File

While Derby is most famous for its delicate porcelain figurines, Royal Crown Derby, its later incarnation, is renowned for its Imari-style decoration. The rich red, blue, white and gold pattern was influenced by the Japanese porcelain and is used extensively on its crockery and paperweights which are very collectable. Later Derby and all Royal Crown Derby are very easy to date. Just look for the symbol (or cypher as it's better known) by the backstamp – every year has a letter eg 'I' represents 1938 which is when Roman numerals first began to be used.

c.1825 printed

BLOOR DERBY

Bloor Derby porcelain figure, 'The Tailor's Wife', from around 1820, with gilt decoration, incised N62 (SWORD)

A&C 62, sold for £580, now worth £500–800

ROYAL CROWN DERBY EWERS

A pair of Royal Crown Derby vases of ewer form, dated 1914. The ovoid bodies are decorated with shaped turquoise reserves Signed C. Gresley. 23cm high (HAMP)

A&C 8, sold for £1,900, now worth £2,000–4,000

MILTON FIGURE

A good, large eighteenth century Derby porcelain figure of Milton, c.1765, 31cm high (DANDO)

A&C 21, est. £825, now worth £1,000–2,000

CERAMICS

DRESDEN

Let me start by saying that this is probably the most confusing area of ceramics. Dresden and Meissen were so close together geographically and many of the Dresden potteries copied Meissen's style that the two names were often used instead of the other. While Meissen was an individual pottery, Dresden had many different ones.

DRESDEN FIGURE

Pair of Dresden ceramic figures (girl figure has broken hand) with an 'AR' mark used by Helena Wolfsohn, c.1870

A&C 1, sold for £150, now worth £300–500

BALLERINA

A Dresden porcelain figure of a ballet dancer, 29cm, the skirt made of lace, hardened by liquid porcelain – other firms used sugar (PH)

A&C 15, est. £100–150, now worth £150–300

HELENA WOLFSOHN FIGURE

Pair of Helena Wolfsohn figures (one damaged), Meissen sued her in 1879 over use of the crossed swords mark which she'd copied from them – as did many potteries

A&C 1, sold for £150, now worth £300–500

PLAYFUL PUTTI

Early-twentieth century Dresden porcelain, putti playing with a goat, 25cm wide with hand-crafted flowers (ROSE)

A&C 60, sold for £550, now worth £500–700

TWO-HANDLED VASES

Pair of Dresden urn-shaped, two-handled vases with covers topped by finials and depicting different scenes, 25cm high (CLEV)

A&C 33, sold for £400, now worth £400–700

HUMMINGBIRD VASES

Dresden schneebalen pair of vases and covers, encrusted in white flowerheads with hummingbirds and a finial in the shape of a parrot, 50cm high (CHEF)

A&C 63, sold for £2,100, now worth £2,000–2,500

FLORAL-ENCRUSTED

Dresden vase and cover,1890–1910, two knarled leafy floral handles with moulded flowers and enamelling, 61cm high (WINT)

A&C 43, sold for £1,600, now worth £1,500–3,000

Fact File

Germany produced some of the best porcelain in Europe. In the nineteenth century, many craftsmen moved to the Dresden area to start their own potteries. At this point, the pottery in Meissen, around twelve miles from Dresden, became known officially as Meissen while the new firms became known as Dresden – although this was not the name of just one pottery. To add to the confusion, the word 'Dresden' also refers to a type of pottery (Meissen-style) and Dresden china was made outside Dresden including Sitzendorf porcelain. Earlier Dresden china tends to be superior, even if the design is imitative. The moulding of individual flowers and the richly painted goods, while not actually Meissen, is certainly good enough to collect in its own right.

FIGURES

Some people prefer to collect themes, not makes and figures are very popular. They can be Deco dancing girls by makes such as Goldscheider and Wade or floral-encrusted figures by Continental firms including Meissen. They are often very evocative of an era with the elegant and romantic Regency period being highly collectable.

NYMPHENBURG THEATRICALS

'Isabella' – a Nymphenburg porcelain Commedia dell'arte figure, late-nineteenth/ twentieth century, on a flat scroll base (SOTH)

A&C 21, sold for £517, now worth £800–1,000

THE LOST SHEEP

Late-eighteenth/early-nineteenth century Ralph Wood type figure, 19cm high (SWORD)

A&C 46, sold for £100, now worth £100–200

RUSSIAN DANCER

Russian porcelain figure of a dancer. Impressed marks 'Gardners Factory', nineteenth century, 22.5cm high (DANDO)

A&C 21, est. £500, now worth £600–800

NODDER

Regency painted 'Brighton Pavilion' terracotta figure with detachable nodding head, 34.5cm. Japan was in vogue at the time (GORR)

A&C 50, sold for £3,400, now worth £3,000–5,000

ROMANTIC OFFERING

Walton Group 'Tenderness' in bright colours c.1820, 21cm high (DREW)

A&C 50, sold for £500, now worth £500–800

Fact File

Figures are very desirable and can be costly with the Goldscheider versions selling for several hundred pounds but, no matter what their cost, there are common dangers to spot. The better made figures are the ones most prone to damage as they are modelled with their arms lifted away from their body, feet sticking out and delicate heads – all of which can get broken. In an ideal world, all auction houses and dealers would warn you about any restoration or damage. In reality, you need to look for yourself and that's great if your eyes are good, otherwise, check the texture – if it changes from smooth to rough (or vice versa for bisque figures), then it's damaged and should be priced accordingly.

CHARLES VYSE

'Punch and Judy', Charles Vyse pottery group, c.1929, ebonised wood base (SOTH)

A&C 16, sold for £6,670, now worth £10–12,000

ROYAL DUX WATER CARRIERS

A pair of Royal Dux figures depicting water carriers, heightened in gilt and carrying vessels showing their trade, 50cm high (SWORD)

A&C 50, sold for £580, now worth £500–700

HIGHLANDER FIGURE

An unusual pottery figure of a Highlander. Probably Scottish pottery, c.1825–30. Scottish pottery is increasing in price (DANDO)

A&C 21, est. £820, now worth £1,000–1,400

CERAMICS

JUGS

These are great to collect. They're not just practical but easy to display, either on shelves or hanging from hooks. The word originates from *jugge* and was first used in 1538 for a servant woman, the type of person who carried jugs for employers or at inns. They can take many forms, not just a bulbous body with lip and handle.

FREEMASONS JUG

Graduated set of three Sunderland lustre jugs with masonic and sailing ship decoration. Masons' goods are very collectable (SWORD)

A&C 56, sold for £380, now worth £300–600

RUSKIN GLAZED JUG

Ruskin jug decorated with a high-fired sang-de-boeuf and mottled purple glaze, date 1933 (late period Ruskin), 20cm high (FELL)

A&C 57, sold for £1,000, now worth £1,000–1,500

RUSTIC DELIGHT

Chocolate sprigged brown Essex jug with ochre wheat ears on the rim, a rustic jug, 35cm high (CHEF)

A&C 61, sold for £200, now worth £200–400

PUZZLE JUG

Red-glazed pottery puzzle jug with ochre slip, possibly Sussex from around 1800. The trick was to pour it without spilling (DREW)

A&C 53, sold for £720, now worth £600–900

ART NOUVEAU JUG

Art Nouveau Bishop and Stonie jug, c.1900, of a medieval lady in a garden (HAMP)

A&C 49, sold for £190, now worth £200–400

Fact File

The handle of a jug is often its most interesting aspect. Burleigh specialised in jugs with novelty handles in the form of people or animals. Although the parrot jug is fairly easy to find, the sporting range is much more desirable, especially the golfer. Wadeheath made two Disney musical jugs, one with the Big Bad Wolf with his large hat (liable to chip) which was also available as a non-musical version and the other, much rarer version, of Snow White. Handles are prone to damage so check carefully before buying. While most people check the sections at the top and bottom, it's also worth checking in the middle which is often the most fragile part.

RELIGIOUS POTTERY

Early-nineteenth century pearlware jug, of bulbous form and decorated with religiously inspired texts. Inscribed 'John Stephens' (b.1825), 22.5cm high (AMER)

A&C 29, sold for £360, now worth £400–800

COPPER LUSTRE

One of six copper lustre jugs, four of the six with moulded floral sprays, nineteenth century and later. Used to be popular (SWORD)

A&C 58, sold for £80, now worth £80–120

COMMEMORATIVE JUG

Liverpool commemorative jug. Printed with a drinking scene of men outside an alehouse. The jug had a hole in the base, big enough to fit four fingers through (DREW)

A&C 45, sold for £680, now worth £600–1,000

MAJOLICA

This is the name given to the heavily glazed pottery and dates from 1555. It was named after Majorca, the largest of three islands which took its name from its size – *major* means 'large' in Latin. Created by several makes, the most collectable of the British versions were made by Minton or George Jones and are often ostentatious.

JARDINIERE

Majolica jardiniere by Holdcroft, decorated with water lilies, restored, 26cm high (GORR)

A&C 48, sold for £380, now worth £400–600

MINTON CRAB DISH

Minton majolica crab dish, with segmented border, the cover in the form of a crab (GORR)

A&C 53, sold for £5,000, now worth £6,000–8,000

GEORGE JONES

George Jones majolica stilton dish and cover with butterflies, lilies and bullrushes, late-nineteenth century (SWORD)

A&C 64, sold for £1,100, now worth £1,000–1,500

Fact File

The thick glaze that makes majolica what it is, is a viscous tin-glaze. It's so thick that the colours do not run during the glazing process. The pottery is earthenware and it originated in the Middle East and came to Europe via trading with Spain before being imported into Italy via Majorca, hence its name. Interestingly, a variation of it is known as Faience in France after the French imported it from Faenza. For purists, true majolica is seen on a white glazed background, instantly recognisable as Faience. For the British and American market, majolica is a thick, rich glaze with a brown or blue background. Putti (cherubs) are a popular form of decoration as are leaves. It is often fantastically ostentatious but can also be very stylish, especially Minton's novelty teapots, including a chicken.

PUTTO COMPORT

English majolica figural comport, modelled as a putto supporting a shallow dish, from around 1880. Estimate £300–£500 (DREW)

A&C 54, sold for £2,400, now worth £2,000–3,000

CANTAGALLI MAJOLICA

Cantagalli Italian majolica painted with figures and cherub before a townscape, 39cm high. Less moulded than British versions (ROSE)

A&C 64, sold for £420, now worth £500–700

FAIENCE MAJOLICA

Italian majolica two-handled cistern of ovoid form, painted in blue with grotteschi, 59cm. Subtle compared to British designs (DREW)

A&C 63, sold for £420, now worth £400–600

LITTLE CHERUBS

A Minton Majolica centrepiece in the form of three Putti acting as supports, 29.5cm high

A&C 11, sold for £4,140, now worth £5,000–7,000

MINTON TOWER JUG

Minton majolica tower jug, with hinged cover moulded with dancing medieval figures, date code for 1868 (DREW)

A&C 63, sold for £250, now worth £300–500

CERAMICS

MASON'S

The pottery is renowned for its ironstone, the heavy ceramic which was strong enough for furniture including a four-poster bed and a garden bench. The pottery is often glazed in Imari-influenced colours of rich blues, red and gold and the same shapes have been used for centuries, including a hydra (snake) handle and octagonal jug.

ORNATE BREAD BINS

Pair of Mason's ironstone dough or bread bins and covers showing Oriental influence (SOTH)

A&C 53, est. £4,000–6,000, now worth £4,000–6,000

REPTILE HANDLE

Fenton jug c 1820 with reptile handle, flower design and vivid blue base (BON)

A&C 53, sold for £587, now worth £550-650

FOOTBATH JUG

Mason's ironstone foothbath jug, from 1815, an age of Oriental influence (SOTH)

A&C 53, sold for £940, now worth £1,000–1,500

IMARI-STYLE COLOURS

Ironstone footbath jug showing Mason's. classic Imari-style colouring (DREW)

A&C 42, sold for £1,300, now worth £1,000–1,800

TREE DISH

Mason's ironstone Tree Dish from around 1820, printed in blue with flowers and bamboo and a blue ground border (BON)

A&C 53, sold for £352, now worth £300–500

Fact File

Mason's was founded in 1813 by two brothers, George and Charles Mason. The creation of the grey ceramic, ironstone, with its heavy glaze led to the 'patent ironstone china' banner which can be seen beneath its most famous backstamp. Mason's strength lay in its shapes and patterns and it is one of the most traditional of the British potteries with its use of old patterns and shapes making it hard to date, though older pieces tend to have a creamier base than the more modern, brilliant white finish.

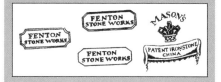

ZOOMORPHIC HANDLE

Fenton jug c 1820 with reptile handle, rarer than a hydra one, and bright colours (BON)

A&C 53, sold for £564, now worth £550-750

DINNER SERVICE

Mason's ironstone part dinner service from 1820, estimated at £4,000–£6,000 (SOTH)

A&C 53, est. £4,000–6,000, now worth £4,000–6,000

IRONSTONE TEAPOT

Rare Mason's Ironstone teapot with large waterlily design and Imari colouring (BON)

A&C 53, sold for £800, now worth £750-1,000

MEISSEN

As you will have read in the Dresden section, Meissen's history is intimately bound with that of the various Dresden potteries. This is partly because it used to be produced as 'Saxony' or 'Dresden' before losing the exclusive right to produce pottery in the Dresden area at which point it became firmly established as Meissen.

RARE MEISSEN VASE

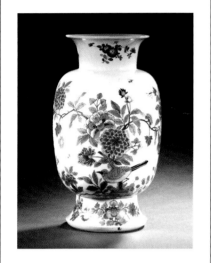

A rare Meissen vase from around 1730 with bird and flower decoration (SOTH)

A&C 44, sold for £75,250, now worth £70–90,000

MEISSEN DRINKING GROUP

A Meissen group of Bacchus and Silenus, the drunken Silenus rides on the back of an ass supported by a standing figure of Bacchus. Late-nineteenth century (WO WA)

A&C 18, sold for £820, now worth £1,500–2,000

PAIR OF JAYS

A rare pair of Meissen models of Jays from around 1740 with moulded detail (SOTH)

A&C 63, sold for £21,600, now worth £15–25,000

PUTTI AND FRUIT VASES

Pair of Meissen vase, c.1870, 36cm high, each campana-shaped body encrusted with fruit and applied with a pair of cherub-form handles. Scenes set in panels in the cylindrical base and body (SOTH)

A&C 31, sold for £3,450, now worth £4,000–6,000

Fact File

In 1719, Meissen became the first European pottery to make 'hard paste' or 'true' porcelain in the Chinese tradition. Its most common form is heavily floral-encrusted porcelain which is much imitated but the quality speaks for itself. Each flower would be individually moulded before being added to main piece and this made each piece unique. As well as its wares being copied, so was its mark, the famous crossed swords backstamp and this can cause a lot of confusion with makes such as Lowestoft, Derby and Bristol all imitating the mark.

The box below shows just some of the examples which continue to confound collectors. As well as the mark, look at the quality of the pieces.

Bellhouse Antiques

Specialists in 18th & 19th Century Meissen

Selection of stock
Including Kaendler Figures circa 1750s

We are always interested in buying items

Bellhouse Antiques
Firs Cottage, Ramsden Park Road
Ramsden Bellhouse, Essex CM11 1NK

Telephone & Fax 01268 710415
Email Bellhouse.Antiques@virgin.net

CERAMICS

MIDWINTER

Back in the 1950–70s, most British people had dinner sets made by Midwinter or Denby. Top designers such as Sir Hugh Casson (eg Riviera and Cannes) and Terence Conran (eg nursery series) created designs for Midwinter which came to typify the era but, in their day, were very fresh and innovative and are now very collectable.

STYLECRAFT SHAPE

Revolutionary 'Stylecraft' shape, forty-three-piece part dinner service, printed and enamelled with Casson's 'Cannes' pattern (RDP)

A&C 62, now worth £300–400

BLACK, WHITE AND RED

The 'Zambesi' range, 1956, turned the trend for black and white designs into a cult clssic by introducing red. The umbrella was a typical motif of the 1950s (RDP)

A&C 62, now worth £200–300

TERENCE CONRAN

The 'Nature Study' range, designed by Terence Conran, founder of Habitat (RDP)

A&C 62, now worth £150–300

RIVIERA – SIR HUGH CASSON

The 'Riviera' pattern, from 1954 by Sir Hugh Casson epitomised the era's Francophilia, equating the nation with sophistication (RDP)

A&C 62, now worth £300–400

RED DOMINO

The 'Red Domino' dinner set showed the 1950s fascination with spotty crockery (RDP)

A&C 62, now worth £400–600

Fact File

Most people have heard of Jessie Tait, Midwinter's prolific designer and the pottery's output is instantly recognisable with its mainly white background never being overwhelmed by the patterns pre-1970s. The work epitomises the 1950s with its shapes and designs but not everyone realises that they also produced animals. Created by Nancy Great-Rex in the 1940s, they are cartoon-like animals including Larry the Lamb and Run Rabbit Run. The decoration was very simple with the trademark eyes being handpainted, along with small details, which allowed for faster production but also a very distinctive finish with many people recognising the animals just by looking at the eyes. Expect to pay £25-40 for an ashtray with three rabbits on it.

JESSIE TAIT

Gay Gobbler meat plate, by Jessie Tait, £150-300

A&C 14, est. £150–300, now worth £200–300

GOING DOTTY OVER SPOTS

'Blue Domino'; 'Blue Domino variant'; eggcup tray 'Green Domino'; 'Blue Domino variant'

A&C 62, eggcup holder now worth £60–80

PRIMAVERA

A selection of Primavera items on the Stylecraft shape, most famous for not using conventional round plates. The shapes were as exciting as the patterns

A&C 14, teapot £120–150, now worth £150–250

MINTON

The founder, Thomas Minton, started his working life at Caughley Porcelain works but opened his own pottery in 1793 in Stoke to be nearer his best customers, including Josiah Spode for whom he created the most famous design ever, the blue and white Willow pattern. It is one of the most exciting and imaginative potteries to collect.

DELICATE DESIGNS

Victorian Minton bone china six-piece dinner service of two comports and four plates. Very different from their heavy majolica (GORR)

A&C 56, sold for £360, now worth £300–500

PUTTI AND HORNS OF PLENTY

A pair of Minton majolica cornucopia vases,

A&C 42, sold for £4,000, now worth £4,000–6,000

CLASSICAL IMAGERY

A large Mintons majolica flower holder, c.1873. Modelled as a classical woman in a robe, reading from a book and resting on a grey tapered column (SOTH)

A&C 17, sold for £8,625, now worth £10–15,000

ORIENTAL INFLUENCE

Minton bowl with Oriental-style decoration, showing the influence of the East (GARD)

A&C 39, sold for £120, now worth £200–300

PUGIN-STYLE PLATES

Set of six Minton Pugin-style plates, 26.5cm with stylised-flowers (PH ED)

A&C 18, sold for £506, now worth £600–900

Fact File

Minton (Mintons from 1873) is one of the easiest potteries when it comes to dating. They used cyphers from 1842, even using a separate symbol for the month. They are also one of the most innovative potteries. Famous for their majolica works, these can reach record prices with a pair of blackamoor figures reaching £146,750 at auction. Minton was one of the few potteries to use pate-sur-pate (paste on paste) a technique created by Minton's Marc-Louis Solon circa 1870. The layering of slip (glaze) created a cameo-effect and Minton's wares of this genre are among the most desirable of all ornamentation produced in the late-nineteenth century.

1876 EXHIBITION

Minton 1876 Exhibition, porcelain bowl with classical foliate scroll figurehead retailed by T. Goode and Co. London (MALL)

A&C 58, sold for £3,300, now worth £3,000–4,000

SECESSIONIST STICK STAND

Minton earthenware 'Secessionist' stick stand, dated 1920. Cylindrical body slip-trailed with stylised flowering stems. Printed no. 62. 58cm high, in sombre colours (BON)

A&C 44, sold for £1,763, now worth £2,000–3,500

RECORD SETTING MAJOLICA

Minton majolica blackamoor figures c 1866., set the world record for majolica (SOTH)

A&C 44, sold £146,750, now worth £150–200,000

Beavis Shops
Est. 1934
Bedford and Isle of Wight

Gatekeepers £4680

Selangor £195

Mountain Kingdom £1875

Rabbits £795

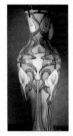

Calla Lily £1750

Jumeirah £390

Visit our website

www.beavis-shops.co.uk

to view over 900 items in stock including
Moorcroft Pottery, Moorcroft Enamels,
Cobridge & Black Ryden

Queens Choice £565

Pyghtle £370

Scrambling Lily £199

Marinka £545

Woodside Farm £395

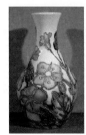

Speedwell £190

We are a small independent family owned retail company specialising in Moorcroft.
We are an official retail partner of Moorcroft PLC. We only sell first quality Moorcroft,
we do not sell secondhand, repaired or seconds.

Buy now for tomorrows heirlooms at today prices.

14-16 The Arcade
Bedford
Tel. 01234 353 741

Upper Saint James Street
Newport, Isle of Wight
Tel. 01983 523 271

Items show a selection of Moorcroft stock available at time of going to press.

MOORCROFT

The pottery is famous for its slip-trailed designs which form thick lines around the patterns of the heavily glazed ware. It was founded by William Moorcroft in 1913, with retailer's Liberty's financial help, after he had worked at James Macintyre and Co. designing their Art Nouveau ware, some of which was sold at the London store.

POMEGRANATES

A 41cm high Moorcroft oviform vase, of pomegranates, signed 'W. Moorcroft' (DREW)

A&C 46, sold for £900, now worth £1,000–1,500

LUSTRE VASE

A rare lustre vase, c.1910. An unusual colour and geometric design by Moorcroft (CHRIS)

A&C 21, sold for £4,700, now worth £5,000–7,000

LEAVES OF FRUIT

Moorcroft 'Leaves of Fruit', baluster vase with continuous design of blackberries and leaves, from around 1930 (GORR)

A&C 53, sold for £950, now worth £800–1,200

POPPIES

A Moorcroft three-handled vase in 'Poppies', the body painted with flowers on a light green ground, 26cm high, signed in green (BON)

A&C 46, sold for £1,670, now worth £1,500–2,500

PANSY

A pair of Moorcroft 'Pansy' oviform vases, signed 'W. Moorcroft'. Both have damaged necks, one having a large chip (DREW)

A&C 46, sold for £450, now worth £400–600

Fact File

It's very easy to date Moorcroft made since 1990 – just look for the cypher. These are based on the alphabet eg the fifth letter of the alphabet is E and the symbol for 1995, the fifth year this method of dating was used, is an eye.

While using traditional methods of production, Moorcroft's work in the 1920–30s was innovative in pattern and designs and these pieces are highly desirable. The best buys are colourful pieces made before the death of William Moorcroft in 1945 and which bear his signature.

W. Moorcroft WM.

MOORCROFT
BURSLEM
1914
M46

FLAMBE DESIGN FOR LIBERTY'S

Cobridge Liberty Flambe: a large two-handled 'Wisteria' vase from around 1925–1926 made by Moorcroft for the London store (SOTH)

A&C 46, sold for £6,110, now worth £6,000–8,000

MOORCROFT PRE-MOORCROFT

Macintyre Hesperian rare 'Carp' jardiniere and stand from 1902, designed by Moorcroft before he had his own pottery (SOTH)

A&C 46, sold for £32,900, now worth £30–40,000

COBRIDGE DESIGN

Cobridge (the site of Moorcroft), a late Florian lustred 'Cornflower' vase, dated 1918 (SOTH)

A&C 46, sold for £4,465, now worth £4,500–6,000

Scotland's Largest Retailer of Moorcroft Pottery & Border Fine Arts

Mail Order Specialists

of CASTLE DOUGLAS

Postage charge of £5.00 for all UK Parcels.
Overseas postage to be advised
**2004 Winner of
"Best Retailer Inititative"**

We are Scotland's Largest Retailer of Moorcroft Pottery & are proud of our extensive stock of Discontinued & Current Designs with many Prestige Pieces also in stock. We are also stockists of Moorcroft Enamels, discontinued, limited editions & current designs.

Only 1 hours drive from Carlisle on the A75 to Stranraer, please feel free to visit our showrooms for a truly unique shopping experience or visit our website on:

www.posthorn.co.uk

We are the **ORIGINAL** Posthorn **ONLY** to be found at 26/30 St Andrew Street, **CASTLE DOUGLAS**.
Straight down King Street, turn right at the Town Clock
Look for our distinctive logo

Call for the additional benefits

of our great new Privilege Card

Tel: 01556 502531   Fax: 01556 503330
26/30 St Andrew Street, **CASTLE DOUGLAS**,
Scotland, DG7 1DE
E-mail: info@posthorn.co.uk

Also Stockists of: COBRIDGE STONEWARE. BLACK RYDEN. ROYAL DOULTON. EDINBURGH CRYSTAL. SPODE.
WEDGWOOD. WATERFORD CRYSTAL. COUNTRY ARTISTS. TUSKERS. HEDGIES. ROYAL CROWN DERBY. HEREDITIES.
AYNSLEY. LLADRO. NAO. LILLIPUT LANE. COALPORT *and many, many more.*

- Moorcroft • Spode • Cobridge
- Bronte Porcelain
- Reproduction Furniture

No. 53 HIGH STREET
MUCH WENLOCK
SHROPSHIRE TF13 6AE

Telephone: 01952 728285
Fax: 01952 728639

www.wenlockcollection.co.uk

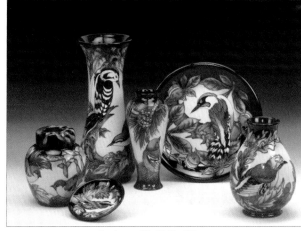

Ingleswood by Philip Gibson

A tantalising selection . . .
one of the best in Yorkshire!

Limited Editions, all current ranges, together with lamps.
Good choice of older pieces.
The miniature delights of enamels.
Cobridge models.

Midsummer Surprise, 2004   *Alhambra, Florian c1903*

Nestling at the foot of the North Yorkshire Moors
the bustling picturesque market town of Helmsley
is home to William Sissons Gallery.

All are welcome — serious collector to browser.

Pottery, Enamels, John Ditchfield (GLASFORM), Paintings
and much more . . .

Mail order with pleasure.

William Sissons Gallery

23 Market Place   Helmsley   York YO62 5BJ
Telephone: 01439 771385
Email: sales@sissonsgallery.co.uk
Open 10.00am – 6.00pm & Sundays 12.00 noon – 6.00pm

www.sissonsgallery.co.uk

CERAMICS

SPANISH VASE

Moorcroft 'Spanish' vase with lavish floral decoration in heady reds (CHRIS)

A&C 30, sold for £2,300, now worth £2,000–4,000

FISH DESIGNS

A pair of 1930 Moorcroft vases with matte glaze one with with fish pattern, the other with Dawn. Very different from their traditional heavy glazes (WINT)

A&C 41, sold for £1,600, now worth £1,500–2,000

SIGNED FREESIA

Baluster-shaped vase decorated with 'Freesia' pattern, c.1930-50, green painted signature of Walter Moorcroft, 33cm high (FELL)

A&C 40, sold for £2,100, now worth £2,000–4,000

SPRING FLOWERS

Walter Moorcroft's Spring Flowers vase, dated 1954, the interior glazed in dark blue (SOTH)

A&C 65, sold for £850, now worth £800–1,200

MACINTYRE VASE

MacIntyre vase designed by William Moorcroft during his time at the pottery, decorated with blue roses and pink poppies, 15cm (GORR)

A&C 48, sold for £1,450, now worth £1,500–2,500

SALLY TUFFIN FOR MOORCROFT

Rainforest design by Sally Tuffin, head designer and saviour of Moorcroft, limited edition, numbered 3 of 150, 42cm (SWORD)

A&C 63, sold for £800, now worth £800–1,200

EVENTIDE

Moorcroft's 'Eventide' pattern of tapered bulbous form, from around 1920, 16.5cm high. Trees were a popular design (LOCK)

A&C 51, sold for £1,850, now worth £1,800–2,500

RARE CARP VASE

A rare 'Carp' vase, akin to the work of Brannam and the Devon potteries (CHRIS)

A&C 30, sold for £4,465, now worth £4,000–6,000

Fact File

One of Moorcroft's top designers was Sally Tuffin who brought a modern, playful feel to the pottery while continuing with their traditional methods of decoration. These included polar bears and penguins, vastly different from some of her more traditional work, based on earlier designs such as peacock feathers, a theme that William Moorcroft himself had produced so successfully for MacIntyre's to sell at Liberty's. Whatever the age, what makes Moorcroft so special is their use of design and colour and that commands top prices but it's worth looking in job lots at auction, one auction house had overlooked a Moorcroft vase and which was found by a lucky buyer in the bottom of a job lot.

CHINACRAFT at BLYTH & WRIGHT

  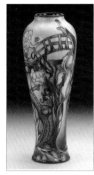

We also stock • Poole Pottery
• Florence Figurines • Cardew Teapots
• Royal Worcester • Portmeirion • Robert Harrop
• Harmony Kingdom to name just a few . . .

Also, new in stock . . . Aynsley China

34–40 Station Road   Sheringham   Norfolk   NR26 8RQ
Telephone 01263 823258   Email: blythwright@btconnect.com
www.blythandwright.co.uk

WEAVERS

"A dedicated fine china & giftware specialist"

Over 150 different pieces of
Moorcroft Pottery and Enamels,
including Limited Editions.

★ ★ ★

A large selection of Black Ryden.

★ ★ ★

A selection of older pieces of
Cobridge Stoneware, including
Rachael Bishop's 'Lascaux' and
'Ox-eye' numbered edition vase.

★ ★ ★

Open Monday to Saturday
9.15am to 5.00pm

Contact: Mrs Melody Carter
24 Church Street, Saffron Walden,
Essex CB10 1JW
Tel: 01799 525950 Fax: 01799 525940

TALENTS OF WINDSOR
Stockists of Fine Luxury Gifts & Collectables

    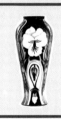 

Daum   LOET VANDERVEEN   HAZLE CERAMICS   JAY STRONGWATER

TALENTS OF WINDSOR
12 Church Street, Windsor,
Berkshire, SL4 1PE.

Tel. 01753 831 459
Email: shop@talentsofwindsor.com
www.etalents.com

OPENING HOURS
Monday – Saturday 10.00am – 5.30pm
Sunday 11.30am – 5.30pm

LOCATION
Adjacent to Windsor Castle
(behind the Guildhall and Crooked House)

Claris's
of Biddenden

Specialist retailer of contemporary Moorcroft Pottery & Enamels.

Always a beautiful display including Limited & Discontinued.

One of the largest selections in the South East.

Torridon by Philip Gibson

Also stocking Caithness Glass, Dennis China, Rye Pottery, Copenhagen, Harmony Kingdom, Staffordshire Enamels, Royal Selangor Pewter, Steiff Club Store.

Our world famous tearoom adds to that special shopping experience

We have gained many awards over our 20 years, including Tea Council Award of Excellence 2004 and Les Routiers Café of the Year for London and the South East 2004

1–3 High Street, Biddenden, Kent
Telephone 01580 291025 Closed Mondays

Mail Order Service

www.collectablegifts.net

GOLDENHANDS
Tel/Fax. 01424 439674

30 George Street,
Hastings,
East Sussex,
TN34 3EA

A family business situated in the charming Old Town, Hastings. We stock a fair range of Moorcroft and happily order items for customers. Club members receive a 10% discount on Moorcroft and we offer a free postal service within the UK. If we can be of assistance we will be delighted to help in any way we can.

21ˢᵗ Anniversary

Just Right
of Denbigh, North Wales

Established since 1983
One of the North West's Leading stockists of Moorcroft Pottery, we are stocking the exciting *new* 2004 ranges of , 'Blue on Blue' and, 'Philip Gibson presents…'

A small selection of the 11 pieces of Philip Gibson's collection,

If you would like any information on these, or any other pieces, please contact Ceri or Terry on 01745 815188
27-31 Vale St., Denbigh, Denbighshire, LL16 3AH
www.justrightcollectables.com

POOLE POTTERY

Like many potteries, Poole Pottery is now named after its location, namely Poole in Dorset but it was not always so and the pottery started life as Carter & Co in 1873 before becoming Carter, Stabler & Adams Ltd. in 1921. While their traditional blue, green, yellow and pink palette is instantly recognisable, they also made animals.

MOON CHARGER

The new Moon charger complement the Planets set perfectly, to make a truly collectable series.

A&C 50, now worth £300–500

ALFRED READ DESIGNS

White earthenwares with contemporary patterns, designed in 1954 by Alfred Read (RDP)

A&C 50, centre vase now worth £100–200

DELPHIS STUDIO POTTERY

Poole 'Delphis' charger, shape No.4. 26cm diameter, their most popular studio pottery design with its vivid colours (GARD)

A&C 7, sold for £30, now worth £200–350

MOULDED ANIMALS

A moulded dogs head by Poole Pottery, one of several which they made (COTT)

A&C 25, sold for £120, now worth £150–200

AEGEAN DESIGNS

Inspiring Aegean designs are evergreen (Picture by Martin Fells)

A&C 50, front dish now worth £50–70

Fact File

Poole's most famous designer was Truda Adams who was married to two of the partners of Carter, Stabler & Adams, first John Adams and then Charles Carter (son of the pottery's founder). Her designs were innovative, jazz-age in style and very fluid, including the 1926, Leipzig Girl which looks like a Roman figure leaping through flowers. Her pale palette with its simple, white-cream background, was continued into the 1960s. The famous dolphin backstamp calling the pottery 'Poole' was first used in 1950 and continues to be used today.

LAVA COLLECTION

Modern Lava vases, a homage to the 1950–60s studio pottery colours and now typical of Poole's recent studio output

A&C 50, sold for £25, now worth £20–30

BLUEBIRD MOTIF

1960s Bluebird vase decorated with the bird and flowers. Colourway first introduced by Truda Carter in the 1920s (GORR)

A&C 46, sold for £140, now worth £150–200

MODERN CROCKERY

Inspired by the tradional hand-painted banding that many Poole plates are finished with, Freehand design prices start from £6

A&C 50, now worth from £6

CERAMICS

CHARLOTTE RHEAD

Charlotte Rhead was born into the Rhead family of potters, one of the Potteries' most innovative families. Like her father, Frederick Rhead, she specialised in tubular style design, a style that Moorcroft are so famous for using with thickly lined glazes forming the pattern outlines. She is one of the most famous of all Art Deco designers.

PERSIAN VASES

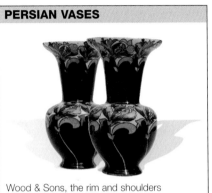

Wood & Sons, the rim and shoulders decorated with stylised flowers, probably by Charlotte Rhead, 33cm high WINT)

A&C 45, sold for £800, now worth £800-1,200

BURSLEY LAMP BASE

A 'second period' Bursley lamp base, c.1940s, featuring the pattern TL30 – heliotropes on a marigold background, signed. Est. £350–400

A&C 12, est £350-400, now worth £500-700

POMELO RIBBED EWER

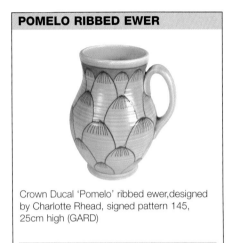

Crown Ducal 'Pomelo' ribbed ewer, designed by Charlotte Rhead, signed pattern 145, 25cm high (GARD)

A&C 8, sold for £200, now worth £XX

PHEASANT CHARGER

A Burleigh, 'Pheasant' design 35cm charger, c.1927/1928. Estimated value £1,500–1,875 (Courtesy of Mervyn and Sandra Dawson, Yorkshire)

A&C 12, est £1,500-1,875, now worth £1,500-2,500

'FLORENTINE' BOWL

A Burleigh bowl, c.1931, 34cm diameter, featuring the 'Florentine' pattern

A&C 12, est £300-330, now worth £300-450

Fact File

Charlotte Rhead was a designer who worked for a variety of potteries including Wood and Sons (where her father also worked) and, from 1926–31, Burgess and Leigh, better known as Burleigh, one of the most collectable of all Art Deco potteries where she created the shapes of the ceramics as well as their decoration. Her later pieces were signed, although her initial work, decorating existing patterns, is not signed but obviously her work because of the quality of design. Collectors tend to stick to signed pieces. Charlotte Rhead's work has never reached the financial heights of Clarice Cliff but prices are rising and pieces can still be bought fairly cheaply at smaller auctions.

JUG AND BOWL

A 'second period' Bursley ware jug and bowl in the 'Trellis' pattern, TL3. Dating from the 1940s, these two separate items were sold as a set. Valued individually, the bowl is worth between £150–180, while the jug is £200–220

A&C 12, est £350-400, now worth £600-800

'AZTEC' COFFEE SET

A rare Richardsons coffee set in Crown Ducal pattern 2800, 'Aztec'. This pattern does not generally sell well because of the lack of decoration

A&C 12, est £500-600, now worth £800-1,000

'HYDRANGEA' CHARGER

A Richardson's charger, 80cm diameter, c.1933, featuring the 'Hydrangea' pattern, no. 3797. This is one of the more sought-after Richardson's patterns

A&C 12, est £300-350, now worth £400-600

ROYAL DOULTON

Like many potteries, Doulton started life making practical goods, in their case, toilets. Now they are one of the most collectable makes with a vast range of goods from studio pottery (Lambeth Ware) to Art Deco figures and a collection of characters including Bunnykins and Brambly Hedge, as well as crockery and toby jugs.

FLAMBÉ VASE

Royal Doulton flambé vae, signed 'Eaton', 20cm high in the distinctive red (CLEV)

A&C 33, sold for £1,100, now worth £800-1,400

STONEWARE VASE

A Royal Doulton stoneware vase in rich glaze with interior detail (HART)

A&C 63, sold for £1,100, now worth £800-1,400

ANNIE HORTON VASE

1884 Royal Doulton baluster vase by Annie Horton. Modelled in relief with flying swans, 27.5cm high (GARD)

A&C 8, sold for £150, now worth £200-250

HANNAH BARLOW JARDINIERE

Royal Doulton jardiniere, Hannah Barlow, with continuous incised frieze of horses, 45cm diameter (GORR)

A&C 45, sold for £2,300, now worth £1,800-2,400

BREAKFAST SET

Rare Royal Doulton 'Gnome' series, heightened in gilt (SWORD)

A&C 48, sold for £5,800, now worth £5,000-7,500

Fact File

Doulton was established in Lambeth, London, in 1815, becoming Royal Doulton in 1902. Lambeth Ware was produced in their London pottery. A former student was Hannah Barlow, possibly Doulton's most famous potter, another George Tinworth, the 'Mouseman'. The potters signed their work but, as there were so many, it is not always easy to identify the signatures. Royal Doulton are now producing a series of modern, limited edition Lambethware in edition sizes of around 100, which makes them worth buying but don't mistake them for the older pieces.

HANNAH BARLOW DONKIES

Royal Doulton Lambethware vase by Hannah Barlow, a good name to collect (CHEF)

A&C 56, sold for £520, now worth £600-800

THE ALCHEMIST

'The Alchemist' a superb Sung vase by Charles Noke , renowned Doulton designer

A&C 7, sold for £4,370, now worth £6,000-8,000

1906 EXHIBITION VASE

This Burslem exhibition vase was created by David Dewsberry for the 1906 New Zealand International Exhibition of Art and Industry

A&C 7, sold for £16,100, now worth £20-25,000

CERAMICS

DOULTON FIGURE

'Fanny', Royal Doulton figure HN 1204, modelled by Leslie Harradine, one of their best designers,19cm high.(SWORD)

A&C 45, sold for £1,100, now worth £800-1,200

ALICE IN WONDERLAND

Royal Doulton's serene Alice, created in 1959 (Picture by Joel Birenbaum)

A&C 46, est £110, now worth £100-180

GLADYS

'Gladys', HN 1740, issued 1935–1949, 12.5cm., unusual shape (SWORD)

A&C 65, sold for £280, now worth £200-400

JACK POINT

Royal Doulton limited edition, 'Jack Point' HN 3925, Number 46 of 85. Based on their popular character (SWORD)

A&C 50, sold for £1,350, now worth £1,000-1,500

IN DREAMLAND

'Dreamland' by Leslie Harradine (1931–1938) featuring figure and toy Pierot (DREW)

A&C 54, sold for £1,500, now worth £1,200-1,800

MASK FIGURE

Mask figure by Royal Doulton, HN 785. 1926-38 (CHRIS)

A&C 66, sold for £3,055, now worth £2,500-3,500

NELL GWYNN

Royal Doulton's 'Nell Gwynn' HN 1887, issued 1938–49, based on a cigarette card illustration of Charles II's mistress and orange seller, 17cm high (LOCK)

A&C 65, sold for £400, now worth £300-500

MENDICANT FIGURE

'Mendicant' by Royal Doulton, HN 1355, printed mark, painted title, number and 'Potted by Doulton & Co' (FELL)

A&C 58, sold for £820, now worth £700-1,000

Fact File

Royal Doulton figures are extremely desirable, especially the Art Deco figures such as 'Sunshine Girl' (HN 1344 and 1348). Doulton's figures are very easy to identify as they have names but also, more importantly, HN numbers. While different figures might bear the same name because of redesigns, the HN number is unique and the best way to identify and date a figure – there are no variations, the HN number is set, a redesigned figure will simply be given a different number. HN does not stand for 'house number' as is often claimed but 'Harry Nixon' who worked for Royal Doulton and was in charge of the painters, as well as suggesting the colours used. HN numbers began in 1913 and have been used ever since.

DOULTON

For all your favourite collectables, why not visit Doulton Home, the new name for Royal Doulton Retail.

We stock a large range of collectables by Minton, Royal Doulton, Royal Albert and Doulton, as well as products from Royal Crown Derby, Preciosa Crystal, Lladro and many more.

For your nearest store, please call 01782 404045 or visit www.royaldoulton.com/website/storefinder/index.isp

The following stores:

LAWLEYS   CHINACAVE

ROYAL DOULTON   DOULTON AND COMPANY

are part of

DOULTON

The **NEW** name for
Royal Doulton Retail

CERAMICS

CHICKEN TEAPOT

An early twentieth-century Doulton Lambeth chicken teapot, 15cm high (DAH)

A&C 16, sold for £85, now worth £200-300

JOHN LENNON

'The Beatles', John Lennon mug, limited edition 1984. 1991 final year of issue. Modelled by Stanley James Taylor.

A&C 8, for sale £150, now worth £150-200

COCKEREL JUG

Late Victorian Doulton Lambeth glazed stoneware jug, fashioned as a cockerel, by Mark V. Marshall, 14.5cm high (AMER)

A&C 35, sold for £620, now worth £800-1,000

BRITISH BULLDOG

Royal Doulton figure of the British bulldog wearing the Union Jack, 10cm high. (GARD)

A&C 8, sold for £100, now worth £100-200

TOADSTOOL MODEL

Flambé model by Bernard Moore for Royal Doulton, printed and impressed marks (restored) (GORR)

A&C 51, sold for £650, now worth £600-800

BUNNYKINS BAND

Royal Doulton Bunnykins, in commemoration of Queen Elizabeth's II Jubilee (discontinued 1990) (GORR)

A&C 51, sold for £260, now worth £250-350

Fact File

Bunnykins were created especially for Royal Doulton by a nun, Barbara Vernon Bailey, for her father, Doulton's general manager, Cuthbert Bailey. She was alleged to have hated drawing them by the end but her designs have always proved popular.

But not all Bunnykins were designed by her, only the pieces bearing her signature (usually on the bottom right corner of the design). The famous dressed rabbits were joined by mice when Walter Hayward started designing them. People often get confused when dating Bunnykins because of the '1936' date on the special Bunnykins backstamp but this is simply the copyright date, not the age of the piece.

If you like Bunnykins, it's worth looking at Doulton's Brambly Hedge range, based on the books by Jill Barklem.

SPIRIT BARREL

Royal Doulton decorative Kingsware spirit barrel, 17.5cm long (CLEV)

A&C 33, sold for £550, now worth £500-750

OWL JUG

Doulton Lambeth stoneware 'Owl' jug

A&C 54, sold for £1,600, now worth £1,500-2,250

WHATEVER YOU COLLECT........

BOBBY'S BOOKS
Specialising in books on Antiques & Collectables

For ALL your book
requirements contact
Judy Smith
Beckley Hill Works
Canal Road
Higham
Rochester
Kent
ME3 7HX

CHINESE SNUFF BOTTLES:
A GUIDE TO ADDICTIVE MINIATURES

This book clearly explains the history of snuff and its specialized bottles from the 17th Century to the present in America, Europe and China.

With over 650 bottles to study, 657 colour photos, prices in $.

Orders taken now.

Price £55 plus postage.

01474 823388 **bobbysbooks@aol.com**

Classic Ceramics

Specialist Suppliers of early Staffordshire & fine English Pottery

Pot Lids • Pastille Burners • Measham
Staffordshire figures & animals • Toby Jugs

Tel: 01278 425752
Email: info@classic-ceramics.com
www.classic-ceramics.com

JUST PUBLISHED

Toby Jug
The most underestimated antique

The only book currently in print devoted entirely to Toby Jugs. Full colour illustrations throughout, a must for Toby collectors and all Staffordshire collectors. Covers Pearlware, Running Glazes, Creamware, Yorkshire and Portobello types and much more.

Getting to Know Your
Toby Jug

RON EARL

Just send £11.50 +£2.00 p&p to
Libra Printing, 14 Fairfield Avenue, Datchet, Berks SL3 9NQ

YOUR BOOK WILL BE SENT BY RETURN

Toby Jug
Antiques & Collectables

South Toll House, Deal Pier, Beach Street, Deal Kent CT14 6HZ

Telephone 01304 369917

Specialising in Toby & Character Jugs.
Wide selection of quality ceramic collectables always available.
Commissions undertaken - we also buy

CERAMICS

SPODE & COPELAND

Spode was founded by Josiah Spode in 1761, came under his sole ownership in 1776 and, despite several owners, is still on the same site in Stoke-on-Trent. The most famous change of ownership was to Copeland whose name was incorporated into the pottery, making it Copeland-Spode. They are most famous for blue and white.

'TOWER' DRAINER

A Spode blue and white 'Tower' pattern earthenware drainer, c.1815–20. Some damage. 32.5cm long (BOO)

A&C 11, sold for £180, now worth £200-400

'TOWER' SPITTOON

A Spode blue and white 'Tower' pattern earthenware spittoon, c.1820

A&C 11, sold for £160, now worth £200-400

INDIAN SPORTING SERIES

'Indian Sporting' series, earthenware vegetable dish and cover, c.1820. This is a very popular pattern

A&C 11, sold for £940, now worth £1,000-1,500

BOTANICAL PLATE

One of four hand painted Bow botanical plates, all with different patterns

A&C 41, est £550, now worth £500-600

TEA AND COFFEE SET

Spode stone china tea and coffee service, c.1815, some cracks and scratches (HAMP)

A&C 38, sold for £920, now worth £1,000-1,500

Fact File

In 1764, Spode bought the pottery of his former employer, William Banks, to which he moved his new pottery and, over three hundred and forty years later, it's still on the same site.

Josiah Spode I was a great innovator, he was the first to create blue and white wares in Britain and, in 1797, Spode discovered the formula for bone china.

The bone aspect was ox-bone which helped to give the fine material its structure. He died before seeing how successful it was to become but part of that success was his forethought in establishing a London showroom and shop where his son, Josiah Spode II, could show their superior clients what made Spode so special.

SCOTTISH POET

Classical Copeland portrait of a Scottish poet, 1871, with impressed marks including 'Ceramic and Crystal Palacert Union', 36cm high (FELL)

A&C 39, sold for £360, now worth £400-600

CLOISSONNE PANELS

Detail from a pair of cloisonné panels in the style of Namakawa Sosuke

A&C 41, sold for £3,050, now worth £3,000-3,700

RARE EGG CUP

A rare Spode Indian Sporting series egg cup from around 1815–25 (DREW)

A&C 48, sold for £520, now worth £500-800

SUGAR BOX

A Spode 'Japan' pattern 'New Oval' sugar box and cover, c.1810, with rich oriental-style panelled decoration

A&C 11, sold for £160, now worth £200-300

SAUCER DISH

A Spode bone china saucer dish, c.1810, featuring three ladies in Etruscan red figure style. Minor wear, some discolouration. Pattern no.1171, not marked Spode. Diameter 23cm (BOO)

A&C 11, sold for £340, now worth £XX

JAPANESQUE SET

A rare Copeland 'Japanesque' style bone china teapot and sugar bowl, c.1874

A&C 11, sold for £100, now worth £200-300

AESOP'S FABLES

A Spode 'Aesop's Fables' series earthenware shaped rectangular dessert comport, c.1830. 30cm long (BOO)

A&C 11, sold for £240, now worth £300-400

OVAL BASKET

Oval basket, two-handled and pierced, printed in black and painted in green and iron-red, from around 1820 (DREW)

A&C 52, sold for £200, now worth £200-300

Fact File

Josiah Spode II made William Copeland his partner. The company came under the ownership of Copeland-Garrett in 1833 before being owned solely by W. T. Copeland in 1847, the company known as Copeland-Spode, still respecting the importance of Spode as a pottery. In 1970, the company reverted to the name Spode, not using Copeland on the backstamp. As the Spode museum shows, the pottery did not suffer but continued to produce good quality wares, especially blue and white and there is a Blue and White Room in the museum to show how the pottery had dominated the market which they helped to create. The Willow pattern, although copied by others, originated at Spode.

SPODE FOOTBATH

Spode filigree footbath, c.1825 (Picture courtesy Gillian Neale Antiques, Aylesbury)

A&C 41, est £2,000, now worth £1,800-2,400

CHELSEA DESSERT PLATE

A Copeland cream-coloured earthenware fluted 'Chelsea Dessert' plate. c.1870, printed in red-brown with an amusing scene. Diameter 21cm (BOO)

A&C 11, sold for £110, now worth £XX

PEARLWARE FOOTBATH

A Spode pearlware footbath, c.1820, printed with the 'Willow', third pattern. Estimated value £1,000–1,500 (DREW)

A&C 11, est £1,000-1,500, now worth £2,000-3,000

CERAMICS

STAFFORDSHIRE

Staffordshire, the county, is the home to the Potteries because of its natural resources. It is also the name given to the distinctive white glazed figures or animals, often with cobalt blue decoration. They are a style, not a make and it is often impossible to identify the potter of these collectable ornaments, spill vases or pastille burners.

DISRAELI GREYHOUNDS

A pair of Staffordshire greyhounds, 'Disraeli' type (PH)

A&C 11, sold for £1,265, now worth £2,000-3,000

CRIMEAN FIGURES

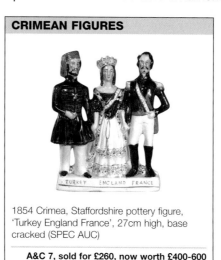

1854 Crimea, Staffordshire pottery figure, 'Turkey England France', 27cm high, base cracked (SPEC AUC)

A&C 7, sold for £260, now worth £400-600

PAIR OF GOATS

Staffordshire goats, a pair, 30.5cm high, some damage (FELL)

A&C 39, sold for £460, now worth £400-600

ENGLISH SETTER

Seated English Setter, decorated with gilt highlights, on a naturalistic base, 27.5cm high (AMER)

A&C 31, sold for £100, now worth £200-300

A GAME OF CARDS

Group of Dr Syntax and a companion playing cards at a drop flap table (GORR)

A&C 51, sold for £1,000, now worth £1,000-1,500

Fact File

Collectors usually limit themselves to a genre within this field such as political, royal, humorous figures or animals, the most popular being dogs.

The most famous of these are the two large, seated spaniels. These are believed to be based on Queen Victoria's King Charles spaniel, Dash and were made from 1837, the year she became queen. In England, they were known as 'comforters', bringing comfort to even the loneliest of homes. Many did not have their backs decorated because these would rest against a wall, thus saving the need for time-consuming decoration.

This was typical of Staffordshire and became known as 'flatbacks'. They also made figures as spill vases, which doubled up as match strikers, 'spill' or 'spile' meaning small pieces of wood.

SMITH & COLLIER

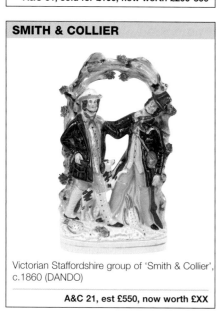

Victorian Staffordshire group of 'Smith & Collier', c.1860 (DANDO)

A&C 21, est £550, now worth £XX

SPILL VASE

Very colourful Victorian Staffordshire pottery figure of a medieval huntsman – converted to an electric lamp (GORR)

A&C 57, sold for £1,100, now worth £800-1,400

HIGHLAND FIGURE

Victorian Staffordshire figure in Highland costume, c.1860 (DANDO)

A&C 21, est £295, now worth £300-450

STUDIO POTTERY

This is a lovely and very diverse area of collecting. For some people, studio pottery is all about shape, the brown colour of the pottery concentrating the eye on the form (eg Bernard Leach) while, for others, it is both tactile (eg Troika) and colourful. Studio pottery is the name given to potteries run by individuals or with few employees.

BERNARD LEACH

Stoneware slab bottle by Bernard Leach (PH)

A&C 31, sold for £4,140, now worth £4,500-6,500

DAME LUCIE RIE

Oval stoneware 'Fluted' bowl by Dame Lucie Rie, a concentration on form (PH)

A&C 31, sold for £11,500, now worth £12-15,000

HANS COPER

Oval stoneware pot by Hans Coper (PH)

A&C 31, sold for £28,750, now worth £26-32,000

MICHAEL CARDEW

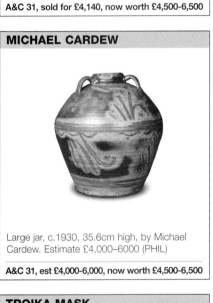

Large jar, c.1930, 35.6cm high, by Michael Cardew. Estimate £4,000–6000 (PHIL)

A&C 31, est £4,000-6,000, now worth £4,500-6,500

LUCIE RIE BOWL

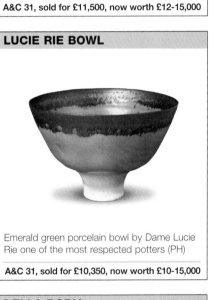

Emerald green porcelain bowl by Dame Lucie Rie one of the most respected potters (PH)

A&C 31, sold for £10,350, now worth £10-15,000

Fact File

Troika means 'tribe', 'triumvirate' or 'three'. It is also the name of a studio pottery which was established in 1963 in the artistic community of St Ives, Cornwall by three people; Benny Sirota, a potter, Jan Thompson, an architect and the sculptor, Lesley Illsley. They were influenced by Scandinavian design and the Cornish landscape. Their work is very tactile and they were completely innovative, the texture similar to stone or slate, not the highly glazed work or smooth surfaces of contemporaries. Troika moved to Newlyn in 1970 but closed in 1983. Prices have risen drastically recently with the larger pieces being the most desirable.

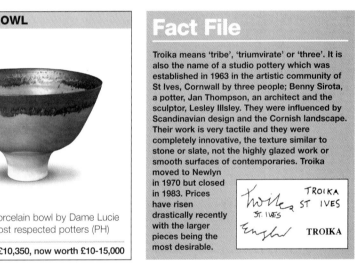

TROIKA MASK

Rare Troika Mask (Picture by David Lay's Auctioneers)

A&C 52, est £1,000-1,500, now worth £1,500-1,800

DELLA ROBIA

Arts and Crafts Della Robbia vase with tulip-shaped rim and neck, decorated with stylised leaves 34cm high (SWORD)

A&C 51, sold for £130, now worth £150-200

JAMES TOWER

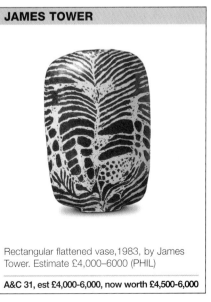

Rectangular flattened vase,1983, by James Tower. Estimate £4,000–6000 (PHIL)

A&C 31, est £4,000-6,000, now worth £4,500-6,000

CERAMICS

HONEY POT

Wemyss pottery from around 1910, with bee decoration, damage and staining (SWORD)

A&C 60, sold for £260, now worth £250-300

TROIKA WHEEL VASE

Troika St Ives Wheel vase, decorated by Honor Curtis (Picture by Paul Longthorne)

A&C 52, est £300-350, now worth £350-400

WEMYSS PIG

Large pig, glazed in apple green, 45cm high, inscribed 'Wemyss' on base. One ear is damaged, chipped snout, body cracked, tail missing - but still a good buy (PH ED)

A&C 34, sold for £450, now worth £500-600

ARTS AND CRAFTS

British Arts and Crafts two-handled vase by Della Robbia with artists' initials LW (Liza Wilkins) and EB.(GORR)

A&C 54, sold for £550, now worth £500-700

MARTIN BROTHERS

Wally bird from Martin Brothers with a hammer price of £40,000 – 'a near world record', according to the auctioneers (WO WA)

A&C 64, sold for £40,000, now worth £38-42,000

Fact File

Potters tend to work in the same locale, not just because of resources but a feeling of community. This was best seen at St Ives (Bernard Leach and Troika) and Aldermaston in Berkshire which was established in 1955 by Alan Caiger-Smith and trained dozens of accomplished potters including Julian Belmont.

Their work was very distinctive and highly influenced by the master potter, Caiger-Smith with his use of decoration and colours.

Although not everyone is interested in pots or understands why some studio pottery commands higher prices than others, the figural studio pottery continues to appeal and amuse and Caiger-Smiths birds are highly sought-after but hard to find. Basil Matthews' work is cheaper (around £80–120 for larger pieces) and highly attractive, ideal for novice collectors.

RUSKIN POTTERY

Ruskin's famous glazes seen in orange lustre vase, 1915, blue speckled lustre vase, 1924, and turquoise vase, 1914. (SWORD)

A&C 63, sold for £180, now worth £400-600

PALISSY-STYLE

Palissy style by Mafra of Caldas de Rainha, with applied lizards, toads, beetles and a frog on extruded clay, 1880 (SWORD)

A&C 64, sold for £1,000, now worth £1,000-1,500

WEMYSS BISCUIT JAR

Wemyss earthenware, biscuit jar painted with strawberries, c 1900. The Queen Mother used to collect Wemyss which was from her native Scotland and often depicted roses (GORR)

A&C 57, sold for £280, now worth £250-350

Gemini Publications Ltd

Publishers

bookbasket

30a Monmouth Street, Bath, BA1 2AN, UK

Telephone: 01225 484877
Fax: 01225 334619
Email: sales@bookbasket.co.uk
Web: www.bookbasket.co.uk

TROIKA CERAMICS OF CORNWALL
By George Perrott
PLUS UPDATED PRICE SUPPLEMENT

Troika Pottery made distinctive moulded shapes, and developed lines in both textured and smooth white surfaces. They existed from 1963 until 1983. Just 20 years.

Their wares today have become very collectable and are fetching high prices at the sales.

This book has been written by George Perrott to meet the demands of collectors and dealers for information on this innovative and desirable pottery.

Packed with useful information, plus over 200 coloured photographs.

It covers shapes, designs and glazes with an informative section on marks.

A Price Guide covering those realised at auction and on the internet plus prices expected in the antique market and at fairs.

A book well worth a space on your bookshelf.

ISBN	0-9530637-3-9
Format	240 x 170mm portrait
Pages	128
Illustrations	200 plus in colour
Binding	Softback
Cover	Gloss laminated
Body	Black text on white paper with coloured illustrations
Price	£17.95
Publication	17th March 2003

SPECIAL OFFER

Troika Ceramics of Cornwall

plus new

Troika Price Supplement

£17.95 Postage Free.

If you would like to purchase this book **PLUS NEW PRICE SUPPLEMENT** for £17.95 postage free. (UK only) please fill in this form and return to the Publisher or contact us by phone.

ORDER FORM

Name

Address

Postcode

Telephone

CERAMICS

TILES

Tiles are now seen as decoration for large areas, for kitchens and bathrooms and generally mass-produced with a repetitive pattern but it was not always so. In the Victorian era, they would be concentrated around smaller areas, such as fire surrounds, and be decorative in themselves, either forming a mural or as a single tile.

WILLIAM DE MORGAN

William De Morgan tile, painted with a fantastic bird, blue painted mark, late Fulham period, 1891–1907 (SWORD)

A&C 65, sold for £1,100, now worth £800-1,200

MINTON CLASSICAL TILES

Pair of tiles Minton Hollies & Co in the manner of John Moyr Smith. Each printed and painted with a classical lady figure, titled 'Mechanics' and 'Botany'. 20.5cm high (WINT)

A&C 31, sold for £520, now worth £500-700

VOYSEY WHITE RABBIT

Framed Minton 'Alice in Wonderland' tile, depicting the White Rabbit, designed by CFA Voysey. (BON)

A&C 29, sold for £210, now worth £300-500

BRISTOL DELFTWARE

Bristol delftware painted polychrome tile, c.1760 (BON)

A&C 29, est £350, now worth £400-500

DE MORGAN CORNFLOWERS

William de Morgan tile painted with cornflowers, Fulham mark. (GORR)

A&C 59, sold for £190, now worth £200-300

Fact File

When it comes to tiles, William de Morgan's work is possibly the most desirable. The Arts and Crafts designer created a vast range of tiles in his trademark style, his main designs being ships, leaves, birds, monsters and animals.

Some of his work shows an Aesthetic Movement style with its Japanese and Persian influences. His work is highly desirable with the better ones worth over £1,000, depending on condition and design. Minton's tiles are also highly sought after with their often Medieval-influenced themes of courtly love, knights and ladies. For those interested in collecting more modern tiles, the work of the late Wally Cole of Rye Pottery is a very good buy as are Victoria Ellis' modern tiles

EDWARD BURNE-JONES

Rare two-tile panel 'Thisbe', designed by Edward Burne-Jones for Morris, Marshall, Faulkner & Company in 1861 (CHRIS)

A&C 29, sold for £16,450, now worth £20-30,000

MINTON PANEL

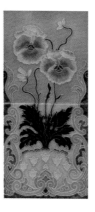

Original Minton tube-lined two-tile panel (BON)

A&C 29, sold for £185, now worth £300-400

SNAKE PANEL

Original William De Morgan three-tile 'Snake' panel, a typical Arts and Crafts motif, in rich blues (RDP)

A&C 29, est £7,000, now worth £7,000-8,000

VASES

Vases make good but practical collectables. You might opt to collect ones by the same make, with similar designs or in the same colour (eg blue) for a more uniform collection or you might just buy what you like – which is the best reason for collecting. As with all china, look for tell-tale hairlines (cracks) before buying.

PINE CONES

Nineteenth century vase, 50cm high (DREW)

A&C 41, sold for £130, now worth £100-200

PILKINGTON VASE

Pilkington vase with lustre glaze, the base with a mark for Gordon Forsyth and year code 1914, 19cm high (CLEV)

A&C 39, sold for £500, now worth £500-700

DOULTON CHINE

Doulton Slaters chine vases with long slender necks, prone to damage, 37.5cm (GORR)

A&C 43, sold for £260, now worth £200-300

WILLIAM DE MORGAN

William de Morgan Arts and Crafts ruby lustre stoneware bottle vase (WO WA)

A&C 59, sold for £2,800, now worth £2,500-3,500

MR PUNCH VASE

An unusual pottery figure, c.1880, modelled as Mr Punch holding a quill within a parchment boat-shaped vase. 39cm x 31cm high (HAMP)

A&C 8, sold for £290, now worth £200-400

Fact File

Vases were made to be used and, if you're thinking of buying one for use, turn it over – ignore the backstamp and look harder. You might notice something called a 'spider crack' on the bottom – that's where a crack carries on cracking down different lines. Another area to look is around the rim where vases often get chipped or cracked. The word 'vase' comes from the Latin *vars* meaning a container. The pronunciation of vase to rhyme with bars dates from the mid-nineteenth century, although Americans rhyme it with base. Different eras adopted different styles and colours and the distinctive black and white stripes date from the 1950s eg Midwinter, Beswick and Hornsea, a tempting collection.

BERLIN PORCELAIN

Nineteenth century porcelain vases, painted with rustic lovers, adapted as lamps, 48cm high (SWORD)

A&C 54, sold for £820, now worth £800-1,200

MOORCROFT LIBERTY TUDRIC

Moorcroft Eventide pattern with Liberty Tudric pewter mount, 23cm high (LOCK)

A&C 61, sold for £2,600, now worth £2,000-4,000

WORCESTER VASES

A pair of ovoid bodied vases with floral panels. in pale colours (SWORD)

A&C 46, sold for £560, now worth £600-800

FRANZ
Hummingbird

The beautiful colours of Franz Porcelain are created by its underglaze decorating techniques; the quality of which is measurable by the fluid shading and reflective depth of colour on each item. The accents of delicate creatures and fragile flowers superbly illustrate Franz Porcelain creators' intricate skills.

FZ00132 Hummingbird Coffee Pot

FZ00134 Hummingbird Sugar Bowl

FZ00133 Hummingbird Cream Jug

FZ00129 Hummingbird Cup & Saucer

FZ00198 Hummingbird Spoon

For more information, contact:
ENESCO
Customer Service & Distribution Centre, Brunthill Road, Carlisle, Cumbria, England, CA3 0EN.
Tel: 01228 404040 Fax: 01228 404041
E mail: uksales@enesco.co.uk

Franz Porcelain © 2004 Seagull Décor Co., Ltd. 2004 ENESCO LTD.

FZ00131 Hummingbird Jug

CERAMICS

WADE

Wade is one of the stalwarts of the collectables world but is best known for its pocket money ornaments which were produced in the 1950s with another series in the 1970–80s, Whimsies. Not many people know that they also produced some of the tiles for the American space shuttles in the 1980s or ceramic fires, part of their industrial line.

WALT DISNEY FIGURINES

Walt Disney figurines – Snow White and the Seven Dwarfs from 1938 painted in celluloid which tends to peel easily

A&C 42, est £2,000, now worth £1,800-2,000

FAUST LANG PARROT

A rare, Faust Lang Parrot model based on the work of the famous sculptor, 1939 (POTT)

A&C 16, sold for £1,350, now worth £1,500-1,800

SNOW WHITE

Walt Disney's Snow White and the Seven Dwarfs, 1980s glazed version.Snow White with an early version of Snow White (FELL)

A&C 54, sold for £400, now worth £1,200-1,500

UNDERGLAZED JULIET

A rare 1930s underglaze porcelain figure of 'Juliet' played by Norma Shearer, designed by Jessie Van Hallen (POTT)

A&C 16, est £400-700, now worth £800-1,200

BILLINGSGATE PORTER

Boxed 'Billingsgate porter', one of four British Characters which included the Pearly King

A&C 42, now worth £60-80

Fact File

Jessie van Hallen, Wade's most famous modeller, was hired in 1930 and created over thirty of the collectable figurines, including Pavlova, Zena, Joy and Springtime. She was related by marriage to Henry Hallen who used to own the Henry Hallen Pottery which was renamed as Wade's Manchester Pottery where she worked. Her most famous work is the 1938 set of Snow White and the Seven Dwarves which was one of her last creations for Wade. She became a freelance potter but never achieved the success that she did at Wade. Her Art Deco figures are great buys.

WADES
ENGLAND
Mark Type 1
Mid 1920's-1927
Ink Stamp

PAVLOVA

Jessie Van Hallen's 'Pavlova', 1930s. This is one of the most common figures and was one of three Wade figures based on the ballerina, Anna Pavlova (C&S Collectables Direct, West Sussex)

A&C 16, est £90-120, now worth £100-150

FAUST LANG

A 1939 Faust Lang Rearing Horse model. Valued at around £1,000 (POTT)

A&C 16, est £1,000, now worth £1,200-1,500

ZENA

Wade Jessie Van Hallen figurine dancing figurine, 'Zena'. This is the easier to find standard model, the miniature is much rare (C&S Collectables Direct, West Sussex)

A&C 16, est £200-250, now worth £300-400

CERAMICS

WEDGWOOD

Wedgwood is one of Britain's greatest potteries, its traditional cameo designs are popular exports. Josiah Wedgwood founded the pottery in 1759 and introduced the famous jasper ware (cameos) in 1767, drawing on antiquity. In the twentieth century, they produced the famous Fairyland Lustre with its colourful designs.

CREAMWARE TEAPOT

A rare globular creamware teapot and cover (lid), with foliate moulded spout and handle, with a portrait of the Marquis of Granby after the engraving by Richard Houston. 107mm high, c.1766 (SPEC AUC)

A&C 7, sold for £3,200, now worth £4,000-5,500

PERFECT PORTRAIT

Wedgwood blue jasper medallions of Lord and Lady Auckland, from 1800 (SOTH)

A&C 51, sold for £763, now worth £700-900

POT POURRI VASE

Wedgwood pearlware pot pourri vase, with a mottled pink-lustre, 1810 (DREW)

A&C 51, sold for £1,000, now worth £800-1,200

BLUE JASPER WARE

Wedgwood three-colour jasper coffee can and saucer. This colour is now known as Wedgwood blue (SOTH)

A&C 51, sold for £998, now worth £800-1,400

ERIC RAVILIOUS

Wedgwood Garden Series tea set, designed by Eric Ravilious, the cult designer and collectable in his own right (SWORD)

A&C 56, est £250-350, now worth £500-800

Fact File

Josiah Wedgwood had a leg injury and could not work as a potter because of it but he was an ideas man who realised that there was a massive market place out there, not just for the rich but all classes and even overseas.

He worked on different forms of pottery and experimented with glazes. One of his earliest creations was black basalte, an unglazed stoneware, which he decorated in line with the neo-classical fervour of the day.

His famous jasper ware, a form of stoneware, was introduced in 1774 and still remains Wedgwood's most famous creation, especially the blue version. The white cameos were decorated with neo-classical themes drawing on Roman and Greek material.

FIT FOR A QUEEN

'Queensware' bullet-shaped cream coloured teapot from 1775, (DREW)

A&C 51, est £320, now worth £250-350

FAIRYLAND LUSTRE

Jewelled Tree pattern vase in Fairyland Lustre, Wedgwood's most colourful creation (WO WA)

A&C 57, sold for £4,200, now worth £4,000-6,000

JASPER VASE

Nineteenth century green jasper vase and cover on octagonal foot, 36cm high (CHEF)

A&C 35, est £250, now worth £200-400

LEAP-FROGGING ELVES

Wedgwood Fairyland Lustre bowl, painted with leap-frogging elves pattern (GORR)

A&C 57, sold for £800, now worth £800-1,400

PAIR OF ELF VASES

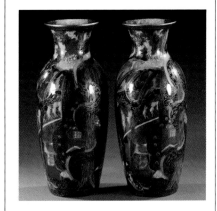

Pair of vases depicting green elves in Wedgwood's fantasy Fairyland Lustre (SOTH)

A&C 57, sold for £6,240, now worth £6,000-7,000

FOOTED BOWL

Wedgwood Fairyland Lustre 'Antique Centre' bowl from 1925 (SOTH)

A&C 57, sold for £3,720, now worth £4,000-5,000

OCTAGONAL BOWL

Wedgwood Fairyland Lustre octagonal bowl, gilding on the interior with 'Smoke Ribbons', (DREW)

A&C 57, sold for £820, now worth £800-1,400

IMPS ON A BRIDGE

Wedgwood Fairyland Lustre plate decorated by Daisy Makeig-Jones, central Imps on a Bridge panel within a floral border (GORR)

A&C 57, sold for £3,400, now worth £3,000-4,000

FAIRYLAND LUSTRE

Wedgwood 1920s Fairyland Lustre octagonal bowl. Estimated at £1,800-£2,200 (SOTH)

A&C 57, sold for £3,290, now worth £3,000-4,000

MAJOLICA PLATE

Wedgwood majolica plate with a date code for 1867 (DREW)

A&C 51, sold for £180, now worth £150-250

QUEENSWARE VEILLEUSE

'Queensware' Veilleuse and fittings, in the Dutch style with shades of iron-red, blue and green, 1884 (DREW)

A&C 51, sold for £160, now worth £200-250

Fact File

In 1769, with a business partner, Wedgwood opened a factory which was named 'Etruria', a name often seen on backstamps and which paid homage to his love of Etruscan pottery whose influence can be seen in some of their neo-classical designs. A more up-to-date product was Fairyland Lustre which typified the lustrous decoration of the Deco era and whose style, if not subject, influenced Carlton Ware and Crown Devon. The Wedgwood version was produced in the 1920s and the most popular paterns were designed by Daisy Makeig-Jones. What sets Fairyland Lustre apart from its competitors is the fantasy landscape they inhabit, filled with elves and fairies.

CERAMICS

WORCESTER

Royal Worcester is just part of the rich heritage of Worcester potteries which have a collective history but different names and owners. The work of Flight and Barr and Worcester and Barr are part of the ancestry of the popular pottery with their own collectors. They are all renowned for the quality of their hand painted decoration.

CUP AND SAUCER

Eighteenth century Worcester polychrome cup and saucer (SWORD)

A&C 58, sold for £200, now worth £150-250

NAUTILUS VASES

Nautilus (shell-shaped) vases by Royal Worcester. Impressed marks and date code for 1885, 22cm high (DREW)

A&C 40, sold for £170, now worth £200-400

URN-SHAPED VASES

A matched pair of early 1900s Royal Worcester vases, Painted to the front with a landscape scene (FELL)

A&C 45, sold for £4,400, now worth £4,000-6,000

FIGURE OF SISTER

A limited edition Royal Worcester figure from the Nursing Sisters series by Ruth Van Ruyckevelt, No. 205 of 500 (small edition) size), with box and certificate (GORR)

A&C 47, sold for £1,700, now worth £1,500-2,000

HENRY AYRTON

Twelve Royal Worcester plates, painted by Harry Ayrton with a named fish, acid-etched gilt borders, 1934 (SWORD)

A&C 66, sold for £1,280, now worth £1,000-1,500

Fact File

Worcester was established in 1751 by Dr John Wall as a place for artists to experiment in ceramics. After he died, the pottery declined and was sold in 1783 to Thomas Flight for £3,000, which although an enormous sum, was a third less than it had been sold for previously. Mismanagement by Thomas's son, Joseph, could have ruined the factory but his brother John interceded and a timely visit by King George III in 1788 led to a Royal Warrant and links with French porcelain companies saw a vast improvement in the quality of decoration at a time when Chamberlain's porcelain company, founded by a previous employer, was threatening their future. Healthy competition led to an exciting output for both firms with several of the craftsmen being employed at different times by both potteries, leading to similar work – which is very confusing when trying to identify unmarked pieces.

BLUE AND WHITE

Worcester, blue and white printed in the pine cone pattern, c 1770, 24.5cm (SWORD)

A&C 62, sold for £330, now worth £300-500

DOUBLE-GOURD VASE

Royal Worcester double-gourd-shaped vase and lizards c 1870 (CHRIS)

A&C 51, sold for £705, now worth £800-1,200

HOUSE OF PARLIAMENT

A Chamberlain's Worcester shell encrusted topographical card tray C 1840, with view of the new Houses of Parliament (SOTH)

A&C 48, sold for £822, now worth £XX

OWL COFFEE SET

Coffee cups were often slender versions of tea cups. This boxed set of six owl cups and saucers comes with six spoons (SWORD)

A&C 58, sold for £580, now worth £500-800

PAIR OF JARDINIERES

Barr, Flight and Barr from around 1810, of flared form. Typically English flowers painted against a salmon pink ground gilt (SOTH)

A&C 44, sold for £7,990, now worth £6,000-10,000

FRUIT PAINTING

Royal Worcester, painted with apples and blackberries, by W. J. Bagnall, 1926 (SWORD)

A&C 50, sold for £280, now worth £300-400

POT POURRI LINER

Large Royal Worcester blush ivory pot pourri liner and cover, date code for 1909, 34cm high (HAMP)

A&C 38, sold for £1,100, now worth £1,000-1,500

CANDELABRUM

Royal Worcester candelabrum, modelled with children with a frog and bird's nest beside trees, designed for three candles each (GORR)

A&C 65, sold for £1,300, now worth £1,500-2,000

ONION-SHAPED VASE

George V, unusual onion shaped vase, with hand painted decoration of highland cattle, 20cm high (SWORD)

A&C 50, sold for £1,400, now worth £1,000-1,800

CYLINDRICAL MUG

A documentary Worcester cylindrical mug, c.1780, 11.5cm high, (WO WA)

A&C 18, sold for £2,500, now worth £2,500-3,500

Fact File

One of Royal Worcester's best painters was Harry Ayrton who started work as an apprentice in 1920 at the age of 15. After the First World War, there had been an influx of apprentices and Harry was part of the 'terrible seven', a group of trainees renowned as trouble makers, playing football when they should have been working. He trained under the esteemed artists, William Hawkins, possibly the pottery's best ever painter. While painting a wide variety of subjects initially, including fish, Ayrton is best known for his fruit, one of Royal Worcester's enduring themes which attracts many collectors. He retired in 1970 but continued to paint until his death in 1976 and his work is greatly admired and collected.

CLOCKS

BRACKET
Whilst other areas of the antiques trade have declined in value recently, clocks continue to rise. Bracket clocks are popular and are often referred to as mantel clocks although, for purists, the mantel clock tends to have a rounder top and bracket clocks are squarer with some devised to sit on brackets on walls… hence their name.

GEORGIAN

Georgian mahogany bracket clock. (HAMP)

A&C 17, sold £1,600, now worth £2,000-3,500

FRENCH GILT

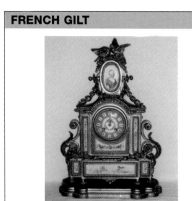

French gilt clock with enamel decoration on porcelain panels, surmounted by birds (LTAY)

A&C 44, sold for £740, now worth £1,000-1,500

ARCHITECTURAL FORM

A 19th-century rosewood bracket clock. Architectural form with brass finials flanked by pilasters and good chiming movement (CRIT)

A&C 13, sold for £3,600, now worth £4,500-6,000

MAHOGANY AND ROSEWOOD

Regency mahogany and rosewood repeating bracket clock, with painted Roman dial signed Slater, resting on ball feet (GORR)

A&C 65, sold £1,350, now worth £1,200-1,500

Fact File

The invention of the pendulum in the 17th century lead to the creation of bracket clocks which were 'spring driven' by the short pendulum. The cases are similar in design to longcase clocks with British versions mainly using wooden cases.

French clocks were much more ornate, often employing other materials such as slate or even a tortoiseshell veneer. Some of the clocks were seen as being portable with a handle attached. In Regency days, these would sometimes come with a lion's head or a cornucopia (shell) mount, similar to the boxes of the day.

Anyone thinking of moving a clock, even off a shelf while dusting, is advised to remove the pendulum first to avoid damage. And be careful not to overwind; it's one of the most common ways to damage a clock.

REPEATING CLOCK

Brass-mounted hour repeating clock (strikes hour and quarter hour) with inner date ring, signed William Evill, Bath (GORR)

A&C 63, sold for £1,000, now worth £1,000-1,500

THOMAS TOMPION TABLE CLOCK

Thomas Tompion No 417, very rare ormolu mounted red turtle-shell grande-sonnerie table clock, London from around 1705 (SOTH)

A&C 54, sold £901,600, now worth £950,000

WALL BRACKET CLOCK

Louis XV Tortoiseshell and brass inlaid, wall-mounted bracket clock, with ormolu mounts and urn and flame finials, circular dial with blue enamel numerals and figural details (MALL)

A&C 47, sold £2,500, now worth £3,000-4,000

AUSTRIAN SCHOOL

Early 20th century Austrian School, secessionist coromandel and satinwood parquetry veneer clock, pyramid form (SOTH)

A&C 52, sold £6,000, now worth £6,000-8,000

Samuel Orr
Antique Clocks

Established 36 Years

OVER 100 CLOCKS ALWAYS IN STOCK

• Good investment clocks • Shipping Worldwide
• Antique Clocks • Barometers
• Restoration Clocks purchased

34-36 High Street, Hurstpierpoint,
West Sussex BN6 9RG

Telephone: 01283 832081
Email: clocks@samorr.co.uk

www.samorr.co.uk

GÜTLIN CLOCKS
& ANTIQUES

*One of London's largest selections
of antique grandfather clocks
& French mantel clocks.*

Full online catalogue at
www.gutlin.com

All types of antique clocks repaired
and restored. FREE ESTIMATES!

606 King's Road SW6 2DX   Telephone: 020 7384 2804
www.gutlin.com   Email: mark@gutlin.com

The
Clock-Work-Shop
Winchester

6A Parchment St., Winchester SO23 8AT
Tel: 01962 842331 Open 9.00–5.00 Mon-Sat
or Mobile 07973 736155 anytime
www.clock-work-shop.co.uk

8 Day mahogany longcase clock
by William Hall of Nottingham

• We offer a wide range of lovingly restored quality
antique clocks
• Full repair/restoration service.
• Delivery and set-up or shipping can be arranged.
• Good prices paid for quality/intersting clocks

All work carries a 3 year written guarantee

LAPADA
MEMBER

THE ASSOCIATION OF
ART AND ANTIQUE DEALERS

P. A. Oxley

Quality British Antique Clocks
& Barometers

Established 1971

The leading UK dealer in quality restored antique longcase clocks

Very large selection always available

Prices from £4,000 to £40,000

P. A. Oxley Antique Clocks & Barometers, The Old Rectory,
Cherhill, Calne, Wiltshire SN11 8UX
Telephone: 01249 816227 Fax: 01249 821285
Email: info@paoxley.com www.british-antiqueclocks.com

Full stock with prices shown on our website

Member of the Association of Art and Antique Dealers

LONGCASE OR GRANDFATHER CLOCK

For most of us, a longcase clock is better known as a grandfather clock. This dates back to a popular song from 1880 called *The Grandfather's Clock* which stopped when the old man died. The clocks actually date back to 1600 and then, as now, were seen as a status symbol. The smaller version is known as a grandmother clock.

PIETER KROESE

Walnut Longcase Clock Dutch, c.1770, 239cm high, the break arch 13.25in dial with silvered chapter ring and signed 'Pieter Kroese, Amsterdam' (SOTH)

A&C 30, sold £5,520, now worth £6,000-8,000

EIGHT-DAY CLOCK

George III oak and mahogany crossbanded longcase clock with eight-day movement and square brass dial and date aperture, pillar decoration 83in high (MALL)

A&C 49, sold £2,700, now worth £3,000-5,000

R TURNBALL WOOLER

George III mahogany eight-day longcase by R Turnbull Wooler, with a painted arched dial and subsidiary seconds and date dials, pillars by face topped by finials 211cm (SWORD)

A&C 46, sold £2,100, now worth £2,500-4,000

Fact File

A true grandfather clock should be at least six feet tall. There is no set value for these clocks and, like most antiques, much of the valuation is based on the maker's name. One of the best clockmakers was Thomas Tompion (1639-1713) whose work was owned by royals, including Queen Anne and Queen Victoria. His most expensive clock fetched £1,200,000 in New York.

As well as names, buyers should look for condition and the quality of workmanship, including the case, works and face painting, if any. Popular themes include the four seasons and the moon. It is possible to sell a longcase without a clock, One in fairly poor condition was sold to a dealer for £700 at a house sale.

SQUARE SURROUND

Early 18th century, the brass dial with subsidiary seconds dial and date, and an eight-day movement, square top (SWORD)

A&C 66, sold £1,400, now worth £1,000-2,000

MAHOGANY LONGCASE

Late-18th century mahogany longcase clock, 80in high, simple form (AMER)

A&C 43, sold £2,600, now worth £3,500-5,000

SWAN NECK PEDIMENT

Oak longcase clock, 19th century with swan neck pediment flanked by two orbs. (87in) (FELL)

A&C 42, sold £1,900, now worth £2,000-4,000

WILLIAM KIPLING

George III ebonised longcase clock, the arched brass dial inscribed 'William Kipling London', topped by urn finials (LOCK)

A&C 61, sold £950, now worth £1,000-1,500

THOMAS STRIPLING

Longcase clock George III oak and mahogany, with eight-day movement by Thomas Stripling of Barwell, 208cm high (WINT)

A&C 40, sold for £4,800, now worth £5-8,000

CLOCKS

MANTEL CLOCKS

The most common mantel clock is the Deco head and shoulders shape in its wooden case with some marquetry. These can be found at every general fair and even car boots and tend to be worth under £40. They were used in most households from the 1930s and their condition tends to be poor but earlier mantel clocks are highly ornate.

AUSTRIAN

Austrian 19th-century ormolu mantel clock, with engraved silvered chapter ring (GORR)

A&C 62, sold £1,050, now worth £1,000-1,200

LOUIS PHILLIPPE

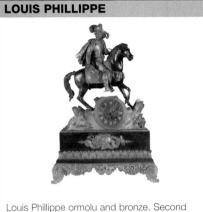

Louis Phillippe ormolu and bronze. Second quarter of 19th century, 54.5cm high (WINT)

A&C 40, sold for £950, now worth £1,000-1,500

VINER & CO

Early Victorian drum-shaped gilt clock with swag decoration, mounted on a marble base, dial marked "Viner & Co London" (FELL)

A&C 57, sold for £780, now worth £800-1,200

MEISSEN PORCELAIN

Meissen porcelain with applied decoration of exotic birds and floral encrustations (SWORD)

A&C 62, sold for £400, now worth £400-800

CHERUBIC CLOCK

Victorian bronze, with a burnished and matt gilt finish and porcelain panels (SWORD)

A&C 56, sold for £1,050, now worth £800-1,400

Fact File

Mantel can also be spelt 'mantle' and refers to the mantle piece above a fire where the clock traditionally stood.

One of the most frequent problems with clocks is that they stop running. If your clock has been wound (but not overly so – overwinding can stop clocks), it probably needs cleaning. If you're not great at DIY, call in the professional – most clock dealers and antiques centres know of specialists.

Realistically, clocks should have their works cleaned at least every five years. You can help to keep them running by the careful application of oil but be careful as this, in turn, attracts dust which causes friction – which stops clocks.

As for buying clocks without keys, don't worry, just ask a specialist dealer if they sell spares.

ART NOUVEAU

An Art Nouveau mantel timepiece, with bronze mounts, with sturdy feet, 33.5cm high (PH BA)

A&C 17, sold for £90, now worth £150-250

GEORGE GRAHAM

A silver-mounted ebony quarter repeating table clock No 775 by George Graham c. 1735, English with seconds face (SOTH)

A&C 17, sold for £80,500, now worth £90-120,000

SKELETON CLOCK

Skeleton clock, brass, mid-19th century, 31cm high. (HAMP)

A&C 38, sold for £500, now worth £800-1,000

CARRIAGE CLOCKS

Carriage clocks are very elegant. They were designed as travelling clocks and would be transported with their owners (or ahead of them, depending on the size of the retinue) in carriages, hence the name. Some can still be found with their specially designed travel cases, made to prevent them from being damaged en route.

TABLE CLOCK

Walnut table clock. English, c. 1770, the break arch dial signed 'George Somersall, London'. The wooden body and finials differentiate this from sturdier carriage clocks (SO STH)

A&C29, sold for £28,750, now worth £30-40,000

PENDULUM ON DISPLAY

Carriage clock 19th century, gilded brass, open cased, 4.5in high (CLEV)

A&C 33, sold £950, now worth £1,000-1,500

Fact File

In France, carriage clocks are known as 'officer clocks' after one of Napoleon's officers reported in late when battle was imminent. He had overslept. After that, the French Emperor ordered all of his officers to carry clocks with them so that they would never be late again.

The clocks are generally rectangular in shape and sturdy, built to withstand the rough roads of the day. The British clocks are generally better quality than their French counterparts as they were generally made to order. They belonged to the aristocracy and the wealthy who could afford to travel in style – and had the time to do so.

Look for decorated versions but beware of any with devaluing, replacement parts.

ATTRIBUTED TO THOMAS COLE

19th century with engraved, silvered dial carriage clock, possibly by Thomas Cole, in gilt-brass case with a leather travelling case (GORR)

A&C 66, sold for £1,200, now worth £1,200-1,800

CARRIAGE CLOCK IN TRAVEL CASE

A 19th-century carriage clock by P and A Drocourt, with repeat and alarm, serial number 15662 in a travelling case (HAMP)

A&C 23, est £300-500, now worth £500-800

AESTHETIC CARRIAGE CLOCK

Aesthetic movement gilt brass faux bamboo clock with a hexagonal dial above an alarm dial c. 1870s (SWORD)

A&C 58, sold for £1,350, now worth £1,500-1,800

DROCOURT GIANT CARRIAGE CLOCKS

Two Drocourt giant carriage clocks with decorative detail, c. 1885 (HAMP)

A&C 5, est £5,000-8,000, now worth £10,000-15,000

COMMEMORATIVES

ROYAL COMMEMORATIVES

In Britain, royal commemoratives have declined in popularity along with that of the royal family. Unless they are by good makes (for example Royal Doulton) or interesting designs (such as 'Spitting Image'), they are often surprisingly cheap. You might collect a particular monarch, royal house or make of china.

GEORGE III

A Wedgwood two-handled cup, cover and stand – celebrating the Golden Jubilee of George III, 1810 (CHRIS)

A&C 25, sold for £2,300, now worth £2,750-3,250

PRINCESS DIANA

A present from Diana, Princess of Wales in 1989, Diana memorabilia was at its peak following her death in 1997 (CHEF)

A&C 53, sold for £1,700, now worth £1,400-1,600

LOVING CUP

Copeland Edward VII souvenir with flaring rim and gilt handles, 1910, retailed by T. Goode & Co., London (SWORD)

A&C 63, sold for £550, now worth £550-600

CHARLES II CHARGER

London Delft dated Royal portrait charger, with a full-length portrait of Charles II (CHRIS)

A&C 53, sold £93,950, now worth £85–95,000

Fact File

Judging by the pieces available royal memorabilia was first created in Britain in the seventeenth century. This was a time of political turmoil for the royal family as Charles I was executed and the monarchy suspended. Charles II must have been rather relieved to see commemoratives celebrating his reign. In those days, pieces such as a Delft charger (sold for £91,000 at Christie's), would have been handmade whereas most of today's commemoratives are mass-produced and, as such, unlikely to have the same appeal for future generations. The exception being the all-white royal pieces created by irreverent 'Spitting Image' designers, Fluck and Law for Carlton Ware. The Prince Charles Loving cup, with his ears as handles, sells for £100–150. Apart from that range, the best buys are from 1901 and earlier.

EARLY COMMEMORATIVE

Commemorative polychrome Delft dish, late seventeenth century (CHEF)

A&C 57, sold for £13,000, now worth £13-15,000

THE KING WHO NEVER WAS

A collection of Royal Doulton figures including King Edward VIII who abdicated. Edward VIII goods are fairly common so stick to good makes (BON)

A&C 54, sold for £800, now worth £700–800

RARE EARLY COMMEMORATIVE

London Delft dated royal portrait mug, 1660, painted with a half length portrait of King Charles II (CHRIS)

A&C 53, sold £71,950, now worth £72–75,000

IMPERIAL FABERGE

Fabergé Imperial Easter egg presented by Tsar Nicholas II to his wife the Empress Alexandra Feodorovna at Easter 1911

A&C 60. £6,000,000-8,000,000

MINIATURE BUSTS

Extemely rare George V and Queen Mary Silver Jubilee toy busts, produced by W. Britain's (CHRIS)

A&C 39, est. £200, now worth £250–350

REGAL TEAPOTS

Two Wedgwood creamware teapots printed in Liverpool, c.1762–63. Left: Frederick the Great, King of Prussia, sold for £2,415. Right: Shows a portrait of Queen Charlotte, sold for £4,600, now worth £4,000–6,000 (PH)

A&C 25, sold for £2,415, now worth £3,000–4,000

SIGNED BOOK

'Silver Wedding – The Record of Twenty-Five Royal Years' by Louis Wulff MVO (Sampson Low, Marston & Co Ltd), full colour plate photographs of King George and Queen Elizabeth, signed by the monarchs. Some damage (FELL)

A&C 40, sold for £200, now worth £250–400

PRINCE WILLIAM

Prince William's 1982 birth loving cup by J & J May (SPEC AUC)

A&C 53, sold £480, now worth £300–500

PARAGON TRIO

Unusual Paragon cup, saucer and plate, for the 1937 Coronation

A&C 40, sold for £160, now worth £200–250

COPELAND LOVING CUP

1937 Coronation mug by Copeland for retailers Goode (SPEC AUC)

A&C 40, sold for £800, now worth £600–800

SOLDIER KING

Rare Britain's figure of King George V, issued to commemorate the Royal Visit to South Africa in 1947 (CHRIS)

A&C 39, est. £1,800, now worth £1,500–2,000

SPITTING IMAGE CHARLES & DI

1981, Fluck and Law, 'Spitting Image' pair of slippers depicting the royal couple in sleeping bags (SPEC AUC)

A&C 53, sold for £85, now worth £60–80

Fact File

Queen Victoria's 64-year reign produced a multitude of collectables, especially for her Golden (1887) and Diamond (1897) Jubilees, the latter leading to more goods than the earlier celebration. In theory, commemoratives mark occasions such as jubilees but today's market seems to produce royal memorabilia all the time with extra goods laid on for special occasions such as The Queen Mother's 100th year – note, not birthday, a cynical marketing device.

Few goods produced are worth collecting except for die-hard royalists. As for modern commemoratives, realistically, most goods produced after the death of Queen Victoria in 1901 are hard to sell which makes them perfect buys for royalists.

COMMEMORATIVES

POLITICAL COMMEMORATIVES

In the Victorian era, politicians relied on commemoratives for self-promotion. There was no television or radio and tankards and plates commemorated absolutely everything as politicians reminded voters that they existed. Political commemoratives are replacing royal ones in terms of collectability.

WARTIME PRIME MINISTER

Lloyd George: a Foley 'Intarsio' caricature teapot and cover, c.1901, printed mark on base, 122mm high, with a tiny chip on the spout (SPEC AUC)

A&C 8, sold for £360, now worth £400–600

POLITICAL MESSAGE

Henry Hunt: a portrait inscribed 'Hunt and Liberty', on the reverse 'No Corn Bill, universal suffrage, annual parliaments and votes by ballot' c.1819, spout restored (SPEC AUC)

A&C 8, sold for £620, now worth £800–1,000

POLITICAL MUG

Henry Thomas Liddell: a pink lustre decorated cylindrical mug with a portrait entitled 'Liddell for ever, independency', c.1826 (SPEC AUC)

A&C 8, sold for £550, now worth £650–800

DRINKING TO SUCCESS

A pair of baluster-shaped brown stoneware cups each moulded with named portraits and inscribed with electoral results from the 1880 Leeds Election. William Gladstone's has the Yorkshire Rose (SPEC AUC)

A&C 7, sold for £320, now worth £350–500

Fact File

The American politicians have made little impact on the British market for political collectables which is why wise dealers are buying the goods here and selling them for a profit on eBay to a more interested audience. Others concentrate on parties (Whigs or Tories in the nineteenth century), areas (for example Yorkshire) or specific politicians with PMs such as the colourful Disraeli being especially popular.

One of the nicest collectables is a series of octagonal plates. They aren't signed but were made by Wallis Gimson & Co. from 1884–90 (which is when the firm existed). Expect to pay £80–120 for the white plates with the brown transfers or £120–150 for the more colourful versions (generally royal).

THE IRON LADY

Fluck and Law 'Spitting Image' Margaret Thatcher teapot made by Carlton Ware, c.1981 – spout and inner rim prone to damage (SPEC AUC)

A&C 7, sold for £200, now worth £200–250

STATUTARY RIGHTS

A fine Derby porcelain figure of John Wilkes, holding a 'Bill of Rights' and a 'Magna Carta' scroll, slightly damaged, c.1768 (SPEC AUC)

A&C 7, sold for £900, now worth £1,500–2,000

KENNEDY BUST

JFK bust by Robert Berks

A&C 33, sold for £80, now worth £100–200

PRESIDENTIAL FIGURE

John F. Kennedy is one of the most collectable modern US politicians

A&C 33, sold for £70, now worth £50–100

MILITARY AND NAVAL COMMEMORATIVES

Great leaders such as Wellington and Nelson were commemorated, often in figural form. They were instantly recognisable in their day. It was a different era where generals and admirals were fighting not just to expand an empire but to save Britain from invasion from the likes of Napoleon Bonaparte.

FIRST WORLD WAR

The 'Peace Plate', 1919, Goss (Goss Collectors' Club)

A&C 39, now worth £50-80

1857, HAVELOCK AND CAMPBELL

Left to right: Sir Henry Havelock; Sir Henry Havelock. A white Parian bust by Copeland sold for £170; Copeland Parian bust of Field Marshall, Sir Colin Campbell (SPEC AUC)

A&C 8, sold £170, now worth £150–250 each

PUTTING THE BOOT IN

1829 'King's College to Wit – A Practical Essay'. A hand-coloured engraving after T. Jones (pub S. W. Fores) depicting Wellington fighting a duel with Winchelsea (SPEC AUC)

A&C 8, sold for £90, now worth £150–200

WELLINGTON ON HORSEBACK

A pearlware jug with equestrian portrait named Marquis Wellington and inscribed Salamanca, with loyal inscription on the reverse, some damage (SPEC AUC)

A&C 7, sold for £620, now worth £700–900

Fact File

Nelson's death at the otherwise triumphant Battle of Trafalgar in 1805 plunged Britain into mourning. The naval admiral was a hero and, in 2005, we are celebrating the bicentenary both of his death and famous victory against the French-Spanish navy aboard HMS Victory, the flagship of the fleet. This means that Nelson-related goods, already commanding high prices, are set to explode – and then come down again.

As with all commemorative ware, buy the event and sell during it or, if you're buying for yourself, wait until the fuss has died down and prices are more realistic. Military and naval goods have a very established market and it's worth doing research to see what you find more interesting – the people or the battles.

WELLINGTON

1852 Duke of Wellington in Memoriam. A pottery jug moulded with seated statues of the statesman, inscribed beneath the spout R & Christina Cross (SPEC AUC)

A&C 8, sold for £75, now worth £100–150

IN MEMORIAM

Duke of Wellington in Memoriam. A Staffordshire figure of the statesman, c.1852, with a small chip to a finger on his right hand (SPEC AUC)

A&C 8, sold for £210, now worth £250–350

NELSON MOURNED

A nineteenth-century creamware jug commemorating Nelson, with a printed description of the battle of Trafalgar (CHEF)

A&C 54, sold £2,000, now worth £2,000–2,500

CHURCHILL COMMEMORATED

Abbeydale bone china Churchill commemoration bowl and cover made in 1965 for retailers T Goode & Co, number 89 of 250 (SWORD)

A&C 60, sold for £540, now worth £500–600

DRINKS & ACCESSORIES

WINE AND OTHER DRINKS

Fine wines are made of the first press of the grapes, cheaper ones have chemicals added to preserve them and fine wines not only keep longer but offer a good investment with collectors often buying not to taste but to lay down (keep for a few years until the wine has matured for taste and as an investment). Champagne, fortified wines and spirits are also collected. Know your vintages for best buys.

MACALLAN WHISKY

The Macallan 1950, distilled and bottled by Macallan Glenlivet Ltd. Distributed by Gordon & MacPhail, bottle no 96, screw cap and capsule. In wooden presentation case with booklet, level high neck, 75cl, 43% proof, Macallan is a good investment or drinking choice (PH ED)

A&C 34, sold for £380, now worth £400-600

LIMITED EDITION WHISKY, 1926-28

The Macallan 50-year-old, bottle no 7 of 500, bottled from three casks distilled between 1926 and 1928. Accompanied by a letter of authenticity signed by Allan G Shiach, in a leather-bound wooden presentation case, 75cl, 38.6% at cask strength. Vintage whisky is a good buy (PH ED)

A&C 28, sold for £4,000, now worth £4,500-6,000

CHATEAU LAFITE ROTHSCHILD

A 1960 Chateau Lafitte Rothschild, with Dolamore silvered label (ROSE)

A&C 64, sold for £160, now worth £150-200

VINTAGE PORT

A pair of vintage ports Quinta do Noval 1945, bottled at Oporto, 1947 by Da Silva and a bottle of 1970 vintage port bottled in 1972 (GORR)

A&C 65, sold for £220, now worth £200-250

PERFECT SERVED COLD

Walnut, oval and brass-bound wine cooler with a metal liner and four outswept legs, 60.5cm high x 62cm wide (DREW)

A&C 47, sold for £450, now worth £400-600

DIRECTOR'S RESERVE WHISKY

Case of Teacher's whisky very unusual director's reserve of 1950, bottled at 24 years old. Twelve bottles (one empty, otherwise all low neck) (BON)

A&C 36, sold for £920, now worth £1,200-1,800

Fact File

There is a modern marketing ploy where some vineyards number each aisle of vines and add the number of the aisle to the label so that you know exactly where your wine was collected. It's a lovely idea and perfect for the novice collector or one buying for show – but connoisseurs avoid such devices, preferring to stick to the established names and vintages.

A vintage depends on the quality of the wine which, in turn, depends upon the weather. Too much rain and that year is best avoided as grapes need sunshine to create the sweetness of the fruit which delivers good wine.

It's worth getting the catalogues for the specialist wine auctions to see which vineyards perform the best and which vintages are the most valued.

CORKSCREWS

The bottle openers were devised from a bulletscrew or gun worm, a device which removed stuck bullets from guns. By the 17th century, they were made by blacksmiths but no one knows who invented the first ever corkscrew or when. This is a specialist area which is great for collectors as most general dealers avoid them.

DOUBLE LEVER

Massive double lever corkscrew. Brass with champagne tap, archimedian screw, square section frame and levers with traces of gilding. Unmarked, possibly late-19th or early-20th century (CHRIS)

A&C 29, sold for £5,175, now worth £5-7,000

RISQUE OPENER

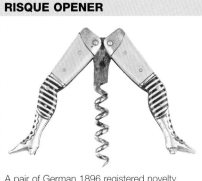

A pair of German 1896 registered novelty folding ladies legs pocket corkscrew, with light and dark green striped celluloid stockings. Striped versions are rarer than plain (CHRIS)

A&C 16, sold for £329, now worth £300-500

KING'S SCREW CORKSCREW

A 19th century King's Screw Corkscrew with a turned bone handle (BON)

A&C 8, est £150-200, now worth £200-400

ROTARY ECLIPSE BAR

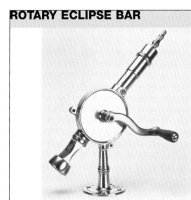

An English Masons brass patent Rotary Eclipse bar corkscrew, 1886 (CHRIS)

A&C 16, sold for £564, now worth £700-1,000

Fact File

One of the most desirable corkscrews is German. The plain, stocking legs open up to expose the corkscrew – bawdy humour which sells for around £200-250 with the ones exposing bare thigh above harder-to-find stripy stockings selling for £300-500. The record price achieved at auction was £18,400 for an 18th century, English silver pocket corkscrew whilst an 1802 Thomason-type (one of the simplest style of corkscrews with double-action screw) corkscrew sells for £3,000-3,500. If you are thinking of buying to use, be advised that these are not generally sold for use but collecting and that the metal might not have withstood the years. Dealers advise people to collect old corkscrews, and buy modern versions for use.

1903 HALF-FRAME

A German W Neues, 1903 half-frame corkscrew with wooden handle (CHRIS)

A&C 16, sold £1,175, now worth £1,200-1,800

FOUR-PILLAR VERSION

A fine English 19th century four-pillar narrow rack King's Screw, with shaped bone handle, an unusual and stylish design (CHRIS)

A&C 16, sold for £1,840, now worth £2-3,000

1842 JONES II

A Jones II registered design, 1842 (CHRIS)

A&C 16, sold £18,400, now worth £20-24,000

1894 MURRAY & STALKER

An English Murray & Stalker, 1894, extractor nickel-plated double-lever corkscrew, marked 'Patent No. 234', wire helix, a forerunner of the modern easy pull (CHRIS)

A&C 16, sold £7,475, now worth £8-10,000

DRINKS & ACCESSORIES

ACCESSORIES

This is a rich area of interest. Some people collect wine labels, others wine barrels, used for storing wine. A 1970s Bonwit and Teller silver-plated ice bucket in the form of a chicken is worth around £200-250 as well as being highly entertaining. Wine coolers are a bit more understated and surprisingly stylish as are goblets (p166)

WINE COOLER

A George III mahogany and brass bound oval wine cooler, still a popular accessory (LAW)

A&C 23, sold £780, now worth £1,200-1,500

PACKING A PUNCH

Victorian gilt bronze bowl mounted, by F & C Osler of Birmingham (GORR)

A&C 50, sold for £1,200, now worth £1-1,500

WINE FUNNEL

George III silver wine funnel with beaded border, made by Fenton Creswick & Co, Sheffield, 1777. Interesting collectable (GORR)

A&C 65, sold for £340, now worth £350-400

CELLARETTE

Regency mahogany cellarette (box to store drink bottles) of sarcophagus form, with brass castors shaped as feet, 79cm high (CHEF)

A&C 35, est £1,500-2,500, now worth £2-3,000

Fact File

Wine, like tea, is ceremonial and, as such, deserves accessorising. Wooden wine coolers with brass banding remind the drinker of the quality of the alcohol, as well as serving to keep it cool. They are more stylish than ice buckets which tend to have a more kitsch appeal, especially the ubiquitous plastic pineapple from the 1950-70s (£15-30 at antiques fairs). Whilst not all are sturdy, some wine coolers have been converted by their owners to plant stands. Wooden barrels, used to store wine, have become accessories and wine pourers, the handled baskets once so popular in restaurants, are not yet collectable for most people. Wine provides many areas for collecting, as do all types of alcohol and drink stirrers are increasing in popularity; affordably kitsch collectables.

TANTALISING TANTALUS

19th century inlaid rosewood tantalus box, containing a two tier lift-out stand with a pair of liquor decanters and six glasses. Originally locked to keep safe from the servants (ACAD)

A&C 5, sold for £290, now worth £300-500

COCKTAIL SHAKER

A novelty 1930s engraved cocktail shaker. Popular collectables of a bygone era (BON)

A&C 8, now worth £40-60

SILVER NEF

A German silver nef (wine carrier) in the shape of a ship, on wheels, it would be pulled down the table for self-service (DREW)

A&C, sold for £4,500, now worth £4-6,000

SPIRIT BARREL

Oak spirit barrel, late-Victorian, with EPNS mounts and tap, opposing lion mask ring handles and separate matching stand (AMER)

A&C 31, sold for £190, now worth £200-400

EPHEMERA

The Greek *ephemeros* from which ephemera is derived, means 'lasting only one day' and refers to pieces of paper and cardboard intended for short-term use, for example letters, cards, food labels, diaries and leaflets. Autographs are covered elsewhere but they form a vital part of this fascinating area.

Fact File

You have probably bought ephemera without realising it, for example an old auction catalogue. It's the perfect excuse for a hoarder. Like most collecting, it can be divided into types – Valentine's cards, postcards related to a specific area (such as Southwold) or subject (such as trains), stock certificates or anything most people throw away. The most interesting area is probably old diaries, which offer an insight into an era, capturing the common concerns of the day such as poor harvests or warfare. What they contain is unique. These are real, not carefully written political diaries and, by collecting them, you get a chance to peek into another time. The same is true for letters.

NELSON'S LETTER

Horatio Nelson's racy letter to Emma Hamilton, recounting his erotic dreams, their affair was scandalous in that era (CHRIS)

A&C 58, sold £117,250, now worth £120-140,000

ROYAL WRITING

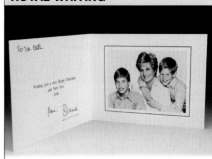

A Christmas card from 1994 bearing Diana's signature. A popular item for ephemera and royal collectors (CHEF)

A&C 53, sold for £750, now worth £600-800

DONALD CAMPBELL

Archive collection of the famous racer, including photograph album of the Bluebird under construction, inscribed 'To Kaye Barry my long suffering and overworked secretary' (GORR)

A&C 45, sold for £1,100, now worth £1,500-2,000

CHURCHILL'S LETTER

Winston Churchill's letter to Pamela Plowden, in which he proposed marriage. The letter set a new record at auction (CHRIS)

A&C 58, sold £77,675, now worth £75-85,000

SPANISH THEATRE

Spanish cardboard theatre from the 1920s, including cardboard figures, play scripts and scenery (SOTH)

A&C 51, sold for £564, now worth £500-700

ROYAL CHILDREN'S CARD

Hand-painted card signed by the Royal children, Edward, Albert (later George VI), Mary, Henry, from York Cottage, Sandringham around 1910 (GORR)

A&C 53, sold for £500, now worth £520–600

WILLIAM AND HARRY

William and Harry are currently extremely collectable – signed royal Christmas card from 1992 (CHEF)

A&C 53, sold for £350, now worth £400–500

DAME LAURA KNIGHT

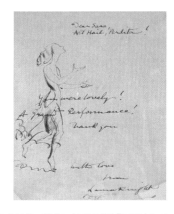

An inscribed letter from artist Dame Laura Knight RA to an actress

A&C 48, sold for £260, now worth £300-400

This is the time to buy furniture. Prices of the average pieces have dropped recently as more buyers move from brown furniture (wood) to later styles such as the metal of the Bauhaus era and plastic of the 1950s

Furniture

ANTIQUE FURNITURE ADDS CHARACTER TO ANY room. The current dip in the mid-range market (up to around £5,000) makes this the best time to buy furniture for years. You can get several pieces of quality furniture for less than it costs to buy mass-produced modern furniture and you have the knowledge that you won't walk into anyone else's house and see the exact same sofa or bookcase but that your home is unique. What you are buying is quality and originality. Modern firms often reproduce period furniture but why not buy the real thing?

When buying furniture, think of your house. This might sound obvious but some of the most tempting antique furniture is not suitable for some houses, especially the more modern ones which have built-in wardrobes and don't have enough room for real ones. Will your doors be wide enough to fit non-foldable tables? Can you get six dining chairs around a table in your dining area? These are very real concerns and the easiest way to get the right goods for your home is to measure up before going out – and always carry a tape measure with you. Continental furniture, while very often cheaper than its British counterparts is also often larger – are your ceilings really high enough to accommodate

a French wardrobe and, if so, are your stairs wide enough? It might sound stupid but some people do buy furniture and then have to sell it quickly after finding that it simply won't fit into their home and, if you've bought the goods at a one-day fair and didn't take the dealer's card, it's up to you to sell it again. Even then, not all dealers can afford to give you your money back. After all, it was your mistake, not theirs.

But, if you know what fits, have you thought about what you want? There are lots of different styles and woods out there. Blond wood is in vogue at the moment with some dealers dying old mahogany pieces to profit from the market. Real blond wood (eg ash) is beautiful and lights up the room whereas darker rooms with smaller windows just seem even darker with mahogany furniture, no matter what the design or quality. One of my tips is Art Deco furniture at auction, especially bedroom sets. If you like the sweeping design and the pale wood, it's an ideal combination of style and affordability – around £500 for the matching double bed, wardrobe, round-mirrored dressing table and chest of drawers. Now all you need to buy is the mattress.

And that's another thing – older beds are gorgeous but will they take modern mattresses or will you have to have a smaller mattress made for you? When buying antique furniture, think the same way that you would for modern furniture – will it fit, can you live with it and is the price right? If the answer is yes, just ask about delivery charges – dealers and centres tend to offer a better rate than most removal firms or even some modern furniture shops, another good reason for purchasing antique furniture. **WIW**

BATHS

Antique baths are all the rage and often much more comfortable than modern versions with deeper backs, perfectly sloped for extra comfort. All of the style magazines point to the same thing – claw-footed, curved back baths are the must-have accessory for any bathroom and, based on Victorian designs, you can get an original – for less.

ORNATE FEET

Roll top bath with ornate feet costs and green enamelling (Picture by Antique Bathrooms of Ivybridge)

A&C 51, sold for £1,200, now worth £1,200

PLUNGER BATH

Edwardian Plunger bath (Pictures by Antique Bathrooms of Ivybridge)

A&C 51, sold for £2,500, now worth £2,500

EARTHENWARE TOILET

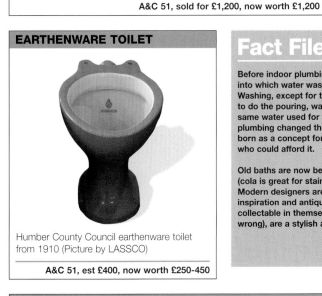

Humber County Council earthenware toilet from 1910 (Picture by LASSCO)

A&C 51, est £400, now worth £250-450

Fact File

Before indoor plumbing, baths were big tubs into which water was poured from buckets. Washing, except for the rich who had servants to do the pouring, was a hurried affair with the same water used for the whole family. Indoor plumbing changed that and the bathroom was born as a concept for everyone, not just those who could afford it.

Old baths are now being reclaimed, cleaned up (cola is great for stains) and resold as designer. Modern designers are looking to the past for inspiration and antique baths, while not collectable in themselves (but we could be wrong), are a stylish addition to any house.

COPPER BATH

French copper bath with tin lining from 1890, (Picture by Lassco)

A&C 51, sold for £2,650, now worth £2,000-3,000

SITZ DOWN

Unusual Sitz bath (Picture by Antique Bathrooms of Ivybridge)

A&C 51, sold for £750, now worth £600-1,000

GORGEOUS GILT

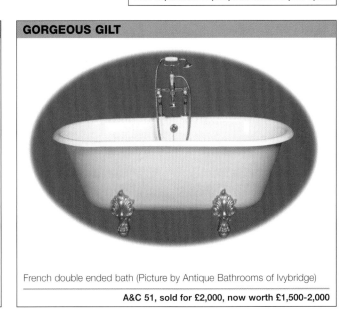

French double ended bath (Picture by Antique Bathrooms of Ivybridge)

A&C 51, sold for £2,000, now worth £1,500-2,000

FURNITURE

BEDS

A trip to any stately home or The Royal Pavilion at Brighton will show you that people have got taller over the years. In the fourteenth century, the average height for a man was just over five feet, it's now around a foot taller and that makes bed buying very interesting – because you need a bed that fits, as well as something stylish.

DAY BED

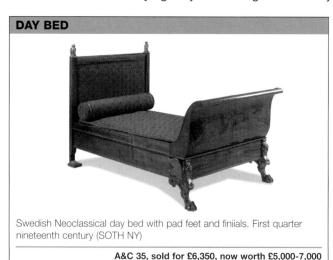

Swedish Neoclassical day bed with pad feet and finiials. First quarter nineteenth century (SOTH NY)

A&C 35, sold for £6,350, now worth £5,000-7,000

EGYPTIAN INFLUENCE

This Bedroom 'Aux Nenuphars', from around 1900, has a double bed, two bedside tables and a wardrobe (SOTH)

A&C 47, sold for £619,500, now worth £500,000-600,000

HOUSE SALE

Sold in situ, this 19th century mahogany four poster bed came with the drapes and bed cover but was smaller than modern beds (CHEF)

A&C, sold for £1,200, now worth £1,200-1,500

BED HEAD

Bed head and foot, on bun feet (DREW)

A&C 41, sold for £280, now worth £200-300

MAHOGANY BED

William IV mahogany four-poster with turned tapering columns and padded head and foot, 254cm high (DREW)

A&C 47, sold for £1,650, now worth £1,500-2,000

WILLIAM IV BED

William IV mahogany four-poster with a moulded cornice on lappet carved columns, with mahogany curtain poles and cotton hangings, 261cm high (DREW)

A&C 47, sold for £2,250, now worth £2,000-2,500

Fact File

Queen Victoria was concerned about fleas and bedbugs in beds. In those days, wooden beds were the norm and they were a haven for bedbugs but they found it more difficult to climb up the iron bedsteads and so she declared that everyone ought to have metal beds.

Some antique bed dealers recommend iron bedsteads for asthmatics – aesthetic values combined with healthcare. Queen Victoria's own bed was brass and went on display at the 1851 Great Exhibition in the Crystal Palace in London's Hyde Park. By the First World War, an improvement in hygiene and the need for metal for the war effort meant that metal beds fell out of favour and wooden ones were back in fashion.

STAVELEY ANTIQUES

BEAUTIFULLY RESTORED ANTIQUE BEDS

OVER 100 BEDSTEADS IN STOCK

BRING AUTHENTIC HERITAGE TO YOUR HOME

**27/29 Main Street
Staveley, Cumbria
Telephone 01539 821393**

www.staveley-antiques.co.uk

ROBERT AMSTAD

HASTINGS *Antique* CENTRE

3 floors full of English & Continental Antiques — one of the largest stock held.

Specialist dealers providing a complete range to satisfy any buyer or seller.

Hastings (01424) 428561

59–61 Norman Road,
St. Leonards-on-Sea,
East Sussex TN38 0EG

Established locally over 20 years

THE SWAN

AT TETSWORTH
Voted **BRITAIN'S 'BEST ANTIQUES CENTRE 2003 & 2004/5'**

40 Showrooms of Fine Quality Antique Furniture displayed in a historic Grade II listed Elizabethan Coaching House

Georgian through to Art Deco - Garden Statuary Area

Silver, Ceramics, Glass, Mirrors, Textiles, Rugs, Clocks

Open every day 10 - 6 including Bank Holidays

Award Winning Restaurant - booking advisable

Full Calendar of Events - Large Car Park

The Swan at Tetsworth

High Street Tetsworth Nr. Thame Oxfordshire OX9 7AB

Antiques: 01844 281777 Restaurant: 01844 281182

for more information and to receive our programme of events, please call or visit our website@ www.theswan.co.uk

FURNITURE

CHAIRS

Every house needs a chair and antique chairs were made for specific rooms as we'll see in the next few pages. The two most important elements when buying a chair for use is that they are safe and comfortable. Never sit in a chair when thinking of buying it without looking under it first – is anything broken? If not, is it comfortable?

OPEN ARMCHAIRS

Four Louis XV style, giltwood armchairs carved with scrolls, flowers and leaves. Seats depicting classical figures and animals (DREW)

A&C 45, sold for £4,200, now worth £3,500–4,000

CEYLONESE THRONE CHAIRS

By repute, these chairs were used by the Queen and Prince Philip at the opening of the Parliament on their first Commonwealth tour in April 1954 (PH ED)

A&C 30, sold for £10,120, now worth £8–12,000

CORNER CHAIRS

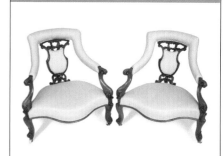

Pair of unusual Victorian corner chairs. Walnut framed, with upholstered and pierced back panels, scroll arms on carved cabriole supports, with casters (CLEV)

A&C 29, sold for £539, now worth £450-650

CHARLES EAMES

This lounge chair and ottoman was designed in 1956 and was the last in the Eames' series of plywood chairs. This design was so popular that it is still in production. A contemporary version will cost around £2,500–3,000 but prices for vintage chairs has risen drastically

A&C 23, if vintage, now worth £3,000-5,000

ROSEWOOD CHAIRS

William IV rosewood chairs. With serpentine crest rails, carved scroll decoration, padded seats on reeded tapered front supports. Frame stamped 'RB' (CLEV)

A&C 29, sold for £1,391, now worth £1,000-1,500

Fact File

People are different heights and weights, we have grown taller and fatter over the years which is an important consideration when buying chairs, not just for your own comfort but that of your family or guests.

Not all chairs will be comfortable for all people, Edwardian chairs are often fragile which rules them out for larger people and nursery chairs, devised to be used when rocking babies, are too low for people with back problems or bad legs.

Rocking chairs might look comfortable but are they really too low for comfort and do you have the extra room needed for when the chair tilts back? All of these matters must be weighed up before parting with any money. Another thing to think about is whether you even get them in your car if the dealer can't deliver?

BUCKET CHAIR

A stylish 1950s Lusty's chair on a tubular steel frame. (From the Vitra Design Museum, in Germany)

A&C 45, now worth £80-120

ARTS AND CRAFTS STYLE

William Morris-style ash and beechwood recliner (SWORD)

A&C 48, sold for £380, now worth £400-600

VICTORIAN GOTHIC

Metamorphic, Victorian Gothic oak library steps and chair, with carpet-covered treads (DREW)

A&C 41, sold for £260, now worth £300-500

SITZMACHINE ARMCHAIR

Josef Hoffmann's Sitzmachine armchair, Wiener Werkestatte, 1905 (CHRIS)

A&C 58, sold for £26,290, now worth £20-40,000

REGENCY DINING CHAIRS

A set of fourteen Regency mahogany dining chairs on sabre legs, panelled ebony and strung bar back, two being carvers

A&C 48, sold for £24,000, now worth £20-25,000

FOLDING COMFORT

George IV mahogany Daw's patent reclining armchair (DREW)

A&C 57, sold for £1,750, now worth £1,500-2,000

BENTWOOD CHAIR

nineteenth century walnut and floral marquetry chair, the back inlaid with foliate scrolls (DREW)

A&C 66, sold for £360, now worth £300-400

STAINED BEECH CHAIR

French chair in stained beech, on slender cabriole legs. Largely eighteenth century, but repaired (DREW)

A&C 41, sold for £190, now worth £150-250

OAK BOX CHAIR

George I oak box chair with arched, panelled back, English, c.1725 (Paul Hopwell Antiques)

A&C 39, now worth £2,000-4,000

BENTWOOD CHAIR

Model No. 3, a bentwood chair by Thonet, the typical scroll frame slung with fabric for the seat seat and back, made in the second half of the nineteenth century (SOTH)

A&C 66, sold for £960, now worth £1,200-1,800

RELAX AND READ

Mahogany library elbow chair with ball and claw feet. Late-nineteenth/early-twentieth century

A&C 58, sold for £1,750, now worth £1,500-2,000

Fact File

Rush and cane seats are very attractive but are often found in poor condition, fraying or even completely broken but that shouldn't deter you as long as they are priced accordingly. It costs around £60 a seat to get these repaired or there are lots of courses where you can learn to do it yourself. If you are thinking of emigrating, be advised that not all countries will accept cane, rush and wickerwork because of risk of disease so find out before shipping them – the same goes for anyone buying in England for their homes overseas, check that the goods are allowed to be imported into your home country before parting with your cash (ring the Department of Trade and Industry for advice – 020 7215 5000).

FURNITURE

ARMCHAIRS

The armchair traveller needs to be comfortable and these chairs were designed for relaxation. Dating back to the Wainscot chairs of the seventeenth century, armchairs used to denote the status of the master and mistress of the house, the extended arms contrasting with the stools or shared seating of the settle used by lesser mortals.

WALNUT WING ARMCHAIR

A George I walnut wing armchair with padded back and outscrolled arms, the needlework extensively restored (CHRIS)

A&C 23, sold for £7,475, now worth £6,000-7,000

LIBRARY ARMCHAIRS

A pair of Regency leather upholstered library armchairs, with deep buttoned scrolling backs, can be too low for comfort (PH ED)

A&C 25, sold for £5,520, now worth £4,000-6,000

CARLO MOLLINO

Carlo Mollino, an upholstered armchair, 1951, for use in the Rai Auditorium, Turin. Red velvet upholstery, with hinged seat, on tubular brass frame (CHRIS)

A&C 23, est £1,500-2,000, now worth £3,000-5,000

MAHOGANY LIBRARY CHAIRS

A pair of Victorian mahogany library armchairs, with waisted overscrolled button-upholstered back and padded arms (CHRIS)

A&C 23, sold for £1,880, now worth £1,500-3,000

PAUL FOLLOT

A pair of walnut armchairs designed by Paul Follot, c.1925 combining Art Nouveau style with Art Deco curves (CHRIS)

A&C 23, sold for £9,200, now worth £10-12,000

Fact File

The armchair is now thought of as a comfortable chair in which to unwind but they used to be wooden chairs with elaborate carvings, the seat softened by the cushion which we now expect to see as part of the chair. The 1930s saw the armchair become an integral part of the style of the day with its curves reflecting that of Art Deco and this was echoed in the Utility furniture of the 1940s, the Government-supervised scheme to ensure the quality and affordability of furniture during the war years.

Art Deco chairs are highly desirable but often have the stuffing knocked out of them. These can be restored, as can all armchairs so don't overlook neglected versions.

OAK PANEL-BACK ARMCHAIR

Rare oak panel-back armchair Anglo-French, mid-sixteenth century, the rope twist carved top rail above a trailing husk and double C-scroll upper panel (SOTH)

A&C 30, sold for £15,525, now worth £14-18,000

HEPPLEWHITE-STYLE CHAIRS

Set of eleven Hepplewhite style mahogany framed chairs, upholstered in green leather. His is one of the top names to buy (ROSE)

A&C 62, sold for £1,300, now worth £1,000-1,500

FRAMED ELBOW CHAIR

Mid- to late-eighteenth century, mahogany with square, upholstered back, padded arms and overstuffed seat, on cabriole forelegs with carved knees, talon and ball terminals (AMER)

A&C 29, sold for £14,500, now worth £12–15,000

DINING CHAIRS

While many families now eat at different times or in front of the furniture, dining used to be an experience with elegant chairs to match. It is traditional to buy either six matching chairs or four chairs with two matching carvers, the armed chairs which, like armchairs, were used to denote status – the master and mistress of the house.

MAHOGANY DINING CHAIRS

Mahogany dining chairs with balloon back, in a set of six (AMER)

A&C 30, sold for £650, now worth £400-600

DOUBLE DESIGN

Set of six nineteenth century painted mahogany, the frames with pierced back above an overstuffed seat. (CHEF)

A&C 65, sold for £1,000, now worth £1,000-1,500

REGENCY DINING

A set of eight Regency mahogany dining chairs (two shown).(HAMP)

A&C 19, sold for £3,200, now worth £2,000-3,00

HEPPLEWHITE SET

Twelve Hepplewhite period mahogany shield back, chairs, including carvers, with buttoned and upholstered seats (GORR)

A&C 50, sold for £30,000, now worth £30-40,000

GEORGE IV CHAIRS

Dining chairs from a set of six. George IV, beech, with drop-in seats and sabre legs (DREW)

A&C 41, sold for £680, now worth £500-700

ROSEWOOD DINING

A set of six Regency rosewood dining chairs, the backs with curved bar top-rails and leaf carved scroll splats (PH BA)

A&C 18, sold for £3,335, now worth £2,500-4,000

GEORGE III CHAIRS

Eight George III mahogany chairs, the Heppelwhite-style shield backs with vertical pierced slats, over drop-in seats (ROSE)

A&C 66, sold for £1,300, now worth £1,000-1,500

CHARLES AND RAY EAMES

Charles and Ray Eames set of three dining chairs, 1974 (PH ED)

A&C 17, sold for £1,150, now worth £1,500-2,000

Fact File

Dining changed in the early-nineteenth century with more courses being introduced which led to longer meal times and the need for more comfortable chairs.

Larger families made for longer tables and more chairs with most sets having twelve chairs, including the two carvers.

It is unusual to find twelve matching chairs today, sets got broken up as families separated through marriage or death and smaller families have led to little need for the large sets although the tradition of buying six chairs is still maintained, for now.

Some people prefer to buy similar chairs, either through need (six decent antique chairs can cost at least £250) or because they liked a particular style but couldn't find matching chairs.

FURNITURE

HALL CHAIRS

Hall chairs and porter's chairs are the perfect examples of British snobbery and were designed for large houses. They were created to stand in the halls to provide seating for servants, either household staff or servants from other households, waiting to deliver or collect a message. They are attractive to look at but not for use.

HALL SEAT

Hall seat with no back to discourage slouching but with attractive turned legs and side support - more for aesthetics than comfort (WO WA)

A&C, now worth £2,000-4,000

PUGIN-STYLE

A pair of early Victorian oak hall stools, in the manner of A. W. N. Pugin, made in the Gothic Revival style with scissor arches (CHRIS)

A&C 21, sold for £5,750, now worth £5,000-7,000

PAIR OF HALL CHAIRS

Pair of William IV mahogany hall chairs either side of a worktable (PH BA)

A&C 18, sold for £1,300, now worth £1,000-2,000

WILLIAM IV

A pair of William IV mahogany hall chairs, each with gadrooned crest (LAW)

A&C 23, sold for £800, now worth £800-1,200

Fact File

They were also designed for lowly visitors who were not to be made welcome lest they misunderstand their status. As such, they were designed not to be comfortable. Servants and undesirables were not encouraged to linger. That said, they would be on open display so they were attractive with their tall carved backs and sometimes elaborately carved seats, more appealing to see than use.

They were made in large sets, often space for over a dozen sitters , and always used without cushions – although modern usage differs. Think carefully before buying to use for more than decoration – there is no padding on the back which can cause discomfort, even if cushions are added to the hard seats. Porter's chairs are generally upholstered in leather and were hooded to shut out draughts.

MAHOGANY HALL CHAIRS

A set of four early-nineteenth century mahogany hall chairs with wheel backs (PH ED)

A&C 16, sold for £5,290, now worth £4,000-7,000

SETTLE

An elaborately carved settle (from which sofas originated). Cushions were only used for important family members

A&C, now worth £800-1,200

CHESTS & COFFERS

'Coffin' comes from the Latin *cofre* meaning a chest and is a grandiose word for a simple concept – a chest in which to store clothes, linen or blankets. Dower chests formed part of a woman's dowry and would bring new linen to her new household which made them significant items from Medieval times to the seventeenth century.

OAK CHEST

Oak chest with moulded rim to the lid, single drawer and bracket feet. Lock inscribed with initials 'EV', 60cm x 31cm x 41cm (FELL)

A&C 39, sold for £1,200, now worth £1,000-1,500

CHEST ON STAND

Late-seventeenth century walnut chest, the upper section with moulded cornice, 107cm wide (CHEF)

A&C 65, sold for £3,000, now worth £3,000-5,000

MULE CHEST

An unusual lacewood plane and walnut mule chest, eighteenth/nineteenth century. Estimated value (HAMP)

A&C 13, sold for £4,600, now worth £4,000-5,000

CARVED CHEST

English oak chest, c.1680, with carved front and three-panelled top, 140cm wide (Paul Hopwell Antiques)

A&C 39, now worth £3,000-5,000

LEATHER CHEST

Brass-bound leather covered studded chest, the hinged top incorporating the Royal cypher believed to be that of Katherine of Braganza, 98cm. Estimate £2,000–3,000 (CHEF)

A&C 35, est £2,000-3,000, now worth £3,000-5,000

Fact File

Chests were known as blanket chests in the eighteenth century and, throughout the ages, have been kept at the end of the bed. Medieval versions were also used for storing valuables which is why they had heavy locks.

Sixteenth and seventeenth century oak chests with their elaborate carvings were often broken up through time and these have been added to more modern wood to create either chests of drawers or other chests and it's easy to get caught out by these 'ringers' or 'marriages' as they are known.

A chest with two drawers below is called a mule or dower chest and would influence the creation of chests of drawers. From the mid-seventeenth century, chests were replaced by chests of drawers which were deemed more sophisticated.

BLANKET CHEST

An Edwardian walnut blanket chest, 112cm wide, 50cm deep and 64cm high. Painted and with carved panels (PH ED)

A&C 23, est £400-600, now worth £300-500

PINE CHEST

Swiss painted pine, the interior fitted with small drawers, eighteenth century (MALL)

A&C 53, sold for £1,500, now worth £1,200-1,800

FURNITURE

CHESTS OF DRAWERS

Chests of drawers succeeded dower chests, their two bottom drawers giving way to three layers of drawers. The word 'drawer' refers to something that can be 'drawn' or 'dragged' out of a cabinet and was first used in 1580 but did not evolve fully until the mid-seventeenth century when they replaced the chests in wealthier households.

DWARF CHEST

George III dwarf chest of drawers, with replacement brass handles, 84cm long, 76cm high. (FELL)

A&C 40, sold for £1,600, now worth £1,200-1,800

OYSTER LABURNUM

Oyster laburnum, William and Mary, c.1700, 79cm high x 99cm wide (SOTH)

A&C 31, sold for £17,250, now worth £12-15,000

SATINWOOD COMMODE

Mid-nineteenth century commode (chamber pot in chest) with satinwood and king wood veneer, 72.5cm high, 127.5cm wide (AMER)

A&C 30, sold for £920, now worth £800-1,200

GEORGE III CHEST ON CHEST

A George III mahogany chest on chest, the moulded dentil cornice above two short and three long graduated drawers (DREW)

A&C 45, sold for £3,000, now worth £2,000-4,000

GILLOWS CHEST

An early Victorian oak chest, by Gillows of Lancaster, after a design by A. W. N. Pugin, c.1850 (CHRIS)

A&C 21, sold for £5,500, now worth £4,000-6,000

Fact File

From the mid-seventeenth century to the mid-eighteenth, chests of drawers were influenced by the earlier chests, some having highly decorative carved front doors which opened to reveal the drawers inside.

The four-drawer version (two long, two short drawers) became the standard from about 1680 and feet also varied with bun feet (like squashed circles) being introduced in 1690. In early chests of drawers, oak was the most common wood and have survived better than yew or elm versions.

As with chests, beware of the marriage where portions of earlier chests or chests of drawers are used on later bodies, this is especially true of the more elaborately carved versions.

QUEEN ANNE CHEST

Queen Anne chest on stand, herringbone banded walnut, 105cm wide (BR AU)

A&C 41, sold for £1,100, now worth £800-1,400

OAK DRESSING CHEST

Oak dressing chest, late-seventeenth century, with brass drop handles, 90cm high (AMER)

A&C 40, sold for £600, now worth £1,000-2,000

BOWFRONT CHEST ON CHEST

Bowfront chest on chest, mahogany, late-George III, with later brass swan-neck handles, 110cm wide x 193cm high.(HAMP)

A&C 33, sold for £1,400, now worth £1,000-2,000

WALNUT CHEST ON CHEST

Early-eighteenth century walnut veneered and feather-banded chest on chest (TF)

A&C 18, sold for £24,000, now worth £18-22,000

ITALIAN COMMODE

Italian commode, walnut, early-eighteenth century, with brass handles in the baroque taste with decorative feet (HAMP)

A&C 33, sold for £4,000, now worth £3,000-5,000

REGENCY CHEST

A Regency mahogany bowfront chest (PH BA)

A&C 21, sold for £480, now worth £300-600

WILLIAM AND MARY

A walnut and marquetry chest of drawers, William and Mary, c.1690. Inlaid throughout with scrolling foliate panels, on large ogee bracket feet (SOTH)

A&C 17, sold for £14,950, now worth £10-15,000

BIEDERMEIER

Ninetenth century Biedermeier walnut chest, with five drawers raised on bracket style feet, with good patina (GORR)

A&C 65, sold for £1,000, now worth £800-1,200

SERPENTINE FRONT CHEST

Late-nineteenth century walnut and satinwood serpentine front chest, with foliate cast gilt metal handles, 75cm high x 60cm wide (AMER)

A&C 35, sold for £460, now worth £400-600

SERPENTINE COMMODE

A George III mahogany serpentine commode. (CHRIS)

A&C 45, est £7,000-10,000, now worth £6-8,000

BOMBE COMMODE

Bombé commode with rouge marble top over a serpentine front, nineteenth century mounted kingwood. A very smart toilet (GORR)

A&C 57, sold for £5,000, now worth £4,000-6,000

Fact File

The majority of chests of drawers are rectangular in design but, if you have room, you might want to opt for the more costly but very attractive bow-fronted or serpentine versions. The bow-fronted version is curved like an archer's bow while the serpentine curves in, then out, then in again – like a snake – and is the most desirable of the shapes because it needed better craftsmen than the more basic rectangular.

Always look for names when buying furniture, they are usually on small plaques screwed on the rim of the top drawer or stamped there.

Some are marked on the back of the piece. A name can add 50% or more to a piece of furniture – Liberty's and Waring & Gillow made beautiful quality, mid-range furniture.

Stocks & Chairs
ANTIQUES

One of the best Antique Shops in the South of England

19thC marquetry rosewood centre table, c.1840

Victorian burr walnut stretcher table c.1870

George III period flame mahogany
open bookcase, c.1790

Georgian style hand dyed leather wing backed chair
made by Stocks & Chairs, c.2004

Victorian style hand dyed leather Chesterfield made by Stocks and Chairs, c.2004

**Associated warehouse of 4,000 sq ft
Visit our website: www.stocksandchairsantiques.com
11 Bank Chambers, Penn Hill Avenue, Parkstone, Poole, Dorset BH14 9NB Tel: 01202 718618**

CHILDREN'S FURNITURE

Children's furniture is eternally popular but not for its original use. Modern health and safety regulations have scared many new parents from using antique cribs or cradles and these are now being bought as plant holders or for exhibiting dolls. Likewise, old prams and children's chairs are now very popular for teddy bears and dolls.

WILLIAM IV CRADLE

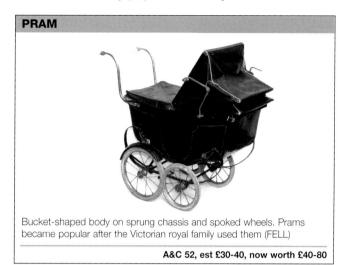

A William IV mahogany cradle in Empire style, 112.5cm long and 47cm wide. A curtain would have hung from the head's hook (HAMP)

A&C 19, sold for £1,200, now worth £1,000-1,500

PRAM

Bucket-shaped body on sprung chassis and spoked wheels. Prams became popular after the Victorian royal family used them (FELL)

A&C 52, est £30-40, now worth £40-80

Fact File

Children's chairs are always popular buys and are often sold by general dealers (not just furniture or toy dealers) because they fit into most cars.

It's important to check that the chairs are in proportion as some unscrupulous dealers have been known to cut the legs off fairly mundane, adults' chairs to make them shorter – and, thus, more desirable children's chairs.

Check that the seats are small and everything else is in proportion. If buying for use, as with all chairs, turn over and ensure that none of the stretchers (the rail between the legs) or legs are broken.

Cane seats are very popular and command a premium as do rocking chairs for children.

DOLLS' HOUSE FURNITURE

Miniature Dutch walnut display cabinet, 100cm high (GARD)

A&C 8, sold for £1,000, now worth £1,000-2,000

LIBERTY CRIB

Oak crib by Liberty & Co, inscribed 'Where soft the footstep falls', 119cm high (BON)

A&C 41, sold for £420, now worth £300-500

SWINGING CRADLE

Swinging cradle, 19th century mahogany and bergere cover (SWORD)

A&C 52, sold for £320, now worth £300-500

GEORGE IV CRADLE

George IV mahogany cradle, with caned arched hood and sides, a slatted base and brass casters. 129cm high x 113.5cm wide (DREW)

A&C 44, sold for £480, now worth £400-600

DESKS, BUREAUX & DAVENPORTS

Nowadays, desks, bureaux and davenports are used more for storage than their original concept as places to write, as well as store documents. The roll-top desk, once the stalwart of the Victorian era, can be found at most regional auction houses. Bureaux are still in demand and the smaller davenports are much sought after.

MAHOGANY BUREAU

A George III mahogany bureau (PH ED)

A&C 16, sold for £4,715, now worth £3,000-5,000

WALNUT DAVENPORT

Mid-Victorian, walnut-veneered davenport, with rising top and sloping serpentine front with hinged lid. 95cm high, 57.5cm wide (AMER)

A&C 33, sold for £2,800, now worth £,2500-3,500

KNEEHOLE DESK

A George II walnut kneehole desk, so-called because of the space for leg room (HAMP)

A&C 23, est £1,000-2,000, now worth £1,500-2,500

ROSEWOOD DAVENPORT

A George III rosewood davenport with fretted balcony, in the manner of Gillows. Signed in pencil under one drawer W. Cooper (PH BA)

A&C 18, sold for £3,600, now worth £3,000-5,000

DUTCH BUREAU

An eighteenth century Dutch walnut and marquetry bombe bureau (PH ED)

A&C 25, sold for £5,750, now worth £5,000-8,000

Fact File

Portable writing slopes had been in use since the Middle Ages but the desk as a standing piece of furniture did not evolve until the seventeenth century when literacy improved.

Desks can be seen in several forms, the most popular being the bureau (see left) but pedestal desks were made for more commercial use, their sturdiness both reassuring the client of their trustworthiness and their importance. The two heavy sides with their drawers would form an archway for the writer, with one or two further drawers within the arch.

A kneehole desk (see top) is a smaller version of this shape, the sides almost squashed together to form a smaller area for the user to sit. These were originally created for use as a dressing table, not a desk.

BUREAU BOOKCASE

George III mahogany secretaire bookcase with glazed panels fronting the bookcase and a series of small drawers in the bureau (BR AU)

A&C 34, sold £2,300, now worth £2,000-3,000

WALNUT DAVENPORT

Mid-Victorian walnut davenport, the ogee fronted fall opening to reveal a fall front interior with leather writing surface, pen trays and inkwell holders (HAMP)

A&C 34, sold for £2,800, now worth £3,000-4,000

QUEEN ANNE BUREAU

A walnut and featherbanded bureau bookcase, Queen Anne with restorations, in three parts, 216cm high, 99cm wide (SOTH)

A&C 25, sold for £15,180, now worth £12-18,000

PEDESTAL DESK

A Victorian walnut fruitwood crossbanded and marquetry gilt metal mounted ebonised pedestal desk. (CHRIS)

A&C 42, sold for £6,110, now worth £5,000-8,000

CYLINDER DESK

A mid-Victorian mahogany cylinder desk, 130cm wide.(MALL)

A&C 42, sold for £800, now worth £800-1,200

OAK DESK

Oak desk by Titmarsh & Goodwin, on block feet, 75cm high, 117.5cm wide (AMER)

A&C 41, sold for £1,000, now worth £1,500-2,500

OLIVEWOOD DAVENPORT

Victorian davenport, olivewood and inlaid, c.1870, the slope inscribed 'Jerusalem', 92cm high (WINT)

A&C 41, sold for £3,800, now worth £4,000-5,000

WRITING DESK

A late-Victorian rosewood and satinwood marquetry writing desk by Collinson and Lock, London and numbered 109. 122cm wide x 63cm deep x 108cm high

A&C 42, sold for £2,115, now worth £2,000-4,000

WALNUT DAVENPORT

Victorian walnut davenport, raised on turned feet, 89cm high, 55cm wide (AMER)

A&C 41, sold for £1,250, now worth £1,500-2,000

KNEEHOLE DESK

Late-nineteenth century kidney-shaped kneehole desk, Sheraton Revival satinwood and marquetry. 107cm wide.(DREW)

A&C 42, sold for £4,200, now worth £3,000-5,000

SHERATON REVIVAL DESK

Late-Victorian Sheraton revival satinwood and marquetry, the roll top enclosing a mechanical writing inset, drawers and recesses (DREW)

A&C 47, sold for £2,200, now worth £2,000-3,000

Fact File

Bureaux evolved in line with literacy, and the bureau bookcase was born, made by the likes of Chippendale and Sheraton and much reproduced over the years.

Prices of the more affordable pieces have dropped in the last few years with a George III bureau bookcase often selling for around £1,200–1,500 at auction. The basic bureau shape has remained unchanged for over 250 years, although, in an age of computers, it is now more ornamental than practical. Some of the most appealing bureaux were made in the Biedermeier period (1820–30 in Germany and Austria) and their appeal lies not just in the quality of their design but the secrets within – most of them contain secret drawers – and not all sellers realise it. When buying bureaux, try to find ones with keys for extra security.

FURNITURE

KIDNEY-SHAPED DESK

Late Victorian satinwood banded mahogany desk, with leather-lined top and nine drawers, on square tapered legs.(GORR)

A&C 48, sold for £2,000, now worth £1,800-2,200

BONHEUR DU JOUR

Walnut and tulipwood parquetry bonheur du jour (DREW)

A&C 52, sold for £550, now worth £500-800

CARLTON HOUSE DESK

A George III satinwood and sycamore Carlton House desk, the top inlaid with purpleheart and floral marquetry spandrels (SOTH)

A&C 42, sold for £53,775, now worth £45-60,000

GEORGE II BUREAU

A George II bureau attributed to J. Gravely, with brass inlaid fall (DREW)

A&C 8, sold for £14,000, now worth £12-18,000

PIANO-STYLE DAVENPORT

Late-Victorian walnut davenport with a piano top style, the pop up section with pierced gallery (GORR)

A&C 56, sold for £2,100, now worth £1,500-2,500

LADY'S WRITING BUREAU

Edwardian mahogany bureau with satinwood inlay, the interior enclosed by a fall front, 70cm wide (MALL)

A&C 50, sold for £660, now worth £600-800

Fact File

The word 'davenport' should never be spelt with a capital unless at the beginning of a sentence, despite these small versions of bureaux being named after the man for whom the first one was created, Captain Davenport. It was made by Gillow in Lancaster in around 1795 and their account books show a sketch of a box-like desk which had drawers on one side, along with a writing slope at the top.

Designed to be used on a ship, it was an innovative space-saving desk which allowed for storage, as well as writing. Its size appealed to women and led to more ornate versions in future, often with a fretted gallery and of colourful woods such as walnut or rosewood. Expect to pay over £2,500 for more attractive versions.

BUREAU CABINET

Mahogany, in two parts, the upper half with break arch pediment and foliate scroll cartouche (MALL)

A&C 64, sold for £3,600, now worth £3,500-5,000

GEORGE III BUREAU

A late George III mahogany cylinder bureau cabinet, banded in satinwood with boxwood and ebony strings (DREW)

A&C 8, sold for £18,000, now worth £15-25,000

Badger Marketing Ltd.
Club Fenders

- **Made to measure to suit your fireplace.**
- **Brass, black or brushed chrome finishes.**
- **Real leather seats.**

Badger Marketing Limited, 2 Chancel Drive,
Market Drayton, Shropshire TF9 3QT
Telephone 01630 655 202 Email: dgb@uk.net

WESTLAND ★ LONDON

First established in 1969 WESTLAND LONDON
offer an extensive & varied range of antique, period
& prestigious fireplaces and architectural elements.

We are always interested in buying suitable fireplaces, grates and other architectural items

ST MICHAEL'S CHURCH
LEONARD STREET
LONDON   EC2A 4ER
(OFF GREAT EASTERN ST)
TUBE: OLD STREET, EXIT 4

TEL: 020 7739 8094
FAX:020 7729 3620
e-mail: westland@westland.co.uk
OPEN MON-FRI 9-6, SAT 10-5
(SUNDAY BY APPOINTMENT)

www.westland.co.uk

FIREPLACES
By Distinction ...

Unit 3b
Yorkhill Quay
Glasgow G3

Tel: 0141 357 5812

www.bydistinction.co.uk

Fire Surrounds
Imperial White Marble
Portuguese Limestone
Sand Stone
Estremoz Marble

Inserts
Polished Mild Steel

Hearths & Panels
Granite
Flat & Riven Slate
Limestone

Fire Baskets

FURNITURE

FIRE SURROUNDS & ACCESSORIES

The hearth was once the heart of a family. In Medieval times, most homes would have fires opening to the skies, the mud cottages not strong enough to take the weight of chimneys but the use of stone and brick changed the history of the fireplace and more ornate fire surrounds were used to denote status as well as be decorative.

GOTHIC REVIVAL

Pair of Gothic Revival sandstone chimney pieces, second half nineteenth century

A&C 33, sold for £4,700, now worth £4,000-6,000

IRON GRATE

A Victorian cast iron fire grate, after the design by Alfred Stevens (CHRIS)

A&C 9, sold for £5,175, now worth £5,000-8,000

ART NOUVEAU

Art Nouveau, with simulated flame and rising smoke decoration and studded surround, 95cm x 105cm (MALL)

A&C 49, sold for £480, now worth £400-600

BRASS FENDER

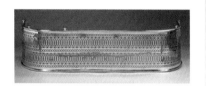

A Victorian pierced brass fender, mid-nineteenth century (CHRIS)

A&C 48, sold for £2,300, now worth £2,000-2,500

CAST IRON FIGURES

Pair of stylised cast iron figures of naked male and female, 1920s (SWORD)

A&C 53, sold for £660, now worth £600-800

IRON FENDERS

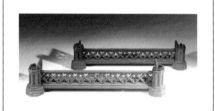

A pair of early-Victorian Gothic revival cast iron fenders, c.1850 (CHRIS)

A&C 9, sold for £1,495, now worth £1,500-2,000

Fact File

In the 1970s, period fireplaces were ripped out in a call for modern design. However, these days people are paying around £400 for Victorian and Edwardian fire surrounds to be returned to their period homes to create a more authentic feel.

Salvage is all the rage and a fireplace gives the home a centre other than a television set. For some people, an open fire is a dream that will never be realised (allows in draughts, difficult for the novice to light and it produces ash and soot) but the fireplace creates an illusion and the right fire surround is essential.

Some can be deemed immoral and US President John Adams ordered that there be no nudes in the fire surrounds at the White House when he went to live there in 1800.

FIRE DOGS

A set of four Victorian polished steel and brass mounted fire irons (CHRIS)

A&C 9, sold for £1,610, now worth £1,500-2,250

STEEL FIRE IRONS

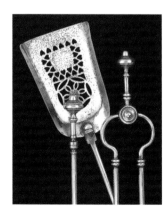

A set of three nineteenth century steel fire irons (CHRIS)

A&C 9, sold for £1,265, now worth £1,500-1,800

WALNUT FIRE SCREEN

A walnut fire screen, nineteenth-century, or Regency style, incorporating an eighteenth-century needlework tapestry. 86.5cm x 125cm. (CHRIS)

A&C 9, est £1,000-2,000, now worth £1,500-2,500

BRASS GRATE

English polished steel and brass grate, late-nineteenth century (CHRIS)

A&C 33, sold for £6,462, now worth £5,000-8,000

MAHOGANY FIRE SCREEN

A Victorian mahogany cheval fire screen with Chinese fine needle work panel of a hare, 65cm wide.

A&C 1, sold for £125, now worth £150-300

GILT METAL FENDER

With foliate scrolls and fruit on bun feet, 113cm wide.(DREW)

A&C 45, sold for £800, now worth £800-1,200

CLUB FENDER

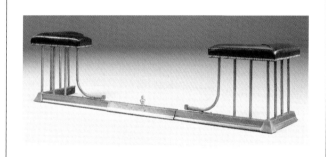

Polished brass adjustable club fender, twentieth century (CHRIS)

A&C 33, sold for £2,820, now worth £2,500-3,500

VICTORIAN FIRE IRONS

A set of three Victorian steel and brass fire irons presented in a stand (CHRIS)

A&C 9, sold for £920, now worth £800-1,200

COMPANION STAND

A French steel and gilt bronze fireside companion stand with fire dogs (CHRIS)

A&C 9, sold for £575, now worth £500-800

Fact File

The Art Nouveau era led to some of the most attractive fire surrounds ever created. The decorative tiles formed scenes or portrayed plants in glorious colours and patterns typical of the era. Some fire surrounds can be bought intact while others have been stripped and the tiles sold separately.

Be careful when buying fire surrounds, some people are painting them black not to refresh them as is often claimed but to hide the fact that they are modern – although you don't want to buy anything too dented or rusty, at least it tends to show their age.

It is not only fire surrounds that should be inspected being buying – check grates very carefully as some will have pieces missing because they have been destroyed over repeated firings and this could be dangerous.

FURNITURE

GOTHIC REVIVAL

The Gothic Revival was based on religious architecture and ecclesiastical furniture of the twelfth–fifteenth centuries. Common motifs included trefoils (hollowed out areas in the shape of a shamrock) while chairs had high backs, their shape similar to a building's gable (the peaked sides). It was high drama in practical form.

THREE SEATER

Victorian Chippendale-style mahogany three seater, with gothic splat, open arms and claw and ball feet (MALL)

A&C 45, sold for £1,400, now worth £1,000-2,000

OAK LIBRARY TABLE

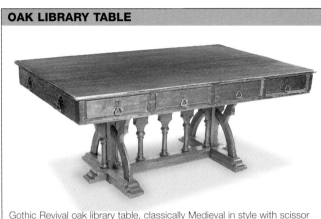

Gothic Revival oak library table, classically Medieval in style with scissor arches at each end, 185cm long and 76cm high (DREW)

A&C 34, sold for £1,900, now worth £2,000-2,500ß

Fact File

This is possibly Britain's most dramatic period of furniture, even outdoing Art Deco's flowing lines for sheer theatricality. The Continent had the Baroque with its ostentatious use of gilt but Britain looked backwards and created light out of the Dark Ages. In reality, the original Gothic movement had three stages (Early English, Geometric also known as Flamboyant or Decorated and, the final stage, Perpendicular). The Gothic Revival took what elements it wanted and turned it to its own use. The furniture from this era is both frivolous and religious. Cardinal's chairs, based on designs for eminent church leaders, were recreated for home use. Reading stands became miniature pulpits for the home and dining chairs became a minor production. This is an exciting style - perfect for any home.

OAK DRESSING TABLE

Neo-Gothic oak dressing table, 106.5cm wide

A&C 34, sold for £270, now worth £300-500

GOTHIC PRODUCTION

Victorian pitch pine in two parts with typical Gothic arches and high drama (MALL)

A&C 48, sold for £2,300, now worth £1,800-2,800

MIXING MOVEMENTS

Late-Victorian Gothic Revival secretaire bookcase, walnut, fruitwood and ebonised, by Holden & Co, Liverpool with a hint of the Aesthetic (DREW)

A&C 41, sold for £190, now worth £800-1,200

HEAVY GOTHIC LOOK

A set of 12 heavy Gothic Revival oak dining chairs with leather back and seat coverings, worn through use

A&C 34, est £1,500-2,000, now worth £1,500-1,800ß

SOFAS, SETTEES & SETTLES

The sofa as we know it is based on an earlier wooden design, the settle which was designed, not for comfort, but for seating. The settle was made of wood, later with loose cushions making its users more likely to settle down. The settee was more comfortable with its padded seat, although the back remained wooden.

MAHOGANY SETTEE

George III mahogany settee, with square back, reeded arms, baluster supports and brass feet (MALL)

A&C 56, sold for £800, now worth £700-900

GILTWOOD SOFA

George IV giltwood sofa with scalloped back, attributed to Gillows, 108cm high x 234cm wide x 90cm deep (DREW)

A&C 41, sold for £82,000, now worth £70-90,000

SATINWOOD SOFA

Early-nineteenth century sofa. Arms, seat rail and sabre legs veneered in satinwood with ebonised detail (DREW)

A&C41, est £2,500-3,000, now worth £2,000-4,000

EBONISED GILT SOFA

Early-nineteenth century ebonised gilt sofa, upholstered in green damask with fluted top rail and turned arm supports.(LOCK)

A&C58, sold for £700, now worth £600-900

WALNUT OTTOMAN

Mid Victorian walnut ottoman, with four outward facing, co-joined quadrant seats, raised on turned legs and castors (AMER)

A&C 40, sold for £670, now worth £600-900

BEECH SETTEE

French beech settee (DREW)

A&C 52, sold for £680, now worth £600-800

Fact File

There were various forms of comfort with chaise longues and day beds as the ultimate form of relaxation. The word 'couch' used to mean a day bed although we now use it to describe a sofa which, from its creation in around 1690, has always been padded throughout, not just the seat. Settles date from around 1500 and were country furniture and, from the seventeenth century, deemed unfashionable except for rural use (for example inns and farmhouses). Settees were much more fashionable and created in a variety of styles and sizes, generally allowing for two, three or four sitters and tended to be very fashion-led and influenced by the top chair designs of the day, such as Hepplewhite's shield (escutcheon) back. Check for comfort and strength before buying.

TWO-SEATER SETTEE

An early-nineteenth century mahogany double chairback, two-seater settee with reeded uprights and scrolled arms on turned legs (COOP)

A&C 23, sold for £520, now worth £500-800

EDWARDIAN SETTEE

Edwardian mahogany framed, small settee, with satinwood marquetry and boxwood string inlaid decoration (AMER)

A&C 35, sold for £420, now worth £400-800

CARD TABLES

Gambling was at its prime under the Prince Regent which led to increasing numbers of the pieces being produced. The most popular was the demi-lune, the D-shaped table which could be placed against a wall when not in use and folded out when needed. They belonged to the gentry and wealthy so were of superior quality.

MAHOGANY CARD TABLES

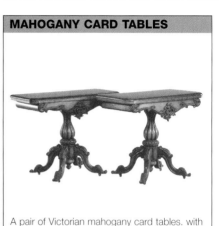

A pair of Victorian mahogany card tables. with carved detail (PH BA)

A&C 18, sold for £3,800, now worth £4,000-6,000

SATINWOOD CARD TABLE

A George III inlaid satinwood demi-lune card table, c.1790 (HAMP)

A&C 11, sold for £3,500, now worth £3,000-5,000

TAPERING, CARVED LEGS

George III maogany card table with rich patina but some damage and restoration. Attractive carvings on the tapering legs

A&C44, sold for £2,700, now worth £2,000-3,000

TRIANGULAR TABLE

Edwardian rosewood with unusually shaped satinwood triangular top on tapering legs with spade feet and castors, 96cm wide (MALL)

A&C 45, sold for £840, now worth £800-1,200

DEMI-LUNE

Late nineteenth century satinwood demi-lune card table with marquetry detail

A&C 44, sold for £2,300, now worth £2,000-2,750

DUTCH CARD TABLE

A Dutch marquetry shaped bow-fronted card table early-nineteenth century 75cm wide x 37cm deep (HAMP)

A&C 29, sold for £1,450, now worth £1,500-2,500

FRUITWOOD AND BURR WALNUT

Mis-eighteenth century fuirtwood and burr walnut concertina style card table with lined interior and storage wells for cards etc.

A&C 44, sold for £6,600, now worth £5,000-8 ,000

GEORGE III TABLE

George III mahogany serpentine fold over type with green baize playing surface (MALL)

A&C 64, sold for £1,100, now worth £800-1,200

Fact File

Gambling-related goods are highly collectable and card tables, especially from the Georgian era (1714–1830), command a premium. The Regency period (1811–20) saw some of the best pieces because virtually every dinner party for people with money would end with card games, cards being the main form of gambling, although betting on horses was huge business.

Some of the most interesting of the tables were made between 1800–50 with 'birdcage' supports – that's where four column supports grew out of a platform.

Baize, the green covering used for card games and removed for general use, is rarely original and be careful, some people will add the covering to ordinary tea tables to make them look like card tables.

CONSOLE TABLES

The highly ornate console table with its gilt frame dates back to the Baroque era (1630–1750). Made to stand against a wall it is a frivolous mark of status and highly ostentatious – which is what makes them so popular. The gilt support would usually be surmounted by a marble top. 'Console' comes from the French for a bracket.

LOUIS XVI TABLE

A French Louis XVI giltwood console table, c.1780. Restoration to gilding (HAL)

A&C 19, sold for £XX, now worth £XX

NEO-CLASSICAL STYLE

Painted overall in neo-classical style with a fan and ribbons on a cream ground, 81cm high x 100.5cm wide.(DREW)

A&C 47, sold for £3,800, now worth £3,000-5,000

GILTWOOD TABLE

A nineteenth century parcel giltwood table, the serpentine top over an elaborately C-scroll carved frieze, 90cm x 105cm (ROSE)

A&C 62, sold for £720, now worth £600-800

MAHOGANY CONSOLE TABLE

George I style carved mahogany with marble top over cabriole supports, 82cm x 100cm (ROSE)

A&C 62, sold for £1,100, now worth £800-1,200

FIGURAL SUPPORT

A Venetian ormulu console table with mermaid support. Figures have been used as supports since the Baroque era (see fact file) but could be too ornate for some households

A&C, now worth £600-800

VENETIAN CONSOLE TABLE

Similar but not identical to the one on the left. Note the different position of the swag (garland). These tables appeal because they are both decorative and practical

A&C, now worth £600-800

Fact File

There are two types of console tables, those which are screwed to a wall on brackets (consoles) or those set against a wall. The most extravagant versions were made by the sculptor, Brustolon and supported on carved human figures. These were created in the Baroque era, famous for its over the top creations. The versions seen in the Rococo era (1730–50) are still dramatic with their use of gilt and carving and most reproductions are based on this period. Expect to pay £2,000+ for one of the more interesting versions and beware of reproductions which have brighter gilding and less detail than authentic versions.

FURNITURE

DINING TABLES

When it comes to dining table, size matters which is why it's best to buy ones which either come with spare leaves (panels used to extend the table). Some tables have to be opened manually to add the extra leaves while others wind out – these tend to be very popular. Above all, will it fit in your house?

ON A PEDESTAL

George IV mahogany triple pedestal dining table on wheels, some damage (BON)

A&C 54, est £6,000-8,000, now worth £6,000-8,000

ROUND TABLE

An early Victorian mahogany round extending dining table (LAW)

A&C 23, sold for £2,800, now worth £2,500-4,000

GILLOWS STYLE

George IV extending mahoghany dining table in the style of Gillows, c 1820 (SOTH)

A&C 54, est £8,000-10,000, now worth £7-10,000

CARLO BUGATTI

Inlaid dining table by Carlo Bugatti, from around 1900 (CHRIS)

A&C 66, sold for £21,150, now worth £20-25,000

EXTENDING DINING TABLE

Mahogany patented extending dining table with a rounded rectangular top with reeded edge, containing three leaves on draw-out stretchers. (PHI)

A&C 11, sold for £46,000, now worth £40-60,000

REFECTORY TABLE

A walnut refectory table, Italian, seventeenth century style, c.1900, the cleated top with a carved border, carved scroll block feet and central stretcher rail (SOTH)

A&C 11, sold for £2,300, now worth £2,000-4,000

MOUSEMAN

An oak dining room suite by Robert 'Mouseman' Thompson, famous for carving mice into his work eg legs of chairs (SOTH)

A&C 16, sold for £4,130, now worth £6-10,000

OAK REFECTORY TABLE

An oak refectory table, Charles I, 1625–1650. Features a triple-plank rectangular top above a carved frieze, and bulbous baluster and block-turned legs joined by peripheral stretchers. Some minor restorations (SOTH)

A&C 11, sold for £14,950, now worth £12-18,000

Fact File

The refectory table at Hatfield House can never be removed, the building was actually erected around it and it's too big to fit through the door.

Dining tables are now getting smaller, squeezed into the corner of kitchens but dining used to be a grand affair and the large eighteenth century household would regularly entertain guests to lavish meals on tables which had to be large enough to entertain in style – at the top end of the market, that is.

There are also farmhouse tables which fulfil the same role but in a more homely style. When looking for the perfect dining table, get on your knees – and crawl under the table to look for the maker's plaque – Waring and Gillow or, for Deco furniture, Epstein, are good choices.

OCCASIONAL AND OTHER TABLES

The phrase 'occasional tables' is a very useful collective for tables with no obvious every day use. They were used occasionally, ie not for tea, dining, working or playing. As such, there are dozens of different shapes and sizes which come under this heading. They are perfect for whatever use you wish to make – in whatever style.

REGENCY SOFA TABLE

An early nineteenth century Regency period mahogany and satinwood cross-banded sofa table, with original gilt metal castors (TF)

A&C 18, sold for £5,000, now worth £4,000-6,000

WRITING TABLE

Walnut veneered ladies' writing table, oval, 1920s, 79cm high, 92.5cm wide (AMER)

A&C 31, sold for £550, now worth £400-800

KNEEHOLE WRITING TABLE

Walnut veneered kneehole writing table, 1920s, 77.5cm high, 120cm wide (AMER)

A&C 31, sold for £600, now worth £600-800

PEDESTAL TABLE

George III mahogany pedestal table, 62.5cm high, 70cm diameter AMER

A&C 35, sold for £720, now worth £600-800

IAN GRANT

Pair of contemporary ripple sycamore console tables, by Ian Grant. The tops centred by four squares of eroded tartan inlays of holly, sycamore and birch, with cherry pine overcheck (PH ED)

A&C 34, est £1,500-2,000, now worth £1,800-2,400

PORCELAIN PLAQUE TOP

Late-nineteenth century French, with gilt metal mounts, the top inset with a painted porcelain plaque (DREW)

A&C 66, sold for £2,700, now worth £2,200-2,800

CIRCULAR TABLE

Regency, with circular slate top inlaid with coloured marbles and three gilded paw feet (GORR)

A&C 56, sold for £9,500, now worth £8,000-10,000

FRENCH JARDINIERE STAND

Ebonised and porcelain mounted French jardiniere stand from 1890 (SOTH)

A&C 52, sold for £423, now worth £350-550

Fact File

Tables are generally – but not always – made of wood. Some occasional tables are made of chewed up paper – better known as papier mâché. This started life as paper before being soaked in water and layered upon itself with glue made of flour and water before being lacquered into a hard and ornate piece of furniture. The decoration, like the legs, is often ornate and worth around £200–400, depending on the quality of the decoration. Other tables have metal or wooden frames and pietre dure tops – hard stones which tend to be semi-precious and are highly sought after. It's also worth thinking whether low lying, marble-topped tables are suitable for your needs – they can have sharp corners which makes them dangerous for children and anyone unsteady on their feet.

FURNITURE

SIDEBOARDS

Sideboards used to be essential pieces of furniture for late-eighteenth–nineteenth century diners. Starting life as a table to rest hot food, they became vital for serving multi-course meals. In addition, there were generally two cupboards – one of which would store the chamber pot, vital for long dinners with only basic indoor plumbing.

MAHOGANY SIDEBOARD

Mahogany serpentine-front sideboard, late-nineteenth century reproduction of a George III sideboard, 87.5cm high, 117.5cm wide (AMER)

A&C 30, sold for £670, now worth £500-800

ART NOUVEAU SIDEBOARD

Art Nouveau oak sideboard, attributed to Wylie & Lochead, Glasgow. Est. £3,000–5,000 (BON)

A&C 36, sold for £3,000, now worth £5,000-8,000

BOW-FRONTED SIDEBOARD

Late Georgian mahogany with satinwood crossbanding and ebony string inlay with lion's head handles, 99cm wide (FELL)

A&C 57, sold for £1,200, now worth £1,000-1,500

OAK DRESSER

Oak dresser, Georgian, with pot-board base, 165cm x 41cm x 85cm (FELL)

A&C 39, sold for £3,100, now worth £2,000-4,000

GOTHIC REVIVAL SIDEBOARD

A Victorian oak sideboard, the panelled gallery carved with masks, fruit and foliage with a rope-twist cresting and reeded finials (CHRIS)

A&C 21, sold for £2,400, now worth £2,000-3,000

GEORGE III SIDEBOARD

George III sideboard, mahogany, 160cm wide with serpentine front and balcony back (CLEV)

A&C 33, sold for £4,200, now worth £3,500-5,500

AESTHETIC SIDEBOARD

Aesthetic rosewood and harewood sideboard, c.1880, in the manner of Collinson & Lock. 161cm high x 198cm wide (SOTH)

A&C 30, sold for £3,450, now worth £3,000-6,000

OAK DRESSER

Oak dresser base, George II, mid-eighteenth century. Some faults and restorations. Dressers were a natural development from sideboards (SOTH)

A&C 11, sold for £6,670, now worth £6,000-8,000

Fact File

You might find it strange that we've listed sideboards under tables and not in their own right but that's because they started life as part of the table family. Sideboard literally means 'long plank'. This dates from their beginnings as serving tables which were first used during the 'Chippendale' era of the mid-eighteenth century. This tallies with when mahogany was first being used and the large trees were ideal for making the long serving tables.

The first sideboard as we know it was introduced in around 1775. There were two cupboards, one in which to store the much-needed chamber pot, the second being been used to store wine, crockery or extra silver.

WORK TABLES

Sewing was not always the work of the seamstress. Ladies of quality sewed to show their accomplishments, creating tapestries or samplers, as well as bookmarks and even adding lace ruffles to their clothes. Materials would be stored away in what we call either work tables or sewing tables, some doubling up as games tables.

WORK AND PLAY

Victorian mahogany work/games table on a pedestal base. The top is reversible and turns over to reveal a chessboard (CAPES)

A&C 60, sold for £650, now worth £500-1,000

TORTOISESHELL WORK TABLE

Louis XV style tortoiseshell mahogany lady's work table, inlaid with mother-of-pearl and ivory, by T. Clifford, Stockholm, c.1860 (CHRIS)

A&C 41, sold for £24,000, now worth £20,000-30,000

INLAID WORK TABLE

A. L. Majorelle, inlaid work table with wisteria and berry inlay, fitted frieze drawer on slender sinuous supports (BRI)

A&C 28, sold for £1,550, now worth £1,200-1,800

REGENCY WORK TABLE

A Regency mahogany and ebony line inlaid rectangular work table, with reeded edge and two rounded drop leaves (LAW)

A&C 23, sold for £2,600, now worth £3,000-4,000

COLONIAL WORK TABLE

Colonial work table in solid tropical hardwood. Estimate £700–900 (HAMP)

A&C 38, sold for £700, now worth £XX

OCTAGONAL TABLE

Victorian walnut work table with octagonal top and tapering trumpet column

A&C 60, sold for £380, now worth £XX

Fact File

Work tables are sometimes confused with tea-poys, expensive tea caddies on stands with lockable lids which would open to reveal the tea-making goods within (two smaller caddies and two bowls, one for sugar, the other for mixing the leaves). Work tables tend to be cheaper but no less appealing. Some sewing tables were also used as writing tables, opening up to reveal small drawers and a writing slope. The tables have two types of bottoms – one with a material work bag (rarely original) or a wooden base. The Victorians liked to use the cone-shaped work table whose octagonal top gave way to a wooden coned base for stylish storage. The better quality work tables sell for around £3,000–5,000 but some decent ones can be bought for under £1,800.

FURNITURE

WARDROBES & CUPBOARDS

Strictly speaking, a cupboard is a place in which to store crockery or food and a wardrobe a place for storing hanging clothes but the two terms are interchangeable as the wardrobe was loosely based on the cupboard's design. Clothes hangers, which make wardrobes viable, did not become popular until 1900.

OAK CUPBOARD

Early-nineteenth century oak cupboard, on bracket feet, 167.5cm high, 100cm wide (AMER)

A&C 35, sold for £1,600, now worth £1,000-2,000

PANELLED CUPBOARD

An oak joined cupboard, the base with two panelled and carved doors on a sledge base (DREW)

A&C 49, sold for £1,400, now worth £800-1,200

SOUTH WEST WALES DRESSER

George III South West Wales oak dresser, the plaque says it belonged to a couple married in Dolgelly in 1774 (BON)

A&C 49, sold for £9,500, now worth £8-10,000

CORNER CUPBOARD

George III mahogany corner cupboard, on bracket feet, 212.5cm x 77.5cm (AMER)

A&C 35, sold for £500, now worth £400-800

SWISS WARDROBE

Swiss painted with polychrome foliate and figure decoration with panel doors, 117.5cm x 195cm (MALL)

A&C 50, sold for £2,000, now worth £1,500-2,000

Fact File

The wardrobe as a word first appeared in 1325 and was a place to keep (or guard) garments but the hanging cupboard space which we now use did not catch on until 1900, clothes mostly being stored in chests and, later, chests of drawers. The coat hangers that enable wardrobes to hang the clothes, although first created by Sheraton in 1790 and called 'shoulders', were not seen again until 1890 and took ten years to catch on – at which point wardrobes became popular. In the meantime, clothes (or linen) presses were created with their drawers in which to store clothes. These were seen in the eighteenth-century and people often mistake them for wardrobes. The large linen presses havedecreased in popularity (and price) in the past five years as people use built-in wardrobes.

BREAKFRONTED CUPBOARD

Large oak breakfront cupboard George III, too large for many modern houses which makes it surprisingly affordable (LOCK)

A&C 52, sold for £750, now worth £800-1,200

AESTHETIC CUPBOARD

Aesthetic movemtn cupboard with panelled doors painted with stylised fruit and flower designs (SWORD)

A&C 54, sold for £600, now worth £600-800

WASHSTANDS

Before most homes had bathrooms, people used washstands in their rooms. These would hold a large jug and bowl in which to wash and often had marble or tile backs which were often splashed during washing. Victorian and Edwardian versions with tiled surfaces are especially popular – and often reproduced.

MAHOGANY BIDET WASHSTAND

Nineteenth century washstand with hinged lids, Inside, is a mirror and bidet (SWORD)

A&C, sold for £780 now worth £800-1,000

MAHOGANY WASHSTAND

Gilt-bronze mounted mahogany washstand. Empire, c.1810, the porcelain basin and ewer, Paris, Nast from the same year

A&C 31, sold for £20,700, now worth £18-22,000

PAINTED CORNER WASHSTAND

George III painted corner washstand c 1800 with honeycomb decoration (SOTH)

A&C 31, sold for £1,800, now worth £1,500-2,300

GEORGIAN DRESSING CHEST

Georgian dressing chest (washstand) with marquetry panels and Gillow stamp (PH BA)

A&C 31, est £180-220 , now worth £200-300

IRISH MAHOGANY WASHSTAND

A George III Irish mahogany and crossbanded serpentine fronted enclosed washstand (LAW)

A&C 23, sold for £3,700, now worth £3,000-5,000

Fact File

The washstand has fallen out of fashion with the growth of en suite bathrooms but, mainly in Victorian and Edwardian times, most middle class homes had a washstand in the bedrooms where the family could clean in the days before everyone had indoor plumbing.

The marble topped washstands, often with tiled back, are very popular but not for washing. Instead, the cool top is said to be the ideal surface for rolling pastry.

Tiled backs are very popular and were created by some of the best makes, including Minton (see below) and these command premium prices. A basic Edwardian tile-backed version costs around £200-250 with prices dropping in the last couple of years - making it a good time to buy.

MARBLE TOPPED WASHSTAND

Victorian mahogany veneered washstand with marble top

A&C 1, sold for £225, now worth £200-400

MINTON TILES

Victorian washstand (used as dressing table). With Minton tiles, c.1860, 106cm high (CHRIS)

A&C 31, sold for £9,500, now worth £8,000-12,000

GAMES

ARCADE AND BOARD GAMES

Games are a social activity whether played at home (board games) or in arcades. The latter are often noisy, competing with each other to attract players and, therefore, money. Pinball games are very popular, their artwork evocative of their era. Horse racing games are very collectable, for example Totopoly.

MARBLES

An unusual and complete Delft pottery game with marbles, the bowl decorated with kakeimon pattern (FELL)

A&C 16, sold £920, now worth £1-1,500

SLOT MACHINE

Slot machine of the popular song, *Roll Out The Barrel,* 63cm high (SWORD)

A&C 58, sold for £400, now worth £400-700

HORSE RACING

Early French mechanical race game with two runners and winner's cup (COL TO)

A&C 29, est £300-600, now worth £400-800

EVEL KNIEVEL ARCADE GAME

Evel Knievel pinball machine, formerly owned by singer Robbie Williams (BON)

A&C 58, sold for £588, now worth £600-800

Fact File

Board games date back to ancient times and were not always played just for enjoyment; some educated or were used to teach morality. These included Snakes and Ladders which originated in India as a Hindu game, *Moksha-Patamu* with the snakes representing a decline into evil and ladders moral accomplishments that needed to be attained to reach a higher order. The squares represented virtues and negatives ranging from generosity to drunkenness. The ultimate achievement was the hundredth square, Nirvana. Monopoly is a popular game with the most expensive version made of gold, diamonds and rubies and worth $1,000,000 (£555,000) although an original board handmade by Charles Darrow, the man controversially credited with creating the game in the 1930s, sold for $71,500 (£39,750). The original games were set in Atlantic City.

TOY PINBALL MACHINE

American Marx tinplate table-top toy pinball machine, arcades at home, 1955

A&C 39, sold for £60, now worth £150-250

PENNY ARCADE

Wonders shooting gallery in a wall-mounted oak case, first half of 20th century, in working order (SWORD)

A&C 64, sold for £400, now worth £400-600

FRUITY SLOT MACHINE

One of the most popular designs for slot machines – part of the thrill is pulling the handle and watching the fruits spin

A&C, now worth £400-700

ROULETTE SLOT MACHINE

German wall Roulette slot machine from the late 1950s, 74cm high (SWORD)

A&C 46, sold for £160, now worth £200-400

BRENTWOOD
ANTIQUE AUCTIONS
Auctioneers & Valuers

45 North Road, Brentwood, Essex CM14 4UZ

Tel: 01277 224599 Fax: 01277 261502

*Auctions held every fortnight
alternating Antiques & Collectables
and Antiques & General*

View illustrated catalogue at
www.brentwoodantiqueauction.co.uk

Viewing Thursday & Friday prior to sale

SPITALFIELDS
ANTIQUE MARKET
Commercial Street, London E1
EVERY THURSDAY 7am - 3pm

COVENT GARDEN
ANTIQUE MARKET
The Jubilee Hall, Southampton St
Covent Garden WC2
EVERY MONDAY from 6am

STRATFORD-UPON-AVON
ANTIQUE CENTRE
60 Ely St, Stratford-upon-Avon
7 DAYS A WEEK 10am - 5pm

YORK
ANTIQUE CENTRE
2a Lendel, York
MON - SAT 10am - 5pm

Tel: 020 7240 7405
Sherman & Waterman Associates

GARRICK COLEMAN
Antique & Collector's Chess Sets

75 Portobello Road, London W11 2QB

Telephone: 020 7937 5524   Fax: 020 7937 5530   Email: coleman_antiques_london@compuserve.com

Visit our website and online showroom at www.antiquechess.co.uk

GAMES

CHESS

The origins of chess are shrouded in mystery. The game with its two opposing armies was first mentioned in a seventh century Persian poem. The idea was vividly portrayed in the form of wizard chess in *Harry Potter and the Philosopher's Stone*, which rejuvenated interest in the game for all generations.

PERUVIAN

Rare late-nineteenth–twentieth century Peruvian alabaster set, carved as Incas (GORR)

A&C 56, sold £1,100, now worth £1-2,000

FABERGÉ

Fabergé chess set from 1905, commissioned as a gift for General Alexei Kuropatkin (Som Hse, Gilbert Collection)

A&C 56, from Royal collections

DUTCH DELFT

Dutch Delft Art Deco chess set (GORR)

A&C 56, sold for £550, now worth £500-800

RUSSIAN LAQUERED WOOD

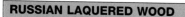

A Russian lacquered wood figural chess set, early-20th century (CHRIS)

A&C 25, sold for £176, now worth £250-450

Fact File

The castle, better known as the *rukh* (which is pronounced rook, deriving from a Persian word), the chess piece which can move up or across the board, was originally an elephant with a tower on its back. This, however, proved rather too time-consuming and costly to make so changed over time to the much simpler castle.

The invasion of Spain by the Moors in the eighth century brought chess to Spain and its first mention in European literature came in 1010 AD. But it was the Europeans who made one of the most significant changes to the game by introducing the board. Beforehand, it had been played without a board with its famous 64 squares. Sets are traditionally found in either red and white/cream or black and white/cream.

RUSSIAN PROPAGANDA

A Russian porcelain propaganda figural chess set, possibly by the famous Lomonosov factory. mid-20th century. King 11cm high, pawn 6cm high (CHRIS)

A&C 25, sold for £9,987, now worth £10–12,000

LAVA AND CORAL

An Italian lava and coral chess set, possibly c 1800. King 8.9cm high (CHRIS)

A&C 25, sold £7,990, now worth £8-12,000

MINIATURE CHESS SET

Mid-19th century, Indian ivory miniature chess set and table (GORR)

A&C 56, sold for £600, now worth £600-800

INDIAN JOHN COMPANY

An Indian John Company chess set, early-19th century, possibly Berhampur. Both sides mounted on bases carved with lotus petal motif. King 11cm high (CHRIS)

A&C 25, sold £28,200, now worth £30-35,000

Glass

Interest in glass has risen significantly in the last few years and the colourful medium is threatening the previously unchallenged dominance of ceramics at general antiques fairs.

FRENCH FAVOURITES

The emphasis on glass has also changed. The market used to be dominated by the traditional, mainly French designs of the 1920-40s:

Baccarat, made Le Roy Soleil, the perfume bottle designed by Dali for Schiaparelli
Daum, (pronounced dome), acid-etched glass designs, plants are a popular theme
Gallé, textured art glass using acid-etching and inlay
Lalique, famous opalescent glass designs, Art Deco ones being the best

TOP BRITISH FIRMS

The traditional British glassworks have their own following:

George Davidson, famous for his cloud glass, used the mark of a lion in a turret
Caithness, famous for their paperweights, vases have distinctive colouring (eg streaky, chalky purple)
Mdina, made on the Isle of Wight or Malta, notable for its blue-green colouring and gold streaks
Monart and Vasart, Scottish glass featuring streaky, pastel colours

Sowerby, carnival glass, including the famous press-moulded chicken pots
Stevens and Williams, cameo vases, iridescent wares
Webb Corbett, good use of texture and colour
Thomas Webb & Sons, one of the many glassworks in the Stourbridge area
Whitefriars, distinctive colours and styles, ideal for first-time collectors

EUROPEAN CONTENDERS

Boda, stylish Scandinavian designs
Bohemian crystal, an area specialising in glass making, not an individual make, stained glass goblets with scenes (eg hunting) are good buys
Holmegaard and Kastrup, heavy-set, stylish Scandinavian glass
Kosta, top Scandinavian make with some outrageous designs
Loetz, shapely iridescent designs, prices rising fast
Moser, superb use of colours
Murano Glass, an area of Italy specialising in glass (sometimes listed as Venetian glass)
Orrefors, famous for their engraved wares

AMERICAN CLASSICS

Depression Glass, a thick, colourful style
Fenton Glass, carnival glass and opalescent glass in pink-yellow designs
Mary Gregory style, cameos of children originated in Hungary but possibly named after an American glassmaker who worked at Boston & Sandwich
Tiffany, famous for his favrile glass, especially the lampshades

'MODERN' DESIGNERS

Geoffrey Baxter at Whitefriars, colourful, textured designs
Carlo Moretti, look for his heavy but clever animals
Zeleznobrodské Sklo, fantastic figural work
Venini, innovative use of colour and design
Vistosi, especially his birds

GLASS

GLASS

This is one of the most attractive and yet frustrating areas of collecting. Most glass is unmarked which means that you need to learn what you're doing or you could miss out. That said, some makes or styles are so obvious that you'll always recognise them and this includes carnival glass, made as prizes for fairs, often in orange.

BRISTOL BLUE

Blue finger bowl with a band of gilt decoration. Signed 'I Jacobs, Bristol', c.1810, 8.8cm high. (Courtesy of Somervale Antiques)

A&C 30, est £800-1,000, now worth £800-1,200

TRUMPET-SHAPED GLASSES

Four trumpet-shaped wine glasses in Bristol blue (Courtesy of Somervale Antiques)

A&C 30, est £400-450, now worth £400-600

BLUE BEAKER

Blue beaker with gilt floral decoration (Courtesy of Somervale Antiques)

A&C 30, est £400-450, now worth £400-600

CARNIVAL GLASS

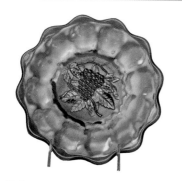

An 8in Imperial amber Heavy Grape plate in marigold, the easiest to find colour

A&C 29, est £90-120, now worth £100-150

Fact File

Not all glass is marked and the pieces that are can be hard to spot – always hold the glass up to the light (if it is not too heavy) and try to look for the names.

Waterford is very hard to read. Baccarat has a distinctive mark of a decanter with a glass on either side. The advantage of buying unmarked goods at auction is that they tend to be very cheap, ask a friendly glass dealer if they can identify the maker.

Glass can be very distinctive so the more original pieces should be easier to identify than more ordinary ones. When it comes to Mary Gregory glass, this is a style not a make so don't expect to see the name underneath – unless it's modern.

CARNIVAL GLASS JUG

Marigold Carnival glass water pitcher, Field Flower by Imperial, good detail

A&C 29, est £150-180, now worth £100-200

BLUE DECANTERS

Two decanters with 'Hollands' and 'Brandy' in gilt (Courtesy of Somervale Antiques)

A&C 30, est £600-800 now worth £700-900

STOURBRIDGE

A Stourbridge 'Rock Crystal' style bowl, c.1910, with cut glass scrolled decoration, on a pedestal base (HAMP)

A&C 23, est £300-400, now worth £400-600

GEOFFREY BAXTER

A Whitefriars glass vase by Geoffrey Baxter, the most desirable modern designer (COTT)

A&C 25, sold for £35, now worth £300-500

F.W. ALDRIDGE LTD.

UNIT 3, ST JOHN'S INDUSTRIAL ESTATE,
DUNMOW ROAD, TAKELEY, ESSEX CM22 6SP
Telephone 01279 874000/874001   Fax 01279 874002
email angela@fwaldridge.abel.co.uk

www.fwaldridgeglass.com

We are a small family run business that specialises in glass repairs
and supplying blue glass liners.

GLASS REPAIRS We undertake all types of glass repairs such as chipped
glasses, decanters, vases, fruit bowls and cruet bottles - both Antique or
modern glass.

GLASS RESTORATION We restore cracked or broken glassware
including claret jugs, lampshades, decanter stoppers
- making pieces which were once useless, perfect again.

BLUE GLASS LINERS FOR SILVERWARE We hold a large stock of
Bristol Blue Glass liners and can fit most condiments from stock.
Alternatively we can have them specially blown, and supply other colours
such as Cranberry, Green, Amethyst and Clear.

SILVERWARE We can silver plate or repair items to a high standard.

Visit our website to see the many other services we offer not listed,
alternatively call Angela on the number above.

GLASS

VENINI

Handkerchief vase by Venini for Murano, early 20th century, worked with latticino muslin and spiral bands, 21 cm high. This inspired the famous Chance glass versions (CHEF)

A&C 60, sold for £360, now worth £400-600

CRANBERRY GLASS

Oval sweet dish in cranberry glass by Elkington & Co, late Victorian. In a cast silver wire carrier with ribbon tied mount, Birmingham, 1898, 8in wide (AMER)

A&C 31, sold for £340, now worth £400-600

ANSOLO FUGA

Polychrome vase by Ansolo Fuga for Arte Vetraria Muranese 'a canne' vase from around 1960 (SOTH)

A&C 52, sold for £3,840, now worth £3,500-5,000

DAUM POPPY VASE

Daum cameo glass poppy vase, oblong shape acid-etched with naturalistic flowers (GORR)

A&C 53, sold for £260, now worth £400-600

OPALINE SPHERE

Opaline (cloudy) glass box (centre) French, 19th century, with cover and gilt metal mounts, 19cm high (DREW)

A&C 40, sold for £480, now worth £600-800

EARLY BOTTLE

Early green glass bottle with tapering neck and natural iridescence (MALL)

A&C 57, sold for £160, now worth £150-250

Fact File

Lalique is possibly the most famous of all glass makes but not all Lalique is equal. The best buys are the ones with the signature of R. Lalique who started his own glass business in 1902.

Pieces were signed R Lalique from 1914-25 and R Lalique France 1925-50. The most popular signature is in script form which dates from 1914-39. The opalescent (colour like opals) designs remain the favourite with the clear, 1960s+ designs selling for significantly less (eg around £100 for a simpler vase).

If you have the money – or are very lucky – the car mascots are superb designs with the cheapest selling for around £8,000 and the stunning Deco figures or heads worth around £35,000+.

CRYSTAL LUSTRES (DROPS)

Clear glass lustres, Victorian pair, with prismatic drops (five drops missing), 30cm high (SWORD)

A&C 50, sold for £320, now worth £300-500

NOBLE BLUE PLATE

Bristol plate, signed ' I. Jacobs'. With crest for the Earl of Veralum, depicting a stag (Courtesy of Somervale Antiques)

A&C 30, est £1,000-1,500, now worth £1,000-1,500

LALIQUE MERMAID

Lalique 'Sirene' mermaid statuette, opalescent glass c 1920 (GORR)

A&C 54, sold for £2,300, now worth £2,000-4,000

IRIDESCENT GLASS

Loetz-type glass vase with inverted baluster shape and wavy bands against a gold iridescent ground (GORR)

A&C 66, sold for £110, now worth £100-180

LALIQUE BUDGERIGARS

Lalique 'Ceylan' opalescent vase, cat. ref. 905, moulded with four pairs of perched budgerigars (GORR)

A&C 63, sold for £2,300, now worth £,2000-2,800

BOHEMIAN GLASS

Bohemian goblet, vase and covers, scent bottle and a candlestick, all etched, most on a faceted stem (SWORD)

A&C 66, sold for £1,200, now worth £1,000-1,500

SATIN GLASS

Thomas Webb & Sons satin glass Queens Burmese ware vase, factory mark to base. This colouring was popular with US firm Fenton as well (SWORD)

A&C 62, sold for £80, now worth £80-120

GABRIEL ARGY-ROUSSEAU

'Farniente', A Gabriel Argy-Rousseau pate de verre vase, (Bloch-Dermant no. 32-01), after 1932, with rich amethyst colour (SOTH)

A&C 66, sold for £15,000, now worth £12-18,000

CAMEO VASE

Cameo vase by Thomas Webb & Sons from around 1885, with etched banner and GEM./CAMEO mark

A&C 60, sold for £28,200, now worth £26-32,000

Fact File

To a certain extent, the colour of glass is one of the determining factors in its appeal – and price.

Cranberry glass remains the firm favourite, worth between two to four times the price of the less popular amber, depending on the style.

Opaline glass (milk glass) is also very popular and can be mistaken for china at first glance because it is painted inside or outside to create the effect of ceramic. If in doubt, hold it, it will feel like glass and it's worth seeing if some of the paint has peeled away as this will devalue it. Buy with care, there are fakes around – they feel too light or heavy to be real and are easy to spot – when you're looking.

THOMAS WEBB & SONS

Cameo vase by Thomas Webb & Sons from around 1885, with etched banner and GEM/CAMEO mark (CHRIS)

A&C 64, sold for £19,975, now worth £18-25,000

GLASS

LALIQUE

Lalique vase In the Doremy pattern no. 979, 21.5cm high (SWORD)

A&C 53, sold for £600, now worth £600-800

GILTY DETAIL

Large plate in Bristol blue with gilt rim (Courtesy of Somervale Antiques)

A&C 30, est £550-600, now worth £550-650

ART NOUVEAU GLASS

Loetz vase with green iridescence, a tapering body and frill rim, mounted within an Art Nouveau pewter stand (GORR)

A&C 66, sold for £360, now worth £300-500

RUBY GLASS

Venetian composite ruby and clear glass table service, enamelled and gilt with figures in 18th century dress (DREW)

A&C 62, sold for £600, now worth £600-800

Fact File

Glass collecting has changed drastically in the last few years with the 'modern' designers such as Geoffrey Baxter at Whitefriars not just being collectable to the connoisseur but recognised by most people interested in antiques. This is partly because of television. The Baxter colours and textures are so vivid that they are a popular choice with those in the media. Frequent television and magazine coverage has made Baxter's designs instantly recognisable, commanding high prices. A large Drunken Bricklayer vase (one brick sticks out from the rest) in kingfisher blue, the most desirable of the colours, can fetch £1,000. It's worth looking for other Whitefriars, especially the work of the Powell family who owned the glassworks which was known as James Powell & Sons which isn't so recognisable – perfect for collecting

DAUM WINTER LANDSCAPE

Daum vase etched and enamelled 'Winter Landscape', early 20th century, mark, 'Daum, Nancy' and cross of Lorraine

A&C 66, sold for £1,560, now worth £1,500-2,000

BOHEMIAN GLASS

19th century Bohemian cranberry and white overlaid, of baluster outline (FELL)

A&C 56, sold for £260, now worth £250-350

BRITSOL BLUE ROLLING PIN

Rare 19th century Crimea rolling pin, printed and painted 'Bristol' blue glass (SWORD)

A&C 58, sold for £100, now worth £150-250

LALIQUE

Statuette 'Thais', Rene Lalique, after 1925 (Marcilhac No 836) in their famous opalescent glass with its distinctive blue finish (SOTH)

A&C 51, est £6,000-8,000, now worth £6,000-9,000

Just Glass

To Include:
**Mary Gregory ~ Vaseline ~ Cranberry
~ Bristol Blue Glass
& Decanters and Wine Glasses**

Telephone 01434 381263
Shop Mobile 07833994948

Opening Hours
Wednesday and Thursday
11.00—12.30 & 1.30—4.00

Saturday
11.00—4.00

Sunday
12.00—4.00

or by appointment

M.J. Graham, Cross House, Market Place,
Alston, Cumbria

SUSAN MEGSON GALLERY

CREATIVE GLASS ART

*The Susan Megson Gallery is dedicated to
original works in a variety of styles and
forms, featuring over 60 artists from all over
the world — including England, America,
Italy, Australia, Iceland and Czechoslovakia.*

*The inherent qualities of hand blown glass
create a unique piece of time. Each piece
of glass is an original, each piece a creation
and which in its final form stands as a
work of art.*

*The profile of the artist or studio
is a testament to the high quality of work
that the Susan Megson Gallery is
associated with.*

***Digbeth Street   Stow-on-the-Wold
Glos. GL54 1BN
Telephone 01451 870484
Email: SueMegsonGallery@aol.com
& SoHo, New York***

GLASS

CLARET JUGS AND DECANTERS

The wealthy people in the 18th and 19th centuries took their dining and entertaining very seriously, most courses being served with a different type of wine. The claret jugs and decanters of this age were made to be used and also expressed status. Some of them were figural, others used brilliant colours and all are collectable.

DUCK-SHAPED CLARET JUG

A fine Victorian novelty silver-mounted claret jug, Alexander Crichton, London, 1881 (SOTH)

A&C 11, sold for £28,750, now worth £30-40,000

EDINBURGH AND LEITH CRYSTAL

Extensive Edinburgh and Leith crystal service, c.1930s, including decanters (PH ED)

A&C 33, sold for £1,725, now worth £1,500-2,500

LALIQUE DECANTER

This decanter, 1930, decorated with a silhouette of Saint Odile and bearing the moulded mark R Lalique (SOTH)

A&C 61, sold for £600, now worth £600-1,000

LIBERTY CLARET JUG

Pewter-mounted claret jug, 1905, with Liberty's Tudric mark, probably designed by Archibald Knox (1864-1933) (CHRIS)

A&C 61, sold for £2,400, now worth £2,000-3,000

Fact File

According to Samuel Johnson (1709-84), "He who aspires to be a serious wine drinker, must drink Claret". Claret is the British word for all red Bordeaux and was used to distinguish it from red wines from other nationalities. It is quite a dry red wine but highly desirable and deserved a distinctive way of being served – the Claret jug.

The traditional shape is tall and thin with a handle and silver or gold-mounted lid or cover (another name for a lid) although they can be animal-shaped or otherwise whimsical and these are often the most sought after.

The jugs were created around 1830 when industrialisation led to the creation of uniform-sized bottles which replaced barrels in which wine used to be stored. These were not smart enough for dining so elegant jugs were crafted.

SCOTTISH DECANTER

Very large Scottish, crystal presentation decanter (PH ED)

A&C 33, sold for £3,680, now worth £3,000-5,000

DRESSER-INFLUENCE

Victorian silver mounted glass claret jug, of Christopher Dresser inspired design with ebonised bar handle (GORR)

A&C 53, sold for £2,600, now worth £2,500-3,500

RUBY GLASS CLARET JUG

Victorian ruby glass claret jug with plated mount with Bacchus' head, engraved with a crane and prunus blossom (GORR)

A&C 44, sold for £440, now worth £400-600

EWER

Victorian glass ewer c 1870, the pear-shaped body etched with trailing vines and baskets of flowers, 31.5cm high (HAMP)

A&C 45, sold for £540, now worth £500-700

MAPPIN AND WEBB

Mappin and Webb silver-mounted, cut-glass claret jug with flower head pattern, Mappin and Webb, Sheffield, 1900 (SOTH)

A&C 61, sold for £850, now worth £800-1,200

WINE CRUET

Silverplated blue glass wine cruet by H Wilkinson and Co. from around 1835, the tri-form stand with fruiting vine rim (ROSE)

A&C 64, sold for £300, now worth £300-500

ELKINGTON-STYLE

Victorian electroplate and gilt claret jug mount, in the manner of Elkington (CHEF)

A&C 62, sold for £420, now worth £300-600

CRANBERRY DECANTERS

Cranberry decanters, Victorian. Decorated with gilt, white enamel and 'jewelled' ribbon swags, each with clear glass stopper (FELL)

A&C 39, sold for £240, now worth £300-500

TANTALUS

Early-20th century oak tantalus or case, the three decanters pinched into hourglass shape below a plated locking handle, the base 47.5cm wide (CHEF)

A&C 35, est £250 now worth £300-400

SILVER-MOUNTED

A pair of mid-Victorian silver-mounted glass Claret jugs, made in London 1873 (BON)

A&C 8, est £1,500-2,000 now worth £2,000-4,000

STOURBRIDGE

Stourbridge engraved, of globular form with slender neck, trefoil spout and loop handle, resting on a foot (DREW)

A&C 64, sold for £420, now worth £300-500

CRANBERRY CLARET JUG

A Victorian cranberry glass claret jug, mounted with a silver plated hinged lid with an acorn finial, the handle and spout moulded with shells and leaves, the cranberry body tapered and ribbed to a clear glass foot (DAH)

A&C 8, sold for £420, now worth £500-800

Fact File

There were various reasons to use decanters from the late 18th century, one being that bottles were seen as being crude and had no place at genteel gatherings.

On a more practical level, decanting separated the wine from its sediment. In the process, air would be added to the wine which allowed the full bouquet and flavour a chance to expand (modern drinkers now use jugs for this reason).

And then there is the scandalous reason, those wishing for private conversation, away from the servants' ears, could serve themselves instead of waiting for the servant to pour the wine.

When using decanters, always pass to the left except when the decanter has been refilled and then pass, once only, to the guest on your right.

GLASS

GOBLETS AND DRINKING GLASSES

When it comes to wine glasses and goblets, 18th century goblets continue to be the most desirable, apart from Art Deco Lalique versions. The goblets with their twisted stems need hands-on experience to differentiate them from their modern counterparts (beware of fakes) but it's a skill worth learning – with lots of potential profit.

BOHEMIAN GOBLETS

Two pairs of Bohemian goblets, one pink, the other green, enamelled with bright leaf scrolls and gilding (GORR)

A&C 66, sold for £550, now worth £500-700

BRISTOL BLUE GLASSES

Nine Bristol blue rummers of tapering form with knopped stems and six glass beakers (SWORD)

A&C 61, sold for £420, now worth £300-500

ENGRAVED GOBLET

A large Dutch engraved wine glass, mid-eighteenth century (SOTH)

A&C 11, sold for £1,437, now worth £1,500-2,500

TWIST STEM

Colour-twist wine glass from 1770 (SOTH)

A&C 52, sold for £6,110, now worth £5,000-7,000

Fact File

The word goblet derives from the Celtic word meaning mouth or gulp down and goblets tend to be bigger than the average wine glass, one of the reasons for their popularity.

Traditionally, red wine glasses should be larger than white which allows for the bouquet and flavour to enrich itself in the air, whereas white wine is served chilled. Wine has been around for over 6,000 years and is now supposedly at its most popular since Medieval times.

When buying glasses, always check round the rim for tiny chips which can cut lips – these can be easily smoothed out by glass files, just ask a friendly restorer for help.

ETCHED GLASSES

An 18-piece set of etched glasses for drinking sherry, port and wine, plus two other glasses (GORR)

A&C 66, sold for £90, now worth £80-100

COURSING BEAKERS

Four, Victorian, embossed coursing beakers chased with acorn and leaf decoration with gilt interiors, used before or after hunting (SWORD)

A&C 50, sold for £1,500, now worth £1,500-2,000

BEILBY ENAMELLED GLASS

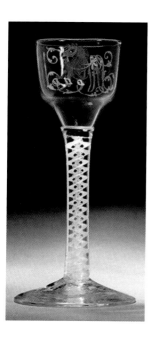

Beilby enamelled wine glass, painted with the crest and monogram of the Horsey family from 1765 (SOTH)

A&C 52, sold for £19,975, now worth £18-24,000

OPAQUE TWIST

Rare two-colour opaque-twist wine glass from 1765 (SOTH)

A&C 52, sold for £31,725, now worth £28-35,000

GLASSES GALORE

From left to right: engraved baluster wine glass, estimated £1,200-£1,800; Dutch-engraved pedestal-stemmed goblet, £400; mid-18th century plain-stemmed wine glass, £820; plain-stemmed wine or cordial glass, £850 (DREW)

A&C 52, est £850, now worth £700-1,000

MARY GREGORY-STYLE

These Mary Gregory-style champagne tumblers, c.1890-1910, are probably Bohemian (Grimes House Antiques)

A&C 39, est £90, now worth £80-120

BEGGAR'S BENISON

Rare 18th century enamelled "Beggar's Benison" opaque-twist wine glass (SOTH)

A&C 52, sold for £16,450, now worth £15-18,000

AIR TWIST STEM

Air twist wine glass on a conical foot (DREW)

A&C 52, sold for £800, now worth £700-1,000

Fact File

Toasting is a ritual form of celebration or respect which dates as far back as 6,000 BC when the ancient Greeks used to add burnt toast to a vessel of wine to remove the bitter taste. Toasting glasses with their thick bodies and short stems are very collectable and most people overlook them, not realising what they are.

The thickness of glass was used to hide how little the glass contained – the idea was to offer respect, not to drink too much. One of the most desirable forms is the Masonic toasting glass. This would bear the symbol of the Freemasons – the square and compass, dating from their times as master builders (stone masonry). Expect to pay £120-150 for normal versions.

GLASS

SCENT BOTTLES

There are two different types of scent or perfume bottles: those created by the manufacturers to sell with the perfume and those created in which to pour the perfume from the previous bottles. Both have a following and some perfumiers such as Guerlain have deliberately created limited edition perfumes for these collectors.

EAGLE-EYED COLLECTOR

Rare yellow glass eagle head scent bottle with hinged lid, 1890s, maker 'D & LS', Birmingham, 18cm (SWORD)

A&C 61, sold for £880, now worth £800-1,200

CAMEO GLASS

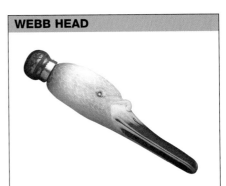

Cameo glass, overlaid in red glass with fruiting foliage and a bronze neck, probably continental, 10cm high (SWORD)

A&C 48, est £400-600, now worth £400-600

WEBB HEAD

A Webb cameo red ground swan's head scent bottle, c.1884, overlaid in white and carved with feathers. Silver hallmarks for 1884, 23cm in length (SOTH)

A&C 25, sold for £5,290, now worth £5,000-7,000

CHINA SCENT BOTTLES

A pair of nineteenth century scent bottles, with enamelled courting couples and hinged, shaped lids (MALL)

A&C 50, sold for £150, now worth £150-200

Fact File

Coco Chanel's favourite number was five. Chanel Number 5 was released in 1921 on May 5 – the fifth day of the fifth month. She was the first couturier who wanted to create a perfume for women who could not afford her clothes but wanted an essence of them.

Chanel's great rival, Elsa Schiaparelli produced one of the most collectable perfume bottles of all time in 1946, Le Roy Soleil. It is linked with three top names – the designer herself, Salvador Dali, the cult artist who designed the bottle and top French glass makers, Baccarat. Named after the famous Sun King (Louis XIV of France), the case is shaped like an oyster shell opening up to reveal a small crystal bottle topped by a sun.

DOUBLE ENDED

Double ended perfume bottles from 1880 with embossed silver lids. (Picture by Lynda Brine, Assembly Antiques)

A&C 53, est £200, now worth £150-250

VINTAGE PERFUME

A Worth perfume bottle (COTT)

A&C 25, sold for £40, now worth £40-70

EDWARDIAN BOTTLES

Pair of Edwardian scent bottles. Silver gilt-mounted glass, 8in high, the screw caps crested with motto. Made by Charles Stuart Harris, London, 1902 (CLEV)

A&C 29, sold for £1,217, now worth £1,400-1,600

STAINED GLASS

Most people think of stained glass in the windows of churches where it was used to depict Biblical stories in an illiterate age. People would know the Bible by heart and the brightly coloured windows would remind them of the stories which best illustrated man's duty to God such as St Christopher bearing Christ on his shoulders.

MORRIS & CO

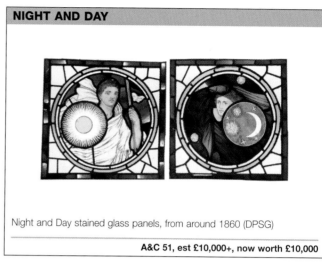

1935 Morris & Co set of stained glass windows from Holyhead's demolished St Seiriol's Church (DPSG)

A&C 51, sold for £40,000, now worth £40,000-50,000

NIGHT AND DAY

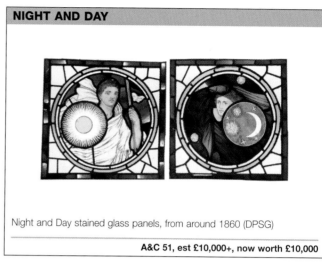

Night and Day stained glass panels, from around 1860 (DPSG)

A&C 51, est £10,000+, now worth £10,000

HERALDIC DEVICE

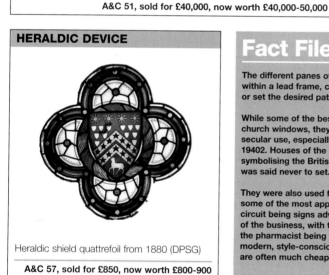

Heraldic shield quattrefoil from 1880 (DPSG)

A&C 57, sold for £850, now worth £800-900

Fact File

The different panes of stained glass would be set within a lead frame, carefully cut to tell the tales or set the desired patterns.

While some of the best examples are seen in church windows, they were also popular for secular use, especially from the 1920s to the 19402. Houses of the era could feature a sun rise, symbolising the British Empire on which the sun was said never to set.

They were also used for shop windows with some of the most appealing on the antiques circuit being signs advertising the name or nature of the business, with the tall colourful bottles of the pharmacist being the best known. For the modern, style-conscious individual, the originals are often much cheaper than brand new versions.

HOME USE

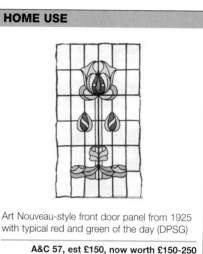

Art Nouveau-style front door panel from 1925 with typical red and green of the day (DPSG)

A&C 57, est £150, now worth £150-250

PAIR OF WARRIOR SAINTS

Pair of very fine Victorian stained glass windows by Burlison & Grylls, 1870, depicting St George and St Michael (Lassco)

A&C 57, est £35,000, now worth £32-38,000

SHEPHERDESS

Shepherdess, part of a larger piece from around 1880 (DPSG)

A&C 57, est £550, now worth £500-700

ST JOHN

Victorian stained glass nave window from 1895, removed from the former Anglican mission Church in Huddersfield, depicting St John the Evangelist (Lassco)

A&C 57, est £9,500, now worth £9,000-11,000

GOLD & SILVER

SILVER
Silver was discovered after gold and copper and has been mined since the Bronze Age for jewellery.
The silver ore also contained lead which poisoned the miners. It was used in coins although its use under the Romans was otherwise fairly limited as it was believed to be sacred. Silver is much cheaper than gold.

SALVER

George III silver salver, engraved with initials 'MC' within a reef. Maker's mark of 'P. Cunningham & Son, Edinburgh 1808' (PH ED)

A&C 34, sold £400, now worth £450-600

PHOTOFRAME

Edwardian silver photoframe by William Comyns, London, 1902. The scrolled mount is pierced with putti (CHEF)

A&C 60, sold for £260, now worth £250-80

GEORGIAN CRUET SET

George III, silver set, in fitted Victorian morocco leather case, all items engraved with 'ATP', possibly by Andrew Fogelberg, London, 1810 (HAMP)

A&C 33, sold for £260, now worth £40-500

Fact File

One of the best all-round designers was Dr Christopher Dresser who was working in silver from about 1878. A skilled craftsman, he rejected the ideals of his contemporaries, the Arts and Crafts movement, and embraced the industrial age, bending the metal to his will and creating designs twenty years ahead of his time. His teapots were not just kettle-shaped but square, angular and one even had a hole in the middle (like the later Polo mint). His work was innovative and has been regenerated in the last 30 years with a teapot selling at Christie's for £80,000. That's the top end of the market but, for more affordable designs, look for Georg Jensen. His stylish teapots, some dating from the 1930s, sell for around £500–6,000 but prices are rising fast so buy quickly.

GOLD MOUNT

A heart-shaped Victorian gold pendant with pavé-set old brilliant cut diamonds (GORR)

A&C 66, sold for £1,400, now worth £1,200-1,800

PIN CUSHION

A novelty silver pin cushion in the shape of a swan. Edwardian, Birmingham 1909 (GORR)

A&C 44, sold for £200, now worth £250–350

PITCHER OF BEAUTY

Jensen & Co water pitcher, 1923, by Jorgen Jensen, Georg's second son

A&C 63, now worth £2-3,000

PEPPER POT

A pepper pot In the form of an owl with red glass eyes, George Fox Victorian silver, London 1852 (GORR)

A&C 62, sold £350, now worth £350-450

TEA KETTLE

A blossom-decorated tea kettle on stand by Jensen dating from 1905

A&C 63, now woth £4-6,000

SCOTTISH SILVER

A Scottish provincial silver bullet teapot by George Cooper, Aberdeen, c1740

A&C 25, sold for £5,750, now worth £7-8,000

GEORG JENSEN

Georg Jensen-designed compote dating from around 1918

A&C 63, now worth £1-2,000

RUSSIAN SILVER AND ENAMEL

Silver and enamel Russian chair, 19th century, by Ivan Saltykov with silver gilt interior, 5.75cm high (SWORD)

A&C 63, sold for £1,450, now worth £1,600

SILVER TANKARD

Late-17th century silver tankard with hollow scrolled handle and hinged domed lid. Makers mark 'H. E.', 17.5cm high (MALL)

A&C 45, sold for £1,500, now worth £2,000

GEORGIAN SILVER

George III silver sugar basket, maker's mark of 'Alexander Gairdner, Edinburgh 1792' (PH ED)

A&C 34, sold for £400, now worth £450-500

DRESSER STYLE

Plated teapot in the style of Christopher Dresser, of circular form with ebonised bar handle, 17.5cm (GORR)

A&C 48, sold for £140, now worth £300-500

GOLD SNUFF BOXES

Gold snuff boxes. Left: Pierre Cerneau, marks of Jean-Jacques Prévost, Paris, 1766. Right: Philippe le Bourlier, marks of Jean-Francois Kalendrin, Paris, 1788. Sold for £7,800 and £3,000 (SOTH)

A&C 66, right sold £3,000, now worth £3,200

GOLD JEWELLERY

Demi-parure in Victorian gold, comprising brooch and earrings (the earrings with later fittings) in a fitted case (FELL)

A&C 41, sold for £700, now worth £800-1,000

Fact File

The letters 'EPNS' stand for electro-plated silver nickel, it means that a thin sheet of silver has been used on top of a nickel base. We call this silver-plate, it's not actually solid silver. A more unusual term is 'EPBM' which is short for electro-plated Britannia metal and is of poorer quality than the EPNS, although it's also plate. Electro-plating involves using electrodes (metal wires) on a piece of metal which is covered by a solution in a tank. A current is passed through the object via the electrodes and this is turned from positive to negative which makes the silver sheet stick to the metal. Initially copper was used but this was replaced by nickel, hence EPNS. The process was used extensively from the 1840s.

GOLD & SILVER

NOVELTY BOX

Russian silver box in the form of a daccha (country house) with finely turned engine decoration, 1874. Russian silver is popular with collectors (MALL)

A&C 52, sold for £2,900, now worth £3-3,500

CANTEEN OF CUTLERY

Standard silver canteen of cutlery, the 12 settings with shaped handles, German late-19th to early-20th century (ROSE)

A&C 60, sold for £580, now worth £550-600

YORK SILVER

Two seal-top spoons. Late-16th to early-17th century, York hallmarks, makers mark indistinct (BRI)

A&C 29, sold for £1,500, now worth £2-2,500

JAMES DIXON & SON

Pair of Edwardian Neo-classical style loaded silver candlesticks, by James Dixon & Son, Sheffield 1903 (AMER)

A&C 35, sold for £770, now worth £800-1000

MAPPIN AND WEBB

A silver dessert set, Mappin and Webb, Sheffield, 1937-38 (SOTH)

A&C 62, sold for £950, now worth £800-1200

MINIATURE

Victorian miniature watering can engraved with initials, Sheffield 1888, by Henry Wilkinson & Co, 4.5cm high x 8.5cm wide (DREW)

A&C 44, sold for £170, now worth £200-250

IRISH DISH RING

An Irish silver dish ring probably John Walker, Dublin, c 1770 (SOTH)

A&C 62, sold for £3,200, now worth £3-3,500

ROMAN GOLD

Gold, garnet and cornelian earrings, third century AD. Quality jewellery is always in demand, these vastly exceeded their estimate (CHRIS)

A&C 64, sold for £23,585, now worth £25,000

Fact File

The Latin word for gold is *aurum* and the word gold refers to its colour, it means 'yellow' although white gold is very popular for jewellery. It is becoming increasingly hard to find old gold except as jewellery because so many older pieces have been melted down. It is a wonderfully rich metal that is seldom pure (24 carats) but tends to be mixed with alloys (for example silver, copper, zinc, lead, etc). 9ct gold means that there are nine parts pure gold and 15 parts alloy. Carat is not an actual weight but a measure of purity, deriving from carob beans (the beans are called Qirat in Arabic) – no one is quite sure why. In Germany and America, 'carat' is spelt 'karat' which can cause confusion.

FABERGE

Carl Peter Fabergé (1846–1920) was born in Russia of French descent. The son of a jeweller, he opened his own workshop in Russia in 1866 before inheriting his father's business. His work with Russian treasures led to the famous Imperial Easter eggs which were made in his workshop.

ENAMEL CLOCK

A silver and guilloche Fabergé enamel table clock from around 1890, signed 'MP' (Michael Perchin), famous for his work on the Imperial eggs (CHRIS)

A&C 64, sold for £23,500, now worth £25,000

RUSSIAN CLOISONNE

Fabergé silver-gilt and cloisonné enamel desk set by Fyodor Rückert of Moscow, a very unusual set (SPI)

A&C 60

CIGARETTE CASE

Carl Fabergé cigarette case, enamelled and set with diamonds 1908 (ROY COL)

A&C 60, from Royal Collection

UNUSUAL FABERGE

Carved hardstone dormouse and snail by Fabergé, 1910 (ROY COL)

A&C 60, from Royal Collection

Fact File

Carl did not create any of the 68 famous Fabergé eggs himself. Instead, they were supervised by two of his employees, Michael Evlampievich Perchin (pieces signed MP until 1903) and Henrik Wigström (signed HW from 1903). His voluntary work at the Russian Hermitage, which contained the precious artefacts of the Tsars, gave him access to Russian treasures. Working with his brother, Agathon, this influenced the work which they exhibited in Moscow where Tsar Alexander III bought a piece. After this, Fabergé became the supplier to the Imperial Court. The first Easter egg was produced for Tsarina Maria in 1884 and the workshop made 56, all containing a surprise, including a carriage for the Coronation of Tsar Nicholas II, Alexander's son. They also produced delicate gold flowers.

DELICATELY CRAFTED FLOWERS

Carl Fabergé, cornflowers and buttercups, 1900 (ROY COL)

A&C 60, from Royal Collection

IMPERIAL CARRIAGE

Fabergé Imperial Easter egg presented by Czar Nicholas II to his wife, the Czarina Alexandra Feodorovna, Easter 1897. All eggs contained surprises such as this carriage (FC)

A&C 60, now worth £10–15,000,000

THE SIZE OF A HEN'S EGG

Fabergé mosaic egg, the colours created by gemstones, 1914 (ROY COL)

A&C 60, from Royal Collection

CUCKOO EGG

Fabergé Imperial Easter egg, 'the Cuckoo' presented by Tsar Nicholas II to his mother, the Dowager Empress Maria Feodorovna, Easter 1900 (FC)

A&C 60, sold for £4–6,000,000

JEWELLERY

JEWELLERY

The emphasis on jewellery has changed from a blatant display of status to more subtle pieces. Costume jewellery has been worn for over 200 years but is now seen as a safer and original alternative to costly precious stones, as well as a stylish choice. When it comes to engagement rings, diamonds are still a girl's best friend.

ART NOUVEAU

Art Nouveau gold locket with a pressed head and shoulders of a lady in period dress (MALL)

A&C 52, sold for £270, now worth £250-350

FRENCH ART NOUVEAU

French silver Art Nouveau pendant with opal and freshwater pearl droppers (FELL)

A&C 39, sold for £240, now worth £300-500

ART DECO

Art Deco 9ct gold necklace, with amethyst line-drop centrepiece, stylish Deco lines (FELL)

A&C 39, sold for £240, now worth £300-400

OPAL AND DIAMOND

Late Victorian brooch or pendant, set with cabochon opal and diamonds, each diamond weighing 0.15-0.5, forming a star (WINT)

A&C 39, sold £9,000, now worth £10-12,000

BASKET BROOCH

Flower basket brooch, openwork design, 9ct white gold and platinum mounted multi-gem set brooch; a common brooch theme (FELL)

A&C 58, sold for £350, now worth £300-500

EDWARDIAN DESIGN

Edwardian brooch or pendant, 9ct gold, set with central amethyst and pearl cluster, with further pearl and amethyst decoration (FELL)

A&C 40, sold for £300, now worth £300-450

PIETRA DURA

Circular Pietra Dura (stone decoration) brooch and matching earrings with shepherd's crook backs, with central floral spray, mounted, and a *pietra dura* brooch depicting doves (MALL)

A&C 45, sold for £320, now worth £300-400

VICTORIAN BROOCH

Victorian gold pendant brooch. Powder blue enamel decoration and pearl detail (FELL)

A&C 51, sold for £400, now worth £350-500

Fact File

As the Birthstone of the Month column in *Antiques and Collectables* shows, there is a lot more to a precious stone than simply its colour. All stones have superstitions, whether you believe them or not but understanding them adds to their appeal.

Garnet, the stone for January, is given to women celebrating their second wedding anniversary or to symbolise friendship. As well as the well-known deep red, it also comes in green and blue which are more costly and attractive alternatives.

And, if diamonds are not colourful enough for you, think again – they come in pink, yellow, champagne, blue and green with pink being the most expensive, while the green sapphire is a much richer colour than an emerald.

RUBY AND DIAMOND

1950s ruby and diamond bracelet (HAMP)

A&C 45, sold £2,500, now worth £3,000-5,000

RUBY CUFFLINKS

Gold mounted cufflinks, set with oval cabochon, synthetic rubies.(GORR)

A&C 56, sold for £150, now worth £180-250

SCOTTISH AGATE BROOCH

Scottish agate brooch In the form of a belt with buckle open centre and silver mounts. Scottish jewellery has a strong following even though they are not expensive gems (MALL)

A&C 44, sold for £250, now worth £250-350

Fact File

Cartier, the famous Art Deco jewellery firm immortalised by Marilyn Monroe (*Diamonds Are a Girl's Best Friend*), was composed of three brothers, Louis, Jacques and Piers Cartier, who inherited the family business. Louis Cartier invented the first man's wristwatch in 1904 for the aviator, Alberto Santos-Dumont. Edward, Prince of Wales, described him as "the jeweller of kings, the king among jewellers".

Their famous Art Deco creations were epitomised by the Tutti Frutti necklace in 1936, composed of emerald, sapphire and ruby stones which looked like large sweets and was made for Daisy Fellowes, the heiress of the Singer sewing machine fortune. The Cartier designs were big, unsubtle and a glorious celebration of how exciting jewellery could be with the right imagination, quality stones and workmanship.

DIAMOND RING

Daisy cluster ring, 18ct gold, nine stones, total diamond weight 2.52ct, popular style (FELL)

A&C 40, sold £1,300, now worth £1,500-1,800

EMERALD RING

Cluster ring emerald 2.66ct and diamonds totalling 1.23ct. Emerald is the birthstone for May and diamond for April (FELL)

A&C 40, sold £1,700, now worth £2,000-2,500

AUSTRO-HUNGARIAN NECKLACE

Mid-19th-century multi-gem necklace from Austro-Hungary, an area famous for its jewellery in this distinct colouring (DREW)

A&C 58, sold for £280, now worth £250-350

CARTIER DIAMOND TIARA

Diamond bandeau by Cartier, c. 1913. Tiaras have come back into fashion for weddings and this one combines top quality stones with one of the best names in jewellery (CHRIS)

A&C 35, sold £131,000, worth £150-200,000

KOKOSHNIK-DESIGN TIARA

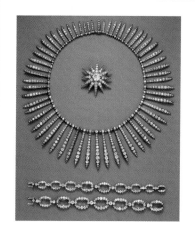

Diamond Kokoshnik-design tiara (CHRIS)

A&C 35, sold £37,600, now worth £50-75,000

KITCHENALIA

KITCHENALIA

One of the most surprising areas of collectables is kitchenalia, old crockery and kitchen implements that most people threw away as soon as the latest gadgets came out. This is one of the many areas of collecting where you can raid your own cupboards because the goods which you're not using could be worth something.

CERAMIC ROLLING PIN

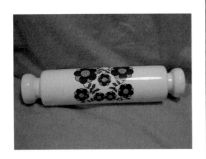

A late 1960s/early 1970s ceramic rolling pin in the style of Midwinter. Plastic stoppers still in each end, no maker's name

A&C, now worth £25-35

T.G. GREEN

Cornish Ware pots by T.G. Green, whilst good starter pieces, they are all fairly common. The flour shaker.is probably the easiest to find

A&C 7, sold for £40-60, now worth £40-60

CHROME GUITAR CRUET

1950s chrome guitar-shaped cruet with blue glass linings to prevent erosion. No markings

A&C, sold for £30, now worth £80-120

JELLY MOULD

19th century copper crown mould, 12.5cm high

A&C 35, est £60-80, now worth £50-60

Fact File

T. G. Green is one of the most sought-after areas of kitchenalia. The company made storage jars, rolling pins, flour shakers and mixing bowls, amongst other kitchen crockery. Their most famous colouring is blue and white, decorated in large stripes. This is Cornish Ware, famously named after one of the sales reps comments on his return from holiday in Cornwall, comparing it to the blue of the Cornish sky and the white of the crests of the waves.

There are a lot of fakes around so be careful when buying – if the pieces look too new or have shiny black backstamps, then leave them. The red and white versions are also being faked. If in doubt, speak to dealers you trust and ask for their advice.

KITCHEN CLOCK

T.G. Green electric wall clock by Smith's, the perfect accompaniment to Cornish Ware

A&C 39, est £500, now worth £300-500

CHROME TOASTER

British-made electric toaster by Hawkins of Drury Lane. Chrome with Bakelite handles, the sides open out to deliver the toast

A&C, sold for £5, now worth £40-50

TONI RAYMOND

Sugar storage jar hand-painted in the distinctive Toni Raymond style, 1951-70s. Attractive and affordable collectables. It's worth buying Toni Raymond animals as well

A&C 7, est £10-15, now worth £10-20

TEA STRAINER

Attractive Art Deco chrome tea strainer designed to sit on the cup. Bakelite handles and an in-built drip-tray

A&C, sold for £2, now worth £20-30

LIGHTS

Period lights add extra style to any house, no matter what the age of your home. Chandeliers are especially desirable. Check that all crystals are there before buying and that your ceilings are strong enough to support their extra weight. The impressive word 'chandelier' replaced 'candelabrum' in 1736.

BENSON

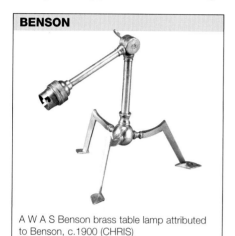

A W A S Benson brass table lamp attributed to Benson, c.1900 (CHRIS)

A&C 23, sold for £293, now worth £400-500

BRONZE

A bronze galleon lamppost finial from the Mall, London. Attributed to Sir Aston Webb, c.1904

A&C 25, sold £1,600, now worth £2,000-2,500

CEILING LIGHT

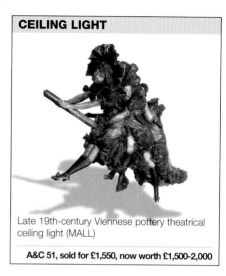

Late 19th-century Viennese pottery theatrical ceiling light (MALL)

A&C 51, sold for £1,550, now worth £1,500-2,000

VICTORIAN GLASS

A pair of moulded Victorian satin glass light shades (SWORD)

A&C 60, sold for £210, now worth £200–250

Fact File

Art Deco lights are very popular because of their curves and chrome finishes. When buying old lights, it's important to check that the wiring has been changed for modern use and is safe. Health and Safety rules mean that it's illegal to sell lights with their original wiring but not all dealers adhere to the rules so ensure that all electrical wires are modernised before plugging in.

Some of the lamps also come with clocks, ideal for use in the bedroom. The large glass Deco light shades which sell for around £80–100 at fairs and auctions (or £30 at car boot sales if you're lucky) are great buys as they jazz up a room and offer an alternative to bland modern cotton or paper shades.

LALIQUE LIGHTING

Boule de Gui, a Lalique hanging light (PHIL ED)

A&C 17, sold for £4,945, now worth £8-10,000

BRONZE LUSTRES

Regency pair of bronze table lustres (lights), supported by eagles on Bristol blue glass plinth bases, 32cm high (SWORD)

A&C 48, sold for £700, now worth £700-900

OIL LAMP

Late 19th-century oil lamp, with a glass reservoir on foliate decorated gilt metal cast column and brass base. Cranberry glass is more desirable (SWORD)

A&C 48, sold for £230, now worth £300–400

BRONZE CANDELABRA

Bronze, black patinated cherubs holding two gilt torches, on a gilt and rouge marble base (SWORD)

A&C 56, sold for £1,750, now worth £2250-2500

Portobello

The world's largest antiques market

Market open every Saturday from 5.30am (shops open Monday to Saturday)

THE RED LION ANTIQUES ARCADE

One this site Susan Garth launched London's First Antiques Market, making Portobello Road an International Institution
Some of the first stall holders are still here!

Red Lion

165–169 Portobello Road

Admiral Vernon
17 39
ANTIQUES MARKET

The Admiral Vernon is the largest, most varied and busiest antiques arcades within Portobello Road.

'The Market in the heart of the the Antique Trading Area'

141–149 Portobello Road

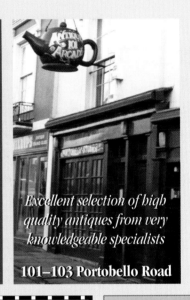

Excellent selection of high quality antiques from very knowledgeable specialists

101–103 Portobello Road

CROWN ARCADE

- 18/19th Century Glass
- Treen
- Boxes
- Paintings • Bronzes
- Sculpture • Silver
- Jewellery • Arts & Crafts • Art Nouveau
- Art Deco

119 Portobello Road

Lipka's
Antiques Gallery

- Advertising Memorabilia • Art Deco
- Art Nouveau • European Porcelain
- Works of Art • Gramophones • Ivory
- Jewellery • Lighting • Music Memorabilia • Period Art Glass • Pewter
- Portrait Miniatures • Prints • Scientific
- Silver • Susie Cooper • Taxidermy
- Tobacco Ephemera • Tortoiseshell
- Toys • Treen • Tribal Art • Watches

282-290 Westbourne Grove

HARRIS'S ARCADE
OPEN ALL WEEK

ANTIQUITIES, COLLECTABLES, ETHNOGRAPHIC, JEWELLERY, LACE, LINEN, PAINTINGS, PERIOD COSTUME, PHOTOGRAPHS, PRINTS, SILVER, TRIBAL, SPORTING MEMORABILIA, MAPS, WATCHES

161/163 PORTOBELLO ROAD

The World Famous
Portobello Market

Totally secured units with steel shutters available, please call
020 7727 5240

www.portobellogroup.com

Dealer stall enquiries 0207 727 5240 or 07956 851 283

MAPS AND ATLASES

The geographical prints show evidence of man's exploration with new countries being added over the centuries. There are versions from the Middle Ages when the world was believed to be flat and explorers travelling too far would fall off the edge. There are even atlases which mark 'here be dragons', denoting the beliefs of the age.

JOHN SPEED, SUFFOLK

Map of Suffolk by John Speed, hand-coloured with crests and pictures (SWORD

A&C 53, sold for £400, now worth £400-500

BERKSHIRE

'Barkshire described', double page engraved map with hand colouring, picture of Windsor Castle, by John Speede (MALL)

A&C 60, sold for £480, now worth £400-600

EAST ANGLIA

Map of Norfolk by John Speed and Christopher Saxton sold with a map of Suffolk by Christopher Saxton (SWORD)

A&C 63, sold for £380, now worth £400-500

MIDDLESEX

Hand-coloured map engraving of Middlesex, a county which has changed its borders several times to include parts of Essex (SWORD)

A&C, est £60-100, now worth £100-200

Fact File

One of the most famous maps is the Mappa Mundi, the map of the world, created in around 1290 and signed by Richard de Haldingham e de Lafford who is believed to be Richard de Bello, Prebendary of Lafford in Lincoln.

It recorded the world in terms of geographical and spiritual meaning with Jerusalem in the centre and Christ at the top of the circular map.

Made of vellum (animal skin), the map is mainly in black 'ink' although the Red Sea is drawn in red. There are also descriptions of inhabitants of the far away lands, including the imaginary Phanesii who are represented as having huge ears which they would wrap around themselves to keep warm. Hereford's location was shown by a drawing of the cathedral.

HERTFORDSHIRE

Hand-coloured engraving of the south-eastern county, showing parts of Bedfordshire and Essex as well, sold with another (SWORD)

A&C, est £100-150, now worth £100-200

ATLAS

A 'New General Atlas', Edinburgh 1821, 74 double page and folding maps (MALL)

A&C 58, sold for £1,900, now worth £1,500-2,000

1777 SUFFOLK

Collection of 16 map sheets from Chapman and André's 1777 edition, including a plan of Colchester and Harwich Harbour (SWORD)

A&C, sold for £60, now worth £300-500

SAMPLER MAP

An embroidered sampler map of Ireland by Susan Campbell Douglas, dated 1818, 53cm x 57cm, in period Rosewood frame (HAMP)

A&C 8, sold for £1,250, now worth £1,000-2,000

METALWORK

BRONZE

The richly coloured metal, bronze has been important throughout the ages, starting with the Bronze Age over 5,000 years ago. This was a period when weapons were crafted out of the metal but bronze is now used for sculpture, heavy metal figures that withstand the elements and are designed for both indoor and outside use.

BUDDHAS

Near pair of 19th-century, gilt-bronze Sino-Tibetan Buddhas on pierced bases with concealed prayer sections (GORR)

A&C 61, sold for £800, now worth £700-900

JAMES OSBOURNE

James Osborne (1940-1992) *Running Rhinoceros*, bronze with 'movement', signed and editioned 4/10 to the underside (RT)

A&C 13, sold £1,800, now worth £2,000-4,000

VERDIGRIS

Italian bronze water fountain in the form of a putto, on a shaped base, oxidised (MALL)

A&C 58, sold for £700, now worth £600-800

HUNTERS

Bronze statue of Pointers from around 1890 by Eglantine Lemaitre entitled *Au Coup De Fusil*, 27cm x 44cm (SWORD)

A&C, sold for £2,700, now worth £2,800-3,200

BRONZE HORSE

Bronze horse by Apul Edouard Brierre, on a naturalistic cast base, 23cm high (DREW)

A&C 40, sold for £140, now worth £150-250

Fact File

Bronze is an alloy of copper with up to one third being tin. This occurs naturally, rendering the metal dark brown. It can turn green in the air (oxidising), this is known as verdigris.

Figures are not carved out of the metal, rather the molten bronze is poured into moulds, based on the original plaster figure which the artists created. They are often made up of several parts which are then melted together to create the whole figure. The same mould can be used for several figures although they would set ever so slightly differently, making each unique.

Some of Rodin's figures were not intended to be cast in bronze but were created posthumously, making moulds from the original statues.

ALEXANDRE FALGUIERE

French bronze figure of *Esclave au Collier*, cast from the model by Alexandre Falguiere, c. 1880. Inscribed *Falguiere d'apres Gerome* and *Goupil et Cie Editeurs 123*, 39cm (CLEV)

A&C 39, sold £1,500, now worth £2,000-3,000

UNIFORMED FIGURES

A pair of figures in uniform, made of metal, probably bronze, and ivory with worn Continental marks (maker BHM) and London import marks for 1922 and 1923 (WINT)

A&C 38, sold for £1,500, now worth £2-2,500

ART DECO FIGURE

Austrian, cold painted, semi nude lady dancing, with coiled snake, on circular onyx plinth, 23cm (GORR)

A&C 45, sold for £400, now worth £800-1,000

THE THINKER

Bronze male seated beside a vice in thoughtful pose on a stepped base to give depth (BRI)

A&C 44, sold for £680, now worth £600-800

BRONZE TAZZA

Described as a bronze tazza (shallow wine cup) and with putti detail (ROSE)

A&C 12, sold for £620, now worth £800-1,200

WARRIOR AND CAMEL

Painted, cold cast bronze model of a Sudanese warrior, seated upon a camel, with impressed marks, by Franz Bergman (AMER)

A&C 35, sold for £820, now worth £800-1,200

SPELTER FIGURES

Male and female farm workers made of spelter – often mistaken for bronze but lighter, not as good quality and cheaper (GORR)

A&C 62, sold for £80, now worth £60-100

MACAW

Large bronze Macaw. Early 20th century, cold-painted, Austrian, painted in polychrome, 76cm (SOTH)

A&C 29, sold £8,050, now worth £12-15,000

MOREAU FAMILY

Bronze cherubs with swags, French, late 19th century, by one of the Moreau family, famous for their bronze figures which are highly sought after (GORR)

A&C 60, sold £2,200, now worth £2,000-3,000

Fact File

Some sculptors would add patinas (in this case, surface of the bronze altered by chemicals) to their bronze figures to create shadows and interest. The acclaimed British sculptor, Henry Moore is quoted as saying that he would apply patina to a figure the opposite way that a woman would apply make-up; he was seeking to intensify the curves. Patina can, however, be badly applied and some of the later Rodin bronzes (cast after the artist's death) have such unsubtle and unsympathetic patinas that they can deter buyers. The simple rule is, it's meant to complement the piece, not look like boot polish. Patina also occurs naturally and is a sign of a piece's age. As such, take care with cleaning as you could ruin a desirable finish.

SANDRINGHAM HOUSE

Bronze bust of young girl, signed A Drury, paper label, 'Sandringham House' (SWORD)

A&C 57, sold £2,300, now worth £2,000-3,000

THIEBAUT FRES FOUNDRY

A figure of a nude with a snake, French, late 19th century. Bronze, brown patina, with the Thiebaut Fres foundry stamp (SOTH)

A&C 17, sold £3,450, now worth £6,000-8,000

MENE BULL

P J Mene, bronze bull with nut brown patination, standing on an oval base cast with vegetation, on black marble plinth (GORR)

A&C 47, sold £2,800, now worth £3,000-4,000

ARAB SCRIBE

Bronze model of an Arab scribe seated on a low chair, Austrian, cold cast tinted (MALL)

A&C 48, sold for £120, now worth £150-200

EQUESTRIAN FIGURE

Bronze horse and jockey after the original by Pierre Jules Mene, 68cm (SWORD)

A&C 62, sold £1,400, now worth £1,400-1,800

MILKMAID

E Barillot, bronze and ivory figure of a milkmaid wearing gilt patinated clothes, signed Gebr. Broodel, Berlin (GORR)

A&C 62, sold £1,300, now worth £1,200-1,500

PUTTI

Bronze putti, representing summer, on marble bases, 19th century, 22cm (SWORD)

A&C 64, sold for £600, now worth £500-700

DANCING FAUN

A late 19th/early 20th-century bronze figure of *The Dancing Faun*. Weathered patination (RT)

A&C 9, sold for £580, now worth £1,000-1,500

JEAN-AUGUSTE BARRE

Figure of the ballerina Marie Taglioni by Jean-Auguste Barre (1811-1896) French (SOTH)

A&C 30, sold £11,500, now worth £12-18,000

Fact File

Some of the most famous bronze figures made for commercial use, not public statuary or private commissions, date from the Art Deco period where bronze was teamed with ivory or an ivory-replacement – cryselephantine.

These are mainly dancers, some based on the performers at the Ballet Russe. The detailing is exquisite, something to check when buying as thousands of copies (fakes or repros) have been produced but the originals are beautifully done.

The two top sculptors were Demetre Chiparus and Ferdinand Preiss and their works are highly desirable and generally signed.

Avoid polishing the bronze as this could ruin the gentle patina. Check that the ivory is not cracked as this will devalue them.

DANCING DECO FIGURE

Art Deco bronze dancing figure by Josef Lorenzl, on green marble plinth base (GORR)

A&C 61, sold for £600, now worth £500-800

METALWORK – PEWTER, BRASS, PLATE AND COPPER

Non-precious metals such as bronze, brass and copper are generally referred to as metalwork. As previously seen, these metals contributed to the Arts and Crafts and Art Nouveau eras, being moulded into fluid shapes, especially with leaves and flowers. The molten metal could be created into wonderful and practical forms.

ART NOUVEAU

Art Noveau log box made of hammered and studded copper with a stylised curvilinear motif to two of the sides. 48cm (FELL)

A&C 44, sold for £320, now worth £300-450

PEWTER

Five Glasgow lidded measures, mid-19th century, largest 18cm, the lids originated to protect the drinkers from the Plague (SWORD)

A&C 38, est £600-800, now worth £700-1,000

TEA URN

Sheffield Tea Urn, early 19th century, with two leaf chased handles, on a square base with paw feet. 27cm x 37cm high (DREW)

A&C 44, sold for £420, now worth £400-600

TAPPIT HEN

Rare Imperial half-gallon tappit hen (a large mug with a knobbed lid) by Robert Whyte of Edinburgh, c. 1830, 30.5cm (SOTH)

A&C 38, est £500-800, now worth £600-800

Fact File

Many rural pubs contain the most basic of metalwork, the horse brass. These were originally used from the late 19th century by the Romanies who would attach them to the harness of their horses to ward off evil. These amulets soon increased in popularity and were even used by the royal family. Although cheap brass was the preferred option, some were made of more costly silver. They were highly decorative and some of the symbols had meanings, including the square and compass which the Freemasons used on their versions. Heraldic versions were made, some grand estates using their family crest on the brasses and these are very collectable among connoisseurs but check that they are nicely moulded as the modern reproductions are crude by comparison.

FLAGON

A pewter Beefeater flagon, c. 1680. Stamped with the William III verification mark, 22.5cm high, some damage (SOTH)

A&C 11, sold £3,680, now worth £4,000-6,000

HOROSCOPE PANEL

Brass panels featuring the Zodiac signs, Pisces, Cancer, Scorpio and Libra for the lift grille at Selfridges, London, before 1928. C A Llewellyn-Roberts (SOTH)

A&C 52, est £5-8000, now worth £10-20,000

TUDOR BRASS

A rare Tudor brass candlestick, English, mid-16th century, 33.5cm (SOTH)

A&C 21, sold £13,800, now worth £15-20,000

PEWTER PLATES

Two single reeded rim pewter dishes, early-18th century, one by William Smith. Marks polished, 42cm (SOTH)

A&C 38, est £300-500, now worth £350-550

MILITARIA

MEDALS

Medals are some of the most meaningful areas of collecting, the most obvious versions rewarding those who risked and possibly lost their lives for their country. The most common date from the two World Wars because of the sheer numbers of those involved. Other medals celebrate achievement in life-saving, work or sport.

BLUES AND ROYALS

Military bar brooch for the Blues and Royals, in enamel and rose diamond (FELL)

A&C 40, sold for £320, now worth £300-400

EGYPT MEDAL

Scots Fusilier Guards. Egypt Medal 1882, Clasp 'Tel El Kebir' and Khedive's Star 1882

A&C 7, est £100-150, now worth £200-400

RNLI

When they do come up for sale, long service medals prove very popular with collectors

A&C 48, est £300-500, now worth £350-550

SOUTH AFRICA SERVICE

South African service medals, 1877-79 (GORR)

A&C 57, sold for £550, now worth £400-600

KNIGHT'S CROSS OF THE IRON CROSS

Knight's Cross of the Iron Cross 48mm x 48mm, excluding the eyelet. Awarded for military leadership and individual acts of bravery. Aproximately 7,300 were awarded (Photo courtesy of The Old Brigade, Kingsthorpe)

A&C 1, est £2,500-3,500, now worth £3,000-5,000

CHILD-BEARING AWARD

Mothers' Cross comes in bronze, silver and gold. Bronze was awarded for four or five children, silver for six or seven and gold (shown here) for eight or more children

A&C 1, sold for £50-100, now worth £100-300

OUTSTANDING BRAVERY

Rare gold medal awarded for outstanding bravery (Picture courtesy of Eastbourne Lifeboat Museum)

A&C 48, est £1,200-2,500, worth £1,500-2,800

Fact File

The British War medal in silver (First World War) and 1939-45 Star in bronze with standard clasp from the Second World War, which were given to all who served to show their service, are still very common and, despite the bravery behind their presentation, often sell for around £8-10 each. The ribbons on their own sell for £3-5 each.

One of the most sought-after medals of recent times is the VC, the Victoria Cross, which was first awarded in 1856 for extraordinary gallantry during wartime.

One sold at Spink's in April 2004 for a record £235,250. It had been awarded to RAF warrant officer, Norman Jackson who crawled onto a wing of his Lancaster Bomber to put out a fire – at 20,000 feet.

UNIFORMS

The army uniform has changed distinctly over the years, the brilliant red of the Victorian era, symbolic of the Empire, giving way to camouflage green as modern soldiers try to be inconspicuous as opposed to dominating. Uniforms hold a fascination with collectors, some of whom wear them, others simply admire.

DRAGOONS 1871

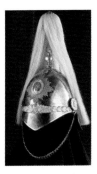

6th Inniskilling Dragoons Officer's helmet. A rare 1871 pattern example (BOS)

A&C 13, sold for £2,600, now worth £2,500-3,500

PERSIAN WARRIORS

A Persian kulah-khud (left), sold for £529. A fur-lined leather dress helmet (right), sold for £138 (PHIL)

A&C 12, left sold £529, now worth £600-800

GRENADIER'S HELMET

A 19th-century grenadier's helmet (SWORD)

A&C 51, sold for £620, now worth £550-700

JAPANESE ARMOUR

Two Japanese cuirass Do breast and backplates, both in good condition. The armour on the left sold for £900 while the other fetched £875 (WA & WA)

A&C 9, left sold £900, now worth £1,500-12,500

Fact File

Jackets and helmets are the most sought-after features of military uniform. Jackets should be checked carefully before buying to ensure that their buttons are from the correct era and are all there. Belts should be attached or their absence calculated into the price (£30+ depending on the era) and look for damage.

And there's the snag; these uniforms were worn into battle, you almost expect to see stains from blood and holes from sabres or bullets. That's part of the thrill, knowing that these clothes had been at some of the fiercest, most historic battles of the last few centuries. People collect the glamour associated with these eras and conflicts. Nazi, and especially Gestapo, uniforms are very good collectables, despite their history.

PERSIAN HELMET

A 19th-century Persian Qjar kulah-khud in good condition (WA WA)

A&C 9, sold for £1,000, now worth £2-4,000

12th LANCERS

A Victorian Trooper's full dress uniform, 12th Lancers, in very good condition (WA & WA)

A&C 9, sold for £775, now worth £1,000-1,250

SPORRAN

79th (Q O Cameron Highlanders) Officer's sporran. A rare, pre-1881 example with three battle Honours 'Peninsula', 'Egypt' and 'Waterloo' (BOS)

A&C 13, sold £1,200, now worth £1,500-2,000

GOVERNOR OF AUSTRALIA

Uniform, ceremonial sword and medals awarded to Colonel Sir William Campion, Governor of Australia 1924-1931 (GORR)

A&C 52, sold for £1,600, now worth £1,5002,500

MILITARIA

WEAPONS

This area of collecting has been subject to bureaucracy in recent years and it is now illegal to sell swordsticks (blades hidden in walking sticks). Part of the pleasure of collecting weapons is the feeling of danger and history that they bring. Swords are very popular (beware of reproductions which have the wrong balance), as are guns.

GEORGE III GUN

George III Tower pattern flintlock muzzle loading gun, with shoulder strap, 140cm (SWORD)

A&C 50, sold for £1,300, now worth £1,000-1,800

REMINGTON REVOLVER

Six-shot army percussion revolver, signed patented 14 September, 1858, E Remington & Son Lion, New York (SWORD)

A&C 57, sold £1,500, now worth £1,500-2,000

BLUNDERBUSS

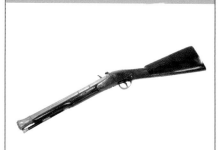

Flintlock blunderbuss Jackson, with struck brass multi-stage barrel belled at the muzzle and full wood stock (GORR)

A&C 61, sold £1,300, now worth £1,500-2,000

LOADED TO THE HILT

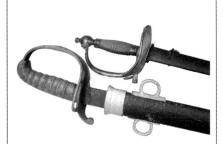

George III infantry officers sword and Royal Artillery officers sword, both with etched blades (SWORD)

A&C 48, sold for £700, now worth £800-1,200

Fact File

If you collect or are thinking of collecting guns, check with the police about whether you need to have a licence. It is illegal to own a gun in the UK without one, even wartime guns.

A Winchester used in the Battle of Little Big Horn raised $648,000 (£360,000) at auction in America but less important guns are very affordable which is part of their appeal. Swords can also make attractive and fascinating collectables; the more decorative the hilt, the higher the price, although their history and age are also vitally important.

Second World War weapons are a niche area with daggers carrying the Nazi Swastika, once a symbol of peace, being highly desirable. Always unsheathe daggers before buying to check for rust and damage. These and similar goods can be found at militaria fairs.

RAPIER

Mid-17th century English rapier with a pierced and stylised shell hilt, later wire grip (SWORD)

A&C 50, sold £2,300, now worth £2,000-2,500

PERCUSSION PISTOLS

Percussion pistols by H James, London, each with flat top barrel, dolphin hammer and Damascus barrels (SWORD)

A&C 58, sold £1,650, now worth £1,500-2,000

DOUBLE-BARREL RIFLE

Double-barrel rifle, No 3452 by Alex Henry Edinburgh, the 65cm barrels with file cut rib (LYON)

A&C 43, sold £1,400, now worth £1,800-2,200

POCKET PISTOL

Pocket percussion pistol, the octagonal barrel with struck marks, engraved brass lock plate and engine-turned wood stock (GORR)

A&C 65, sold for £160, now worth £100-200

GENERAL MILITARIA

Some of the most attractive forms of militaria are the centrepieces for the officer's dining table. These are lavishly decorated items, generally silver, which have symbols to show the regiment's history, for example elephants for those that have served in India. Hat badges are also popular and affordable collectables and sell for £8 or more.

LOVE TOKEN

Royal Air Force 1950s 'Sweetheart' brooch in 9ct gold, red and green enamel with diamond-set wings. Given to loved ones (Picture courtesy of Pragnell's Antiques)

A&C 41, est £1,100, now worth £1,000-1,500

SMUTS

Rt Hon J C Smuts, Shorter & Son prototype character jug, 15cm high (POTT)

A&C 34, sold for £210, now worth £400-600

MOUNT AUSTIN BARRACKS

Nineteenth-century primitive oil on canvas depicting Mount Austin Barracks, 45cm x 53cm (CLEV)

A&C 35, sold £3,200, now worth £3,500-5,000

SNUFF BOXES

Early 19th-century Stobwasser, snuff box made of papier mâché, commemorating military victory by the allies, 1813 (GORR)

A&C 56, sold for £600, now worth £500-800

Fact File

When it comes to militaria, some people collect a theme such as medals or everything connected to a regiment. With so many changes being made to regiments in recent years, including the demise of some of the older or more popular regiments, there is additional nostalgia attached, especially among those who once served.

Some of the most poignant items are ephemera, letters or postcards from those who were serving, letters of citation with medals or, most tragically, the telegrams informing their loved ones of their death or that they were missing in action. Books are also extremely popular, with collectors often choosing one particular conflict on which to concentrate. The Crimean War and Boer War offer a lot of potential.

WARTIME CHESS SET

Unusual German carved wood political set, Allies versus Germans (GORR)

A&C 56, sold for £900, now worth £800-1,500

SATIRE

Types Militaires Angleterre 1862 Highlander, coloured caricature lithograph, by Draner. 29cm x 20cm, stained in margin, framed and glazed (PH ED)

A&C 34, sold for £350, now worth £350-500

RECRUITMENT POSTER

Clever WWI recruiting poster in the form of a theatre bill for The Buffs in *The Road to Berlin* at The Empire. Attracted the interest of David Dickinson from BBC's *Bargain Hunt* (CANT)

A&C 35, sold for £190, now worth £200-400

ROYAL HORSE GUARDS

Copeland figure of an officer of the Royal Horse Guards. His uniform, dating from the era of the Battle of Waterloo, bears the mark of T Goode & Co, the retailers (BOS)

A&C 13, sold for £600, now worth £800-1,000

NAVAL

MARITIME HISTORY

2005 is a big year for anyone interested in naval memorabilia. It marks the bicentenary of the Battle of Trafalgar and the death of Admiral Nelson and there will be lots of limited edition collectables being released for the occasion as well as, far more exciting, genuine memorabilia – of all naval battles, not just Trafalgar.

HORATIO NELSON

19th-century reverse glass print celebrating Admiral Lord Nelson (CLEV)

A&C 35, sold for £560, now worth £600-900

ADMIRAL VISCOUNT DUNCAN

Medallion of Admiral Viscount Duncan, 1798, a naval hero and popular figure (SOTH)

A&C 51, sold for £681, now worth £600-900

WOOLWORK PICTURE

Woolwork picture of three masted Naval vessel flying the White Ensign (MALL)

A&C 57, sold for £750, now worth £700-900

MARITIME PAINTING

Oil Boats By Ronald Ossory Dunlop

A&C 33, sold £950, now worth £1,200-1,500

Fact File

While maritime collectables from the famous luxury liners such as Titanic, Queen Mary and Queen Elizabeth are big business, naval collectables are bought by those fascinated by war at sea. The trouble with naval memorabilia is that some of the best pieces went down with the ships when they sank which is why it's such a challenging area to collect.

The great heroes such as Field Marshall Horatio Kitchener, who drowned when his ship, HMS Hampshire, was sunk off the Orkneys in 1916 during the First World War sea battles, have been preserved in poster or figural form. Kitchener's most famous offering is the recruitment poster with his face and finger pointing above the famous slogan, 'Your Country Needs You'.

MAN OF WAR

An early Victorian woolwork picture of a British three masted man-of-war, 36.5 x 48cm (CHEF)

A&C 48, sold for £950, now worth £1,000-1,200

PRATTWARE PLAQUE

A rare oval Prattware plaque moulded with portrait of Admiral the Earl Howe in uniform flanked by trophies of war. 212mm high, c. 1794, some restoration (SPEC AUC)

A&C 7, sold £1,600, now worth £2,000-4,000

1930'S SILVER MASCOT

A 1930s silver lifeboat mascot

A&C 48, est £130, now worth £200-400

NELSON MINIATURE

This miniature of Nelson by Henry Bone is very collectable and was painted in 1812 (BEA)

A&C 48, sold £12,500, now worth £15-20,000

Freephone: 0800 169 1066 • Freephone: 0800 169 1066

Coins of the Realm©

Dealers in Precious & Historical Coinage

• **2004 Bullion Sovereigns still available** •

2005 Bullion Sovereigns available from mid January 2005

We also carry in stock:

• Shipwrecked Gold •

• Ancient Coins •

• Proof Sets •

• Kruggerands •

and many others. Please call our freephone number below for more details.

Freephone: 0800 169 1066 • Freephone: 0800 169 1066

Coins of the **Realm** Ltd P.O. Box 2662 Romford RM6 6WJ • Fax: 0208 911 8247
www.coinsoftherealm.com   email: admin@coinsoftherealm.org

ORIENTAL CERAMICS AND DESIGNS

For most people, Chinese ceramics can be summed up by blue and white, and Japanese by the red, blue and white of Imari design. Their styles have contributed greatly to the history of ceramics and influenced the West, including the famous blue and white colouring. But they created far more than just that one colour combination.

JAPANESE CLOISONNE

Japanese Cloisonne wall plaque, depicting a peacock displaying to a pea hen (MALL)

A&C 52, sold £1,150, now worth £1,000-1,500

IMARI DISHES

Two square Japanese Imari dishes from the Meiji period, 1868-1912 (WO WA)

A&C 34, sold for £600, now worth £600-800

IMARI CHARGER

19th century Imari charger, 47cm span (LW)

A&C 34, sold for £1,500, now worth £1,500-2,500

IMARI PLATE

Pierced-edge Imari plate with attractive blossom design, c.1900, 25cm diameter (LW)

A&C 34, est £150-180, now worth £160-220

Fact File

Tea originated from the East. Chinese and Japanese teas are lighter in colour and more delicate in taste than their Indian counterpart. Whereas in the West we drink tea out of cups, in the East they use tea bowls, reminiscent of our sugar bowls but smaller and more delicate. These sometimes came with covers (lids) and sometimes with saucers.

Blue and white originated in China in 8AD, almost 12 centuries before Spode discovered its secrets and some of the most desirable pieces in that colouring date from the Ming Dynasty (1368-1644). Chinese ceramics are a very specialist area and their value is often overlooked at general auction houses, which is why it's a great area to learn – take advantage of other people's lack of knowledge and you could pick up some attractive bargains.

LIBATION CUP

Libation cup made from Chinese rhinoceros horn, the sides carved in relief with a stylised band of lotus (GORR)

A&C 56, sold for £1,700, now worth £1,500-2,000

CLOISONNE VASE

Japanese, from around 1880, the metal body has panels of hawks, prunus flowers and cranes (SWORD)

A&C 60, sold for £1,400, now worth £1200-1600

FUKUGAWA VASES

Pair of 19th century Japanese Imari vases, made by the Fukugawa factory (WO WA)

A&C 34, sold for £1,200, now worth £1,800-2,200

CHINESE IMARI-STYLE TEAPOT

18th century Chinese Imari-style teapot. The colours are harsher than the original Japanese Imari and the pattern stronger (WO WA)

A&C 34, est £200, now worth £500-700

POTTERY JAR

Black-painted red Neolithic pottery jar, 14 inches high, 2500 BC, probably used to carry wine or water (Image by Nicholas S Pitcher)

A&C 62, est £1,800-2,000, now worth £1,800-2,200

FISH BOWLS

Chinese pottery pair, modern, on hardwood stands, 52cm diameter (SWORD)

A&C 63, sold for £420, now worth £400-600

QIANLONG DYNASTY VASE

Qianlong dynasty porcelain vase 17th century with some damage and faulty glaze (BEAR)

A&C 42, sold £110,000, now worth £100-150,000

MING DYNASTY

Pair of beautiful Ming Dynasty blue and white 'meiping' with original covers, 11 inches high. Dating from the first half of the 16th century (Image by Nicholas S Pitcher)

A&C 62, est £6,000-6,500, now worth £6,000-6,500

ANDO VASE

Ando vase from the Meiji/Taisho Period, worked in silver wire of varying gauge with nine butterflies and moths, 23.5cm (SOTH)

A&C 48, sold for £7,637, now worth £8,000-10,000

Fact File

Japan's most famous ceramic export was Imari which influenced many English potteries including Mason's, Royal Crown Derby, Welsh Gaudy and even Wadeheath. Whilst the pottery was based in Arita in the Hizen Province on the island of Kyushu, it was named after Imari, the small port where it was shipped to other parts of Japan and where the Dutch would export it. Korean artisans were kidnapped and forced to create the famous porcelain. It was the Korean prisoners in the early 17th century who first created porcelain in Japan and their skill was greatly admired. China, the traditional supplier of porcelain to the West, stopped trading because of politics and Imari took over until renewed Chinese competition and a trade embargo stopped exports from Japan.

ARITA DOGS

A pair of rare Arita dog figures late 17th century, each seated and wearing a collar tied in a bow at the back (SOTH)

A&C 48, sold for £32,900, now worth £30-45,000

MING DYNASTY FIGURINES

These glazed Ming Dynasty (1368-1644) figurines, originally part of a long ceremonial procession. Valued at £175 each (From the 'Kingdom of the Dragon' Exhibition at Fortnum & Mason)

A&C 62, sold for £175, now worth £300-500

STONEWARE TERRAPINS

Unusual Japanese stoneware model of three terrapins, Meiji period, brown glazed, in imitation of bronze, two character seal mark to base, 31.5cm long, some damage (HAMP)

A&C 34, sold for £400, now worth £500-800

A rare and massively potted Chinese white-glazed pottery wine ewer. Tang Dynasty, c. 8th century AD. 18 inches. Oxford Test.

A pair of attractive Chinese cloisonne enamel censers. 18th century. 6 inches wide.

NICHOLAS S PITCHER
Oriental Ceramics & Works of Art

Telephone 0207 499 6621
Fax 0207 499 6621
Mobile 07831 391 574
Email nickpitcher@aol.com

www.asianart.com/pitcher

ASIAN ART
IN LONDON

Participant in Asian Art in London. Gallery exhibition 4–12 November 2004
Also exhibiting at Arts of Pacific Asia Show, New York, March 31–April 3, 2005

Lamont Fine Art

Francois Richard de Montholon, French Born 1856
oil on canvas, 18x12 inches

Lamont fine Art established in 2003. We are dealing with fine paintings from the 19th century along with British and Irish Art and modern Sculpture.

We aim to supply our clients with the best quality art along with value for money and an efficient service before and after sales. We are able to offer a home viewing service but if you would like to view paintings we can arrange for you to do this in relaxed surroundings on a private estate in Leicestershire.

We hold a wide range of stock in both price and style and hope we have something for every collector.

Raymond Desvarreux, French 1876–1961
oil on canvas, 18x13 inches

To contact Michael Brew please call 07790 006347
or email: info@lamontfineart.com

www.lamontfineart.com

IVORY, NETSUKES AND FIGURES

Ivory is made from the tusks of elephants and prices have risen after a ban was imposed on the selling of any ivory less than 50 years old. Buyers are being advisedly cautious at the moment with some refusing to buy anything not obviously old or without a guarantee. Already high ivory Netsuke prices have risen still further.

WOODEN HORSE

A recumbent wooden horse by Tametaka, Nagoya, dated late 18th century (SOTH)

A&C 12, est £3,750-4,000, now worth £4,000-6,000

IVORY MICE

Meiji ivory mice, scrambled together in various positions, with coloured stone eyes (GORR)

A&C 50, sold for £900, now worth £1,000-2,000

EBONY HORSE

A recumbent horse in ebony by Tanaka Minko, Tsu, 1735-1816, a popular pose (SOTH)

A&C 12, est £1,600-1,800, now worth £3,000-4,000

DEVIL ON A FISH

A 19th century ivory netsuke by Masa-Tsugu of Osaka. This netsuke depicts an oni (devil) on a fish

A&C 12, est £1,100, now worth £2,000-4,000

Fact File

Netsukes are actually toggles and would be worn by the wealthy Japanese man to prevent the sash (obi) around his kimono falling open.

Kimonos didn't have pockets and so the men would keep everything we would keep in pockets (such as money) in a pouch tied to the sash. Without the netsukes, the sash would unravel and the pouch fall to the ground. The word means 'root for fastening' and was so-called because many were made of wood although they were also carved out of ivory, bone, amber, pottery and bamboo. Worn from the early 17th to the mid-19th century when fashions changed, they were considered status symbols with the more elaborately carved ones denoting their owner's wealth or importance. The Asian Zodiac symbols were very popular (for example, dog, dragon and horse).

MASK NETSUKE

Front and side views of a 19th century devil mask with oni (devil) in ivory

A&C 12, est £2,500, now worth £3,000-5,000

ARCHER NETSUKE

An 18th century ivory netsuke, depicting a Mongolian archer

A&C 12, est £2,500-3,000, now worth £4,000-5,000

ITTAN OF NAGOYA

A wood sashi netsuke of monkeys by reclusive craftsman Ittan, of Nagoya, c 1820-1877. The monkeys eyes are inlaid (SOTH)

A&C 12, est £2,500-2,800, now worth £3,500-4,500

JAPANESE BELIEFS

Japanese ivory netsuke in the form of an immortal, 9cm high (SWORD)

A&C 45, sold for £1,500, now worth £1,800-2,800

ORIENTAL

KIMONO WEARER

Ivory okimono, Japanese, Meijing period, carved as a standing lady wearing a kimono, brightly decorated with flowers, signed, (damaged), 15cm high (HAMP)

A&C 46, sold for £460, now worth £500-700

BAKU

A very rare unsigned ivory study of the mythical Baku, 19th century. The ivory is dark stained and worn. The work shows some affinities with artists from Osaka, working in the middle of the 19th century. Staining reminiscent of Shukosai Anrak (SOTH)

A&C 12, est £15-20,000, now worth £20-30,000

NETSUKE HORSE

Ivory Netsuke Shibayama; horse on oval base, inlaid in mother of pearl, coral, horn, stained ivory and metal work (CHEF)

A&C 48, sold for £1,500, now worth £1,500-2,250

RABBIT NETSUKE

A 19th century rabbit netsuke. This piece is made in mother of pearl, a rare material

A&C 12, est £3,500, now worth £5,000-7,000

FIGURAL GROUP

Japanese ivory group of figures, Meiji period, male and female peasant, Tokyo School, red lacquer seal insert (FELL)

A&C 58, sold for £1,400, now worth £1,500-2,000

TOMOAKI

Ivory study of Benten, Meiji period, signed 'Tomoaki', 13.5cm wide (HAMP)

A&C 36, sold for £420, now worth £700-900

THE WISEMAN

An 18th century ivory netsuke, depicting Gama-Sennin (a legendary wiseman in rags with a toad on his shoulder)

A&C 12, est £4,000, now worth £6,000-8,000

GOLD LACQUER

A 19th century gold lacquered inro with Kagamibuta type-netsuke

A&C 12, est £3,500-4,000, now worth £5,000-8,000

Fact File

The rules concerning the selling of ivory have changed fairly recently. It is now illegal to sell ivory which is less than 50 years old. If you are not sure about the age of a piece, it's safer to leave it. Not all dealers are aware of the change in law unless they are specialists.

Ivory can get grubby due to handling. Never immerse it in water or try to clean it with water-based products. Instead, use methylated spirits on a soft cloth to remove dirt. When the piece is clean, simply handle it with clean hands – the natural oil in your skin will counteract any dryness caused by the cleaning product.

METALWORK

Bronze was the most common non-enamelled metal used in both China and Japan, used for practical goods such as vases and incense burners as well as figures. The decorations are distinctly Oriental. But the most famous Oriental metal of all was the decorated form – cloisonné, the vividly coloured enamel hiding the metal underneath.

BRONZE HAWK

Japanese bronze hawk sculpture, late Meiji period, with inset amber glass eyes, moulded character marks to base, 43 cm high (FELL)

A&C 57, sold for £1,200, now worth £1,200-1,800

SHIBAYAMA (INLAID STONE) VASE

A Chinese silver and 'shibayama' bottle vase, Meiji Period, much reproduced style (HAMP)

A&C 23, est £400-600, now worth £650-850

BRONZE WINE FLASK

Unusual Han Dynasty (202 BC-8 AD) bronze wine flask, 13 inches wide, from 100 BC

A&C 62, est £3,000-5,000, now worth £3,000-5,000

ENAMEL IRISES

Pierced silver and enamel Japanese lidded pot, the oval body decorated with two shibiyama (using precious stones) inlaid panels of figures and birds, reserved on a ground of silver and coloured enamel irises and foliage, 12.5cm high, some damage (PH ED)

A&C 30, sold for £1,610, now worth £3,000-5,000

Fact File

Cloisonné is named after the wire areas (cloisons) which are laid on the metal vessel and then set in place by using vegetable glue before being fired in the kiln. The wires would form the shape of the pattern which would be inlaid on the pot. Next, these wire shapes would be filled with glaze (enamel) which would set in the kiln after another firing.

Early examples are quite rough but with very colourful, imaginative designs. Later designs are more standard due to the demand and, from the 19th century, large amounts were exported to the West.

This prolific production was not a sign of quality, however but the designs are still popular and its a generally affordable area of collecting. Avoid any with damaged enamelling as these are difficult (and costly) to repair successfully.

VERDIGRIS AGEING

Bronze Tang Dynasty (618-906 AD) food bowl with ladle (Image by NICHOLAS S PITCHER)

A&C 62, est £3,000-3,500, now worth £3,000-3,500

BRONZE TIGER

A Japanese bronze model of a tiger, signed Kunryusai, Meiji period (1868-1912), 57cm paw to tale (PH BA)

A&C 18, sold for £690, now worth £1,000-2,000

PAINTINGS

PORTRAITS

Before photography, the only way to preserve people's likenesses was through portraiture. This was especially popular among the wealthy and ruling classes. There were two ways to paint someone: it could be done either accurately or through flattery. For example, the short, fat and ugly Queen Anne became prettier and younger.

CONTINENTAL SCHOOL

Oil on copper, eighteenth century Continental School portrait of Hugo Crotius (WINT)

A&C 31, sold £1,200, now worth £1,500-2,500

MINIATURES

Pair of portrait miniatures on ivory, in ornate gilt wooden frames (FELL)

A&C 38, sold for £400, now worth £500-600

POSTHUMOUS PORTRAIT

Oval miniature of Shakespeare by W Essex, signed and dated 1849 (FELL)

A&C 54, sold £1,100, now worth £1,200-1,800

Fact File

The background of a portrait tells us as much about a person as their face and name. The artist would carefully pose the subject and add objects showing their trade or distinction. Naval men were shown with ships in the background and invariably wearing their uniform with their rank clearly pictured. Country houses would be painted in the background of idyllic scenes with husbands and their new wives sitting by trees, a popular device used in the 19th century. With the exception of artists like Vermeer, the subjects were wealthy, few ordinary people could afford such luxury. Some rich sitters chose to have their servants added to their portraits, as a symbol of their wealth. These pictures are important for socio-economic historians and interesting for collectors as are any that contain animals, especially horses or dogs.

LADY IN BLUE

Portrait miniature watercolour on vellum (calf skin) by English School, c.1650 of a lady wearing a blue dress (BON)

A&C 63, sold for £478, now worth £450-600

PORTRAIT OF A CHILD AND PETS

Thomas Weaver (1774-1843) oil portrait of a boy on a donkey in a park with terrier, signed and dated 1883 (DREW)

A&C 63, sold £2,600, now worth £3,000-5,000

PORTRAIT OF A CHILD

Jacob Gerritsz Cuyp (1594-1651) oil painting, *Portrait of a Child* which quadrupled its estimate (CHRIS)

A&C 16, sold £20,700, now worth £30-40,000

THEATRICAL ENDEAVOURS

Madame Cavalaszzi in the role of Faust, dated 1896 and signed 'Wilhelm'. Theatrical art is very popular (DREW)

A&C 40, sold for £420, now worth £400-600

LORD RUSSELL

Half length portrait after Reynolds, of a young boy called Lord Russell. Oil on canvas, 59 x 48cm (DREW)

A&C 40, sold for £460, now worth £450-650

MATERIAL DETAIL

Portrait in the style of John Theodore Heins (1697-1756), thought to be Mrs James Beevor, 52cm x 44cm (DREW)

A&C 62, sold for £700, now worth £800-1,200

FLESH TONES

Circle of Sir Godfrey Kneller, portrait of a boy in a green cap, oil on canvas with beautiful flesh tones and red lips (CHEF)

A&C 48, sold £4,000, now worth £4,000-6,000

SUMMER ROSE

A Summer Rose, oil on canvas by Emile Vernon, fetched the highest price ever for the chocolate box-style artist (FELL)

A&C 39, sold for £30,000, now worth £40-60,000

SLEEPING SITTER

A watercolour by popular artist, Sir William Russell Flint, *The Silver Frock.* His work is escalating in price (BON)

A&C11, sold £42,000, now worth £60-80,000

PRETTY IN PINK

Lady Maud Carrington, in pink flowing dress in ornate gilt frame (CRIT)

A&C 13, sold £1,000, now worth £1,500-2,500

TWO BROTHERS

Oil painting by the circle of Sir William Beechey (1753-1839), *The Vaughan Boys,* delightful childhood study (GORR)

A&C 53, sold £5,000, now worth £5,000-7,000

FRENCH MINIATURE

French portrait miniature in 18th-century style, depicting an aristocratic lady and set in a brass frame, 16cm x 20cm (FELL)

A&C 39, sold for £460, now worth £450-650

Fact File

Ideally, artists worked to commissions, knowing that they would be paid for their work and that they would not have to find buyers afterwards. For struggling artists, portraits were very important, whether they liked their subjects or not. Most would make sketches and then paint afterwards, their sitters being too busy to sit for long. The alternative was to use models and then try to sell the painting. Artists fell in love and married their models, including Pre-Raphaelite artist Dante Gabriel Rossetti's doomed marriage to Elizabeth Siddall. This meant that they often used the same model for years, showing the ageing process, which is an ideal subject for a collection. Others, such as Rembrandt and Van Gogh, could not always afford models and so painted self-portraits, a fascinating study but not affordable for most.

WELSH ART

Portrait of a young lady in a yellow dress by Penry Williams (1798-1885, oil on canvas, in ornate frame (MALL)

A&C 63, sold £1,850, now worth £1,500-2,000

Exquisite Hand Made Original Serigraphs

'My Favourites' by Sophie Coryndon
Paper size 103 x 100 cm
Created by the artist using 20 individual colours
In an edition of 90 original serigraphs

'Water Marks' by Sally McGill
Paper size 83 x 80 cm
Created by the artist using 9 individual colours
In an edition of 50 original serigraphs

ARTIZAN EDITIONS

We welcome visitors to our
Brighton & Hove City workshop, by appointment.

Contact Sally Gimson 01273 773959

www.artizaneditions.co.uk

MOUNT GALLERY

18th to 20 Century watercolours, oils and prints

David COX Junior Loading Sand watercolour 7.25 x 10.5 ins S&D 1878

William WIDGERY Crossing the Bridge watercolour 13 x 20 ins S&D 1869

By Appointment : phone & fax 0208·904·5184
e-mail : stanley.collister@btinternet.com

Enjoy a little piece of Heaven in Piccadilly
St. James's ANTIQUES
and collectors
MARKET
OPEN
TUESDAYS 10a.m. ~ 6p.m.

Tube: Piccadilly Circus
or Green Park
Bus: 3. 6. 9. 12. 14.
15. 19. 22. 38
Rail: Victoria/Charing Cross
197 PICCADILLY
LONDON W1J 9LL
Tel: 020 7734 4511
Fax: 020 7734 7449

ANIMAL ART

Animals provide some of the most attractive and sellable paintings, from Stubbs' horses to Maud Earl's dogs. When buying animal portraits for investment, look at the animals; the more detailed and accurate they are, the better – especially for dogs, cattle and horses which remain the best sellers.

FRANZ VAN SEVERDONCK

Simple farm scene showing rural bliss, oil on board by Franz Van Severdonck (1809-1889), 22.5cm x 17cm (FELL)

A&C 40, sold £1,300, now worth £1,000-2,000

EUGENE REMY MAES

Chocolate box oil on panel of *Rabbits Feeding*, by Eugene Remy Maes, reverse signed and inscribed, 26cm x 35cm (CLEV)

A&C 29, sold £3,652, now worth £4,000-4,500

CATTLE AND SHEEP

Pair of oils on canvas by the circle of Thomas Sidney Cooper. *Cattle and Sheep in a Landscape*, a popular theme (SWORD)

A&C 48, sold £1,300, now worth £1,500-2,500

Fact File

Dog paintings are some of the hardest to value. These are the sleepers at auctions – unless the auctioneer is a dog lover or knows their area. When it comes to canines, the artist has to be highly accurate to get top prices. One of the best was Maud Earl (1844-1916) who painted Queen Victoria and Edward VII's dog, one of her most poignant being the late Edward VII's wire-haired fox terrier, Caesar, as he waited for his dead master's return. She was an accomplished artist, capturing the essence of the dog as well as its shape. She also painted a Bedlington terrier, Clyde Bay, an unusual breed for artists which is what made it so collectable. In poor condition, it raised around £7,000. Even unsigned paintings, if the dogs are detailed enough, are very good buys. If you like dogs!

LOUIS WAIN CATS

The Cats' Boat Race on the Thames by Louis Wain (1860-1939). Pen and ink annotated drawing by the famous cat artist (crease to centre) (CHEF)

A&C 35, est £300-500, now worth £600-800

EDWIN SMITH CAT

Untitled oil on canvas of a cat painted by Edwin Smith, 56cm x 76cm (CHEF)

A&C 48, sold for £80, now worth £150-250

COLIN GRAEME ROE

Stable Mates, Colin Graeme Roe, 1983. Hunting paintings are very collectable, even with non-hunters (CHRIS)

A&C 21, est £1000-1500, now worth £3,000

JAMES STINTON

Cock and hen pheasants in an autumnal landscape, signed lower right (WINT)

A&C 45, sold for £520, now worth £400-600

JOHN ARNOLD WHEELER

Heads of Two Hounds and Heads of Two Terriers, John Arnold Wheeler (1821-1903), oil on board, popular breeds with appealingly alert expressions (LOCK)

A&C 51, sold £2,800, now worth £2,500-4,000

Godolphin

Chagford   Devon

The Return of the Missing Boat, St Ives   Richard Harry Carter   1840–1911   Watercolour   28.5" x 52"

Fine Paintings & Watercolours
from the 18th Century
to the Present Day

Full colour catalogue
available upon request

Interesting News   Tom McEwen   1846–1914
Oil on Canvas   18" x 14"

Fishermen Gossiping as They Work   Nicholas Condy
1793–1857   Oil on Panel   12" x 10"

Open Monday – Saturday 10.15am – 5.15pm
11 The Square, Chagford, Devon Telephone/Fax 01647 433 999

LANDSCAPES AND SCENES

Landscape artsist got to capture an ever changing scene in all seasons without having to pay for model fees. Over the course of years, they recorded the developing landscape which makes for an interesting collection. Oil paintings command higher prices than watercolours and maritime scenes are highly collectable.

ALFRED STANNARD

Crown Point Wood by Alfred Stannard. First exhibited in Norfolk in 1829 and on the market for the first time (BEAR)

A&C 45, sold £30,000, now worth £30-40,000

HEYWOOD HARDY

Drawing Cover by Heywood Hardy, ARWS, RPE (1843-1933), signed (CHEF)

A&C 60, sold £49,000, now worth £45-60,000

H. GRESLEY

Watercolour of Monsal Dale in Derbyshire by H. Gresley. Signed lower right and titled in pencil to the mount, 27.5cm x 37.5cm (WINT)

A&C 33, sold £1,050, now worth £1,000-2,000

Fact File

We've differentiated between a landscape and a scene as scenes can contain and focus on human life (for example harbour scenes). Landscapes are strictly views, although purists might disagree.

One of the most famous landscapists was John Constable, whose most famous painting, *The Hay Wain*, was exhibited at the Paris Salon of 1824, three years after it had been painted, achieving the success that had eluded him in England. It influenced French artists, such as Delacroix and the Barbizon School, who started painting outdoors because of his work. He would sketch outside but finish the paintings in his studio. Unlike artists such as Gainsborough, he painted the reality of nature, not picturesque fluffy clouds but stormy skies. He even painted the sky itself; no landscape, just sky.

ALEXIS DE LEEUW

Foresters with horses, 19th century oil on canvas, by Alexis de Leeuw. Rural workers were a common theme (CLEV)

A&C 40, sold £4,000, now worth £5,000-7,000

CARISBROOKE CASTLE

Carisbrooke Castle on the Isle of Wight. English School, oil on board, mid-19th century, 10cm x 14cm (DREW)

A&C 40, sold for £980, now worth £800-1,200

HEYWOOD HARDY

At the Gate Showing the Way, by hunt artist, Heywood Hardy (HAMP)

A&C 40, sold £39,000, now worth £40-60,000

MYLES BIRKET FOSTER

A Mill Pool, watercolour by Myles Birket Foster (1825-1899), attractive rural scene signed with monogram (DREW)

A&C 11, sold £15,000, now worth £18-22,000

EDWARD WILKINS WAITE

Edward Wilkins Waite *Rustic Scene with Geese and a Cottage* signed and dated 1891, 46cm x 31cm (SWORD)

A&C 48, sold for £4,000, now worth £4-6,000

PAINTINGS

DOROTHEA SHARP

Oil painting, *Children Paddling in a Rocky Pool* by Dorothea Sharp, renowned for her pictures of children (SOTH)

A&C 11, sold £9,200, now worth £18-25,000

PENELOPE BEATON

Holiday, oil by Penelope Beaton (1886-1963), influenced by French Impressionists 24cm x 102cm (DREW)

A&C 62, sold for £3,100, now worth £3-5,000

F C B CADELL

F C B Cadell (RSA) (1883-1937), *Iona Looking Towards Mull*, signed, oil on panel, interesting use of colour (PH ED)

A&C 25, sold £34,500, now worth £40-50,000

WILLIAM ALFRED DELAMOTTE

Pen drawing in sepia ink and wash, heightened in white. Signed by William Alfred Delamotte, 1825 (DREW)

A&C 39, sold for £160, now worth £200-250

JOSEPH THORS

Cattle Grazing Beside a Stream, rural landscape by Joseph Thors (British, 1863-1900) oil on canvas (FELL)

A&C 5, sold for £1,800, now worth £4-6,000

DAVID BATES

The Carters, 1910, oil by David Bates, influenced by Contsable (WINT)

A&C 38, sold for £2,500, now worth £3-4,000

PERCY DIXON

Percy Dixon (1862-1924) watercolour *Among the Tumbled Fragments of the Hills*, tactile landscape (GORR)

A&C 53, sold for £2,000, now worth £2-3,000

BENJAMIN WILLIAMS LEADER

1908 painting *Evening on the River Severn* by Worcestershire-born artist Benjamin Williams Leader (BK)

A&C 44, sold for £8,000, now worth £8-12,000

Fact File

As the two paintings on the left show, there are two different types of landscapes: warm and inviting or cruel and rugged. They both have a market, the former being more popular for peole buying art as decoration although they are also useful investments if they are good quality. Dawn and dusk, sunrise and sunset add an extra dimension to any painting as the Leader painting shows (see left). The soft or dramatic colours that these create can transform an otherwise fairly mundane setting. The reds and purples make the painting more interesting and, therefore, easier to sell – always useful when thinking of buying to invest. Bad weather, such as storms or snow, also add to a painting's appeal.

PAINTINGS

MODERN ART

The term modern art is very broad. In this category, we're concentrating on paintings but it could also cover video, sculpture, furniture or any other form of design. Strictly speaking, modern art is anything from the mid-20th century, not just made in the last few years and covers many styles.

ANNE REDPATH

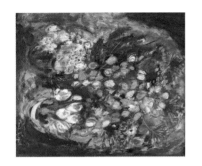

Anne Redpath (RSA, OBE) (1895-1965), *Winter and Spring*, oil (PH ED)

A&C 25, sold £20,125, now worth £24-30,000

VITTORIO EMANUELE BRESSANIN

Vittorio Emanuele Bressanin (1860-1941), *The First Dance*, signed and dated oil by the cult artist with photographic detail (SOTH)

A&C 25, sold £43,700, now worth £45-65,000

JOHN DUNCAN FERGUSON

John Duncan Fergusson (RBA) (1874-1961), *Through the Trees*, South of France, signed oil on canvas (PH ED)

A&C 25, sold £46,000, now worth £50-80,000

Fact File

Pablo Picasso epitomised modern art: he turned portraiture on its head – literally. Ears and noses could be placed anywhere, which unsettled the established art world. His work was exciting. That's what modern art is about, it rejects tradition in return for innovation. It does not have to be outrageous or shocking but can be both pleasurable and a good investment. One of the most notable modern artists is Jack Vettriano who has exhibited at the Royal Scottish Academy and Royal Academy and whose work, *The Singing Butler*, sold for a record £744,800 at auction in 2004. The painting, like the rest of his art, has an almost photographic quality to it and is the best-selling art print. Some of his work can be a bit explicit for all tastes but is a fantastic investment; his limited edition prints are worth buying.

CAPTAIN SCARLET, CULT TV ART

Artwork board no. 7 *Captain Scarlet in Chamber*. Used as a backdrop for the end credits on the TV show c.1968 (CHRIS)

A&C 42, sold for £3,995, now worth £8-10,000

BARBARA HEPWORTH

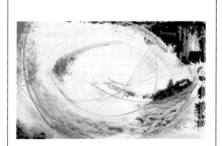

Dame Barbara Hepworth (1903-1975), *Stone From, (Tresco)*. Oil and pencil by the famous sculptor (MALL)

A&C 48, sold £23,000, now worth £30-60,000

BERYL COOK

Oh to Be in England, by Beryl Cook, 1980 45cm x 37.5cm, paint cracked (SWORD)

A&C 29, sold for £6,000, now worth £8-12,000

LAWRENCE STEPHEN LOWRY

A Lancashire Woman Sitting Down, oil by Lawrence Stephen Lowry, RS, signed and dated, 1961. Exhibited in the Walker Art Gallery, Liverpool in 1973 (SWORD)

A&C 29, sold £14,500, now worth £18-25,000

LADY BEATRICE GLENAVY

Lady Beatrice Glenavy, Irish School – *Poet and Shepherdess*, oil on canvas, signed with monogram. With the original receipt of purchase, dated 30 July 1936, some restoration (RT)

A&C 13, sold £7,800, now worth £15-25,000

PAINTINGS

STILL LIFE

Most artists start by painting still lives. These scenes do not move, they teach the painter about shadows and proportion, as well as colours and textures. They tend to show flowers or fruit, especially apples. Some have meaning, often about death, others are just attractive and bought for pleasure.

FLORAL PAINTING

Flowers in a Vase by Virginia Battaile Betts, c.1930, 120cm x 90cm (SWORD)

A&C 50, sold £2,700, now worth £2,500-3,500

FRUITY PAINTING

An English rectangular plaque, painted in coloured enamels, with a still life of fruit, signed 'E Steele' and dated 1881. 23cm x 30.5cm (WO WA)

A&C 18, sold for £2,100, now worth £3-5,000

FASHION LEAD

Trellis Pattern from a series depicting Royalty and Admiralty, Stephen Farthing (b.1950), oil on canvas (MALL)

A&C 51, est £8-10,000, now worth £8-12,000

Fact File

Dorothea Sharp (1874-1955) painted colourful still lives, landscapes and figures, especially children. She studied art in London and Paris and was part of the British Impressionist School. Her work has an attractive simplicity which makes it appealing, especially the flower still lives. She lived in St Ives, Cornwall, with its huge artistic community, and is a good example of what to look for when buying art. She exhibited at two prestigious locations, the Royal Academy (RA) which is notoriously difficult to get into and the highly respected Paris Salon. That means she has to be good and that there are records of her as an artist, an important aspect to consider when buying art for more than pleasure. Above all, buy what you enjoy.

MODERN ART

Nature Morte a l'Artichaut by Henri Hayden (1883-1970), stylistic (SOTH)

A&C 58, sold for £8,400, now worth £8-12,000

MARY FEDDEN

Mary Fedden (b.1915), a jug and fruit on a chequered table cloth, modern art focus on style over detail (MALL)

A&C 48, sold for £5,400, now worth £6-8,000

NATURAL STILL LIFE

Daisies at the Window, a simple still life, oil on board by Denis William Reed (RWA) (1917-1979), affordable art (BRI)

A&C 47, sold for £150, now worth £150-300

IRISES, LILIES AND ROSES

Oil on plywood panel. *Irises, Lilies and Roses*, by John E Nicholls, signed. An interesting combination of flowers (LEV)

A&C 29, sold for £1,043, now worth £2-4,000

PHYLLIS HIBBERT

Carnations, Roses and Gypsophila by Phyllis Hibbert (RSA) (b.1903), a traditional British floral display (CHEF)

A&C 60, sold for £620, now worth £800-1,200

PHOTOGRAPHS

Photographs can be surprisingly valuable, providing a pictorial record of ordinary people, events and buildings that would not normally have been painted. Important events and fashions were captured as they happened and, for the first time, accurate portraits were created and in an affordable format.

THE KISS

Le Baiser de l'Hotel de Ville by Robert Doisneau, 1950. This gelatin silver print was made later and signed and dated by the photographer (CHRIS)

A&C 61, sold £4,465, now worth £4,500-6,000

WORLD RECORD PRICE

Athens, by Joseph-Philibert Girault de Prangey, 1842, set the world record for a photograph sold at auction (CHRIS)

A&C 54, sold £565,250, worth £550-600,000

CLASSIC IMAGE REPRINTED

Femme aux Renards by Jacques-Henri Lartigue, 1911. This silver print was printed later and signed (SOTH)

A&C 61, sold for £2,640, now worth £3-4,000

CARTIER-BRESSON, 1932

One of Henri Cartier-Bresson's best-known images, it was also one of the first to be taken with a 35mm camera. This later silver print is signed (SOTH)

A&C 61, sold for £3,360, now worth £5-6,000

Fact File

The first ever picture was created in 1826 by the Frenchman, Joseph-Nicephore Niepce. His 'heliograph' (as he called it) was of a barn and took eight hours to expose – modern cameras take a fraction of a second – but it was a huge advance. The innovative set designer, Louis Daguerre wrote to him. He was fascinated by the procedure and longed to create permanent pictures of events. In 1839, he unveiled his daguerreotypes, early 'photographs' which, by 1850, were seen as fairly commonplace as people sought to capture all aspects of modern life. His process used a twenty-minute exposure, still long but a huge advance on Niepce's eight hours. Daguerreotypes fade over time and if not stored properly. They are often more valuable than the general dealer or auctioneer realises.

HISTORICAL MOMENT

Captain Scott's birthday dinner (6 June 1911) photographed by Herbert George Ponting (1871-1935) (CHRIS)

A&C 56, sold for £3,107, now worth £3-5,000

SCREEN GODDESS

Marilyn Monroe. Originally taken by Bert Stern in 1962, this Iris print, a superior inkjet print, was made in 1992 (CHRIS)

A&C 61, sold for £1,880, now worth £2,000

THE REAL ALICE

Alice Liddell pictured in the 1850s, part of a scrapbook with 58 albumen 'Alice' prints by Charles Lutwidge Dodgson (Lewis Carroll) (SOTH).

A&C 46, sold £465,500, now worth £500,000

NORMAN PARKINSON

Jerry Hall, Russia 1975. These colour prints, two studies of the model/ex-Mrs Jagger by Norman Parkinson, were signed and dated by Parkinson (SOTH)

A&C 61, sold for £14,400, now worth £12-16,000

PHOTOGRAPHY

CAMERAS

Most old cameras are worth surprisingly little which is why many dealers overlook those that are, such as former MP, Noel Pemberton Billing's Phantom Photographic Unit, which was designed in 1946 but never went into production. It sold for £146,750 at auction in 2001. Leicas are good quality buys.

OLYMPUS

An Olympus Pen F 135mm, half-frame camera with 100mm lens. Made in Japan 1963–66, a good, solid make (BON)

A&C 8, est £120-180, now worth £250-350

FOLDING BED DESIGN

A Zeiss Super Ikonta, model B. A folding bed design with model number on case. Produced in the 1930s-1950s (BON)

A&C 8, est £100-150, now worth £150-250

ALPA CAMERA

A Pignons Alpa camera, model 9D, made in Switzerland 1965-69 (BON)

A&C 8, est £400-500, now worth £400-600

SPY CAMERA

A Russian concealed coat button camera, perfect spying equipment (CHRIS)

A&C 25, sold £2,115, now worth £2,500-3,500

GUN CAMERAS

Gun cameras make good collectables. This Japanese Doryu 2-16 gun camera from the 1950s, no.1027, 16mm, with film cassette, almost tripled its original estimate of £4,000-6,000 (CHRIS)

A&C 25, sold £16,450, now worth £18-22,000

UNUSUAL SHAPE

A Ticka Focal-plane camera with a Cooke lens, produced between 1908 and 1914 by British firm Houghtons Ltd (CHRIS)

A&C 25, sold for £1,880, now worth £3-4,000

POLITICAL PHOTOGRAPHY

The prototype 'Phantom' camera, 1946, designed by Noel Pemberton Billing (former MP) set a new world record when it sold for £146,750 (CHRIS)

A&C 25, now worth £150,000-200,000

RETRO-STYLE

A retro-style Olympus, 1980s (CHRIS)

A&C 25, sold for £188, now worth £250-350

Fact File

One of the most common questions sent to the Antiques Advice column in *Antiques and Collectables* is about Kodak's ubiquitous Box Brownie, one of the first mass-produced consumables which sold in its millions after being introduced for five shillings (25p) in 1900.

You can buy them for £2-3 at auctions or car boot sales or for around £20 at fairs, where they do much better. Although the film is no longer made, you can alter a modern film to make it useable. This is a good way to recycle the otherwise cheap collectable.

One of the most attractive cameras is German and concealed within an enamelled compact. It's worth £150-200.

IESA

Institut d'Études Supérieures des Arts
fully recognised by the French Ministry of Culture
and Communication since 1998

European post-graduate diploma
History and Business of Art
and Collecting

> six-month studies in London
> six-month studies in Paris
> two study trips in Florence and Brussels

This European post-graduate course offers a professional training in the fine
and decorative arts, set within the context of the history of collecting.
The business side of the course is taught in three modules: French law
and the continental art market, the role of the European Union,
and English approaches to law, marketing and sponsorship.

**IESA Campus also offers graduate courses
(2 or 3 years) in the art market, heritage,
art events and multi-media publishing**
The qualification is the equivalent of a BA

the European
world of art

in partnership
with the Wallace
Collection

the course is taught in English
and French and can be joined
at any time of the year

IESALondon c/o the Wallace Collection
Hertford House Manchester Sq. London W1U 3BN
t +44 (0)20 7221 9645 w www.iesa.edu e iesa-london@iesa.edu

IESAParis
5, avenue de l'Opéra 75001 Paris
t +33 (0)1 42 86 57 01 w www.iesa.fr e iesa@iesa.fr

Camera Manuals

Instruction manuals – for almost every
camera (film or digital) and accessory ever
made. It doesn't matter if your camera is new
or 50 years old. We will have a manual for it.

We have over 14,000 different manuals
available. The largest supply in the World.

Focal Camera Guides – the perfect follow on
to instruction manuals for cameras made in
the 50s, 60s and 70s.

Repair manuals – for thousands of cameras.

Test reports – copies of every one ever written
in Amateur Photographer and What Digital
Camera.

Call OTC Ltd on: 01707 273773
Order online at: **www.oldtimercameras.com**

The John Leach Gallery
at Muchelney Pottery
Ceramics   Sculpture   Paintings
for the discerning collector

David
Leach

John
Leach

Gallery
Interior

Peter
Hayes

Benedict
Leach

Ian
Gregory

Muchelney Pottery, 2m south Langport, Somerset Tel. 01458 250 324   www.johnleachpottery.com
Gallery open all year, Monday to Saturday 9am-1pm & 2pm-5pm

PRINTS

PRINTS

The most important thing to remember is that prints are not originals but copies and, as such, not unique.
If buying a limited edition, always ask about the limited edition size – the smaller the better (for example, 50).
Prints can be a wise investment but are also attractive decorations and cheaper than originals.

CLASSIC 1960S

Allen Jones, *Life Class*, lithograph printed in colours, 1968 (CHRIS)

A&C 23, sold for £4,700, now worth £5-8,000

MODERN ART

Victor Pasmore, *The Dance of Man in Modern Times*, aquatints with an etching printed in colours, 1972 (CHRIS)

A&C 23, sold for £1,175, now worth £3-4,000

ALLEN JONES

Allen Jones, *Magic Moment*, lithograph printed in three colours, 1981 (CHRIS)

A&C 23, sold £940, now worth £1,200-1,500

POLIAKOFF

Colour screenprint by acclaimed artist Serge Poliakoff (1900-1965) (BR AU)

A&C 34, sold £700, now worth £1,500-2,500

Fact File

It can be difficult to spot the difference between a painting and a print unless you know what to do. Look at the picture very closely. Can you see lots of small dots? Unless it's obviously pointillism (paintings created by dots such as Seurat's *The Bathers at Asnieres*), it's a print.

Another way is to look at the texture. Prints will be completely flat. (Let's ignore the fake textured versions as these are obviously fake because the texture is too even, colours too bright.) You'll be able to see the artist's individual brush strokes on a painting.

Old prints tend to have cream surrounds and backgrounds and the dealers often sell them in plastic wrappers with stickers guaranteeing that they are over 100 years old.

BUILDING AN INVESTMENT

Coloured print by John Piper, architecture is a popular theme for collectors (CLEV)

A&C 33, sold for £200, now worth £300-500

SCREENPRINT

Tom Phillips, *Benches*, screenprint in colours, 1982, signed and numbered 52 out of 85, a small edition size (CHRIS)

A&C 23, est £200-300, now worth £350-450

STEREOSCOPIC VIEWER

Victorian peep show in pyramidal form with mirrored viewer, complete with nine German colour lithographic world views and 53 stereoscopic slides (GORR)

A&C 42, sold for £1,700, now worth £2-2,500

PART OF A COLLECTION

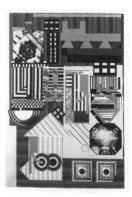

Eduardo Paolozzi, *Artificial Eye*, from the *As Is When* portfolio, offering an ideal way to build up a collection (CHRIS)

A&C 23, est £400-600, now worth £650-850

JAPANESE WOODBLOCK

Seventeen signed Japanese woodblock prints with colourful figures. Woodblock prints are very popular, signed are best (HAMP)

A&C 42, sold for £580, now worth £600-800

FAMOUS NAMES AND IMAGES

Andy Warhol's classic, *Lavender Marilyn* sold for $4,629,500 (£2.5 million) and is one of the enduring classics (SOTH NY)

A&C 46, now worth £3-4,000,000

HOCKNEY GOES TO HOLLYWOOD

David Hockney's famous Hollywood Series, lithograph of Melrose Avenue printed in colour, 1965 (CHRIS)

A&C 23, sold £2,115, now worth £3,000-5,000

MOTHER AND CHILD

Kathe Kollwitz lithographic print, *Mother and Child,* signed in pencil. A simple but effective and popular theme (SWORD)

A&C 53, sold for £1,150, now worth £1,000-1,500

COMICAL CAT

Cheshire Cat by Frances Broomfield, one of a limited edition print of 200
(Picture by David Morcom/Chie Ando)

A&C 46, sold for £125, now worth £200-300

MARILYN MONROE

Signed photo of Marilyn Monroe. Her premature death means that her signature commands high prices, especially on photographs such as this one

A&C 46, now worth £4,000-6,000

Fact File

You might want to collect themed prints or those by the same artist.

The late Al Hirschfeld's witty prints and original drawings are good investments. He sketched Broadway greats and other entertainers, always hiding the name of his daughter, Nina, somewhere in the picture. His Beatles drawings or prints are probably the best buys at the moment for British investors.

Prints (lithographs) are generally limited editions. When buying at auction, you'll come across the letters 'F & G' this means framed and glazed, ie, it's in a frame with a glass front.

Prints at smaller auction houses can be a great buy, often for around £2 and worth at least ten times that – an easy way for a fast profit or a cheap way to decorate your walls.

REGENCY SHOPPING

A Bonnet Shop plus two other etchings with hand colouring, by Thomas Rowlandson (1756-1827) (MALL)

A&C 58, sold for £210, now worth £250-300

RAVILIOUS ENGRAVING

One of a collection of 14 wood-engraved plates by The Cresset Press, 1929 by Eric Ravilious, Blair Hughes-Stanton, Stephen Gooden and others (CHRIS)

A&C 60, sold £2,350, now worth £2,500-3,000

RELIGIOUS

RELIGIOUS ARTEFACTS

Religion used to be an important part of all people's lives, especially in the Tudor period where the wrong beliefs could be fatal. This spirituality led to carefully crafted goods whether it be for the church or temple or for home use. You don't have to be religious to appreciate religious artefacts or art.

RUSSIAN ICON

Small Russian icon depicting Christ, painted on wood with a silver oklad (surrounding frame) (FELL)

A&C 38, sold for £190, now worth £350–450

RELIGIOUS MESSAGE

Early Victorian rosewood firescreen with glazed and framed needlework picture between spirally turned supports (LOCK)

A&C 54, sold for £200, now worth £150–250

WATERCOLOUR

L. Riva painting of *The Rosary* (LOCK)

A&C 54, sold for £400, now worth £400–600

VICTORIAN CHALICE

Victorian silver Gothic revival chalice with agate cabochons. Marked 'TP' for Thomas Peard, London 1873 (DREW)

A&C 34, est £300–400, now worth £500–700

Fact File

Icons are religious paintings which were especially popular in Russia. Some of the simple paintings that depict Christ, the Madonna or saints have a silver frame which spans most of the picture, moulding itself around the face or the face and shoulders. This is known as an oklad. It would be moulded over the wooden board on which the icon was painted.

One of the most ornate was a golden oklad created by goldsmiths for Tsar Ivan the Terrible for a wooden-board icon of The Madonna and Child. Started in 1557, it took three years to complete, the jewels nestling in the gold frame. Icons and the worship of saints are an important part of Russo-Byzantine tradition. Other religious artefacts include richly bejewelled sarcophagi which were created to house the relics of saints.

GOTHIC REVIVAL CHALICE

Silver-gilt Gothic revival chalice by Keith & Co, along with a diamond-set floral plaque. Made in London in 1895 (DREW)

A&C 34, est £400–600, now worth £500–700

VICTORIAN PULPIT

Pitch pine carved Victorian pulpit with cast iron railings, salvaged from a church in Oxfordshire (MAS)

A&C 51, now worth £1,500–2,500

LIMESTONE FONT

Limestone font with Gothic Revival fluted column and carved cover (SWORD)

A&C 34, est £300–500, now worth £500–800

GOBLETS

A pair of mid-18th century, German hallmarked, silver-gilt Kiddush wine goblets, decorated in relief with bands of hearts, hallmarked (RT)

A&C 13, sold for £5,400, now worth £6–8,000

THE BEATLES

The Fab Four were the most successful band in the world and launched an unprecedented wave of memorabilia, not just records and concert programmes but dresses, blankets and, most desirable of all, their autographs. A complete set of John, Paul, George and Ringo's signatures is now worth around £8,000. Singly, John is best.

AUTOGRAPHED ALBUM

Signed copy of the album *With The Beatles*. This would have been collected by a fan so is likely to be real – beware of fakes (SOTH)

A&C 59, sold for £11,750, now worth £10-14,000

SIGNED LOVE ME DO

Love Me Do, record signed by Paul McCartney surpassed sales of a set of Beatles' autographs (BON)

A&C 57, sold for £13,513, now worth £10-12,000

THE FIFTH BEATLE

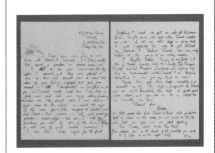

A letter from George Harrison to Stuart Sutcliffe, the fifth Beatle, 1960 (SOTH)

A&C 59, sold for £8,225, now worth £8-10,000

WORCESTER TRAY

Early 1960s Beatles tray by Worcester Ware UK (from www.mtmglobal.com)

A&C 42, sold for £125, now worth £100-180

Fact File

The Beatles dominated the 1960s, scoring 17 number one hits, including four at Christmas. The Fab Four with their mop-top hairstyles were John Lennon, Paul McCartney, George Harrison and Ringo Starr but it took two years for them to create their famous mix. Stuart Sutcliffe, the fifth Beatle, had left the band in 1960 and died two years later, just before Ringo Starr became their drummer. Previous drummers had not worked out, including Pete Best who was initially seen as the group's sex symbol and whom George Martin is believed to have suggested they replace. Ringo turned down an offer to join Gerry and the Pacemakers to become one of The Beatles, partly because the latter had a recording contract. The band split in 1970.

HELLO GOODBYE

A Dick James seven-inch 45rpm demo disc for The Beatles' *Hello Goodbye* (COOP)

A&C 42, sold for £500, now worth £1,000-2,000

YELLOW SUBMARINE MONO

Yellow Submarine (Apple) January 1969. The most expensive album cover made at the time

A&C 42, est £200-250, now worth £200-300

BEATLES TOY GUITAR

Selcol 1960s plastic Beatles toy guitar (SPEC)

A&C 53, est £60, now worth £200-300

CEL OF THE CENTURY

Three *Yellow Submarine* cels from the revolutionary Beatles cartoon film, King Features Studios, 1968. (SOTH)

A&C 21, sold for £3,120, now worth £5,000-8,000

Beatles & Pop Memorabilia Wanted!

Top prices paid! Anything considered!

Also: Stones, Hendrix, Pink Floyd, The Who, Sex Pistols, Punk, 60's, 70's Etc

Concert Posters; Handbills, Programmes, Tickets, Flyers, Contracts, Merchandise, Novelties, Signatures, etc, etc.

Please contact DAVE FOWELL
Collectors Corner, PO Box 8, Congleton, Cheshire CW12 4GD

Tel. 01260 270 429   Fax: 01260 298996
Email: dave.popcorner@ukonline.co.uk

We buy & Sell original pop memorabilia

Beatles & Pop Memorabilia WANTED

Up To **£2000** PAID FOR BEATLES AUTOGRAPHS ON ONE PAGE

Up To **£4000** PAID FOR AUTOGRAPHED BEATLES PROGRAMMES AND PHOTOS (ON THE IMAGE)

Up To **£5000** PAID FOR BEATLES CONCERT POSTERS

Beatles, Stones, Hendrix, Zeppelin, Who, Dylan, Floyd, Marley, 60's, 70's
Any Pop Memorabilia Considered

Programmes, Posters, Handbills, Tickets, Negatives, Lyrics, Personal Effects, Toys, (Sorry No Records)

Free Quotations - Selected Items Purchased
TRACKS, PO Box 117, Chorley, Lancashire, PR6 0UU
TEL: 01257 269726 - FAX: 01257 231340 - e-mail: sales@tracks.co.uk

BEATCITY
BEATLES & POP MEMORIBILIA

BEATCITY ARE LEADING SPECIALISTS IN BEATLES AND ROCK & ROLL MEMORABILIA.

We are always keen to purchase any Beatles items, ie signed material, programmes, tickets, handbills, posters, plastic guitars, novelty items, photographs and negatives.

Any other 60s music memorabilia considered
(ie. Stones, Hendrix, Who, Queen etc.).

WORLDWIDE MAILORDER AVAILABLE

BeatCity   PO Box 229   Chatham   Kent   ME5 8WA
Telephone & Fax 01634 200 444   Mobile 07770 650 890

WWW.BEATCITY.CO.UK

ELVIS

Elvis Presley, a contemporary of The Beatles, outraged American parents with his hip-swinging moves but he remains the single most successful solo artist of all time with his last number one *A Little Less Conversation*, the record eighteenth, gained posthumously. His films and their posters have added to his musical memorabilia.

KING CREOLE

A *King Creole* postcard autographed by Elvis Presley c. 1958 (BON)

A&C 43, sold for £350, now worth £300-400

LOVE ME TENDER

Poster 'introducing Elvis Presley' in *Love Me Tender*, seen with Debra Paget (SPEC AUC)

A&C 39, est £500, now worth £400-600

CHRISTMAS CARD

A 1966 Christmas card signed and dedicated 'To Mary' in blue ballpoint pen (COOP)

A&C 43, est £300-400, now worth £300-400

FAMOUS BELT

Elvis' famous white belt worn with his white suits from his Vegas shows (SOTH)

A&C 59, sold for £5,875, now worth £6,000-8,000

Fact File

An Elvis collector caused outrage when they decided to sell an original Elvis tooth and lock of hair on eBay, creating fears that the King could be cloned, but the pair failed to reach the reserve (£64,000) and remained unsold. Initial hoax bidding had reached £1.28 million before being withdrawn. Elvis memorabilia is more valuable than any other solo artist, including Michael Jackson. His career spanned the 1950s-70s until his death in 1977 and later memorabilia is epitomised by his famous white costume. There are three types of memorabilia – mass-produced merchandise, event specific goods eg film posters or concert tickets, and goods belonging to The King himself. By the end of 1957, £17 million worth of Elvis merchandise was being produced and it is still being made.

AUTOGRAPH

Signed record sleeve. His premature death in 1977 at only 42 has kept prices high (COOP)

A&C 59, sold for £300, now worth £300-400

VIVA LAS VEGAS

Table menu from Elvis' first Las Vegas show in 1969, he spent the 1970s there wearing his famous white suits (Picture by Guy Harrington)

A&C 43, est £300, now worth £300-400

RARE DOLL

One of the rarest 1950s Elvis merchandise, an Elvis doll (Picture by Quintet Publishing)

A&C 43,est £1,000+, now worth £800-1,200

RETURN TO SENDER

Elvis cards, showing stills from the all-singing, all-dancing film *Clambake* (COOP)

A&C 59, sold for £90, now worth £80-100

ROCK & POP MEMORABILIA

THE ROLLING STONES

The group remains one of the most exciting British bands ever. Led by Mick Jagger, the band is still touring meaning that merchandise continues to be produced and signatures are still signed, making them more affordable than many other rock and roll legends. Jagger's autograph on a standard photo sells for around £20.

AUTOGRAPHS

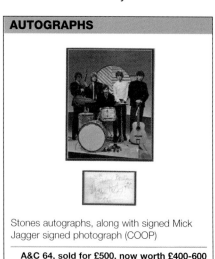

Stones autographs, along with signed Mick Jagger signed photograph (COOP)

A&C 64, sold for £500, now worth £400-600

YUGOSLAVIAN SINGLES

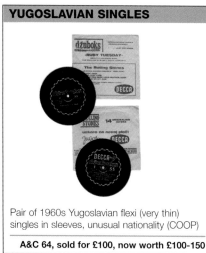

Pair of 1960s Yugoslavian flexi (very thin) singles in sleeves, unusual nationality (COOP)

A&C 64, sold for £100, now worth £100-150

STYLISH POSTER

A signed Rolling Stones Groundhogs UK tour poster, 1971 in classic 1940s style (SOTH)

A&C 21, sold for £840, now worth £1,500-2,500

SIGNED STONES ALBUM

Rolling Stones signed LP (COOP)

A&C 64, sold for £300, now worth £300-400

Fact File

With so much memorabilia, fans can get satisfaction and for surprisingly little compared to their contemporaries and friends, The Beatles.

A guitar signed by the group sold for £900 which makes it a great investment. A full set of autographs, including the late Brian Jones, can fetch around £400-600, ideally signed on the same piece of paper to show that they're from the same era. The most valuable of these is Brian Jones, the group's founder, who died in July 1969, less than a month after leaving the band because of creative differences. Before he resigned, he bought A A Milne's house in Sussex. His autograph sells for around £80-120.

A 1962 reel-to-reel recording of Mick Jagger and Keith Richards made a staggering £78,500 at a recent auction.

STONES PROM

Stones poster for the Great Pop Prom (COOP)

A&C 64, est £1,500-2,000, now worth £1,500-2,000

AUTOGRAPHED GUITAR

Guitar signed by the Stones (COOP)

A&C 64, sold £1,300, now worth £1,200-1,800

ROLLING STONES AUTOGRAPHS

This autographed *Rolling Stones* album cover of 1964, sold along with a number of Stones-related items. Good long-term investments from a great band (BON)

A&C 58, sold for £340, now worth £300-400

LONGEVITY KEEPS DOWN PRICE

Rolling Stones signed guitar (COOP)

A&C 64, sold £900, now worth £1,200-1,600

POSTERS

Rock and pop posters created for concerts are very desirable and often costly as they were created in limited numbers for a very specific event. Collectors try to get as many of these as possible, especially for world tours such as Michael Jackson's first solo tour, Bad (1987-89). Handbills and tickets are also good buys.

BOB MARLEY SIGNED POSTER

A rare, signed Bob Marley concert poster, 1980 (SOTH)

A&C 21, sold for £1,920, now worth £2,500-3,500

SEX PISTOLS

Sex Pistols concert poster displaying their anarchic reputation (SOTH)

A&C 59, est £500-600, now worth £500-800

Fact File

Concert posters list the name, dates and often times of the event. Some of these have been reproduced in tin form, like the old advertising signs, and are being sold as genuine. These are never real and, had they been designed to hang outside buildings as they claim, then they would be rusty and have hammer marks.

The ones which we've seen are obviously fake – but their buyers didn't always realise and have paid up to £60 for the scam.

The real paper/card posters should have signs of use to show that they are real. This often takes the form of folding or slightly ripped corners. Slight damage is acceptable, more is not unless you really want the poster.

GEORGE FORMBY HANDBILL

Rare handbill for a George Formby concert (Picture by The George Formby Society)

A&C 57, sold for £50-100, now worth £60-100

JIMI HENDRIX

Rare cartoon-style Jimi Hendrix Experience Swiss concert poster, 1968 (BON)

A&C 61, sold for £4,230, now worth £4,000-5,000

INFAMOUS QUOTE POSTER

Evening Standard reporter, Maureen Cleave, with The Beatles for the notorious 'we are more popular than Jesus' interview (SWORD)

A&C 67, sold for £170, now worth £200-300

MADONNA 1980s ICON

1980s cardboard cut-out of singer Madonna

A&C 53, est £150, now worth £60-100

BUDDY HOLLY AND OTHERS

Rare handbill for Buddy Holly and the Crickets UK concert, featuring Des O'Connor (SOTH)

A&C 59, sold for £294, now worth £300-400

ROCK & POP MEMORABILIA

COSTUMES

Musicians are performers and they need to entertain their audience at concerts with more than just music which has lead to some fantastic costumes. A simple suit worn by John Lennon to the premier of *A Hard Day's Night* sold for £55,000 while country and western singers' simple costumes of jeans and shirts fetch around £2,000.

PUCCI DRESS

Long-sleeved silk Pucci dress worn by Marilyn Monroe (COOP)

A&C 46, sold for £3,300, now worth £3,500-5,000

BUDDY HOLLY

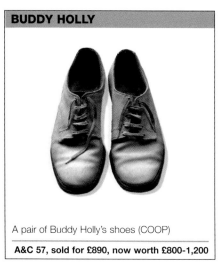

A pair of Buddy Holly's shoes (COOP)

A&C 57, sold for £890, now worth £800-1,200

PRINCE'S HAT

Trilby once belonging to The Artist Formerly Known as Prince (CHRIS)

A&C 67, est £400-600, now worth £500-700

GENTLEMEN PREFER BLONDES

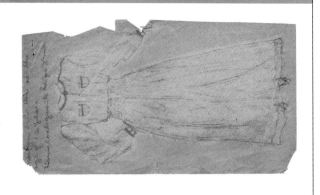

Sketch for singer and actress Marilyn Monroe's costume (COOP)

A&C 46, sold for £1,100, now worth £1,200-1,800

ELTON JOHN'S HEADGEAR

Elton John is renowned for his extravagant outfits and accessories such as this fur, feather and flower hat (CHRIS)

A&C 67, est £400-600, now worth £800-1,000

Fact File

When it comes to modern stars, only The Darkness seem to go for the more outlandish jumpsuits once so popular with rockers such as Freddie Mercury and Elvis. The latter loved his white jumpsuits in the 1970s and one made for him by Judy of Nashville – but not guaranteed as being worn by him – is worth around £1,200-2,500. It would have been worth more with that all important provenance – proof of use, ie, a photo of him wearing it.

One of the most important costume designers was Nudie Cohn, the first designer to use rhinestones on clothes. He even had them added to his Cadillac. Cohn created Elvis' 24ct gold suit and his clients also included Elton John, Cher, Jimi Hendrix... and Ronald Reagan.

RINGO STARR

Ringo Starr's black suede boots (LIV)

A&C 9, sold for £2,450, now worth £3,000-5,000

JAMES BROWN

James Brown felt fine in his checked stage costume from the 1960s (SOTH)

A&C 59, sold for £705, now worth £600-800

MEMORABILIA

Rock and pop is a massive area for collecting and it's often easy to overlook the real reason these musicians have become so famous – their records. Valuing records is a very specialist industry and much depends not only on the condition of the record but the cover. Concert tickets, handbills and programmes are also collectable.

LITTLE RICHARD

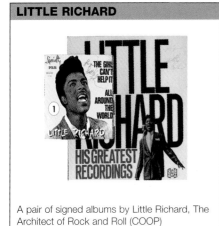

A pair of signed albums by Little Richard, The Architect of Rock and Roll (COOP)

A&C 59, now worth £300-500

PAT BOONE

1950s heart-throb Pat Boone record holder, the clean-cut star still has a following (BON)

A&C 11, sold for £5, now worth £80-120

ROCK AROUND THE CLOCK

Bill Haley was credited with kickstarting rock and roll with *Rock Around the Clock* (COOP)

A&C 59, now worth £200-300

JERRY LEE LEWIS

Jerry Lee Lewis autographed photo (COOP)

A&C 59, sold for £50, now worth £150-300

Fact File

Contracts are some of the most interesting forms of memorabilia. The original contracts, signed by the artists, are proving very popular. Madonna's theatre role in *Goose and Tom-Tom* with her then husband Sean Penn earned her only $364 (around £200) per week in 1986 and the contract for this performance is now worth £600-800.

Jerry Lee Lewis (*Great Balls of Fire*) stipulated that he be paid in cash, amongst other demands (all listed) in his 1985 contract for a concert in Florida and this fascinating memorabilia should fetch £250-300, the same price as the Bee Gees' contract for a 1975 pre-recorded show, *Midnight Special* and Frank Zappa's appearance on *Late Night with David Letterman* in 1982. Interestingly, Moon Zappa's contract for the same show is only worth £60-70.

GEORGE FORMBY

Signed photo of George Formby
(Picture by The George Formby Society)

A&C 57, est £250-300, now worth £200-300

BUDDY AND THE CRICKETS

Rare Coral promotional card from 1958, signed by rockers Buddy Holly and The Crickets (The Ian Higham Collection)

A&C 53, sold £1,500, now worth £1,500-2,500

GEORGE FORMBY

Original sheet music for George's theme tune *Chinese Laundry Blues*
(Picture by The George Formby Society)

A&C57, est £15-30, now worth £10-15

HENDRIX GUITAR

Fender Stratocaster played and burnt on stage by Jimi Hendrix at the 1968 Miami Pop festival. Given to Frank Zappa by Hendrix, it was restored and played on the Zappa album, *Zoot Allures*. Unsold at auction (COOP)

A&C 44, unsold, now worth £350-400,000

ERNA HISCOCK

Specialising in Antique Samplers

Individual & Collections Eagerly Sought

Chelsea Galleries, 69 Portabello Road, London W11
Saturdays 7am–3pm
Tel: (01233) 661407   erna@ernahiscockantiques.com

www.ernahiscockantiques.com

Witney Antiques

96-100 Corn Street
Witney
Oxfordshire
OX28 6BU

Tel.   01993 703902
Fax: 01993 779852

www.witneyantiques.com

Leading Dealers in Historic Samplers & Embroidery

Established over 40 years

Fully illustrated catalogues available by post

Open Wednesday–Saturday 10am–5pm

Other times by appointment

SAMPLING STYLES

In Victorian times, it was customary for girls to create samplers where they would literally 'sample' different sewing stitches, creating pictures often with religious mottos and these would then hang above their beds to remind them of the sayings. They are surprisingly detailed and accomplished for their age.

1832 SAMPLER

Little Archer by Miss E. Nicholas (SOTH)

A&C 35, sold for £5,287, now worth £6,000

QUEEN ANNE SAMPLER

Queen Anne era sampler dated 1713, signed Sussana Russell (GORR)

A&C 50, sold for £1,800, now worth £1,500-2,500

HOUSE AND GARDEN

English sampler by Ann Welling, 1828 (SO)

A&C 35, sold for £4,230, now worth £5-6,000

MORAL MESSAGE

Embroidered sampler by Mary Ann Franey, 1842 (SOTH)

A&C 35, sold for £5,287, now worth £5-7,000

Fact File

Samplers are very collectable and their price is determined by colours, condition and subject matter. The more colourful the sampler, the more appealing, but note that the once vivid threads would have faded over time. Samplers fade if kept in sunlight, as well as through ageing. If the material was not properly framed and kept away from dust any folds would devalue the piece and dirt can be difficult to wash in such a delicate textile, ask a restorer first.

Check that the threads and edges of the material have not frayed and that there are no stitches missing – modern thread will look out of place and any restoration needs to be sympathetic. Historical subjects such as the American Civil War command the highest prices with recognisable landmarks also being desirable, as are garden scenes or maps.

KNOW YOUR ALPHABET

Sampler with alphabet, numerals, house, motifs and pattern bands by Mary Ann Ainsworth, aged ten, 1846 (GORR)

A&C 49, sold for £750, now worth £850-950

1846 SAMPLER

Mid-Victorian sampler worked in coloured silks to a wool ground, dated 1846. Mounted, glazed and framed (BON)

A&C 60, sold for £1,250 now worth £1,400

ADAM AND EVE

A tablet sampler by Susannah Platt, aged ten, dated 1776. Estimate (SOTH)

A&C 21, sold for £7,820, now worth £8-10,000

VIRTUOUS MESSAGE

Sampler by Mary Ann Upson, 1820 (SOTH)

A&C 52, sold for £470, now worth £500-700

SCIENTIFIC INSTRUMENTS

EXPERIMENTAL COLLECTING

Science, while not studied as much as it used to be, is becoming more popular as a hobby and scientific instruments are appealing collectables for this new-found interest. They can range from globes to telescopes (exploration being important) to electricity-creating whimshurst machines.

POCKET GLOBE 1815

A Lane's two and three quarter-inch pocket terrestrial globe, dated London 1815, enclosed in a wooden case, covered in black-stained fishskin (CHEF)

A&C 48, sold for £2,600, now worth £2,800-3,000

ALL AROUND THE WORLD

The Terrestrial Globe and Newton's Improved Pocket Globe, miniature table versions on fruitwood columns (CHRIS)

A&C 29, sold £2,000, now worth £2,500-3,000

POCKET GLOBE c.1830

Lane's terrestrial pocket globe c 1830, in black fishskin-covered wooden case (GORR)

A&C 53, sold for £1,500, now worth £1,500-2,000

THE WORLD GETS SMALLER

Miniature globe on an ebonised stand, inscribed 'A Paris chez C F Delamarche rue de Foin St Jacq' (SWORD)

A&C 58, sold for £1,600, now worth £1,400-1,800

Fact File

Barometers were used to tell the weather. They often sell for surprisingly high prices at auction. This is a specialist field where the maker is all-important, as well as the design, age and quality.

The earliest versions, dating from the late 17th century were made by clockmakers, hence the similarity in their faces. There are three basic shapes – stick (often the most desirable), banjo (with a round wheel by the base of a long stick) and, more unusually, round.

Early versions used mercury, which is now known to be dangerous to handle although it used to be worn by the Elizabethans for make-up. In the 1840s, aneroid barometers were invented which didn't contain liquid (ie, mercury) but used sealed chambers to determine pressure changes – high pressure predicted storms.

CELESTIAL GLOBE

'The Navisphere' patent, created by Commander M H DeMagnac of the French Navy (GORR)

A&C 62, sold for £1,300, now worth £1,500-1,800

GEORGIAN BAROMETER

Rare and large George III barometer with tulipwood crossbanding and a convex mirror concealing a clock (SWORD)

A&C 29, sold for £3,000, now worth £5-8,000

POCKET BAROMETER

Late Victorian aneroid compensated barometer, in gilt metal case, by John Barker & Co of Kensington (GORR)

A&C 57, sold for £120, now worth £150-250

STICK BAROMETER

Walnut stick barometer from 1705. Stick barometers command high prices

A&C 52, est. £11,000, now worth £12-15,000

BRASS TELESCOPE

Negretti and Zambra 19th century brass telescope on a tripod with a fitted mahogany case (SWORD)

A&C 51, sold for £1,500, now worth £1,200-1,800

LADIES' TELESCOPE

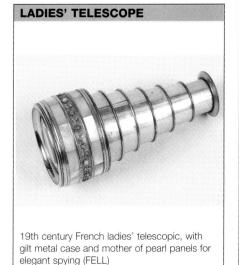

19th century French ladies' telescopic, with gilt metal case and mother of pearl panels for elegant spying (FELL)

A&C 54, sold for £120, now worth £200-300

ZOGRASCOPE

Victorian magnifying glass (zograscope), mahogany and chequer banded on turned column, 60cm high (DREW)

A&C 40, sold for £80, now worth £150-200

SEXTANT

A brass sextant (instrument for measuring distances) by Cary in mahogany case (CN)

A&C 13, sold for £1,000, now worth £2-3,000

STETHOSCOPE

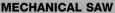

An unusual ivory and fruitwood stethoscope, 27cm long (CHRIS LA)

A&C 23, sold for £2,800, now worth £3-4,000

SLIDE CABINET

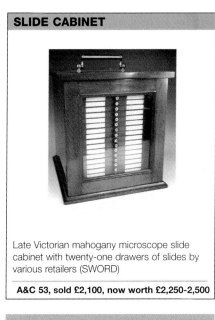

Late Victorian mahogany microscope slide cabinet with twenty-one drawers of slides by various retailers (SWORD)

A&C 53, sold £2,100, now worth £2,250-2,500

FLEMING'S DISCOVERY

A science lover's delight, a sample of penicillium mould presented by Alexander Fleming to his friend Douglas MacLeod in 1935. It doubled its estimate (CHRIS)

A&C 23, sold £14,950, now worth £18-22,000

MECHANICAL SAW

A very rare and fine mechanical steel and ivory chain saw, used for amputations and made by Charriere (CHRIS)

A&C 23, sold for £23,000, now worth £25-28,000

Fact File

Telescopes and microscopes are very popular scientific instruments. The price is determined by maker, quality (power of the lens, as well as the workmanship), age and condition. Both use lenses but for opposite reasons: the former to see items far away, the latter close up. The word 'lens' comes from the Latin word for lentil bean because that's what early versions resembled.

Microscopes were invented in 1590 and succeeded the magnifying glass (once known as the 'flea glass' because they showed the bugs in such intimate detail) which was discovered by accident in the first century AD by Romans experimenting with their new discovery – glass. They saw that distorted pieces of glass made objects appear larger. Galileo is credited with inventing the telescope in 1609 although this was vigorously disputed by Hans Lipperhey, who claimed he was first.

SEWING ACCESSORIES

ALL SEWN UP
At one time, virtually all women sewed, clothes being recycled among families and passed from mistresses to servants. As was seen with samplers, the skill was taught early. For the wealthy woman, it was an accomplishment, not a necessity and attractive sewing accessories complemented this skill.

SEWING TABLE

19th century parquetry lady's sewing table with drawer and sliding silk bag (SWORD)

A&C, now worth £1,300-1,600

SEWING NOVELTIES

Rare Victorian silver novelty sewing étui (small case) in the form of a policeman's lantern, Birmingham, 1899 (BON)

A&C 60, sold for £1,450, now worth £1,600

Fact File

One of the most desirable forms of sewing accessories is the sewing box. We covered worktables in the furniture section (p151). These sewing box tables were stationary but sewing boxes were portable, being carried between the bedroom and the drawing room where the women would gently sew, possibly attaching lace to their dresses to refresh them. Many sewing boxes contained hidden treasures set in special compartments, for example, ivory and mother of pearl accessories or finely turned bobbins. All collectable in themselves but whose absence from an otherwise complete sewing box can devalue it slightly. Check for the delicately moulded scissors and thimbles. Best buys are tortoiseshell or intricately carved sewing boxes. Buttons are also very collectable and affordable accessories which can add vintage style to modern clothes.

NEEDLE CASES

Four ivory umbrella-shaped needle cases, carved as furled umbrellas (GORR)

A&C 60, est £200-250, now worth £200-250

TEDDY BEAR PIN CUSHION

Rare articulated Birmingham silver teddy bear pin cushion (BON)

A&C 60, sold for £840, now worth £800-1,000

REGENCY WORKBOX

Regency 'Brighton' workbox, with transfer printed views of the Royal Pavilion, Steyne and beach (GORR)

A&C 60, sold for £580, now worth £550-600

TORTOISESHELL NEEDLE BOX

Victorian tortoiseshell, wedge-shaped needle box, with ivory-lined interior and a silver thimble (GORR)

A&C 60, sold for £210, now worth £200-250

SPINNING WHEEL

Mahogany spinning wheel on a tripod platform base. The foot pedal is signed by William Richardson, Edinburgh (PH ED)

A&C 34, est £200-300, now worth £300-500

COMPANIONABLE SEWING

Unusual 19th century table 'sewing companion' made from a tropical nut with turned detail (HAMP)

A&C 45, sold for £420, now worth £350-450

CIGARETTE CARDS

These had a huge following in the 1970s but the negative health implications of smoking has affected all areas of smoking related collectables, including cigarette cards. Where they used to be sold in sets, in books or individually, now they are trying to appeal to a different market, often sold in frames as attractive displays.

SAFETY FIRST

Wise advice from the Safety First series by W.D. and H.O. Wills, 50 in set

A&C 49, sold for £50 for 50, now worth £50-70

BOXING CLEVER

Six cards from a set from The Rocket – Rising Boxing Stars, from the 1920s (GTH)

A&C 49, sold for £340, now worth £300-500

STANLEY MATTHEWS

One of Wills's most collectable sets, 'Association Footballers', 1939 issue, a set of 50, featuring Stanley Matthews, Stoke City

A&C 16, sold for £2, now worth £2-4

GRAND NATIONAL

John Player's 'Grand National & Derby Winners', 1933. Grand Parade, Derby, 1919

A&C 16, sold for £1.50, now worth £1.50-3

Fact File

Collecting cigarette cards is known as cartophilly. They started life as blank cards, intended to stop the fragile cigarette packets from getting crushed. For this reason, they were known as stiffeners. In 1886, US cigarette firm created the first advertising card by printing their details on the stiffeners. W.D. & H.O. Wills copied the idea in Britain in 1888 and the first cigarette cards, as we know them, followed. One of the rarest is the Taddy & Co. 20-card set of Clowns and Circus Artistes which sells for £600-650 per card. Sets tended to consist of around 50 cards, encouraging consumer loyalty and books were created in which the cards could be inserted and this increased their desirability. Attractive women, especially actresses, were very popular sets, as were footballers and vehicles.

TRAIN ENGINES

A complete set of 50 Railway Engine cards issued by W.D & H.O. Wills in 1924. Trains are very collectable (Picture by Lee Towersey)

A&C 49, sold for £50, now worth £50-60

CIRCUS LIFE

Lusby Scenes from Circus Life set (BON)

A&C 64, sold for £3,055, now worth £2,500-3,500

NAVAL SKITS

Collection including Young Naval Skits Captain 1735, Cope's Golfers (BON)

A&C 61, sold for £494, now worth £450-550

RECRUITMENT CARDS

A collection including sought-after Lambert & Butler World's Locomotives, Recruiting Posters, and Aviation series (BON)

A&C 62, sold for £317, now worth £250-350

SMOKING ACCESSORIES

SMOKING AND SNUFF

Some smoking accessories have fallen out of fashion because of the hazards attached to smoking but others, such as lighters and pipes, remain collectable. You don't have to be a smoker to appreciate the designs and craftsmanship of some of these goods. Whilst not included here, opium pipes are also highly collectable.

DUNHILL LIGHTER

A Dunhill 18ct gold unique sports watch lighter, Swiss, with London import mark for 1931. Petrol fill with felt pouch (SOTH)

A&C 17, sold for £5,060, now worth £5-6,000

SNUFF MULL

Silver mounted Scottish ram's horn made into a snuff mull (storer) with a cairngorm mounted hinged cover (CHEF)

A&C 63, sold for £1,600, now worth £1,200-1,800

SNUFF BOX

Charles II silver and boxwood carved snuff box with the royal coat of arms, dated 1661. Old snuff boxes can be hard to find (GORR)

A&C 52, sold for £5,400, now worth £5-6,000

PIPE RACK

Stained beech pipe rack with a lithograph panel of Old King Cole, by Hassell, 56cm x 76cm. Use pipe racks for display (SWORD)

A&C 53, sold for £320, now worth £300-500

Fact File

17th century, plain white clay pipes are still popular finds for amateur archaeologists and are very cheap at £3-5, despite their age.

Tobacco did not arrive in Britain until Hawkins and Drake brought it back from the Americas in 1565. Before that, people smoked rolled up leaves, the Romans being particularly fond of pear leaves. The use of the pipe declined in the 18th century with the growth of snuff and then in the 19th century with the introduction of more convenient cigarettes.

Meerschaum was used to create some of the most beautiful pipes. The hard white mineral, often mistaken for clay, absorbs the tobacco and, over time, takes on a yellow-brown hue, almost like amber. It was often beautifully carved, generally as a man's head. Expect to pay £100+.

CIGARETTE CASE

Enamelled silver cigarette case, depicting an ocean going sloop, the case with gilt interior, Birmingham, 1946, 14cm x 8.5cm (FELL)

A&C 45, sold for £520, now worth £500-600

MR PUNCH TOBACCO JAR

Mr Punch tobacco jar. This popular figure was also used for vestas (metal matchboxes)

A&C 31, sold for £275, now worth £300-500

SHOP DISPLAY

Framed shop display of tobacco products and clay pipes of various ages from Bacon Brothers, 16 Market Hill, Cambridge (CHEF)

A&C 48, sold for £130, now worth £120-180

TOBACCO LEAF

Tobacco leaf with painting of a girl (BON)

A&C 62, sold for £1,034, now worth £800-1,200

VESTAS

The Roman goddess, Vesta, was the goddess of the hearth, the fireplace which was at the centre of the home. Matchcases were named after her, the most appealing being figural. As well as keeping the matches from getting wet or snapped, they also had a rough edge for striking but got replaced by cheap, disposal cardboard versions.

CARTRIDGE SHAPE

Victorian silver vesta with enamelled numerals, in the form of a cartridge, by Sampson Morden, famous for their pens (MALL)

A&C 54, sold for £2,800, now worth £2,500-4,000

BOOK FORM

Victorian vesta, shaped like a book and enamelled with the words 'My last', Birmingham, silver, 1886 (PH KN)

A&C 29, sold for £391, now worth £350-550

TUBULAR VESTA

Silver vesta in the form of a tube with a finial of a soldier, 12in long, sold together with a twisted silver pencil (MALL)

A&C 43, sold for £250, now worth £200-400

ENAMELLED SHIP

Edwardian vesta with an enamelled panel depicting a galleon at sea. By Messrs. Holder, Birmingham, 1908 (PH KN)

A&C 29, sold for £311, now worth £300-400

VICTORIAN GIRL

Victorian vesta case of rectangular form. The cover depicts a girl with long dark hair, dressed in a blue and yellow bodice. By C.H. Cheshire, Birmingham, 1896 (PH KN)

A&C 29, sold for £759, now worth £800-1,200

Fact File

Vestas are generally made of silver but can also be found in brass. This includes Mr Punch, the famous puppet character and it's probably the most faked vesta. The faked version is either too light or heavy and very crudely moulded. Real ones sell for £200-400, fakes, generally not sold as such, are around £15.

Gambling was a popular theme for vestas with cards and dice a favourite, the latter sometimes being enamelled. Most vestas are plain metal so enamelling adds interest and value. One of the most appealing is a late-Victorian vesta in the shape of an envelope with a Penny Blue stamp. The date on the postmark matched the hallmark, 1891 and it was very detailed, selling for £400.

WARTIME MEMORIES

The silver matchbox used in the First World War, now back in its original family's ownership after 80 years, some wear (APEX)

A&C 61, now worth £40-80

ASPREY'S

George V Asprey & Co silver smoker's compendium (storage) with graduated tiers for matches, cigarettes and cigars, 1912 (GORR)

A&C 53, sold for £1,500, now worth £1,500-2,500

SPORTING GOODS

CRICKET

Cricket is one of the most appealing sports for collectors but no one is sure quite how or why it originated. It was first mentioned in 1300 when Prince Edward played his friend, Piers Gaveston. The first recorded match took place in Kent in 1646. Roger Fenton took the earliest known 'photographs' in 1857 and team photos are popular.

PORTRAIT OF A CRICKETER

A rare mid-nineteenth century 'Portrait of a Cricketer', English School (CHRIS)

A&C 45, sold for £11,750, now worth £12–15,000

W. G. GRACE

Watercolour of W. G. Grace by Walked Hodgson, together with his ink drawing of Grace's cricket bag. Mounted with Grace's autograph (BON)

A&C 62, sold for £823, now worth £800–1,000

SIGNED POSTCARDS

A fine album of autographed portrait postcards of 'golden-age' cricketers, dated 1904 (SOTH)

A&C 45, sold for £8,225, now worth £8–10,000

GOOD GOLLY

Silver Crane teapot for Robertson's Jam showing the golly playing cricket (GORR)

A&C 45, sold for £70, now worth £250–500

Fact File

Cricket is a game for gentlemen and was very popular during the Civil War of the seventeenth century when the nobility would play games between battles or when hiding from Parliamentarian forces.

Bats in those days looked like sticks and were swung like baseball bats. The current shape was created in 1853. Ones played at top games or by the best players are highly desirable with values to match.

The record price of £54,257 was set by Sir Garfield Sobers' 1968 bat with which he scored six consecutive sixes in an over. In the same auction, another of his bats was sold for £47,476 from his 1958 world-record setting 365 runs against Pakistan in Kingston.

1948 ENGLAND TEAM

The 1948 England cricket team and Sir Donald Bradman, limited edition, signed by all the players (GORR)

A&C 45, sold for £130 now worth £150-350

CANTERBURY CRICKET WEEK

Photographic montage depicting Canterbury Cricket Week 1877, 318cm x 564cm. Sold along with Canterbury Cricket Week, Jubilee Meeting 1891 (CANT)

A&C 35 sold for £390, now worth £300-500

SILVER SALVER

A decorative silver salver with scalloped edges presented to cricketer Roger Kynaston by the M.C.C. in 1858 (CHRIS)

A&C 21, sold for £2,232, now worth £2,500-3,000

ROYAL DOULTON

A Royal Doulton miniature two handled pot – The All Black Team (FELI)

A&C 20, sold for £620, now worth £600-1,000

1930s AUSTRALIAN TEAM

Signed mounted-photograph of the 1930s Australians, 37cm x 43.5cm. (SOTH)

A&C 45, sold for £352, now worth £300-500

CRICKET IN PRINT

Annuals and magazines including *Cricket Quarterly* and press cuttings' albums (SOTH)

A&C 45, sold for £881, now worth £800-1,200

JUVENILE BAT

A juvenile-size bat signed by the 1934 England and Australia test sides and the 1933–34 Chelsea football squad. (SOTH)

A&C 45, sold for £646, now worth £600-800

GRACE PORTRAIT

Portrait of cricketer W. G. Grace wearing the princely turban of his friend Prince Ranjitsinhji, by Henry Scott Tuke R.A., R.W.S., signed by the artist and autographed by W. G. Grace. (BON)

A&C 62, sold for £21,150, now worth £20-30,000

Fact File

Top cricketers include W. G. Grace (1849–1915), the grandfather of cricket and the legendary Australian Don Bradman who played in the infamous 1932–33 'Bodyline' series.

One surprise name is Sir Arthur Conan Doyle, creator of Sherlock Holmes, who played for the Marylebone Cricket Club and even bowled out W. G. Grace who invited him to become the president of London County Cricket Club's new bowling club. A portrait of W. G. Grace wearing 'Ranji's' turban, painted by Henry Scott Tuke in 1908 sold for £21,150 and was accompanied by a photograph of Grace with Ranjitsinhji, the Indian Prince and English batsman.

Cricket balls are also good buys. A very modern cricket ball sold in July 2004 for around £20,000, shortly after Shane Warne bowled it to equal the world record in a World Test match.

SPORTING GOODS

FISHING

Fishing collectables have a dedicated following with fishing reels increasing in popularity in recent years, a 1930s limited edition reel by Hardy fetching £10,000. Other people's lack of knowledge makes this a good area to collect, just like stuffed fish. Old fishing books are also good buys as are prints, often listed under hunting.

SEA REEL

Walnut reel from around 1910, with brass star back centre pin and horn handles, 17.5cm (GORR)

A&C 60, sold for £160, now worth £150–200

WICKER WORLD

A Hardy 'Perfect' brown wicker creel, with leather strapped front net and canvas shoulder strap, brass plaque with makers details (BON)

A&C 29, sold for £130, now worth £200–300

BRASS REEL

Turned and stained ivory handle and engraved C. Farlow & Co, Makers, 191 Strand, London. (GORR)

A&C 42, sold for £100, now worth 150–200

J. COOPER & SONS

A tench mounted in bow front case bears Cooper Label. Case inscribed, Tench 4lb 8 1/2 oz. caught by Ken Eastmead at Bowood Lake Caln 23 August 1951 (BON)

A&C 29, sold for £880, now worth £1,000–2,000

Fact File

There is an episode of *Lovejoy* where the infamous rogue dealer finds a rare stuffed fish. It's feasible because it's an obscure area for non-collectors who would probably overlook the dusty cabinets with their large stuffed and mounted fish in scenic displays.

These dried fish would have been taken to specialist firms by the fishermen who caught them, including J. Cooper & Sons (taxidermists famed for using bow-fronted cases) who would inscribe the display with the name of the fisherman and the date and size of their catch.

The more stylish displays in good condition sell for £1,000–1,500. It is worth mentioning that not all of the fish seen are real but are actually carved versions of the original fish, some of these can fetch £3,000–5,000.

PIKE

A stuffed pike in a presentation case. The large fish are ideal for displays (CLEV)

A&C 23, sold for £1,350, now worth £1,500–2,000

SALMON FISHING

Salmon Fishing by J. J. Hardy, 1907 Black cloth binding with gilt decoration. Some foxing (BON)

A&C 29, sold for £120, now worth £200–300

REEL BARGAIN

An Allcocks Match Aerial reel with twin black handles optional check and adjustable brake. (BON)

A&C 29, sold for £120, now worth £150–250

DISPATCH BOX

Of blue leather, stamped 'Royal Commission on Salmon Fisheries, John Fell Esq.' (GORR)

A&C 53, sold for £300, now worth £200–400

FOOTBALL

The nation's favourite pastime has spawned a huge range of memorabilia. The best memorabilia comes from the top matches including FA or World Cup finals or players such as Pelé or George Best. Football programmes from the 1970s and earlier are very collectable as most people threw them away, again, top matches are best.

LEAGUE CUP FINAL

A League Cup Final programme, 1972, Stoke versus Chelsea, autographed by Gordon Banks

A&C 14, est £8, now worth £20-30

BRONZE FIGURES

Two fine silvered bronze figures of footballers, c.1940. Each stands on a grey marble base, 25cm high. Believed to be G. O. Smith and C. B. Fry (HAMP)

A&C 14, sold for £800, now worth £1,000-1,500

1966 AND ALL THAT

Programme for the 1966 World Cup Final

A&C 14, est £50, now worth £60-80

AFTER MUNICH AIR DISASTER

Manchester United verus Nottingham Forest, 22 February 1958, the first home match after the Munich air disaster

A&C 14, est £35, now worth £50-70

Fact File

Football memorabilia hit the headlines recently when Beckham's boots sold for £2,350 although he wears so many which get resold that prices have settled around the £500–800 mark with big matches fetching more. His shirts sell for £700–2,500 depending on the game. Attention is now moving to Wayne Rooney who will provide the next must-buy goods, although he lacks the visual appeal of the photogenic Beckham so it's unlikely that his prices will equal the England captain's. The top scorer is Pelé whose World Cup final shirt from the 1970 final sold for £157,750 compared to £91,750 for Geoff Hurst's shirt in his hat-trick winning 1966 World Cup final. Pelé's boots worn when scoring his 1,000th goal in 1969, sold for £12,000 and his 1960 contract with Santos FC is worth £10,000–15,000.

FOREVER BLOWING BUBBLES

Billy Bonds' testimonial match programme, 1978, West Ham vs. Spurs

A&C 14, est £5, now worth £10-15

GEORGE BEST

Green Northern Ireland number 11 match-worn international jersey signed by George Best (SOTH)

A&C 62, sold for £6,240, now worth £6,000-7,000

ENGLAND V BRAZIL

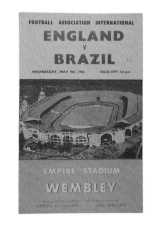

England v Brazil, 1956. Valued at £5

A&C 14, est £5, now worth £30-50

PRESENTATION FOOTBALL

A Tottenham Hotspur football from the 2002/03 season signed by the players with approximately thirty signatures (SWORD)

A&C 53, sold for £100, now worth £100-150

SPORTING GOODS

CENTENARY CUP FINAL

Centenary FA Cup final programme, 1972. Leeds versus Sunderland. Valued at £4

A&C 14, est £4, now worth £20–40

FOOTBALL FIGURE

Royal Dux porcelain, 30cm high.(HAMP)

A&C 50, sold for £200, now worth £200–300

ARSENAL PROGRAMME

An Arsenal programme, 1929–1930

A&C 14, est £35, now worth £50–70

IN RESERVE

Programme for Arsenal Reserves v Southampton Reserves, 1935

A&C 14, est £25, now worth £40–60ß

PELE PRINT

Limited edition signed print of Pele during the 1970 World Cup Final, Brazil versus Italy, after an original by American artist C. M. Dudash. Signed by Pele (BON)

A&C 62, sold for £93, now worth £100–200

1934 WORLD CUP

Very rare official 1934 Football World Cup tournament programme, fine condition (SOTH)

A&C 62, sold for £7,800, now worth £8–10,000

Fact File

The first FA Cup played at Wembley was in 1923, shortly after the famous stadium had been opened. A complete ticket (they would normally have been ripped in half) from this match sold for £3,200 and football fans are advised to keep everything from the important games they visit including tickets and programmes.

The top price for a match programme is £14,400 for the 1901 FA Cup final between Tottenham Hotspur and Sheffield United, while a collection of early football programmes reached a price of £100,000 at auction.

Medals awarded to players are also very desirable and Ray Wilson's 1966 World Cup medal was sold for £80,750. FA Cup final medals tend to sell for between £4,500–22,000 depending on the players. And, when it comes to teams, Manchester United are still the favourites.

RANGERS FIGURE

Rare Rangers footballer ceramic figure, 35.5cm, reg no. 366136 (BON)

A&C 36, sold for £820, now worth £1,000–1,500

CIGARETTE CARD

Scotland's A. James from the Player's Football Caricatures By 'Mac' series of 50. Picture by The London Cigarette Card Co. Ltd

A&C 49, now worth £10-15

GOLF

The origins of golf are much debated with both the Scots and the French claiming to have invented the game. It was officially started in 1744 in Edinburgh with St Andrews Golf Club being started shortly afterwards. In terms of collecting, clubs, balls, programmes, autographs, photographs, books and trophies are the best options.

GOLF BALL MARKER

A rare golf ball marker, c.1870s.(CHRIS)

A&C 19, sold for £47,700, now worth £50–60,000

BISCUIT BARREL

Biscuit barrel by W. Wood & Co, early-twentieth century. Pewter rim and silver plated lid, 18cm high (FELL)

A&C 39, sold for £960, now worth £1,000–1,500

TOAST RACK

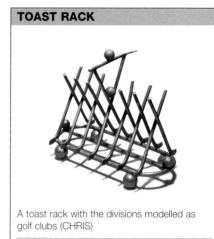

A toast rack with the divisions modelled as golf clubs (CHRIS)

A&C 20, sold for £258, now worth £350-500

THE RULES OF GOLF

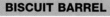

Illustrated Rules of Golf by Charles Crombie, published 1905, red lettering on green cloth boards, 30cm x 46cm. Estimate £300–£400. (SWORD)

A&C 50, sold for £320, now worth £XX

Fact File

The best golf clubs, in terms of collecting, date from before 1920 when the steel shaft was introduced. An exception is those owned by famous people, including John F. Kennedy, whose set of clubs in a bag inscribed 'JFK, Washington, DC' sold for around £450,000, ten times their estimate.

The world record for an individual club was set by a long-nose or 'scared' head version which sold for £106,000. Top makers include:
• Dunn
• Dickson
• Jackson
• Wilson
• Hugh Philp, the most desirable of them all (expect to pay around £10–15,000).

THE RULES OF GOLF

Illustrated Rules of Golf by Charles Crombie, a much reproduced humorous text (CHRIS)

A&C 19, sold for £1.997, now worth £2,000–3,000

RAKE IRON

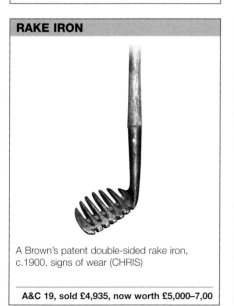

A Brown's patent double-sided rake iron, c.1900, signs of wear (CHRIS)

A&C 19, sold £4,935, now worth £5,000–7,00

THOMPSON MEDAL

The Thompson Medal for the Musselburgh Merchants Golf Club, c.1900, 9ct gold (BON)

A&C 36, sold for £660, now worth £600–1,000

SCARED-HEAD CLUB

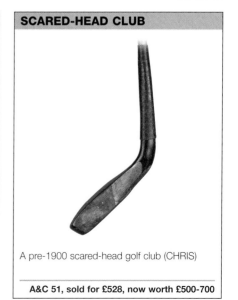

A pre-1900 scared-head golf club (CHRIS)

A&C 51, sold for £528, now worth £500-700

UNIQUE CENTRE OF THE NORTH

Wentworth
Arts Crafts & Antiques

We feature a good range of furniture, antique & reproduction, decorative antiques, collectables & crafts

We buy antique furniture, collectables & curios

Ample on-site parking & wheelchair access

Dine in our coffee shop

Open every day 10am–5pm

To rent units & display cabinets call 01226 744333

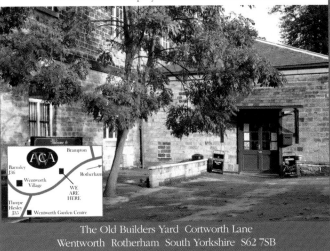

The Old Builders Yard Cortworth Lane
Wentworth Rotherham South Yorkshire S62 7SB

The Antiques Warehouse

A wide range of antiques, fine & country furniture, collectables and garden artefacts set in two stunning Elizabethan tithe barns.

Large Free Car Park

Coffee and homemade cakes served at weekends — often accompanied by live piano music.

Telephone : 01252 317 590

Open 7 days 10.00am–5.30pm

Bagshot Farm, St George's Road, Runfold, Farnham, Surrey GU9 9HR

www.theantiqueswarehouse.com

The largest auction house in the world specialising exclusively in golfing memorabilia

Old Golf Auctions is dedicated to bringing the world's most valuable golfing memorabilia to the attention of private and professional collectors and enthusiasts worldwide, via our regular online auctions. We also act as a highly attractive sales channel for those looking to dispose of high quality memorabilia, either individual items or entire collections. Established in 2000, we have already achieved six world records.

For buyers, we offer access to a wide range of the highest quality golfing memorabilia from our global clientbase of sellers – balls and ball-related items, clubs, books, artwork, programmes, ceramics and glass, postcards and other ephemera. Registering to bid in our auctions is quick, easy and completely free. We don't even require any credit card details.

For sellers, we offer exposure to a global client-base of over 1,000 registered bidders, in 28 countries, including some of the most highly respected collectors of premium quality golfing memorabilia in the world.

We consistently succeed in selling over 90% of the lots consigned to us - roughly double the level achieved by traditional auction houses.

We also offer lower commission rates than any other auction house – internet-based or otherwise – in the world.

Our rates, for both buyers and sellers are: Sale price £2,000 or less - 10%, Sale price over £2,000 - 7.5% So why not give us a try! We look forward to hearing from you.

Prospective buyers can register to bid on our future auctions by logging on to our website at any time: www.oldgolfauctions.com

Sellers should contact us by telephone on 44 (0)1384 75438 or 44 (0)1384 261616, or by e-mail at: enquiries@oldgolfauctions.com

Visit our golf memorabilia catalogue site too at: www.oldgolfmemorabilia.com

GOLF MEDAL

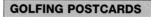

15ct gold golf medal (CHRIS)

A&C 44, sold for £493, now worth £400-600

GOLFING POSTCARDS

Edwardian humorous golfing scenes dated 1908, published by Langsdorff & Co, Series No. 710. (SWORD)

A&C 66, sold for £100, now worth £100-150

PENFOLD FIGURE

Penfold golfing ad figure from the 1930s

A&C 56, sold for £550-650, now worth £500-700

ROYAL DOULTON

Royal Doulton stoneware vase painted with a golf scene. (CHRIS)

A&C 58, sold for £4,465, now worth £4,000–6,000

WINNER'S BOWL

Silver punch bowl, late Victorian, engraved 'Bowdon Golf Club Ladies Prize 1898 won by W. G. Clegg'. London 1897, by Wakely and Wheeler, 29cm diameter, 37oz. (DREW)

A&C 40, sold for £150, now worth £150-250

STAFFORDSHIRE PLATE

Transfer decorated Staffordshire plate with a golfing scene and inscribed 'Full Swing', from around 1910 (SWORD)

A&C 65, sold for £110, now worth £100-150

Fact File

Old balls are also worth money, the record being £20,000 for a late nineteenth century hexagonal, hard rubber, dimpled one. One of the most sought-after is the tiny feathery ball. An early nineteenth century version fetched £7,000 at auction. The early rubber balls were prone to damage and this affects their value. A terrestrial globe ball sold for £10,500 while one with a fine crack reached only a tenth of that.

Books and ephemera also command high prices. A rare programme from the 1923 British Open Golf Championship sold for £1,500. The first book to introduce and describe the game was *The Goff*, published in Edinburgh in the mid-eighteenth century, a third edition from 1744 fetched £19,975. The 1842 Golfiana made £9,400 at a specialist auction.

GOLFING POSTER

Dorette Muller, Golf Club D'Alsace (CHRIS)

A&C 19, sold for £2,937, now worth £3,000–6,000

JOHN WHYTE-MELVILLE

A portrait of John Whyte-Melville of Bennochy, playing at St Andrews golf course. Painted by Sir Francis Grant (PH)

A&C 19, sold £150,000, now worth £180-200,000

SPORTING GOODS

HUNTING

One of the most controversial of all sports, hunting collectables have a firm following, even among those who are anti-hunting. Part of the appeal of the sport is for the costumes and items celebrating the start of the race with hunters in their rich red jackets. Also, items set around the actual riding and jumping are very popular.

JAMES STINTON

Watercolour of a cock and hen pheasant by James Stinton (1870-1961) (LOCK)

A&C, sold for £560, now worth £500-800

STIRRUP CUP

Victorian stirrup cup. Silver fox mask with gilt interior and the mark of James Barclay Hennell & Sons, London, 1881, 12.7cm long, used by riders before a hunt (PH ED)

A&C 29, sold for £1,495, now worth £1,500-2,500

ROYAL DEER

19th century English school of deer resting within a woodland landscape. The castle beyond is believed to be Windsor (RT)

A&C 13, sold for £3,000, now worth £3,000–5,000

SPODE INDIAN SPORTING SERIES

A Spode Indian Sporting series oval, earthenware dish c 1820 (BOO)

A&C 13, sold for £290, now worth £400–600

Fact File

Hunting is not just about foxes and stags. Shooting (birds and rabbits) is part of the way of life for hunters, as was badger baiting and chicken fights, although these latter two are not so popular among collectors because of the gory nature of the related goods. Strictly speaking, fishing should also be thought of as hunting, although we have listed it separately.

One of the most surprising markets is in decoys, used by hunters to lure ducks and other birds. The highest price achieved at auction was around £400,000 for an Elmer Crowell sleeping Canadian goose. The carved decoy by one of the most collectable makers, almost doubled in price in just ten years. The previous record was around £225,000 for a Mason factory wooden duck.

SET OF FOUR NAPKIN RINGS

Four silver napkin rings signed Stinton, Birminham, 1928 with enamel decoration of game birds

A&C, sold for £720, now worth £800–1,000

FIGURAL STOPPER

A Royal Brierley decanter with figural stopper and hand colouring on transfer picture (SOTH)

A&C 61, now worth £400–600

FACE SCREENS

Face screens were used to stop women's make-up from melting when they sat close to the fire. These papier mâché versions were painted in the style of Richard Andsell (BON)

A&C 40, sold for £500, now worth £400-800

HUNTER ON HORSE

20th century Nyphenburg porcelain figure of Hunter on Horse

A&C 1, sold for £130, now worth £200-400

ROYAL WORCESTER

Four Royal Worcester cups and saucers with pheasants painted by different artists including James Stinton and dating from between 1924-35 (WO WA)

A&C, sold for £500, now worth £400-600

PAPIER MACHE TRAY

Papier mache tray with a hunting scene with awkwardly painted horse and rider (SWORD)

A&C 64, sold for £720, now worth £600-800

THOMAS BLINKS

1886 oil painting of A Burning Scent by Thomas Blinks (1860-1912) (DREW)

A&C 8, sold for £19,000, now worth £20–30,000

STIRRUP CUP

19th century Staffordshire stirrup cup, with yellow eyes and black muzzle 12 cm (WO WA)

A&C, sold for £320, now worth £200–400

HIGHLAND HUNTER

Bronze highlander showing a fox to a hound, by Pierre-Jules Mene (1832–1874). Signed, 53cm high, (PH ED)

A&C 34, sold for £10,000, now worth £10–15,000

MINTON RED DEER

A Minon bone china plate with hand-painted red deer and a pierced trelliswork border. The painting is initialled 'HM", c 1870 (WO WA)

A&C, sold for £240, now worth £200–300

Fact File

Cecil Aldin (1870–1935) is renowned for his appealing studies of dogs, which were sketched as book illustrations but, according to his obituary in 'The Times', he was also one of the leading sports artists, specialising in hunting. He created two very different styles. The serious, highly detailed prints capture the essence of the horse and rider with a real sense of movement. Some of these would have been created in sets of four to show the progress of the hunt, a common feature of hunting prints. These sell for around £250–350 a print. His chromolithographs, colourful prints with an oil-base (ie very colourful and not obviously prints) are very comical, gently mocking the seriousness of hunters and the sport. They are wonderful, colourful studies worth £350–450 each.

STONEWARE MUG

George III stoneware loving cup with hunting scene in relief, signe W.C. Rugbag, 1785, some damage (MALL)

A&C 56, sold for £1,400, now worth £1,000–2,000

GAME BIRDS

PAair of stuffed game birds set in a scene and mounted on a plinth

A&C, now worth £500-700

SPORTING GOODS

RUGBY

England's success in the 2004 World Cup has led to an increased interest in rugby and its memorabilia. William Webb Ellis is believed to have created rugby when playing football in 1823, after he picked up the ball and ran with it. But there has been a similar Cornish game since the Bronze Age and there are Irish and Welsh versions.

RUGBY LEAGUE CAPS

Four rugby league caps: a red England cap inscribed 1928–29, two red Great Britain Tour caps inscribed 1932 and 1936, and a black and white cap inscribed 'Test Match', 1937; with a black and white photograph of Martin Hodgson (SOTH)

A&C 62, sold for £1,320, now worth £1,000–1,500

HOW TO PLAY RUGBY

1930s rugby book with dust wrapper (Rugby Relics Ltd)

A&C, sold for £50, now worth £50-80

Fact File

William Webb Ellis was a pupil at Rugby School which gave the game he created its name. William Gilbert began making balls for Rugby school after Webb's famous game. He had a shoemaking shop near the famous school and sewed four strips of leather over a pig's bladder. The bladder gave the ball its distinctive shape, although it is now more ovular than it was originally. Gilbert's balls are very collectable.

Jonny Wilkinson famously used a Gilbert ball in the World Cup final. It was said to be worth £500,000 (a slight exaggeration, we feel) and was controversially kept by the Australian team after the match. An Australian newspaper offered to return it for the Ashes.

MOST CAPPED PLAYER

Eight international rugby shirts were offered for sale as one lot by Jason Leonard OBE, the most capped rugby player in history, but failed to reach their estimate of £100,000–£150,000 at Christie's South Kensington

A&C 62, est £100–150,000, now worth £80–90000

MATCH PROGRAMME

New Zealand versus the British Lions match programme, 1971 (Rugby Relics Ltd)

A&C, sold for £30, now worth £30-50

HONOURS CAP

A Cornwall Schools honours cap, 1937–1938 (Rugby Relics Ltd)

A&C, sold for £150, now worth £150-180

WILL CARLING

A signed photograph of former England captain Will Carling in his Harlequins colours (Rugby Relics Ltd)

A&C, sold for £15, now worth £15–20

CADBURY'S COCOA

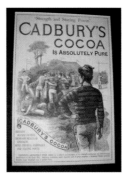

1888 print advertising Cadbury's Cocoa displaying a rugby scene (Rugby Relics Ltd)

A&C, sold for £65, now worth £70–100

STAINED GLASS WINDOW

Stained glass and lead interior window panel depicting a rugby match, from around 1910 (SOTH)

A&C 62, sold for £7,200, now worth £7,000-9,000

TENNIS

One of the most famous players was Henry VIII. The game has evolved since then. The most popular tennis shirt used to be by Lacoste with its trademark crocodile badge. The shirt was designed by legendary tennis player, Jean René Lacoste (1904–96) – nicknamed 'The Crocodile', and is one of the first examples of a designer logo.

TILT-HEADED RACKETS

Three early tilt-headed rackets, extremely rare. The racket on the right sold for: £18,800 (CHRI)

A&C 42, sold for £18,800, now worth £16–24,000

TENNIS BROOCH

Victorian silver and gold-mounted ladies tennis brooch by Thomas Smith of Birmingham, 1883 (SOTH)

A&C 62, sold for £352, now worth £300-400

LOVE MATCH

A watercolour by Violet Beatrice Kell, *A Break In Play* (CHRIS)

A&C 19, sold for £1,410, now worth £1,500–2,000

EARLY RACKET

An early 1870s tennis racket (CHRIS)

A&C 19, sold for £998, now worth £1,000-2,000

SILVER TROPHY

Davis Cup 1912, modelled as a kangaroo (CHRIS)

A&C 45, sold for £3,525, now worth £4,000-5,000

Fact File

Tennis rackets from the 1880s sell for £1,000–2,500, relatively little compared to golf clubs from the same era. The game has seen some of the most colourful characters of all sports and their memorabilia is very collectable, while not commanding the high prices of other games such as cricket and football.

One of the best players was Arthur Ashe (1943–93) who became the world number one in 1975 when he beat Bjorn Borg to win Wimbledon. His autograph sells for £150–200 and is one of the most sought-after of modern players.

Bjorn Borg went on to win Wimbledon for the next five years (1976–80), finally being defeated by John McEnroe before retiring in 1983, aged 26. His autograph fetches £80–120 because of his premature retirement.

COLOUR LITHOGRAPH

A lithograph in colours, entitled *The Art Of Tennis* (CHRIS)

A&C 19, sold for £470, now worth £600-800

SPORTING WINDOW

K. S. Ranjitsinhji sporting window from 1910, depicting a tennis match (SOTH)

A&C 57, sold for £12,000, now worth £10–15,000

RUGSTORE
Specialists in Kilims

Fine Decorative, Oriental, New, Old and Antique Carpets, Rugs & Runners.
Specialising in a wide selection of Old & Antique Turkish Kilims.
Kilim Cushions & Kilim-Upholstered Furniture.

**Professional Hand Cleaning & Restoration Services.
We Buy Old & Antique Carpets - Even Damaged Rugs.
Part-exchange & Evaluations.**

637 FULHAM ROAD • LONDON • SW6 5UQ • UK • TEL & FAX: +44 (0)207 610 9800
329 UPPER RICHMOND ROAD WEST • EAST SHEEN • SW14 8QR • UK
TEL: +44 (0)208 876 0070

email: info@rugstore.org   www.rugstore.org

---

the Rug centre
ONE OF THE BEST SELECTIONS IN THE SOUTH OF ENGLAND

**AN ENORMOUS RANGE OF HANDMADE
RUGS & KELIMS** LARGE CARPETS, RUNNERS,
SADDLEBAGS, ETC.
~ **OVER 30 YEARS' EXPERIENCE** ~
INSURANCE VALUATIONS & REPAIRS ~
FREE HOME TRIALS

**68 SOUTH STREET, DORKING, SURREY RH4 2HD
01306 882202**

NORTHCOTE ROAD
ANTIQUES MARKET
155A   0207 228 6850   155A

45 dealers offering a wide variety of ANTIQUES & COLLECTABLES

Furniture, polished, painted & pine ~
China ~ Glass ~ Art Deco & Clarice
Cliff ~ Lighting ~ Mirrors ~ Silver &
Plate ~ Flatware ~ Jewellery ~ Pictures
& Prints ~ Victoriana ~ Kitchenalia

GALLERY CAFE
Open Monday–Saturday 10–6
Sunday 12–5
**155A Northcote Road,
Battersea, London SW11 60B**

GLOUCESTER
ANTIQUE CENTRE

Come and visit the Antiques Centre in Gloucester Docks

Spend a few hours browsing our wonderful selection of antiques & collectables, you're sure to find something of interest.

Furniture, Silver, Glass, China, Jewellery, Stamps, Cards, Toys,
Games, Books, Railwayana, Linen and much, much more . . .

And while you're here enjoy a snack or meal in our restaurant.

**Open Monday–Saturday 10.00am–5.00pm
Sunday 1.00pm–5.00pm**

**1 Severn Road, Gloucester GL1 2LE
Tel: 01452 529716**

www.antiques-center.com

CLOTHS AND WALL, WINDOW AND FLOOR COVERINGS

Rugs and carpets are offering some of the biggest surprises at the moment, especially pre-19th century versions. A scrap of a 1630 Mughal carpet recently fetched £57,360 because of its quality. The Mughal piece had over 2,000 knots in a square inch, making it one of the densest woven carpets in the world.

PERSIAN RUG

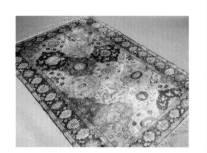

Persian silk rug with central Arabesque motifs, 122cm x 160cm (SWORD)

A&C 47, sold for £950, now worth £1,200-1,500

COLOURFUL RUG

Early 19th century bocha (silk ottoman, a heavy fabric) in an unusually bright yellow, with floral motifs (CHRIS)

A&C 60, sold £3,290, now worth £3,500-3,800

WILLIAM MORRIS STYLE

Large carpet in the style of William Morris with plant motifs (SWORD)

A&C 64, sold for £480, now worth £400-600

17th CENTURY OTTOMAN

Patterned 17th century embroidered linen ottoman (heavy fabric) (CHRIS)

A&C 65, sold £60,950, now worth £60-65,000

Fact File

The Ottoman (Turkish) Empire, former Soviet countries, various north Asian and some Middle-Eastern nations had a very strong tradition in rug and carpet making. It's possible to identify the region where the floor coverings were made by studying the patterns and colours used. A 17th century rug with medallion patterns from Ushak in Turkey sold for around £32,500, the rich red colourings and repeated pattern typical of the quality of the era.

The increase in European dominance from the late-18th, early-19th centuries, lead to a decrease in quality with the rugs becoming rougher and coarser as more were needed for export, allowing less time for production. Beforehand, they were created for the royal palaces and mosques as well as export. Persian rugs remain the best known.

1630 MUGHAL CARPET

This rare fragment of carpet is surprisingly valuable because of its quality, density of knots and age (BON)

A&C 66, sold for £57,360, now worth £57,360

DRAUGHT EXCLUDER

An attractive Aubusson tapestry portière (door curtain) with gold detail (CHRIS)

A&C 40, sold for £2,350, now worth £3,000-5,000

WEST PERSIAN CARPET

A Bakhtiari carpet, West Persia in shades of red, c.1910 (SOTH)

A&C 18, sold for £7,590, now worth £12-15,000

1785 CLOTH

Cover of toile de Jouy, c.1785 (CHRIS)

A&C 40, sold for £940, now worth £1,000-1,200

TINS

BISCUIT TINS

Packaging is very important in a competitive field and biscuit manufacturers, led by Huntley and Palmer, tempted their buyers by creating figural or beautifully decorated tins in which to sell their wares. This device was especially popular at Christmas and would often be presented as a present, the tin worth more than the actual contents.

CHAD VALLEY

Chad Valley London Double Decker bus with 'Chad Valley Toys' advertisement. Also acting as a tin for Carr's Biscuits.

A&C 19, sold for £500, now worth £400-600

HUNTLEY AND PALMER TINS SPEAK VOLUMES

Huntley & Palmer's biscuit tins, designed as a bundle of leather-bound novels. The tin on the left is disguised as Scott's novels (CHEF)

A&C 25, each sold for £185, now worth £200-300

ALICE IN BISCUITLAND

Biscuits for Alice in Jacobs' 'Through the Looking Glass' biscuit tin (SOTH)

A&C 46, sold for £6,815, now worth £6,000-8,000

Fact File

One of the most notorious tins is the Huntley and Palmer Kate Greenaway tin from the 1980s. According to popular legend, the designer was dismissed and it is believed that no one checked his final artwork which is why it was released – covered in sex and swearwords. Admittedly, the intimate figures are not immediately clear but it has meant that this naughty tin is worth £30-50, despite being a normal round shape. The most exciting tins are figural in the shapes of trains and clocks. A Huntley and Palmer tin in the shape of a Georgian longcase clock, complete with moving hands and printed chinoiserie decoration, is worth £250-350 whilst a Crawford's biscuit bus from the 1920s can fetch £1,200-1,500. As with all tins, invest in some plasters – the edges can be sharp.

SHAPELY TIN

Decorative Huntley & Palmer biscuit tin from around 1914

A&C 56, est £600-750, now worth £600-750

HUNTLEY AND PALMER LORRY

LORRY TIN Huntley & Palmers Breakfast Biscuits and Ginger Nuts, with lithographed detailed front with driver to sides, NP H P 1937 (BON)

A&C 58, sold for £3,170, now worth £2,800-3,800

COLLECTION OF DAMAGED TINS

A collection of 20 biscuit tins, all damaged, including H.O. Serpell & Co. Ltd. Military Ambulance (SWORD)

A&C 63, sold for £700, now worth £800-1,200

TINS

They are a convenient form of packaging which prevents their contents from getting crushed or damp. They were used by toffee and chocolate manufacturers, enabling larger quantities to be sold in an appealing presentation and used to commemorate events such as Coronations and Royal Weddings in all shapes and sizes.

NOTORIOUS TIN

The notorious Huntley and Palmer tin supposedly portraying the idyllic world of Kate Greenaway, there are at least seven problems

A&C 66, now worth £30-50

CHOCOLATE TIN

Belgian chocolate tin showing the chocolatier's factory, Chocolat du Desert

A&C 67, sold for £400, now worth £350-500

BOURNVILLE

Bournville chocolate tin, about an inch high in bright, enticing colours

A&C 67, sold for £35, now worth £30-40

CHOCOLATE BOX

Chocolate is traditinally sold in boxes rather than tins, like this Lyons 'Nippy' chocolates, appealing to their majority women customers

A&C 67, sold for £15, now worth £15-20

OXO

As the page on advertising showed (p 37), OXO tins are very collectable. Despite its condition, it will still appeal to some collectors

A&C, now worth £10-15

EDIBLE OFFERINGS

Confectioners vied with each other to increase sales. Attractive tins are sitting in a chocolate shop display at Newark antiques fair

A&C 67, cabinet £650, now worth £600-800

TIN ART

Vintage tins turned into modern art at Art in Caly at Hatfield House.. A novel way to display your tin collection or buy some more

A&C 66, sold for around £35

Fact File

Tins were first used for storing tobacco in 1764 but, at the time, were not considered safe for food use. It wasn't until the 1830s, after improvements in preservation, that they were first used for biscuits and matches before being used for other foodstuffs.

One of the most common tins contains record needles. Produced for firms such as HMV (His Master's Voice), the one inch tins can sell for £15-35, depending on condition. The problem with tins is that they rust so this determines price.

A similar sized Bournville Chocolate tin fetches £35 whilst an Edward VII Coronation tin (1902) made for Cadbury's is worth £30-50. A 1920s toffee tin with a large Swastika on the side, symbolising peace, its new meaning increasing its value to £400-600.

TOYS

Toys

The role of toys has changed over time. Dolls' houses used to be for adults, not children and handmade wooden toys have given way to mass-produced fashion-led items which has led to vintage toy prices regularly reaching record prices.

Steiff skittles set was knocked downfor £6,810 (CHRIS)

TV-RELATED merchandise is increasingly popular, echoing the primary market which has released collectables from favourite 1970s children's programmes to cater for the 30 year old professionals who are having children later and spending money on themselves, especially nostalgia. *Bagpuss, The Clangers, Sooty, Thunderbirds* and *The Magic Roundabout* are thriving and having a knock-on effect on the secondary market.

TV programmes such as *Cash in the Attic, Life Laundry* and *Everything Must Go* have encouraged people to take their old toys to auctions or dealers, not simply throw them away or sell them cheaply at car boot sales. On a positive note for buyers, this means that more toys have been released on to the eager market.

Like all other areas of collecting, top names command the top prices.

TEDDY BEARS AND SOFT TOYS:
Steiff **Merrythought** Dean's **Schuco** Chad Valley **Wendy Boston**

MODEL AND TOY VEHICLES
Hornby I Tri-ang (later part of Hornby) I Mårklinl Dinky I Corgi I Matchbox and Lesney I Meccano I Schuco I Chad Valley I Tonka

DOLLS
House of Nisbet I Madame Alexander I Dressel, Cuno and Otto I J.D. Kestner I Kåthe Kruse I Rosebud I Schultz I Pedigree I Palitoy I Sascha I Barbie I Sindy I G.I. Joe and Action Man

And, when it comes to toy collecting, it really is worth seeing what you or your children used to play with if it's not too late. Those old jigsaw puzzles, especially wooden ones by Victory, are very popular whilst *The Magic Roundabout* jigsaw from the 1970s, complete and in its original box, can fetch £30-40. And as for toy cars, it's best to speak to a friendly expert before giving any away, you could be sitting on a fortune.

CORGI

Mettoy, short for metal toys, was founded in 1933 with its factory being opened in Swansea, Wales, in 1944. The company started producing die-cast toys in the 1950s and, in 1955, founded Corgi. The sub-division was named after the new queen's favourite breed of dogs, a short, sturdy Welsh dog which suited their location.

BASIL BRUSH

TV's favourite fox, Basil Brush was issued by Corgi during 1971-73 along with Boom Boom laughter tapes and a soundbox

A&C 19, set £200, now worth £150-250

HERALDING CORGI

The Corgi Toys Chipperfields Circus Land Rover Parade Vehicle. It's fitted with loudspeakers and passengers are a clown and monkey (Vectis)

A&C 49, now worth £60-100

THE MAGIC ROUNDABOUT

Corgi 807 Dougal's car issued in 1973 with Dougal, Brian and Dylan

A&C 12, sold for £55, now worth £200-300

ON THE ROAD

Corgi Bedford AA Van, 1957, in its original box

A&C 39, sest £15-50, now worth £40-60

CIRCUS COMES TO TOWN

The picture box of the Corgi Toys Chipperfields Circus Gift Set issued in 1964, (Vectis)

A&C 49, est £450, now worth £400-600

Fact File

Corgi was created to make die-cast vehicles and, as such, was competing directly with Dinky. To beat the competition, founder, Philipp scott, this seems to be right spelling Ullmann wanted to make a better product and used a fairly new material, plastic to set his cars apart from his rivals. Corgi's cars became the 'ones with windows'. They also had boots, bonnets and doors which opened, an irresistible idea for children. He even advertised the cars on television in 1957, only two years after Corgi was founded. Cheaper imports from the Far East led to bankruptcy in 1983 and the firm has had three owners since then, including Mattel. They are continuing to produce one of their most famous licensed products, James Bond cars and concentrating on the collectors market.

ALPINE RESCUE

A Citroen 'Alpine Rescue' in its original box (Photo courtesy of Mike Ennis)

A&C 15, sold for £250, now worth £250-325

BEST BUY BONDS

Junior Bond set from Corgi, MIB

A&C 65, sold for £6,570, now worth £6,000-7,000

SPORTY CORGI

Boxed Chevrolet Impala, classic 1950s Corgi

A&C 39, est £15-50, now worth £40-80

TOYS

TOY VEHICLES - DINKY

Dinky started life as Modelled Miniatures in 1933, becoming Dinky Toys in 1934. Their vehicles catered for the affordable die-cast toy market compared to the costly tinplate versions by firms such as the German company, Schuco. They are one of the most collectable toy car makes with most children from the 1940-80s owning one.

TOO MUCH LOVE

Condition is vital, this Delivery Van 'Seccotine' issued between 1935-39 is suffering from fatigue and paint loss (COLL)

A&C 65, sold for £187, now worth £150-200

BEETLE

Dinky Volkswagen Beetle which, in1956, cost only 2/- (10p in today's money)

A&C 39, est £15-50, now worth £20-60

RARE BUT TIRED

Rare Dinky Toy pre-war Sportsman's Coupe showing signs of age, with fatigue and paint chips, still fitted with is original rubber tyres but in general poor condition (WA WA)

A&C 65, sold for £210, now worth £150-250

RAC BOX

DINKY TOY Pre-war diecast model set no.43, of R.A.C. hut, motor cycle patrol and guides in original box (FELL)

A&C 54, sold for £500, now worth £500-600

DINKY LAWNMOWER

Dinky Lawnmower from 1950

A&C 39, est £5-50, now worth £20-60

Fact File

Whilst thought of as a very British company, the model vehicles were actually produced in both Liverpool and in Bobigny, in France. By 1938, Dinky, part of the Hornby Meccano business, had over 300 different models and dominated the market.

Production ceased during the war, some models being brought out in 1945 and it was after the war that significant differences between the two factories began to show. Post-war rubber shortages in France led to the French vehicles using all-metal wheels whilst the British cars had more moulded tyre hubs. From 1947, treaded rubber tyres started to be used to make a more realistic pattern. Competition came in the 1950s, first from Matchbox toys and then from Corgi before Mattel's Hot Wheels started to be imported from 1968.

FRENCH VERSION

Austin Healey which was issued during 1960-61and made in the factory at Bobigny near Paris

A&C 65, est £120, now worth £100-150

MODELLED MINIATURES

The set of six model vehicles which started the famous range of Dinky Toys issued between 1933-35, called Modelled Miniatures (VEC).

A&C 65, sold for £11,000, now worth £10-12,000

AVRO 'YORK' AEROPLANE

Dinky Toy model of the Avro 'York' Airliner issued during 1946-49 and has a current value of between £85-£100

A&C 65, est £85-100, now worth £90-100

RECORD PRICE

Foden Flat truck, version with chains, went for a record price

A&C 65, sold for £12,000, now worth £10-12,000

DINKY GIFT SET

Popular Dinky Toys Gift Set issued during the early 1950s, in very good condition

A&C 65, Est £750-950, now worth £800-1,000

RECORD PRICE

Dinky Leyland tanker sold for a record price of £9,200 (Vectis)

A&C 65, sold for £9,200, now worth £8-10,000

SOUTH AFRICAN SPORTS CAR

A Dinky TOY South Afrian red 113 MGB sports car (CHRIS)

A&C 42, sold for £2,232, now worth £2,000-2,500

GIFT SET

One of a range a Gift Sets containing a number of similar models that were issued during the 1950s. This set dates from 1952 and is valued between £3,000 and £4,000

A&C 65, est £3,000-4,000, now worth £3,000-4,000

DELIVERY VAN

Kodak van, one of the early Dinky Toys delivery vans (CHRIS)

A&C 65, sold for £4,100, now worth £3,500-4,500

TWO-TONE MORRIS

Two tone Morris Oxford issued in 1954, in turquoise and cream green hubs (CHRIS)

A&C 65, sold for £820, now worth £700-900

THUNDERBIRD 2

Second version of Thunderbird 2 by Dinky Toys issued 1974 to 1977, slight damage to the box

A&C 51, sold for £50-70, now worth £60-90

Fact File

One of Dinky's most popular ranges is advertising and, as well as the vehicles themselves, this immediately help to determine the age of the car.

One of the most sought-after is the 28-series Bentalls vans, that being the name of a department store. The original version dates from 1937 and only three are known to exist with most getting lost over time. The rare green van with its yellow upper panels and white roof sold for a record £12,650 at auction. There are later versions which have longer bodies and tend to be green all over.

Be careful of goods being painted different colours to appear rarer than they are. At a recent Internet auction, an advertising van had been repainted to increase its value. If in doubt, don't bid.

TOYS

TOY VEHICLES

Vehicles have captured children's imagination since the creation of trains, planes and cars. Millions of models have been produced to take advantage of this fascination with cars and trains being the most popular and boats, tractors, trucks, planes and motorbikes etc offering plenty of choice. Some of these models are now collectable.

MATCHBOX FIRE ENGINE

Land Rover Fire Truck with tinted windows and rare grey wheels. Versions with black wheels cost around £45.

A&C 42, sold for £990, now worth £800-1,200

RARE FLYING BOAT

One of W. Britain's rarest pre-war models, a flying boat (VEC)

A&C 47, sold for £10,800, now worth £8-12,000

ZXCZXCZXCZC

The popular 1950's Ford Zodiac Convertible car in pink. (Picture by George Kidner.)

A&C 42, est £260, now worth £250-300

ALFA ROMEO

C.I.J. tinplate Alfa Romeo (ROSE)

A&C 12, sold for £1,700, now worth £2,000-2,500

TRACTOR

Lesney Moko Toy, of the Massey Harris Tractor, first issued in 1950.

A&C 42, sold for £225, now worth £200-250

Fact File

Commercial and military planes are very popular with the most desirable being British Airway's Concorde which inspired a range of toys with the famous hook nose of the supersonic plane, including a Corgi version which was only sold in-flight and is now worth £20-30. The sleek lines of that plane are vastly different to the almost stumpy shapes made in cast iron by A.C.Williams whose UX 33 and UX 99, both made in the 1920s-30s, fetch around £100-150 each, the same as most Dinky versions from that era. Some collectors opt for the same airline through the decades which is an interesting way of studying the change in aviation, British Airways and its various previous names (Imperial Airways, BOAC and BEAC) being especially collectable.

BOXED TRACTOR

Fordson Tractor by Britains, with metal red spud wheels, No.127F with driver, boxed, good condition, 10cm long (DREW)

A&C 45, sold for £190, now worth £150-250

ENSIGN

A pre-war 'Ensign' airliner, issued in 1938/41 (Photo courtesy of Mike Ennis)

A&C 15, sold for £70, now worth £80-120

TROLLEY BUS

Taylor and Barrett, 204 Trolley Bus toy (BON)

A&C 56, sold for £223, now worth £200-250

SPOT-ON TRIANG

Spot-On 108 Triumph TR 3 (COLL)

A&C 12, sold for £130, now worth £150-250

70'S MATCHBOX

American Pontiac sports car model (VECTIS)

A&C 66, sold for £4,000, now worth £3,500-4,000

FRENCH BUS GOES HOME

A French C R tinplate model of the Renault Paris Bus. Poor condition, sold in France (Photo courtesy of Mike Ennis)

A&C 15, sold for £950, now worth £800-1,400

1960 VAUXHALL

Matchbox Vauxhall Victor, 1960

A&C 53, est £200, now worth £150-250

BOXED UP

The rarest of seven versions of ths lorry issued in the 1950's. Perfect, MIB (mint in box) ones can cosy up to £1,500.

A&C 42, now worth £400-600

MATCHBOX TROLLEYBUS

Matchbox Trolleybus, 1960

A&C 53, est £200, now worth £150-250

POND YACHT

Scratch built, pond yacht,1920s, twin masted with sails and rigging, named 'Zigzag' (MALL)

A&C 63, sold for £800, now worth £800-1,000

AUSTIN

Austin A40 in mint/boxed condition (Barry Potter Auctions)

A&C 65, sold for £172, now worth £150-200

Fact File

Some vehicles came in kit form, the most famous being made by Airfix which was created in 1939 to make cheap rubber toys.

In 1947, they started to make plastic hair combs and quickly became the main producer in Britain.

Ferguson Tractor asked them to make a promotional toy for them in 1948 but they couldn't afford to make a proper one, only a kit which is how their first toy was made. They are renowned for their planes, the first being the Spitfire MK1 which was released in 1953.

Changing times led them to alter their boxes, removing the more violent wartime scenes. The most collectable and valuable Airfix kits are those which were never made up, such as Stingray (£500-700).

TOYS HORNBY

HORNBY

Hornby, the most famous of all train models, was named after Frank Hornby who also owned the Meccano factory. Their first trains were produced in 1920 but his work dates back to 1901 when he manufactured the kits for which Meccano was later to become famous. He also created Dinky Toys., dominating the toy market..

SOUTHERN REGION

Locomotive Hornby Series gauge 0 electric No. 2, Southern Region, No. 2091, 4-4-2 wheel arrangement. (GORR)

A&C 58, sold for £130, now worth £120-160

CLOCKWORK 'TANK'

Clockwork 'Tank' locomotive - one of the last models built under the Hornby name. Issued in the 1950s (COLL)

A&C 34, est £55, now worth £60-80

1930s TRAIN

Popular London, Midlands and Scotland locomotive, from the late 1930s (LOD)

A&C 34,est £250, now worth £200-350

RARE ELECTRIC MOTOR

One of the very rare Hornby locomotives, driven by a 20v AC electric motor. It was produced in the early 1930s and displays the green livery of the Southern Railway with the unusual running number B28.

A&C 7, sold for £2,150, now worth £2,000-3,000

HORNBY AND DINKY

Rare Hornby Series Modelled Miniatures, Set No. 22, c.1933. Dinky, part of Hornby, is currently making record prices (SOTH)

A&C 11, sold for £4,945, now worth £10-12,000

Fact File

There were originally three trains with truck, tender and engine, made in three liveries; green representing Great Northern, red Midland railway and North Western in black. By 1925, Hornby had also produced an electric train.

Increased competition led to mixed fortunes and, by 1964, Meccano and Hornby were taken over, leading to the renaming of Hornby as Tri-Ang Hornby when they merged with their competitors.

The record price for a Hornby train is £3,175 for the Number 1 Special, a tank locomotive from the 1930s with a clockwork engine in the rare New Zealand livery (black), with NZR (New Zealand Railways) on the side. A photo of Frank Hornby sold for £4,100.

DUCHESS OF ATHOLL

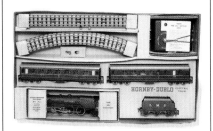

Hornby Dublo EDP2 Passenger Train Set, 'Duchess of Atholl', with two carriages, track and transformer. With original box and paperwork (FELL)

A&C 40, sold for £360, now worth £350-425

PRINCESS ELIZABETH

The Princess Elizabeth, produced between 1937 and 1939 (Loddon Auctions)

A&C 34, est £2,000, now worth £2,000-2,500

HORNBY WATER TOWER

Water tower, along with two model factories. (Barry Potter Auctions)

A&C 34, sold for £3,100, now worth £3,000-3,500

TRAINS

Whilst Hornby dominated the British market, other model trains are highly collectable, including the German firm, Märklin and British make Tri-ang which was later bought out by its rival, Hornby. Train sets could be built up over time which made them more affordable, tracks could be extended and accessories such as stations added

BASSETT LOWKE LMS

Bassett-Lowke '0' gauge railway modell of a London, Midland and Scottish Railway Express Locomotive 5701 'Conqueror', made in the mid-1930s

A&C 7, sold for £3,400, now worth £3,500-5,000

HORNBY STATION

Hornby Tinplate Station - 'Reading' first icost 8 shillings (40p) when it came out in 1936 (Photograph courtesy of Patrick Illife)

A&C 13, est £130-160, now worth £200-400

LONDON AND NORTH EASTERN

A 27 1/2 inch gauge 1 London and North Eastern Railway Class A4 'Mallard', fired live model steam engine by Aster

A&C 21, sold for £9,987, now worth £8-12,000

BASSETT LOWKE

Bassett Lowke 'Duke of York' train (COTT)

A&C 25, sold for £250, now worth £200-400

BLACK PRINCE

Extremely rare Schoenner gauge 3 Black Prince locomotive and tender c 1904 (BON)

A&C 61, sold for £11,163, now worth £9-12,000

Fact File

Märklin were founded in 1859, making tinplate accessories for dolls' houses. They are renowned for their quality trains with electrical versions introduced in 1925.

One of their most desirable ranges is the executive train set which was contained within a briefcase, the carriages and engines set in special compartments in the top of the case and the track within the base and was battery operated to entertain businessmen on long journeys. The Z-gauge train was built to an exact 1:220 scale using the real train manufacturer's plans and photographs. The starter set had four carriages and an engine with more compartments available for expansion. They even created solar-powered versions for better climates. Expect to pay £200+ for a set on the secondary market.

GREAT WESTERN

Clockwork train, A Bing for Bassett-Lowke Great Western 4-4-0 locomotive 'Sydney' and six-wheeled tender No. 3410, c 1907 (CHRIS)

A&C 49, sold for £1,645, now worth £1,200-1,800

STEAM LOCOMOTIVE

STEAM LOCOMOTIVE "Hybrid", 5" gauge coal-fired, with super-heated copper boiler and speed regulator, 2ft. long (GORR)

A&C 52, sold for £950, now worth £800-1,400

HORNBY

Hornby Dublo EDPB electric train inc. a 2-6-4 tank passenger train and two plastic locomotives, rolling stock rails and transformers.(SWORD)

A&C 46, sold for £50, now worth £100-200

TOYS

STEIFF

Th German firm was founded by disabled seamstress Margarete Steiff in 1880, the first animal not being a bear but a felt elephant whose pattern she had cut out of a magazine. The arrival of her nephew, Richard, in 1902 changed the direction of the already successful company when he introduced the now famous bears.

GEORGE

George, a 19 in Steiff Teddy bear c.1908.(CHRIS)

A&C 20, est £4,000-6,000, now worth £5,000-8,000

ROLY POLY

'Roly Poly' an unusual Steiff teddy bear (CHRIS)

A&C 12, sold for £8,865, now worth £8,000-12,000

CENTRE SEAM BEAR

A Steiff centre seam bear, c.1908 (CHRIS)

A&C 20, sold for £1,995, now worth £2,500-3,500

CINNAMON BEAR

Popular cinnamon-coloured bear believed to have been made around 1908 (CHRIS)

A&C 15, est £4,000-6,000, now worth £6,000-8,000

BEAR ON WHEELS

STEIFF BEAR Teddy on wheels from around 1950, with light brown mohair plush, growler and glass eyes (GORR)

A&C 61, sold for £320, now worth £500-600

Fact File

Richard Steiff loved bears and wanted to create life-like toy animals. His articulated bears were revolutionary.

They were not the first teddy bears but they were the best and the fear of competition led them to create their famous trademark 'button in the ear' in 1904, the first ones having the symbol of an elephant, Steiff's first toy creation, although the company having started as a felt clothes maker.

They also made advertising animals, including the Milka cow and exclusives for shops such as FAO Schwartz in Las Vegas and London's Harrods. Their licensed products, such as Disney's Mickey Mouse as Steamboat Willie and the Wind in the Willows series have proved popular and Steiff limited editions are always a good buy because of their quality.

1908 BEAR

Steiff teddy bear c1908 (CHRIS)

A&C 58, sold for £9,987, now worth £8,000-12,000

MOHAIR

Mohair Steiff bear (BON)

A&C 65, sold for £4,063, now worth £3,000-5,000

RARE DOLLY BEAR

Rare Steiff Dolly-Bear, 1913-16.(CHRIS)

A&C 57, sold for £4,112, now worth £3,000-6,000

PROVENANCE

1909 Steiff bear with a photo of its original owner (BON)

A&C 65, sold for £5,019, now worth £4,000-6,000

TITANIC BEAR

A very rare 'Black' Steiff Teddy Bear, 1912, made to commemorate those who lost their lives on the Titanic (CHRIS)

A&C 23, sold £91,750, now worth £90-110,000

CHRISTIE'S BEAR

James, a bear produced exclusively for Christie's in a limited edition of 1,766 representing the year that the auction house was founded by James Christie (CHRIS)

A&C 20, now worth £150-250

BOWLED OVER

Steiff skittles set in the form of rabbits (CHRIS)

A&C 65, sold for £6,810, now worth £6,000-8,000

POLAR BEAR

Steiff polar bear, blonde plush, boot button eyes and jointed limbs, button in left ear, 12" (GORR)

A&C 46, sold for £1,400, now worth £1,500-2,500

STEIFF MICKEY

Rare Steiff Mickey Mouse (CHRIS)

A&C 43, sold for £1,645, now worth £1,500-2,500

MICKEY MOUSE

A rare Steiff Mickey Mouse, c.1931 (CHRIS)

A&C 20, sold for £3,220, now worth £4,000-6,000

Fact File

Steiff are the best bears on the market with prices to match. The 1904 Teddy Girl, one of the earliest jointed bears, sold for £110,000 at auction, more than the black bear which was made to mourn the loss of 1,523 lives when the Titanic sank in 1912, one of which made £91,750 at auction.

The record price for a Steiff bear was achieved in a charity auction when a year 2000, Louis Vuitton, special, limited edition bear, dressed in its namesake's designer clothes fetched £130,000. Prices are high because of the quality of workmanship and design and because they were innovative.

One of the most unusual ranges Steiff made was skittles in the form of bears, rabbits, monkeys and cats.

TEDDY BEARS

of Witney

In 1908 George Michailovitch, Grand Duke of Russia, gave his daughter a red Steiff teddy bear. She christened him Alfonzo and her nanny made him a Cossack outfit. In 1914 Princess Xenia, then eleven years old, brought him to Buckingham Palace for a summer holiday. War broke out preventing their return. They stayed on in London so avoiding the Revolution, during which her father was assassinated at the Peter and Paul Fortress in St Petersburg. This tragedy drew the princess still closer to her little red bear, the only present from her father that she had brought from Russia.
Alfonzo remained near her until she died in 1965.
In 1989 Ian Pout bought Alfonzo at Christie's, London for a world record price.
Ever since visitors from all over the world have come to Witney to see him.

Baby Alfonzo is a 23cm (two thirds size) replica of the original bear.
Made by Steiff exclusively for Teddy Bears of Witney in a limited edition of 5000,
he comes decoratively boxed with a certificate at £165.

Xenia (45cm), named after Princess Xenia, is inspired by a circa 1915 bear in the Witney museum.
Xenia is made by Steiff exclusively for Teddy Bears of Witney in a limited edition of 1500
and comes boxed with a certificate at £245.

Teddy Bears, 99 High Street, Witney, Oxfordshire, OX28 6HY
Tel: 01993 706616 E-mail: ordersonly@witneybears.co.uk

Our shop is open 7 days a week

Our 2005 catalogue, featuring over 400 bears, including 5 Steiff exclusive limited editions,
is available at £5 or comes free with Baby Alfonzo or Xenia.

www.teddybears.co.uk

CUDDLY TOYS

Cuddly toys provided children with comfort and were often much loved which shows in the patches through their 'fur', missing eyes and limbs and general wear and tear. This is what makes the ones in better condition so valuable. Toys were made to be used and were often thrown away or thrown out when the children grew up.

BROTHERS IN ARMS

'Grubby' and 'Young', went to war with their owners, brothers Colonel Sir Guy Campbell and Major David Campbell and were awarded the Military Cross for their actions (SOTH)

A&C 7, sold for £26,450, now worth £20-30,000

CHEEKY BEAR

A Merrythought Cheeky Bear from the late 1950s, their classic bear (CHRIS)

A&C 49, sold for £529, now worth £500-700

MERRYTHOUGHT GUARDSMAN

A Merrythought Bingie Guardsman from the 1930s. Prices are going up so it's a good time to buy while you still can (CHRIS)

A&C 49, sold £1,762.50, now worth £1,800-2,200

MILLENNIUM BEAR

Centre: White mohair Steiff 'Millennium' Bear, 29cm, issued by Danbury Mint. One of thousands of goods to be released for the event but Steiff's quality ensured that buyers had something worth buying

A&C 40, sold for £75, now worth £80-120

CHAD VALLEY

Complete set of seven Chad Valley Hygienic Toy Dwarves, wearing original costumes, together with figure of Snow White (LOCK)

A&C 50, sold for £820, now worth £600-1,000

Fact File

Merrythought are Britain's best known make of cuddly toys. Founded in Ironbridge, Telford in 1930, the company are producing several limited editions in 2005 to mark their 70th anniversary and these are a good investment because the edition sizes are being kept small (eg 100). Merrythought is the word for a wishbone which used to be their trademark. Their most famous creation is the large-headed Cheeky Bear which was revealed at the Toy Fair in 1956. A rare version with an open mouth reached £2,000 at auction with 1960-70s versions currently selling for £200-300. Merrythought also made a set of graduated hippos and, from the 1930s, various gollies, based on the work of children's artist, Florence Upton. Look for their 1950s Noddy and Big Ears (£150-250 each).

J.K. FARNELL JABEZ BEAR

Rare, British 'Jabez' bear, 36cm by the J.K. Farnell Company, who began producing bears in 1908 (BON)

A&C 40, sold for £1,235, now worth £1,000-1,500

WILFRED BUNNY

'WILFRED' BUNNY Gold plush mohair with wood-wool filling, possibly J. K. Farnell 1920, from the Daily Mirror comic strip (GORR)

A&C 58, sold for £260, now worth £250-350

1920S STEIFF BEAR

Rare 1920s Steiff bear, valued at £6,000-8,000 Christie's

A&C 40, est £6,000-8,000, now worth £6,000-9,000

TOYS

PADDINGTON BEAR

1970s Gabrielle 'Paddington Bear'

A&C 40, sold for £210, now worth £400-600

RARE MOURNING BEAR

Rare black Steiff plush teddy c 1915, boot button eyes, mohair good (GORR)

A&C 51, sold for £23,000, now worth £20-28,000

PLUSH BEARS

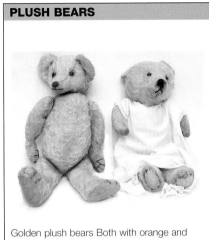

Golden plush bears Both with orange and black glass eyes, swivel head and jointed limbs. (43cm & 51cm high).(FELL)

A&C 43, sold for £340, now worth £200-400

FARNELL TEDDY BEAR

Large Farnell teddy bear

A&C 7, sold for £620, now worth £800-1,200

TALKING TEDDY

Unusual talking teddy bear with Swiss-made musical boxes inside, c.1920 (BON)

A&C 40, sold for £630, now worth £600-800

MUCH-LOVED STEIFF BEAR

Classic Steiff Teddy bear, c.1912 (CHRIS)

A&C 40, est £3,500, now worth £3,000-5,000

CHAD VALLEY

CHAD VALLEY BEAR Pink and white plush Teddy Bear with what look like later blue foot pads, 2ft 6ins, worn condition (GORR)

A&C 50, sold for £25, now worth £20-30

SCHUCO YES/NO BEAR

German Schuco bears. A miniature '2-face' bear (left) valued at around £400 and a miniature 'Yes/No' bear valued at around £200. Schuco also made toy cars (BON)

A&C 40, Yes/No est £200, now worth £200-400

Fact File

The most desirable hair for teddy bears is mohair, the fleece of angora goats.
Some cuddly toys also doubled up as nightdress cases in the 1950-60s. These were predominantly dogs with poodles and Scotties being the most popular. Wendy Boston's versions fetch £50-75 whilst the others tend to sell for £25-30. Most of these have very worn plush where they were cuddled by their young owners.
There were also toys for adults. About four inches high and made by Schuco in the shape of bears and monkeys, amongst others, their heads would pop off either to reveal perfume bottles or a compact (see p.33). These highly desirable accessories are worth £350-450 each with the compacts being the rarer of the two.

CLOCKWORK TOYS

Clockwork is a very old idea and is believed to have been suggested first by the philosopher Aristotle, 4th century BC. The Ancient Chinese and Greeks had moving statues, and clocks in the Renaissance period had moving figures, like dancers or 'clockworks'. The movement was known as automaton, clockwork is similar.

CLOCKWORK BUS

Clockwork tinplate double decker by S Günthermann, Germany, with printed decoration, 35 cm x 17.5cm. Est. £400-£600. (SWORD)

A&C 60, sold for £520, now worth £XX

TIPP & CO.

A rare clockwork single engine highwing monoplane by Tipp & Co, Germany. 26cm long, 31cm wingspan. (WA WA.)

A&C 46, sold for £760, now worth £800-1,000

MARKLIN CLOCKWORK CAR

Märklin tinplate clockwork car of an early two seat open tourer. Repainted, some damage, three tyres missing, 18 cm long and 11 cm high (SWORD)

A&C 58, sold for £2,300, now worth £2,000- 2,750

SCHUCO CAR

Schuco command car A.D. 2000, finished in green with clockwork stop-start motor and instructions, in original box (GORR)

A&C 46, sold for £90, now worth £200-300

TIPP & CO AMBULANCE

A 1930s clockwork military ambulance by Tipp & Co, Germany. Rear door opens for two soldiers on stretchers. Clockwork motor working. 24cm long (WA WA)

A&C 43, sold for £425, now worth £400-600

Fact File

Robots are some of the most collectable clockwork and battery-operated toys. The term robot was first used in a Czech play in 1921, dominated the 1950s toy industry and now commands some of the highest prices for toys.

Machine Man Robot from 1955 made £28,000 at auction whilst the 1960s, battery-operated Radar Robot by Nomura went for £18,000. It is also known as Topolino from the days when no one knew its real name, before one of the original boxes was found.

The word is Italian for Mickey Mouse because the robot had protruding 'ears'. One of the most collectable robots is Robbie the Robot from *The Forbidden Planet*, the 1956 toy went for £7,000 at auction. A reproduction version was made by Masudaya in 1986.

CLOCKWORK TRAINS

Two German clockwork toy trains from 1902 (Picture by Barry Potter Auctions.)

A&C 50, est £2,500, now worth £2,000-3,000

RACING CAR

Kaye Don's Sunbeam 'Silver Bullet' Record Car, a Günthermann clockwork 'De Luxe Edition'

A&C 60, sold for £1,645, now worth £1,500-2,000

TOYS

FRENCH CYCLIST

Boy on Clockwork Velocipede', probably, French, c.1890, depicting a bisque porcelain-headed tri-cyclist. The heavy-gauge tinplate tri-cycle has cast, spoked wheels and is in good condition, 22cm in length.(SOTH) f £800 - 1,000. Sotheby South

A&C 28, est £800-1,000, now worth £1,000-1,500

CLOCKWORK DONALD

A French-made clockwork driven ice cream cart with Donald Duck as the salesman, 23cm long. (Photo courtesy of Mike Ennis.)

A&C 15, sold for £81, now worth £100-150

ALFA ROMEO TINPLATE

Clockwork model of a 1929 Alfa Romeo P2 motor car, tinplate, 21in long. (AMER)

A&C 36, sold for £1,400, now worth £1,500-1,800

HAD VALLEY TINPLATE

One of the early Chad Valley tinplate models - a Clockwork-driven Steamroller, made during 1930.

A&C 19, sold for £45, now worth £100-200

ZXCZXCZXCZC

A Shackleton model clockwork Foden F.G.6 Tipper with Dyson Trailer in their original boxes (CHEF)

A&C 5, sold for £320 now worth £400-600

SHACKLETON FODEN TRUCK

A Shackleton model clockwork Foden F.G. flat truck in its original box (CHEF)

A&C 5, sold for £200, now worth £200-300

DISTLER MONKEY DRUMMER

A Distler clockwork standing monkey drummer c1925. Est. £300-£400. (CHRIS)

A&C 64, sold for £411, now worth £400-500

Fact File

When buying clockwork toys, check that they have a key or can be wound up by moving the wheels backwards and forwards a few times. Versions without keys, unless particularly cheap or desirable, are not as good buys.

Some of the best clockwork toys come from Japan which mass-produced toys for the export market (which is why the writing on the side is in English). Nomura is one of the best makes.

Helicopters can be found for £5 and under at car boot sales, simply wind the propeller blades or wind up the wheels on the bottom to get it moving.

One of the nicest clockwork toys is a row of three ducks who, once wound up, scuttle along together and sells for £35-45.

TINPLATE TOYS

Tinplate toys have been around since the 1830s, some were even exhibited at The Great Exhibition of 1851. The thin metal made the toys very light to handle but also meant that they could bend if held too tightly or thrown which is why so many are dented. The tinned sheet steel was cheap to produce but made expensive toys.

CHARLES ROSSIGNOL

A 1920s model by Charles Rossignol, France, based on a Paris bus (COLL)

A&C 43, sold for £3,760, now worth £XX

CHAD VALLEY TINPLATE BUS

A Chad Valley bus, mid-1930s. Valued at £400.

A&C 16, est £400, now worth £400-600

LONDON BUS

Japanese tinplate toy. London bus with open upper deck and battery operation (12.5" high). (GORR)

A&C 43, sold for £90, now worth £100-150

BING BUS

One of the best known Tinplay toys made by the German company Bing. The clockwork model of the London 'General' bus made around 1910. Rusty

A&C 13, sold for £1,000, now worth £1,500-1,800

CHAD VALLEY BUS

A tin-plate bus made by the Chad Valley company in the 1930s

A&C 16, est £400, now worth £400-600

Fact File

Schuco is one of the best makes of tinplate toys. They are renowned for the smooth lines of their cars. This created a trademark look. One of the most common cars was the Examico which was first seen in 1936 and was operated by a key. The smooth lines of the sports car with its one-coloured body is very collectable, despite its lack of rarity and sells for £200-300 MIB (mint in box). The red fireman's car, one of many versions of the Mercedes 190, often has the cover missing on the working light on top of the car. When it's wound up, the officer inside moves the mike up and down as though talking on the radio. It's ingenious and sells for £400-500 MIB.

ZXCZXCZXCZC

A 1940s clockwork limousine by Mettoy. It has battery powered headlamps, a sliding sunroof and a chauffeur. About 37cm long (CHRIS)

A&C 43, sold for £350, now worth £300-400

MECCANO

Popular Meccano Constructor Car Kit No. 2 from the late 1930s with the original box and made up - ideally, find one which isn't (SOTH)

A&C 43, now worth £200-300

BURNETT CAR

An open tourer made of nut and bolt, produced by British manufacturer Burnett (Picture by Vectis)

A&C 43, now worth £200-300

TOYS

STUDEBAKER

1950S Japanese model of the America Studebaker car (COLL).

A&C 43, est £100, now worth £100-200

MODEL OF HITLER'S CAR

A rare model of Hitler's Mercedes Benz's from around 1935 with the wartime leader in the back. It is missing its steering wheel (WA WA)

A&C 43, sold for £560, now worth £500-800

VESPA SCOOTER

The popular 60s Vespa Scooter, made in France (Picture by Collectoys).

A&C 43, sold for £350, now worth £350-400

MARKLIN

Tinplate Märklin battleship c 1905-1910, single screw clockwork mechanism, deck with eight gun turrets (GORR)

A&C 61, sold for £2,300, now worth £2,000-3,000

MOTORCYCLE

Tinplate motorcycle with clockwork mechanism. Watch out for fakes - lots about

A&C 60, sold for £7,050, now worth £6,500-8,000

EARLY GERMAN TINPLATE

German painted tinplate clockwork model, 9in long, in original cardboard box with printed paper label, c 1900-20. (AMER)

A&C 35, sold for £320, now worth £500-700

TIPP & CO

Clockwork-driven model of a fire engine, produced by Tipp & Co,the collectable German make, during the early 1920s (BON)

A&C 7, sold for £138, now worth £500-700

FIREBIRD RACE CAR

A 1950s Japanese Tinplate, battery-operated racing car in its original box

A&C 7, est £275-325, now worth £300-500

Fact File

Tinplate toys are good investments if you buy now, prices have risen abruptly but there are still plenty of bargains to be had. The Russian exports from the 1950-70s are good buys, especially the cars. Beware of fakes and repros. Some firms are recreating the old-fashioned tinplate toys for modern, adult collectors. They are selling them as modern but beware of those selling them on who are not. One of the most common fakes which can be found at most large car boot sales and on the Internet is the motorbike and rider. Genuine versions sell for over £7,000 (although most buyers don't know it) and the fakes are generally priced at £15-30. Be careful when handling the old toys as they can be sharp and rusty - take plasters with you.

DISNEY TOYS AND GENERAL

The Walt Disney studio produced some of the most memorabilia animated films ever made and some of the most loved characters, most of whom have been made into toys. These include Mickey Mouse who had his first adventure in Steamboat Willie (1928) and Snow White and the Seven Dwarves (1937), the first full-length cartoon.

GOOFY-ING AROUND

Marx Goofy the Walking Gardener (BON)

A&C 53, sold for £493, now worth £500-750

MICKEY MOUSE MONEYBOX

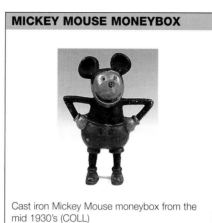

Cast iron Mickey Mouse moneybox from the mid 1930's (COLL)

A&C 47, sold for £1,200, now worth £1,000-1,500

MICKEY'S FIRE BRIGADE

A rare British Charbens model of a fire engine with 'Mickey Mouse' firemen figures. Produced in collaboration with the Disney Company (Picture by Vectis)

A&C 47, est £650, now worth £600-1,200

CLOCKWORK DONALD

Celluloid clock work Donald Duck (BON)

A&C60, sold for £153, now worth £100-200

SCHUCO DONALD DUCK

A 1958 Schuco clockwork 984 Donald Duck, in original box (CHRIS)

A&C 58, sold for £329, now worth £300-500

Fact File

One of the highest prices ever achieved for a Disney product was £51,000 for Mickey and Minnie Mouse on a motorcycle. One of only ten known examples to have a five-fingered hand, the boxed tinplate clockwork toy was made by Tipp & Co in 1929 and is typical of the early Mickeys with the big grin, long nose and very wide set ears. This does not compare with the 24ct gold statue of Mickey sold for £450,000 which was created to celebrate what would have been Walt Disney's 100th birthday but does show his enduring appeal. A more affordable toy, the Donald Duck Pelham puppet sells for £40-50 in its box whilst a shop display Pelham Goofy is worth £150-250.

GRUMPY AND HAPPY

Disney dwarves French pottery dwarves Happy and Grumpy (DREW)

A&C 58, sold for £350, now worth £300-450

WALT DISNEY DRAWING

Drawing of Mickey Mouse by Walt Disney, dated 1932 (CHRIS)

A&C 53, sold for £7,050, now worth £6,000-9,000

MICKEY MOUSE PHONE

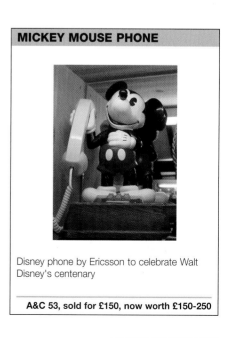

Disney phone by Ericsson to celebrate Walt Disney's centenary

A&C 53, sold for £150, now worth £150-250

"A gift inside a gift inside a gift..."

The Traditional Russian Doll

The 'Zagorsk' Doll, is the traditional style of Russian Matryoshka Doll, originating in the City of Sergiev Posad from the 1890's.

Today this Doll is still hand produced in one of the original craft workshops of Sergiev Posad, within **The Golden Ring of Russia**™

Classic Dolls
A wide range of traditional Russian Dolls are always available in many different styles, including 5, 7 and 10-piece sets.

Collectables
From animals, folk & fairytales to the famous Russian Presidents Doll, our range of collectables is a source of enjoyment to all.

Connoisseur Dolls
The finest painted one-of-a-kind "Author Dolls". Unique masterpieces of the highest standards of artistic quality and very collectable.

Christmas
It's Christmas all year round, with Santa & Snowman Dolls to tree decorations.

Expand your collection today by ordering our new 24-page **collectors catalogue** with over **350 Russian Dolls.**
- just **£2.95** (inc p+p)

contact:

russian-crafts.co.uk
info@russian-crafts.co.uk

4 Church Villas
Vicarage Road Penn
Wolverhampton WV4 5HU

01902 344234

MATRYOSHKA

Visit our NEW website and order online!

russian-crafts.co.uk

OXFORD STREET ANTIQUE CENTRE

Proprietors: Paul & Linda Giles

WE OFFER A VAST SELECTION OF ANTIQUE, TRADITIONAL AND REPRODUCTION FURNITURE & ACCESSORIES, DISPLAYED IN 14 LARGE SHOWROOMS OF 4 FLOORS COVERING 30,000ft²

Open Monday–Friday 10am–5.30pm,
Saturday 10am–5pm
& Sunday 2pm–5pm

FREE ONSITE PARKING

16–26 OXFORD STREET LEICESTER
TELEPHONE 0116 255 3006

DOLLS

From the late 17th century, most dolls were created as toys for children, the exception being the relatively recent collectors' dolls by firms such as Royal Doulton and Franklin Mint which have capitalised on our desire to collect and are generally too good or fragile to be playthings. Dolls have a strong religious background as well.

KATHE KRUSE DOLL

A rare Kathe Kruse 'Schlenkerchen' Smiling baby doll with a painted muslin head, wire skeleton body wrapped with cotton wool and overlaid with knitted fabric (BON)

A&C 33, sold for £1,000, now worth £1,000-2,000

GEORGIAN DOLL

A George III wooden doll, English, c.1760, part of a collection of dolls and accessories which was sold at auction (SOTH)

A&C 13, sold for £9,200, now worth £10-14,000

LENCI-STYLE FELT DOLL

A Italian 'Lenci' style pressed felt doll, with painted features, smart clothes and a feather trimmed hat (PH KN)

A&C 33, est £200-300, now worth £300-40

1775 DOLLS' HOUSE

English Georgian country house, c.1775, 159cm high (BON)

A&C 30, sold for £18,800, now worth £20-25,000

DOLLS' HOUSE

German Moritz Gottschalk 'blue roof' dolls' house, c.1885. 84cm high, 49cm wide, 40cm deep with attractive detailing (BON)

A&C 30, sold for £7,650, now worth £7,000-9,000

Fact File

In France, they have two types of dolls – bébé for ones looking like babies and poupée for older-looking dolls. A 1913 Marque Bébé made £56,500 at auction whilst an early 19th century simple wooden, folk art doll's head sold for £20,000.

Wooden dolls were the earliest type, some destroyed in the Protestant fervour of Tudor England as idolatrous images whilst others have been found in tombs, buried to keep the dead company. The collectable, pre-1920s dolls which we know best with their fancy clothes and delicate features were the Sunday dolls, used to keep the girls quiet in church. These were not the rag dolls and other simple, comforter dolls with which they would play in the house.

GERMAN DOLL

Black celluloid German doll, with moulded wavy hair and inset brown glass eyes (FELL)

A&C 54, sold for £600, now worth £500-700

GIGI

Faerie Glen Gigi model doll

A&C 39, est £65, now worth £60-80

MALIBU BARBIE

Malibu Barbie from 1971. In original box, with blue side glancing eyes, coral lips, blonde hair, tanned skin, twist 'n turn waist, blue swimsuit with wrist tag (Vectis)

A&C 44, est £100, now worth £80-140

TOYS

OTHER TOYS

There are lots of other toys worth collecting, including jigsaws. The best of these are wooden, made by Victory and contain the shapes of animals The jigsaw was developed in 1760 by a mapmaker but, until power arrived in the 1870s to work nachinery, work was costly and carried out by hand which is why early ones are collectable.

RACE TO THE BARGAIN

Late Victorian/Edwardian rocking horse, 130cm wide.(SWORD)

A&C 48, sold for £320, now worth £500-800

ROCKING HORSE

Carved wooden and painted rocking horse on a pine trestle, 105 cm high (SWORD)

A&C 56, sold for £250, now worth £500-600

Fact File

Marionettes or puppets are wonderful toys to collect and the top make is Pelham, the firm started by Bob Pelham in 1947 under the name Wonky Toys Ltd. No one knows how many puppets were made because the records were destroyed in a devastating fire in 1961 when over 10,000 puppets were burnt. Some of the most collectable Pelham's are The Alice in Wonderland series and Noddy and Big Ears.

Famous characters are good buys as they would have been licensed for a short time only which means that not as many were made as the most common such as the witch and the gypsy. The stringed puppets are more popular than the finger puppets (even of Dougal from *The Magic Roundabout*) and the rather cumbersome ventriloquist dolls.

BENDY RUPERT

RUPERT THE BEAR A foam rubber model yellow aeroplane and detachable figure from the 1970s made by Bendy Toys (LOCK)

A&C 51, sold for £22, now worth £20-30

JAPANESE ROBOT

A boxed Japanese robot, built with an engine as a chest, with piston rods as arms, 1960s (Photograph courtesy of Mike Ennis)

A&C 16, est £70, now worth £200-300

PELHAM SHOP DISPLAY

Motorised Pelham Disney shop display, c.1960. Wallis & Wallis

A&C 38, sold for £990, now worth £1,000-1,500

EARLY PELHAMS

Nine early Pelham puppets (flying pigs on brown boxes), six with lead hands, the others wooden, all but one boxed (SWORD)

A&C 53, sold for £2,400, now worth £2,000-2,800

FRENCH THEATRE

A French puppet theatre from the late nineteenth century by Gignol, made from wood with wooden puppets (SOTH)

A&C 51, sold for £1,560, now worth £1,500-2,000

PUPPET ON A STRING

PELHAM PUPPETS All 1950's, four in original brown boxes, including televisions 'Mr Turnip'. The skeleton is now worth £60-90 (SWORD)

A&C 48, sold for £280, now worth £300-400

CLASSIC CARS

Whilst modern cars offer extras such as air conditioning and electric windows, classic cars are stylish, their owners wanting something different, some believing it makes them more interesting. As classic car conventions and automobilia sales show, there is an active trade in classic cars and it might not be as expensive as you think.

FRANK SINATRA'S CAR

Actor and singer Frank Sinatra's sporty red 1970 Lamborghini Miura P400S (CHRIS)

A&C 56, sold £94,100, now worth £90-100,000

LALIQUE CAR MASCOT

1930s clear glass falcon car mascot, by René Lalique, 1930s, *the* make for mascots (AMER)

A&C 33, sold £1,350, now worth £4,000-8,000

PANTHER J72

PANTHER J72 One of the first built for sale. In Ferrari yellow with hard top and 3.8 Jaguar engine. Full service history, new MOT, genuine mileage of 12,950 (GORR)

A&C 44, sold for £11,500, now worth £15-18,000

MESSERSCHMITT CABRIOLET

1961 Messerschmitt KR-200 Cabriolet in silver, restored; new body panels, rebuilt engine, new hood and interior (BR AUC)

A&C 11, sold £5,175, now worth £6,000-10,000

Fact File

MGs, Morris Minors, old Beetles and Minis are some of the most affordable classic cars, depending on condition, good versions sell for around £2,000-plus, less than many modern, second-hand cars.

A 1935 Noble Duesenberg with only 15,000 miles on the clock and two previous owners, sold for $1,045,000 (around £600,000). The Auto Collection in The Imperial Palace in Las Vegas has a whole room devoted to Duesenbergs.

Other cars are collectable not just because of their style but their previous owners. The Vegas museum houses cars owned by the likes of Marilyn Monroe and President Eisenhower, their most popular exhibit currently being 'Eleanor' from the Nicholas Cage cult film, *Gone in Sixty Seconds*. When buying classic cars, it's worth considering the availability of parts.

CLASSIC MINI

First registered in London in June 1966, this classic Mini has the short-stroke 998cc engine introduced in 1964. Professionally restored, 88,000 miles, a firm favourite (BR AUC)

A&C 11, sold £5,980, now worth £4,000-6,000

RAC BADGE

The Princess Victoria Mary (later Queen Mary) Royal Automobile Club life member's badge. Created c 1910, second design, made by Elkington & Sons, London, finished in gold, possibly given to Princess Mary (BR AUC)

A&C 13, sold £5,520, now worth £7,000-10,000

MOUNTBATTEN'S MASCOT

The Semaphore Sailor car mascot 'HMS Daring'. Believed to have once been owned by Lord Louis Mountbatten as the mascot on a Rolls Royce car in his possession (BR AUC)

A&C 13, est £2,000-3,000, now worth £4,000-6,000

DISNEY MASCOT

A very rare Disney Mickey Mouse car mascot by Desmo (signed). Original cold-painted bronze with yellow shoes, white gloves, red jacket and black body c 1935 (BR AUC)

A&C 13, est £1,200-1,800, now worth £2,000-4,000

TRANSPORT & TRAVEL

LARGE MODEL VEHICLES AND VEHICLE PARTS

These large model vehicles are definitely not toys, although some are sold as such. They include steam engines by the likes of Stuart Models (est 1898) and larger trains which appeal to the would-be engineer of all ages. Some are set on boards and only the pistons move whilst some can actually be ridden – by children.

RACING BOAT

Straight Line Racer, a 1950s scale model with a steam-driven motor, 48in long (AMER)

A&C 36, sold for £620, now worth £500-800

NAUTICALIA

Hardwood ship's wheel with brass mounts, ideal for designers, 77cm diameter (SWORD)

A&C 54, sold for £290, now worth £200-400

PARIS BUS

A 1920s model by Charles Rossignol, France, based on a Paris bus (COL TO)

A&C 46, sold £3,760, now worth £4,000-6,000

PLANE CAR

A child's pedal car in the form of an aeroplane (ROS)

A&C 19, sold for £570, now worth £700-850

FLEISCHMANN SHIP

A rare Fleischmann ship, 51cm long, in pink, not dated (COL TO)

A&C 12, sold for £550, now worth £600-800

CONCORDE CAPTAIN'S SEAT

Concorde captain's seat sold at the British Airways Concorde charity auction (BON)

A&C 60, sold £26,000, now worth £15-20,000

PENNY-FARTHING

19th century penny-farthing bicycle by Howe of Glasgow, cycles are collectable (BON)

A&C 44, sold £3,000, now worth £4,000-6,000

Fact File

Pond yachts were very popular in Edwardian times. The wooden models, over a foot long, would have been floated, as the name suggests, on ponds and pushed along with the stick which, hopefully, should still be with the boat. The sails have often come loose or torn over time but these are very simple creations, dating from an era when Britain and her Empire were linked by the sea and, as such, there was a fascination with all types of boats. An idea that would later be replaced by a love of aeroplanes.

Good Victorian and Edwardian pond yachts are worth £100-150. Later versions are more detailed, many being built from scratch and being remote controlled. Whilst impressive, they often lack the appeal of the simpler version.

TRAVEL POSTERS

Posters would be exhibited at railway stations and in towns to tempt people to travel. Time and money were restricted, which is why, until the 1980s with the growth of foreign package holidays, most people stayed in Britain, with only the wealthy able to travel abroad. Posters would celebrate the joys of places like Bristol.

CAR TRAVEL

A large lithographic poster advertising Jenatzy Pneus at 10 Rue Stephenson Bruxelles by J.E. Goossens of Brussels. Framed and glazed, 50x30inches (BR AUC)

A&C 13, sold £5,060, now worth £8,000-12,000

UNDERGROUND POSTER

For All Theatres Travel Underground, 1930, by Edward McKnight Kauffer

A&C 7, sold for £184, now worth £500-600

LMS RAILWAY POSTER

Southport LMS, c 1930, by artist Fortunio Mantania, evocative of the era (CHRIS)

A&C 7, est £1,500-2,000, now worth £3,000-4,000

ST MORITZ

Emil Cardinaux design for Palace Hotel, St Moritz. Lithograph in colours, 1920 (CHRIS)

A&C 25, est £4,000-6,000, now worth £6,000-10,000

Fact File

Some of the most exciting travel posters were Continental. Aimed at the wealthy, they showed richly clad women skiing or relaxing in exotic-sounding locations such as the Cote d'Azur. Only the rich could afford to fly or had the time to travel and these posters are aimed at a certain type, their extravagance irresistible.

The ones in a distinctly Art Deco or Art Nouveau style are best. In contrast, British travel posters of the 1950s depicted caravan holidays as action-packed fun for the whole family.

Railway posters are particularly collectable. Those from the 1950s in good condition can be worth £500-800, depending on location. The train operator GNWR (Great North Western Railway) is still one of the most popular and prices are high.

RAILWAY SEASIDE ADVERT

Morecambe, c 1955, by an anonymous artist for British Railways (CHRIS)

A&C est £400-600, now worth £600-800

MONT BLANC WINTER SPORTS

E J Kerley design for Chamonix-Mont Blanc, PLM, Lithograph in colours, 1910. (CHRIS)

A&C 23, est £700-900, now worth £1,500-2,500

WINTER SPORTS

Roger Broders design for Les Sports D'Hiver A St Pierre De Chartreuse, PLM Lithograph in colours, 1930 (CHRIS)

A&C 21, sold £5,520, now worth £7,000-10,000

PICASSO

Cote d'Azur, c.1962, by Pablo Picasso

A&C 7, sold for £575, now worth £2,000-4,000

TRAYS

SERVING TRAYS

The word 'tray' comes from the Old English word *treow* meaning 'wood' or 'tree' and trays were originally wooden. Smaller versions would be used for glasses and tin trays are especially popular in pubs which has led to advertising tray collections, especially for drinks such as Guinness or Coca Cola.

PAPIER MACHE

Papier mâché tray. Of shaped rectangular form, 77.5cm and decorated with an urn of flowers and with gilt decoration (BRI)

A&C 29, sold for £1,250, now worth £1,000-1,500

SALES TRAY

A nineteenth century tole peint salesman sample tray, painted with a central landscape and a leaf border (DREW)

A&C 66, sold for £600, now worth £500-700

KIDNEY-SHAPED TRAY

A fine 19th century mahogany marquetry inlaid kidney-shaped tray, inlaid with symbols of the arts within a foliate and scroll surround (DAH)

A&C 8, sold for £400, now worth £500-600

VICTORIAN TRAY

Tole peint cartouche shaped tray, painted overall with exotic birds and scrolls around an urn of flowers in monochrome and gilt (DREW)

A&C 45, sold for £400, now worth £450-550

Fact File

Some of the more attractive and expensive trays are made of papier mâché. This is a French phrase meaning 'chewed paper' and is made using paper hardened with a glue made from flour and water. It was invented by the Chinese in the second century using papyrus reeds. It's a very strong substance and has been used for many items, not just trays but clocks, boats and even houses. The French first used it commercially in the 17th century and its use spread to England in 1670. Japanese goods were in vogue at the time and papier mâché was created with the distinctive black lacquer finish so popular in Japan. It was also very popular in Russia with two of the largest collectors being Peter the Great and the art-loving Catherine the Great who collected snuff boxes.

VICTORIAN PAPIER MACHE

Mid-Victorian tray made of papier mâché and mother of pearl, together with another, smaller tray (DREW)

A&C 41, sold for £340, now worth £350-450

REGENCY PAPIER MACHE

Regency papier mâché tray, painted with a shepherd family, representing rural bliss by Henry Clay (GORR)

A&C 53, sold for £1,200, now worth £1,000-1,500

SILVER SALVERS

George III silver salvers with gadrooned borders and engraved armorials, makers Thomas Hannam and John Crouch, London 1806 (GORR)

A&C 65, sold for £1,400, now worth £1,800-2,200

JAPANESE CLOISONNE

Japanese cloisonné tray. Enamelled with a view of Mount Fuji (DREW)

A&C 43, sold for £3,800, now worth £3-5,000

FILM POSTERS

This genre is probably the most collectable of all posters because they have such mass appeal and, unlike rock and pop concerts, would have been nationwide. With so much competition from other films, they had to be gripping or stylish. And Bond did it best, especially the 1962 *Dr No* poster which influenced so many others.

SIGNED POSTER

Poster of cult film *Reservoir Dogs*, signed by director, Quentin Tarrantino and stars, Harvey Keitel and Tim Roth (CHRIS)

A&C 11, sold for £1,495, now worth £2,000-3,000

SINGING IN THE RAIN

Collectable classic *Singing in the Rain* (CHRIS)

A&C 11, sold for £6,325, now worth £12-15,000

BOND IS BACK

Triple-O-Seven UK promotion poster for three Bond films. Bond is always collectable (COOP)

A&C 45, sold for £180, now worth £400-700

Fact File

The image of Sean Connery as Bond in *Dr No* with a smoking gun and a smoking cigarette would not be acceptable now because of the ban on smoking in adverts but it is one of the defining moments in poster history. *Dr No* was the first Bond film and no one knew how successful the now cult film would be.

Mitchell Hooks designed the first poster, released in the US, with the smoking Bond surrounded by scantily clad women. Joseph Caroff added the 007 logo which was to become synonymous with Bond memorabilia. It's interesting to compare the US version to others. One of the Japanese posters has a woman wearing Bond's shirt (and nothing else) and playing golf while the debonair spy looks on from a distant doorway. Expect to pay £2,500+ for a UK version but less for the other Bond films.

HITCHCOCK

Hitchcock's *Vertigo* designed by Saul Bass to recreate the dizziness of the illness (CHRIS)

A&C 11, sold £2,300, now worth £3,000-5,000

STAR WARS REPRODUCTION

Tenth anniversary limited edition poster of cult sci-fi film, *Star Wars* (CHRIS)

A&C 11, sold for £230, now worth £200-400

DRACULA

Dracula, the rarest of all Hammer Horror posters (CHRIS)

A&C 11, sold for £6,900, now worth £10,000-15,000

EALING COMEDY

The artwork for the Ealing classic *The Lavender Hill Mob* was by artist and cartoonist Ronald Searle (CHRIS)

A&C 11, sold for £805, now worth £1,500-2,000

HIGH SOCIETY

Frank Sinatra and Grace Kelly classic *High Society* (Picture by Movie Market)

A&C 56, now worth £300-500

ELVIS

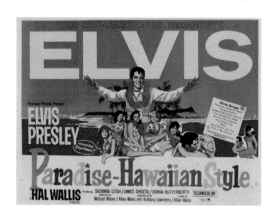

Paradise Hawaiian Style, one of Elvis' many films for Paramount Pictures, 1965. 76cm x 102cm and affordable because of mass showings (BON)

A&C 43, sold for £140, now worth £150-200

BOB HOPE

Posters for the 1963 comedy adventure *Call Me Bwana* (Pictures by Movie Market)

A&C 56, sold for £30, now worth £50-80

JANE RUSSELL

The Outlaw, 1943, Howard Hughes/TCF, US six-sheet (CHRIS)

A&C 56, sold for £52,875, now worth £45-60,000

NORTH BY NORTHWEST

Film poster for Alfred Hitchcock's classic *North By North West* (CHRIS)

A&C 11, sold for £552, now worth £1,000-1,500

KING KONG

This Swedish poster of *King Kong* recently sold for £12,075

A&C 11, sold £12,075, now worth £20-30,000

BARBARA STANWYCK

1964 *Roustabout*, Barbara Stanwyck film (Picture by Qunitet Publishing)

A&C 43, est £60-80, now worth £60-100

Fact File

Horror and sci-fi are some of the best-selling genres while, according to Christie's, bankers love James Bond. Their first pop art sale saw a set of 1965 James Bond posters, still mounted to the cinema door panels, sell for £18,500 but horror prevailed when *The Mummy* (1932, Boris Karloff version) went under the hammer for £80,750, over £25,00 more than cult Humphrey Bogart tearjerker, *Casablanca* (£54,300). Another poster of the horror film set the world record price by selling for £252,000, possibly being a larger size or different country's version.

Another classic, *The Invisible Man* sold for £36,700, climbing higher than *King Kong* which reached the dizzying heights of £28,750. Style icon, Audrey Hepburn, notched up a respectful £13,145 when posed holding a cigarette on the poster of the classic *Breakfast at Tiffany's*.

Look for classic films which have been are about to be remade eg *The Poseidon Adventure*, *Manchurian Candidate* or *Dawn of the Dead*.

BREAKFAST AT TIFFANY'S

Breakfast At Tiffany's/Fruhstuck Bei Tiffany
1961, Paramount, German film poster with unusual, colouring, 84cm x 58cm (CHRIS)

A&C 48, sold for £998, now worth £3,000-4,000

42ND STREET

42nd Street, stylishly naughty poster commanding a high price (CHRIS)

A&C 11, sold £17,250, now worth £20-30,000

AUDREY HEPBURN

Classic image of Audrey as Holly Golightly in *Breakfast at Tiffany's*. This version with the cigarette and cat is the most desirable and costly of the cult classic (Moviemarket)

A&C 48, est £4,000, now worth £15-20,000

BOND BEAUTY

From Russia with Love could be bought for £100 only 5 years ago but poster prices have gone up recently, especially for cult films (CHRIS)

A&C 11, sold for £1,610, now worth £1,500-2,000

SOME LIKE IT HOT

A reproduction of *Some Like It Hot* movie poster to promote a 2000 relaunch. Originals sell for around £2,250 (Moviemarket)

A&C 46, sold for £1,500, now worth £1,500-2,000

Fact File

What's the difference between re-released posters and reproduction? Films which have been re-released also have updated posters to capture the current audience and not appear old-fashioned. One of the most appealing is Al Hirschfeld's 1972 poster for Chaplin's 1936 film, *Modern Times*. The original stressed how new machinery was whilst Hirschfeld's version (worth £400-500) captured the whimsical essence of the star.

Re-releases can be good investments, depending on the design. Reproduction posters faithfully reproduce the original poster, often on a smaller scale as they're being made for home, not commercial, hanging.

Look for a date of issue in the corner of the poster or ask the dealer if you're not sure. Reproduction posters are an affordable way of decorating but not for investment.

ELVIS IN CLAMBAKE

Elvis' 1967 movie poster *Clambake* (Picture by Guy Harrington)

A&C 43, est £50, now worth £100-120

TEMPTING VIEWERS

Hotel For Women, 1934 film poster (CHRIS)

A&C 51, sold for £293, now worth £250-350

TV & FILM

PROPS

There was scandal when the props from the first *Harry Potter* film were being sold on the Internet as they had not been officially sanctioned but it showed how much people wanted to own something from their favourite character or film. Visitors to Universal Studios in America can buy props and a photograph of them being used.

BOND WEAPON

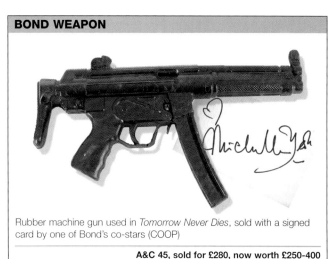

Rubber machine gun used in *Tomorrow Never Dies*, sold with a signed card by one of Bond's co-stars (COOP)

A&C 45, sold for £280, now worth £250-400

ROMEO AND JULIET

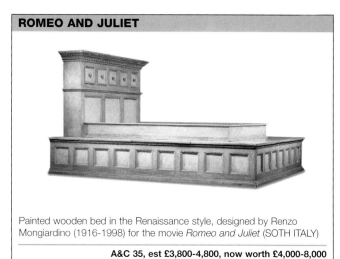

Painted wooden bed in the Renaissance style, designed by Renzo Mongiardino (1916-1998) for the movie *Romeo and Juliet* (SOTH ITALY)

A&C 35, est £3,800-4,800, now worth £4,000-8,000

SPITTING IMAGE

Bob Hope original puppet from the cult TV series *Spitting Image,* designed by Fluck and Law and sold after the series ended (SOTH)

A&C 56, sold £822, now worth £1,000-1,500

Fact File

When it comes to props, provenance is everything. Ideally, you need to have the props signed by the star or a photo of them with it. The most desirable props are the ones which played a large part in the film, eg, the ruby slippers in *The Wizard of Oz* (1939). There are at least nine pairs known to exist which would have been used for publicity purposes or over the course of filming to ensure that they looked perfect at all times. Debbie Reynolds owns a pair which cost her £150 while another pair sold twice. These were originally won in a contest after the film and the owner decided to sell them in 1988. They made around £92,000 ($165,000) and were resold in 2000 for £334,000 ($600,000) – plus the £33,400 commission, of course.

HARRY POTTER

A Howler (shouting letter) from the film *Harry Potter and the Chamber of Secrets* (BON)

A&C 58, sold for £620, now worth £600-1,000

GOLDFINGER

Oddjob's steel-rimmed bowler used as a deadly weapon in *Goldfinger*, 1964 and which more than tripled its estimate (CHRIS)

A&C 13, sold for £62,000, now worth £50,000-80,000

TOMORROW NEVER DIES – SECRET WEAPON

An Omega stainless steel diver's automatic calendar wristwatch from *Tomorrow Never Dies*, 1997 and one of Q's secret weapons (CHRIS)

A&C 45, sold for £8,225, now worth £8,000-10,000

COSTUMES

Clothes are an essential part of a film and often their budget. Joan Collins' large shoulder-pads from *Dallas* lead to similar over-sized creations becoming part of everyday fashion, proving the influence of TV and film on the real world. Fans are eager to buy part of their favourite programmes or characters and even wear an actor's clothes.

BUNGLED ROBBERY

Bungle was sold with Zippy and George as a job lot before being stolen, then returned to his old presenter and now owner (CHRIS)

A&C 30, sold £6,800, now worth £4,000-6,000

ELVIS FILM SHIRT

Floral patterned stage shirt worn by Elvis in the 1970s film *That's The Way It Is*. (CHRIS)

A&C 20, sold £19,500, now worth £20-25,000

BOND BRIDE

On Her Majesty's Secret Service, 1969. A wedding coat of ivory chiffon made for doomed bride Diana Rigg (CHRIS.)

A&C 45, sold for £5,640, now worth £5,000-8,000

BOB HOPE

Glamorous costumes worn by Bob Hope in the 1946 movie *Monsieur Beaucare* (SOTH)

A&C 56, sold £1,875, now worth £1,500-2,500

RAINBOW RETURNED

Original Zippy puppet (in job lot with the other two) from children's TV series *Rainbow* bought by their presenter Geoffrey Hayes (CHRIS)

A&C 30, sold £6,800, now worth £4,000-6,000

FRANK SINATRA

This suit from one of Sinatra's final film roles, as Joe Leland in 1968's *The Detective* (SOTH)

A&C 56, sold £2,430, now worth £3,000-5,000

Fact File

One of the most extravagant productions ever was the Taylor-Burton epic, *Cleopatra* (1965) which, costing $40 million (£22,500,000), bankrupted Fox studios. The original designer was Oliver Messel at Pinewood but this changed to Irene Sharaff. The armour which Taylor wore as the Egyptian Queen was made of real gold and was so heavy that she could only wear it for a short time. It cost $1,000,000 (£556,000) and remains the most expensive film costume ever made and one of the most ostentatious.

Dr Spock's tunic from *Star Trek*, worn by actor Leonard Nimoy, made £73,500 at auction, proving the enduring appeal to the sci-fi series. But most costumes from TV series are affordable and can be found at specialist auctions or on the Internet; try to find ones with photographs of them being worn.

The popular TV series, *Sex and The City* was famous for its use of designer labels and those clothes were quickly snapped up when production finished in 2004.

TV & FILM

THUNDERBIRDS

The release of the *Thunderbirds* movie, using people instead of puppets, has increased interest in the popular sci-fi series which has always had a firm following. Gerry Anderson's 1965 creation was only meant to be 30 minutes-long but Lew Grade said that they should be an hour which allowed for extra characterisation.

LADY PENELOPE'S CAR

Lady Penelope's pink Rolls Royce, issued by Dinky Toys during a ten year period between 1966-76 (VECTIS)

A&C 51, sold for £200, now worth £200-300

THE TRACYS

Scott, Virgil, Alan, Gordon and John Tracy figures in their famous outfits (CHRIS)

A&C 51, sold £1,050, now worth £1,000-1,500

THUNDERBIRD 2

First Dinky Toys model of Thunderbird 2, issued between 1967 and 1973 (VECTIS)

A&C 51, sold for £330, now worth £300-400

THUNDERBIRD 4

Battery-operated model of Thunderbird 4 by Rosenthal Toy Company of Hong Kong, in its original box (CHRIS)

A&C 51, sold for £360, now worth £350-400

Fact File

Thunderbirds memorabilia continues to make record prices. Although the merchandise itself is still relatively affordable, buyers have been snapping up the original puppets. Saved from a rubbish dump when filming finished after 32 shows, the only known remaining head of John Tracy sold almost 30 years later for £37,600, with Virgil Tracy's head, one of several still in existence, fetching £11,750. Puppet sex symbol, Scott Tracy's cap went for £2,600.

One of the favourite characters was Lady Penelope who was meant to be based on Gerry Anderson's wife (now ex), Sylvia. A replica version of the puppet which she once owned made £28,000, less than her famous chauffeur, Parker. The top lot was the FAB 1966 model of the Pink Rolls Royce car with its bubble canopy for easy puppeteering; it sold for £80,000.

THUNDERIRD 2 – THIRD MODEL

Third version of Dinky Toys Thunderbird 2 issued between 1977 and 1980 (CHRIS)

A&C 51, est £80-110, now worth £100-150

JOHN TRACY'S BODY

John Tracy's head pictured here on what is called a 'stock' body in the Thunderbirds uniform The body was sold by itself (CHRIS)

A&C 51, sold £2,600, now worth £4,000-6,000

THUNDERBIRD 3

Thunderbird 3 with wooden body detailed in brass and Perspex (CHRIS).

A&C 51, sold for £880, now worth £800-1,200

THUNDERBIRD 1 PROP

Original launch bay of Thunderbird 1, used for the production of the *Thunderbirds* comics and also on video sleeves, trading cards and other publicity items (CHRIS)

A&C 51, sold for £820, now worth £1,000-2,000

JAMES BOND

Ian Fleming's popular secret agent novels were turned into a series of films in 1962 with *Dr No*, although this was actually the sixth book. Bond's debut was in *Casino Royale* in 1953, a first edition book with perfect dust jacket, sells for £15,000. While there was a lot of merchandise released for the films, original props are the best buys.

FIRST BOND BOOK

Casino Royale was the first of the Bond books and the most valuable of them all (HAMP)

A&C 13, est £4,500-5,200, worth £3,000-4,000

SIGNATURES

You Only Live Twice – featuring related signatures: Sean Connery, Donald Pleasance and Roald Dahl. Connery's autograph is the most desirable of the Bond actors (COOP)

A&C 45, sold for £400, now worth £450-600

AIRFIX KIT

A 1965 1/24th scale Airfix kit of Bond's DB5, still in its original box and complete with instructions. The box is not perfect which does devalue it

A&C 45, est £100-120, now worth £200-300

CORGI CLASSIC

Corgi James Bond's Aston Martin,1966, still in its original box (SPEC AUC)

A&C 53, sold for £180, now worth £300-400

Fact File

James Bond is renowned for many things but most people remember only three – Martini, women and cars. And, when it comes to memorabilia, cars come out on top. The real 1965 Aston Martin DB5 which was driven by Pierce Brosnan in *Goldeneye* (1995) sold for £157,750 whilst its Corgi counterpart from the 1960s can fetch £300-400. An Airfix version, still unmade in its original box, is also worth £300-400. Bond was also famous for his 'toys', weapons created by the long-suffering Q. One of these, an adapted genuine Rolex, fetched £25,850.

And, when it comes to costumes, as the Bond girls discovered, less is more. The first Bond girl was Ursula Andress who walked out of the sea in a bikini which recently made £41,150.

ASTON MARTIN

James Bond's Aston Martin DB5, Corgi No 261, in mint condition with its two figures and original box with 'Secret Instructions' package, the most popular Bond car (GORR).

A&C 45, sold for £300, now worth £300-450

FIRST EDITION

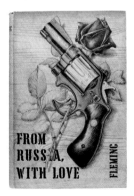

From Russia, With Love by Ian Fleming. Jonathan Cape, 1957 first edition, written five years before the first film (SOTH)

A&C 45, sold for £1,057, now worth £800-1,600

GEORGE LAZENBY

George Laznby's face is hidden under the ironic declaration that 'James Bond 007 is Back' because he was the only actor to play the famous spy just once (CHRIS)

A&C 13, sold for £230, now worth £300-500

THE FIRST BOND FILM

An original 1962 UK poster for the first Bond film *Dr. No*, neither as sexy nor as costly as the American version (Movie Market)

A&C 45, est £1,500, now worth £1,500-2,000

TV & FILM

MEMORABILIA

TV and film have inspired a wealth of collectables. Modern versions are mass-produced although some of the limited editions are good buys. Cult films such as the *Lord of the Rings* and later *Star Wars* films led to millions of goods being produced – but look for early memorabilia from their stars instead as this is where the money lies.

MARILYN MONROE

Ring, earrings and bracelet once belonging to Marilyn Monroe and sold individually as part of her foster-sister Eleanor 'Bebe' Goddard's collection, priced here collectively (COOP)

A&C 42, sold for £9,100, now worth £10-12,000

THE DALEKS

Louis Marx's toy versions of Dr Who's arch-enemy, The Daleks, 1965 (CHRIS)

A&C 54, est £200-300, now worth £400-600

BATMOBILE

Corgi toys Batmobile, No 267, first issue with bat logo on wheels, damaged (CHEF)

A&C 34, sold for £170, now worth £200-400

MARILYN'S CHEQUE

Cheque signed by Marilyn Monroe (FRAS)

A&C 57, est £5,000, now worth £5,000-6,000

Fact File

One of the most controversial British TV series was *Spitting Image* which made politicians household names. The puppets, designed by Fluck and Law, satirised modern events and no one was safe. The series' merchandise is still very collectable, long after the show ended. The original puppets were sold and Michael Winner proved that he knew star quality when he bought Sir John Gielgud for £5,400. Griff Rhys Jones bought an original drawing of himself with his comedy partner, Mel Smith, for £600. Slippers featuring Charles and Diana sell for around £50-80 but best buys are the all-white Carlton Ware depictions of royals and politicians. Rarest of these is Labour shadow leader, Michael Foot (£100-200) while the Diana egg cup is £40-60.

DR WHOS

Limited edition commemorative cover to mark Doctor Who at the Stamp Show in 2000. Signed personally by all surviving Doctors, with facsimile signatures of the others

A&C 54, est £100, now worth £100-150

SHIRLEY TEMPLE

A pressed cloth Shirley Temple doll with painted features (PH KN)

A&C 33, sold for £185, now worth £200-250

DR WHO STAR

Signed photo of Louise Jameson as Leela, one of the Dr Who co-stars

A&C 54, est £20-30, now worth £20-40

STAR WARS

A *Star Wars* Wampa statuette, 1996

A&C 9, est £30, now worth £20-40

Fact File

George Lucas' *Star Wars* trilogy burst onto the screens in 1977 and brought sci-fi to the masses. It was no longer exclusive but part of a strange set of worlds which everyone could imagine. Full of appealing characters from R2-D2 the cheeping robot to wise Yoda, one of the mysterious band of Jedis whose job was to save everyone from the Dark Side, lead by Darth Vader.

But the characters which no one liked, such as the repulsively fat Jabba the Hut were the ones left on the shelf after frantic merchandising and it is these which command the most money. Expect to pay £500+ for an original one still in its original packaging. The second trilogy saw mass-production on a scale and few of these goods have the investment value of those from the first three films. However, they did serve to rejuvenate the cult market and generate new collectors.

BOBA FETT

Return of the Jedi Boba Fett action figure, Kenner (unopened box). Sold in the shops for £2.99 in 1983

A&C 9, sold for £250, now worth £300-500

PRINCESS LEIA

Return of the Jedi Princess Leia of Organa action figure, General Mills, 1983 in unopened packaging,1983.

A&C 9, sold for £250, now worth £300-500

STAR WARS MUGS

Star Wars character mugs – Princess Leia, Chewbacca, C-3P0 and Darth Vader, 1977

A&C 9, sold for £35 each, now worth £35-45

DARTH VADER HELMET

Darth Vader helmet. Released in time for the Special Edition Trilogy, 1996

A&C 9, sold for £125, now worth £70-90

R2-D2

R2-D2 soap in original unopened box, 1977. Originally bought for 99p in 1977

A&C 9, sold for £5-10, now worth £10-20

C-3PO

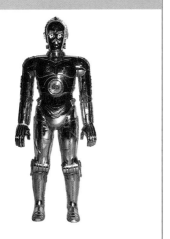

C-3PO toy by General Mills, 1978

A&C 9, est £45, now worth £50-80

YODA

Yoda hand puppet by Applause, 1999

A&C 9, sold for £20, now worth £10-20

STORMTROOPER

Stormtrooper toy by Kenner, 1978, still unopened in packaging

A&C 9, sold for £50, now worth £60-100

WATCHES

ROLEX

One of the best-known makes of watches is Rolex, originally founded in London in 1905 as Wilsdorf and Davies, becoming Rolex three years later. It is a company of firsts for wristwatches – first to receive official chronometer certification in Switzerland (the centre for clock making), first waterproof, and first to show date automatically.

SPORTING PRINCE WATCH

A rare gold and steel Rolex Sporting Prince wristwatch, c 1930s (CHRIS)

A&C 20, est £10,000-15,000, now worth £15,000-25,000

JEWEL-ENCRUSTED WATCH

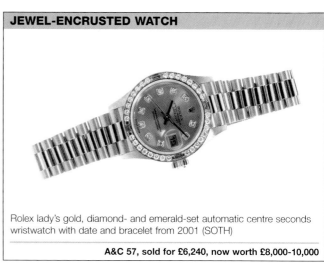

Rolex lady's gold, diamond- and emerald-set automatic centre seconds wristwatch with date and bracelet from 2001 (SOTH)

A&C 57, sold for £6,240, now worth £8,000-10,000

ROLEX OYSTER

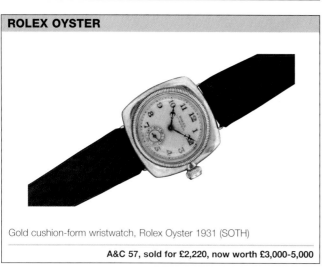

Gold cushion-form wristwatch, Rolex Oyster 1931 (SOTH)

A&C 57, sold for £2,220, now worth £3,000-5,000

OYSTER PERPETUAL

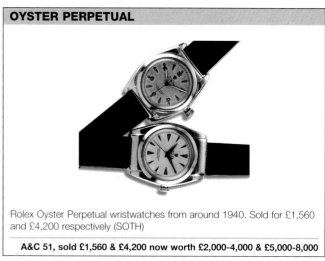

Rolex Oyster Perpetual wristwatches from around 1940. Sold for £1,560 and £4,200 respectively (SOTH)

A&C 51, sold £1,560 & £4,200 now worth £2,000-4,000 & £5,000-8,000

Fact File

Rolex received fantastic publicity when Mercedes Gleitze wore the Rolex Oyster – the first ever waterproof wristwatch – when he swam the English Channel in 1927, a year after it had been released. The 1931 Perpetual Rotor was another legendary creation and is seen as the basis for self-winding movement in watches whilst the 1945 Oyster Datejust inspired other designers by being the first to set the time automatically.

International travellers benefited from a 1955 watch which showed two time zones for the first time, although this has limited appeal for most users. Some dealers specialise in just selling Rolexes because of the demand and quality of the work. The record price for a Rolex was £142,300 for the 'Jean-Claude Killy' watch, a 1952 Oyster chronograph.

RARE 1940s ROLEX

Rare Rolex stainless steel chronograph with register and tachometer, from 1940 (SOTH)

A&C 57, sold £3,600, now worth £5,000-8,000

1960 ROLEX

Rolex watch stainless steel, c 1960 with 26-jewel movement. 'Silver' dial and Jubilee bracelet, case no. 1500 (FELL)

A&C 39, sold £600, now worth £1,000-1,500

FIGURAL, MUSICAL WATCH

A rare enamel- and pearl-set, gold musical two-train pocket watch in the form of a rose with exquisite detailing and colouring (CHRIS)

A&C 17, est £10-15,000, now worth £20-40,000

POCKET WATCH

18ct half hunters pocket watch on chain with whistle on the end, c 1890 (CHRIS)

A&C 40, sold £1,527, now worth £1,500-2,000

Fact File

When it comes to money, the most collectable make of all is Patek Philippe, founded in Geneva in 1839. The company's 1939 platinum world time wristwatch achieved £2,914,000 at auction, a similar price being fetched for the white gold calibre 89, a pocket watch which is said to be the most complex watch in the world.

One of the most attractive watches ever made was arguably from Piguet and Capt. It's shaped like an amphora (urn and lid) and made of gold, set with pearls and beautifully decorated with enamel. The musical watch, one of a pair, also has an automaton (clockwork) scene, despite its small size. Made in 1805, it sold for £1,775,000.

At the other end of the market, delicate ladies' wristwatches from the 1920s-30s, can be bought for as little as £25.

HALF HUNTER POCKET WATCH

Half hunter pocket watch, 18 ct gold, the case engraved and enamelled in blue, signed 'Dent, Watchmaker to the Queen', keyless (GORR)

A&C 63, sold for £330, now worth £350-450

PIGUET

White gold, diamond-set, minute repeating tourbillon wristwatch, Audemars Piguet, from 1995, part of the value being the gems (SOTH)

A&C 57, sold £89,000, now worth £80-90,000

OMEGA

Omega Seamaster Professional stainless steel gentleman's watch, with foldover clasp (FELL)

A&C 41, sold for £440, now worth £400-600

WHITE GOLD AND DIAMONDS, 1998

Impressive white gold, diamond-set bracelet watch with regulator style dial, power reserve and oversized date, A Lange & Soehne, Glashuette, 'Lange 1' and made in 1998 (SOTH)

A&C 57, sold for £24,000, now worth £20,000-30,000

PATEK PHILIPPE

Fine gold wristwatch with flared sides called a Pagoda, made by probably the most collectable make, Patek Philippe, in 1997 (SOTH)

A&C 57, sold for £8,400, now worth £10,000-12,000

HARPERS
Jewellers

2-4 Minster Gates,
York YO1 7HL
Tel. 01904 632634 Fax: 01904 673370

www.harpersjewellers.co.uk

The Old Coach House,
1 Montpelier Street,
Harrogate HG1 2TQ

www.vintage-watches.co.uk

We pride ourselves on our extensive range
of new and second hand watches.

From vintage to modern timepieces,
from Patek Philippe to original Heuer, we buy,
sell and part-exchange.

If you have a collection you wish to dispose of, or
add to, then please contact us for more information.

WOODEN GOODS

Wood is often overlooked as a collectable but comes in a variety of shapes, uses and, using different woods, colours. The Bavarian carvings from Victorian times, often used as Christmas ornaments, are very cheap for the amount of detail, a small bear costing only £5-15. Others, like wine coolers, are attractive accessories.

NUT CRACKER

Horned carved and stained wood figural nut cracker, 6.5in high, popular collectables (GORR)

A&C 43, sold for £200, now worth £200-300

SCOTTISH WOOD

Napkin rings In the tartan colours of Gordon, Stuart, Drummond, Caledonia, MacBeth and Prince Charlie, popular designs (SWORD)

A&C 48, sold for £160, now worth £200-300

WALL BRACKETS

19th century wall brackets, gilt painted wood and gesso, in Neoclassical style, 43cm x 34.5cm, appeal to interior designers (DREW)

A&C 40, sold for £550, now worth £600-800

ORIENTAL FIGURE

Oriental figure, early-20th century, carved hardwood, 17in high (AMER)

A&C 36, sold for £140, now worth £100-200

Fact File

One of the greatest wood carvers was the Bavarian, Faust Lang, an Olympic bronze medallist (skiing) most famous for the animals he created for Wade in 1939. He was not a potter and carved these animals in wood from which moulds would be taken. He always signed his pieces and the high prices being commanded for his Wade figures (£500-2,500) will soon see his wooden carvings increase in price. As well as smaller carvings such as a horse, he also made pieces for churches, including a statue of St Ia in the church of Sacred Heart and St Ia on Tregenna Hill, St Ives, Cornwall which is where he moved after Wade stopped producing luxury goods because of the war.

NORWEGIAN BOX

Norwegian chip carved box and lid, probably for carrying food, part lot (SWORD)

A&C, sold for £150 lot, now worth £150-250

MONEY BOX

19th century marquetry money box shaped as a house, some damage (SWORD)

A&C , sold for £100 , now worth £100-150

HERALDIC DEVICE

Early-17th century, carved oak heraldic newel (staircase) post finial, English (CHRIS)

A&C 39, sold £12,925, now worth £15-20,000

TORCHERE

Hardwood torchere (tall stand for holding a candelabrum), late-19th century, Anglo-Indian, lavishly and well carved with fruit, flowers and foliage, inscribed 'Madras' and 'J.D.' (SWORD)

A&C 45, sold for £5,000, now worth £5-7,000

WOODEN GOODS

TREEN

The word treen is derived from Treow, the Old English term meaning tree or wood. It is used for small, very smooth wooden objects which are not jointed (eg not furniture). The term can be used for any wood, although it is generally used for lignum vitae, the heaviest, densest tree in Britain, an evergreen with a twisted trunk.

COFFEE GRINDER

Lignum vitae coffee grinder, late-18th century, 22.5cm (9in) high, lovely rich wood (SOTH)

A&C 31, sold for £632, now worth £800-1000

CEDARWOOD

Rare, large cedarwood footed cup, late-17th century, 20.5cm (8in) (SOTH)

A&C 31, sold for £1,035, now worth £1-1,500

LIGNUM VITAE

Lignum vitae coffee grinder, second half of the 18th century, 15.5cm (6in) high (SOTH)

A&C 31, sold for £667, now worth £800-1,000

DECORATIVE WOOD

Decorative burr wood, lidded pot with turned finial, part of a job lot (SWORD)

A&C, sold for £150 lot, now worth £150-250

Fact File

There is some debate over whether Tunbridge Ware, with its colourful wooden decoration, is really treen but what you will see if that people who sell treen also tend to sell Tunbridge Ware and Mauchline Ware, the Scottish tourist pieces. Treen is simple but beautifully carved, often with turned wood (deep grooves) as decoration. The rich polish and patina of age should not be ruined by washing or over-eager polishing. Fruitwoods are very popular although they also appeal to woodworm. If pieces show evidence of worm, turn them wormhole down and tap, any dust coming out means that it's active. Treat it with special products available at larger fairs. One way to test the age of treen is to smell it – modern fakes smell fresh, often of olive wood.

COLOURFUL BOX

19th century parquetry box, rosewood edging, style known as Tunbridge Ware (SWORD)

A&C, est £200-300, now worth £150-250

RARE WASSAIL BOWL

Fine and large lignum vitae wassail bowl, English, 17th century, from Phillip Wacher collection (SOTH)

A&C 31, sold for £6,670, now worth £6-9,000

TUNBRIDGEWARE

Tunbridgeware rectangular paperweight. The colouring with different coloured woods is distinctive of the collectable style (SWORD)

A&C, sold for £90, now worth £100-200

COLLECTION OF TREEN

Small, early-19th century sundial in a domed box, three turned boxes, book box and a wooden barrel with lid (SWORD)

A&C, sold for £100, now worth £100-200

PENS

These can be great buys if you know what to spot as they are often overlooked by general dealers and auctioneers. Fountain pens are named after the container which holds the ink, saving the need for repeated dipping. Dipping pens from the 19th century are very desirable but costly, some were even made of real gold.

WATERMAN'S

Waterman's two-colour 18KR 42, Italian pen with floral filigree work, 1920-30s (BLOOM)

A&C, sold for £680, now worth £600-700

ROYAL WEDDING

Parker 105 'Royal Wedding', limited edition pen (1,000), English, 1981, commemorating Charles and Diana's wedding (BLOOM)

A&C, sold for £600, now worth £550-750

TIGER'S EYE

Conway Stewart No. 58 Tiger's Eye, named after the semi-precious stone because of the colour, English, early 1950s (BLOOM)

A&C, sold for £70, now worth £50-100

EVERSHARP CORONET

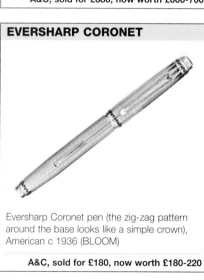

Eversharp Coronet pen (the zig-zag pattern around the base looks like a simple crown), American c 1936 (BLOOM)

A&C, sold for £180, now worth £180-220

Fact File

One of the most famous names in pen history is John Jacob Parker who patented his version of the fountain pen in 1832 – he is not related to the current Parker pen family. His patent was for a self-filling pen, a great advancement for its day. This idea was adapted by L.E. Waterman Company, an American firm whose pens are some of the most collectable. They developed the safety pen which, when it works, stops the pen from leaking. The world record was set by a 1920s Dunhill-Namiki Giant Dragon fountain pen by Shogo which sold for around £150,000. One pen which will appeal to writers is the Lucky Curve (£500-1,000), patented in 1894 by George Safford Parker which was bought by Sir Arthur Conan Doyle, George Bernard Shaw (which he used to write Pygmalion) and Puccini.

SILVER PARKER

Parker white-metal Jack-Knife Safety pen, American c 1919-25 (BLOOM)

A&C, sold for £170, now worth £180-220

RMS QUEEN ELIZABETH

Limited edition of 5,000, a Parker 75 pen 'RMS Queen Elizabeth', American, 1977. Created for the Queen's Silver Jubilee and named after the luxury liner (BLOOM)

A&C, sold for £520, now worth £400-600

PELIKAN SET

Pelikan 400 demonstration pen and pencil by the collectable German firm, 1955-56, in attractive green (BLOOM)

A&C, sold for £160, now worth £150-200

BASKET WEAVE

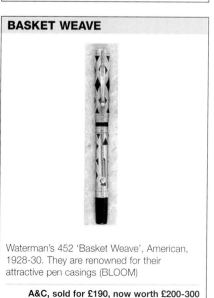

Waterman's 452 'Basket Weave', American, 1928-30. They are renowned for their attractive pen casings (BLOOM)

A&C, sold for £190, now worth £200-300

WRITING ACCESSORIES

TYPEWRITERS

Typewriters were first patented in 1867, although people had tried to create a writing machine since the 14th century. The 1867 models had the famous QWERTY keyboard but they were not produced commercially until Remington and Steel, the famous sewing machine creators, made a sewing machine-like one in 1873.

COLUMBIA

Columbia, 1885, a rare index machine with a round typing wheel on a nickel base (L COL)

A&C 63, est £1,500-2,300, now worth £1,750-2,250

WILLIAMS

Williams No. 2, 1891, with unusual typing movement. The first version is rarer because of its curved movement (L COL)

A&C 63, est £150-450, now worth £300-450

SMITH

Smith Premier double keyboard machine first used in 1889, many models (L COL)

A&C 63, est £30-300, later models worth £20-40

BLICKENSDERFER

Blickensderfer, 1893, which was made in France as Dactyle but both are quite common, even if innovative at the time (L COL)

A&C 63, est £50-150, now worth £50-100

Fact File

The majority of vintage typewriters are worth £25 and under. Makes such as Viceroy and Royalty sound a lot grander than they are and that is why it is possible to pick up fantastic bargains (such as a 1885 Columbia index machine worth £1,500-2,500) because most dealers overlook the typewriters that are worth anything. The original Remington and Steel versions had attractive floral decorations and went on to inspire a 1980s detective series starring Piece Brosnan (later to play James Bond) as the titular character, Remington Steele, a James-Bond style private detective. One of the most expensive typewriters ever was gold-plated and commissioned by James Bond author, Ian Fleming, from the Royal Typewriter Co. in New York in 1952. It was sold at auction for a record £50,000.

HAMMOND

Hammond, 1890, with a curved keyboard, although they also made straight versions. Later became the Varitype (L COL)

A&C 63, est £900, now worth £600-800

MALLING HANSEN

Malling Hansen writing ball, 1867, created by Hans Johan Malling Hansen, director of Denmark's deaf and dumb institute. 180 were made, considered a lot at that time (L COL)

A&C 7, sold for £36,000, now worth £40-50,000

CRANDALL

Crandall, 1884, with mother-of-pearl inlay and a curved keyboard (L COL)

A&C 63, est £1-4,000, now worth £1-2,000

SALTER

Salter Standard version No. 10, the most desirable model was No. 5 (L COL)

A&C 63, est £250-370, now worth £200-250

WRITING ACCESSORIES

There are plenty of accessories to consider when thinking about collecting writing-related goods. These include pen-holders, inkwells, writing tables or slopes, blotters, ink bottles and advertising merchandise, including Swan Ink metal signs. Some of these are innovative, including blotters shaped like elephants and pen holders as cars.

PRESENTATION INKWELL

Victorian silver presentation inkstand. Plaque reads 'presented to Lieut. Verney Lovett Cameron R N by the people of Shoreham on his return home from his exploration expedition in Africa, May 5th 1876' (PH ED)

A&C 29, sold for £2,990, now worth £2-4,000

GEORGE BULLOCK

Rare and decorative tortoiseshell, brass and mother-of-pearl inlaid inkstand made by English cabinetmaker and designer George Bullock (1777-1815), some damage (SWORD)

A&C 63, sold for £15,500, now worth £12-18,000

BAROQUE PAPERKNIFE

Baroque paperknife made of gold and metal and decorated with pearls rubies (CHRIS)

A&C 29, sold for £15,275, now worth £15-20,000

Fact File

The earliest ink used to be made from soot in vegetable oil or animal glue. 17 centuries ago, the Chinese created solid ink in stick form, an idea still used today and these could be broken up and added to water when needed for use without the risk of leaking pens.

In Britain, all school desks before the 1950s would have had inkwells in the corner. These very simple, white ceramic inkwells now sell for around £5-8. More desirable are the shaped versions which would have been self-contained on top of desks. Glass ones are very collectable with an 1820-30 hand-blown version by the Boston and Sandwich Glass Works fetching £5,600. It's also worth looking for good ceramic inkwells as a rare Bobbins inkwell by Clarice Cliff is worth £1,000-1,500.

PAPERWEIGHTS

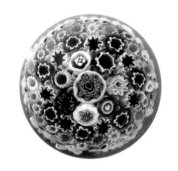

Mid-19th century Bacchus paperweight with millefiori canes, an attractive accessory (BON)

A&C 53, sold for £1,135, now worth £1-1,500

CLICHY PAPERWEIGHTS

Clichy paperweights c 1845, with millefiori canes, 6cm and 4.5cm (SWORD)

A&C 60, sold for £600, now worth £500-800

GOTHIC REVIVAL

Mid-Victorian flat-bed printing press by Hughes & Kimber, Gothic design, painted cast iron frame, manually operated, 52in high (AMER)

A&C 30, sold for £800, now worth £1,200-1,800

EDWARDIAN INKWELL

Pressed glass Edwardian inkwell of a wrythen (twisted), square shape with hinged, star cut cover and brass collar (GORR)

A&C 66, sold for £55, now worth £100-150

FARMAN CARS

Icarus deskpiece inkwell, designed by Georges Colin based on their famous symbol and kept in the boardroom of Farman Automobile Company in Paris (BRO AUC)

A&C 13, sold for £3,450, now worth £4-6,000

ALAN
STEELE

fine tribal arts

87 EAST HOUSTON STREET
NEW YORK
tel/fax (212) 966-3735

by appointment only

discover antiques for your home...

...at the best antiques fairs in the UK

Newark

February, April, June, August, October, December

The Newark International Antiques & Collectors Fair

Up to 4,000 exhibitors at the Newark & Notts Showground, Newark, Notts.

Detling

January, February, April, July, September, October

The Detling International Antiques & Collectors Fair

Up to 500 exhibitors at the Kent County Showground, Detling, nr Maidstone, Kent

Newmarket

February May June August October & November

The Newmarket Antiques & Collectors Fair

Up to 250 exhibitors at the Rowley Mile Racecourse, Newmarket, Suffolk.

Shepton Mallet

January, March, May, July, September, November

The Shepton Mallet Antiques & Collectors Fair

Up to 600 exhibitors at the Royal Bath & West Showground, Shepton Mallet, Somerset. 100's of outside pitches July & September only.

Ardingly

January, March, April, July, September, November

The Ardingly International Antiques & Collectors Fair

Up to 1,700 exhibitors at the South of England Showground, Ardingly, West Sussex.

Malvern

Every month

The Malvern Antiques & Collectors Fair

Up to 200 exhibitors at The Three Counties Showground, Malvern, Worcestershire.

dmg FAIRS ANTIQUES

For more information on the fairs and dates for 2005 please call **01636 702326** or visit **www.dmgantiquefairs.com**
To buy visitor tickets in advance call **01636 605107**

ROBERT BAILEY FAIRS

Organisers of quality

ANTIQUES & FINE ART FAIRS

for the more discerning collector

Venues include
Claridge's, Harewood House, Tatton Park, Hatfield House, Buxton Pavilion Gardens, Seaford College, Pavilions of Harrogate

For our full list of nationwide events please view our website at www.baileyfairs.co.uk or telephone 01277 214 677 to request a copy of our latest catalogue

PENMAN ANTIQUES FAIRS

FAIRS OF DISTINCTION, OFFERING GOOD QUALITY & VALUE
FURNITURE, ART AND ARTIFACTS FROM THE LAST 400 YEARS.
EVERYTHING VETTED FOR AUTHENTICITY AND ATTRACTIVELY
DISPLAYED FOR SALE BY RESPECTED DEALERS & GALLERIES.

January 13 - 16
WEST LONDON ANTIQUES & FINE ART FAIR
Kensington Town Hall, Hornton St, London W8

February 11 - 13
PETERSFIELD ANTIQUES FAIR
Festival Hall, Heath Rd, Petersfield, Hampshire

February 17 - 20
CHESTER ANTIQUES & FINE ART SHOW
County Grandstand, Chester Racecourse, Cheshire.

March 11 - 13
MORRIS to MACKINTOSH 1860-1925
Chelsea Old Town Hall, Kings Road, SW3

April 21 - 24
CHELSEA ART FAIR
(modern art) Chelsea Old Town Hall, Kings Rd, SW3

June 3 - 5
DULWICH ART FAIR
(modern art) Christisson Hall, Dulwich College, SE21

August 19 - 21
THE ANGLIAN CONTEMPORARY ART FAIR
Cressing Temple Barns Nr Braintree, Essex

September 2 - 4
BURY ST EDMUNDS ANTIQUES & FINE ART FAIR
The Athenaeum, Angel Hill, Bury, Suffolk

September 9 - 11
PETERSFIELD ANTIQUES FAIR (as February)

September 16 - 25
CHELSEA ANTIQUES FAIR
Chelsea Old Town Hall, Kings Rd, SW3

October **UCKFIELD** ANTIQUES FAIR to be confirmed

October 27-30 **CHESTER** ANTIQUES & FINE ART SHOW

Tel **0870 350 2442** info@penman-fairs.co.uk
Details, Exhibitor Lists & Complimentary Tickets via
www.penman-fairs.co.uk
or write for brochure to Caroline Penman,
Widdicombe, Bedford Place, Uckfield, E Sussex TN22 1LW

Jopson's Jewellers

Border
F I N E A R T S

Your largest local stockist

3 Carlyles Court, Fisher Street, Carlisle CA3 8RY
T: 01228 525042   F: 01228 525088
E: malcolm@jopsonsjewellers.co.uk

The Grosvenor House Art & Antiques Fair

UNDER THE PATRONAGE OF
HER ROYAL HIGHNESS
PRINCESS ALEXANDRA

16-22 June 2005

Grosvenor House
Park Lane   London W1

Private Preview 15 June
Charity Gala Evening 16 June

From Pharaohs to Frink —
5000 years of fine art

telephone +44 (0)20 7399 8100
www.grosvenor-antiquesfair.co.uk

Devon County Antiques Fairs

01363 82571

www.antiques-fairs.com

Westpoint Exhibition Centre, Exeter

The South West's Premier Antique, Fine Art,
Decorative and Collectors Fair
Up to 500 stands including Furniture
Fri 5th to Sun 7th Nov 2004

2005: Jan 8/9, Mar 5/6, Apr 30 - May 1, Jul 2/3, Sep 3/4, Nov 5/6

The Matford Centre, Exeter

The Largest Saturday Fair in the Country
230 inside stands plus up to 100 outside and
250 undercover outside stands
Sat 27th Nov 2004

2005: Feb 5, Mar 19, May 28, Jul 23, Oct 1, Nov 26

Westland Sports & Social Complex, Yeovil

100 plus Stands
Sun 24th Oct & 19th Dec 2004

2005: Feb 13, Apr 17, Jun 12, Jul 31, Oct 23, Dec 18

The Salisbury Leisure Centre
140 Stands
Sat 4th Dec 2004

2005: Feb 26, May 21, Sep 17, Dec 3

Royal Cornwall Showground, Wadebridge
250 Inside Stands
Plus Unlimited Outside Pitches
Thur 31st Mar & Fri 1st Apr 2005
Fri 19th & Sat 20th Aug 2005

Devon County Antiques Fairs Ltd
The Glebe House, Nymet Tracey, Crediton, Devon Ex17 6DB

WEST DEAN
COLLEGE

Graduate & Postgraduate Diploma Programmes
validated by the University of Sussex

Conservation–Restoration of:

ANTIQUE CLOCKS
ANTIQUE FURNITURE
BOOKS & LIBRARY MATERIALS
CERAMICS & RELATED MATERIALS
FINE METALWORK

New full-time diploma programmes available:

MA CONSERVATION STUDIES
Accessible through Postgraduate study

PGDip CONSERVATION OF BUILDINGS, INTERIORS AND SITES

- Students work on objects of historical importance from museums & private collections

- The low number of students allows for a high level of personal tuition from practising professionals

The department also runs professional development short courses:

BUILDING CONSERVATION MASTERCLASSES
PROFESSIONAL CONSERVATORS IN PRACTICE

For the prospectus and further details contact:

Admissions Office, West Dean College, West Dean, Chichester, West Sussex, PO18 0QZ, UK
T +44(0)1243 818299
E diplomas@westdean.org.uk
www.westdean.org.uk

A Coven of Witches . . . a journey into a delightfully interesting and unique escape from everyday life into a world of intrigue and mystic wonder. A shop like no other with a world of talents and surprises and many superb originals by local artists.

A Coven of Witches is situated in the tiny village of Burley, a village saturated with history dating back to the Bronze age.

The New Forest has always had a history of witchcraft but Burley had its own famous witch.

We have a range of gifts made especially for A Coven of Witches which includes cauldrons, bats, pot-bellied stoves, oil burners, lucky witches, dragons, peg bags, aprons, oven gloves, T-towels and shopping bags. We also have a large collection of antique witches balls and the occasional antique cast iron cauldron. Also available are a large range of New Forest Deer Antlers sold in pairs or singles.

We have a large range of Holistic and magical books, tarots, besoms, runes, crystal balls, Alterware, hand blended oils and Pagan/witch artwork, Reiki candles, hazel wands and special crystal healing wands, handmade by an experienced practitioner of the Craft and various spells created by local hedge witches We also stock the obligatory witches cats, bats, frogs, owls, moles and a fantastic range of mushrooms and toadstools

Our ranges are so vast that it would be impossible to include everything — therefore we invite you to visit the wonderful New Forest and sample the unique atmosphere of our mystical, magical shop. Also, there are several pleasant walks around Burley village for you to enjoy.

Go on - we won't put a spell on you!

The largest Border Fine Arts stockist in the south of England — supplying these exquisite figurines to our collectors for 25 years.

Large selection of discontinued pieces always available.

Are you looking for that rare out-of-production figurine? Why not enlist on our free seekers column?

Mail order available

The Cross, Burley, Ringwood,
Hampshire BH24 4AA
Telephone: 01425 402 449
Email: tuckerheadwitch@aol.com

www.covenofwitches.co.uk

A Coven of Witches

FOUR IN ONE PROMOTIONS

MAMMOTH

Antiques and Collectors & Specialist Collectors Fairs

Established organisers of regular events at the following venues . . .

DONINGTON PARK
EXHIBITION CENTRE, DERBYSHIRE
Next to Nottingham East Midlands Airport

EDINBURGH
ROYAL HIGHLAND CENTRE, INGLISTON
Adjacent to Edinburgh Airport

THE BRITISH INTERNATIONAL COLLECTORS FAIR
DONINGTON PARK, DERBYSHIRE

KELSO
SPRINGWOOD PARK KELSO
Scottish Borders

Visit our website for more information and dates

Telephone (0116) 277 4396   Fax (0121) 360 3649   Email: fourinonepromotions@btinternet.com

www.antiquesnews.co.uk/mammoth

EAST BERKSHIRE

ANTIQUES FAIR

BERKSHIRE COLLEGE OF AGRICULTURE
HALL PLACE • BURCHETTS GREEN • MAIDENHEAD

SPRING & AUTUMN FAIRS

- Over 50 Quality Exhibitors
- Wide Variety of Antiques
- Free Car Parking
- Bar and Refreshments
- AA Sign Posted — M4 (J8/9) M40 (J4) then A404M

(Near Maidenhead)

CONTACT US FOR DETAILS ON THE NEXT FAIR

Admission £4.00 including catalogue

Organised by Fair Antiques 07967 631518

★ THE QUALITY EVENT OF THE COUNTY ★

MALVERN
THREE COUNTIES SHOWGROUND - M5 JUNCTION 7/8
GIANT FLEA & COLLECTORS FAIR
Pre-booked Inside Stall £35 Outside Pitch £25 on gate
Admission: Trade 7.30am Public 9.00-4.00pm £2.50

CHELTENHAM RACECOURSE
M5 JUNCTION 10/11
ANTIQUES & COLLECTORS FAIR

Single Stand £32 pre-booked
Admission:
Trade FWC 8.00–10.00 am
Public 9.00–4.00 £2

WESTON SUPER MARE
WINTER GARDENS PAVILLION
ANTIQUE & COLLECTORS FAIR & FLEA MARKET

Single Stand £25
Admission:
Trade FWC 8.30–10.00 am
Public 9.00–4.00 £1

For details or a booking form please contact Town & Country Fairs Ltd
21 Market Street, Wellington, Telford
Tel: 01952 242019 Fax: 01952 245863 Mobile: 07979 243266
Email: suegoodall@townandcountrymarkets.co.uk

PORCELAIN
RESTORATION COURSES

The Mowbray School offers:

SHORT COURSES

In Basic China Mending, suitable for anyone seeking a leisure interest restoring their own damaged pieces.

EXTENDED COURSES

From Beginners to Advanced Level, ideal for those wishing to pursue Porcelain Restoration on a more professional basis.

Further details:

The Mowbray School of Porcelain Restoration, Flint Barn, West End Lane, Essendon, Hatfield, Herts AL9 5RQ

Telephone 020-8367 1786 or 01707 270158

Email mowbraycourses@btopenworld.com
www.mowbrayrestoration.com

❖ **TWO FABULOUS FAIRS** ❖

Antiques & Collectors Fairs with 'Drive-Ins'

Goodwood Racecourse
GOODWOOD, Near CHICHESTER, WEST SUSSEX

Admission from 7am (T/Card) £5pp & from 9am £2.50pp (B/Hols £3pp)
Concessions from 9am, £2pp (B/Hols £2.50pp)

❖ **INSIDE STALLS • OUTSIDE PITCHES AT BOTH VENUES** ❖

Lingfield Park
RACECOURSE, LINGFIELD, SURREY
(M25 junction 6, then 5 miles south on A22)

Trade are very welcome — FWC from 7am until 9am only
Admission from 9am, £1.50pp — Lots of easy parking

REGULAR FAIRS AT BOTH VENUES ON BANK HOLIDAYS & SUNDAYS – PLEASE CONTACT US FOR DETAILS

ENQUIRIES AND BOOKINGS
TELEPHONE: 01737 812 989   MOBILE: 07802 768 364
email: orchard.cottage@clara.co.uk

Bourne & Son ltd
Traditional Handmade Furniture
Every Piece a Work of Art

Anything can be made using traditional and modern day materials to your own design, fitted or freestanding. Every piece is made with care and an eye to detail, a work of art.

Fitted bedrooms, kitchens, even to a fitted office for those who work from home. Display cabinets, TV units, coffee tables, reproduction furniture produced to name but a few.

We also undertake leathering and repairs. Very competitive prices.

Telephone 01273 491554 Mobile 07710 272532
or visit www.bourneandson.com

Unit 23a Firsland Park Ind. Est., Henfield Road, Albourne, Sussex BN6 9JJ

COTSWOLD PINE
ANTIQUE TRADE WAREHOUSE

The Old Poultry Farm, Middle Aston,
Oxfordshire OX25 5QL
Telephone & Fax: 01869 340963

ANTIQUES BOUGHT & SOLD

NEW STOCK
A SUPERB SELECTION OF HANDMADE IRON
DOOR AND CABINET FURNITURE FOR SALE

Furniture for sale in all states, finished,
ready to go or needing restoration.

Have a go yourself, or pay us to do the restoration.

We also offer a restoration, stripping and wax finishing service.

Hours: Monday–Saturday 9am–6pm, Sunday 10am–4.30pm

Penny Arcade MACHINES

Relive those fun days of yesteryear!

THE FABULOUS 'ALLWINS'

Beautifully recreated amusements from the past

- Available from stock
- Each machine incorporates a solid hard wood frame
- All 6 styles now in stock
- Available for 2p standard play,
- Adjustable for money only return, or money and free game

Prices from £190.00 + VAT (£223.25)

'Kickers'

A completely new style of machine in 2 great designs

Punch & Judy

Shoot

Send For FREE Colour Brochure

NOSTALGIC MACHINES
P.O.BOX 32
WOMBOURNE,
WOLVERHAMPTON
WV5 8YS
Tel/Fax:
01902 897879

Please send me my FREE colour brochure

Mr/Mrs/Miss _____

Address: _____

_____

Postcode: _____

Telephone: _____

Registration No. 3267027

www.nostalgicmachines.com

TRADE ENQUIRIES WELCOME

Sue Pearson
Dolls & Teddy Bears Est. 1975

Rare Cinnamon steiff, circa 1905 (left) with 'Centre Seam' face - superb - POA

Early 'boot-button-eyed' Bing (right), excellent original condition - POA

Vintage bears are guaranteed to be as stated – backed up by 30 years of experience and numerous published books

Appolonia – 72cm, 'The Toy Shoppe' (USA) Exclusive edition of 1500 – £375 + £10 P&P. Named for Appolonia Margarete Steiff, Appolonia is a 'Toy Shoppe' Exclusive edition and companion for the very special 2003 bear Maxmilian.

He is also still available, though soon to sell out, he is a huge 80cm and is £399.

We are now the exclusive UK Stockist of the top US Steiff retailer 'The Toy Shoppe'.

Richard Steiff Bear – 18 inch, 'Toy Shoppe Exclusive', Edition of 1500, £225 + £10 P&P.

A stunning recreation of Richard Steiff's 1905 bear – truly the father of all teddy bears.

Comes with a copy of his sketch book containing many wonderful drawings a photo of him at work.

R. John Wright – White Rabbit. Fully jointed and constructed of the finest mohair plush with molded felt hands with individual fingers. He has leather-covered eyes and hand-embroidered features.

He appears as Alice first saw him at the beginning of Alice's Adventures in Wonderland dressed in a beautifully tailored felt tattersall jacket, fitted brocade waistcoat, and plaid felt ascot – £495.

We buy and sell previous years Steiff and R. John Wright, as well as being stockist of all the major bear manufacturers. Huge range of artist bears available from around the world.

We also offer a Teddy Hospital service with expert restorers.

For new bears and to enter our monthly competition, visit us online: www.suepearson.co.uk

For our vintage bears: www.sue-pearson.co.uk

18 Brighton Square 'The Lanes' Brighton BN1 1HD Tel. 01273 774 851 Email: jasper@suepearson.co.uk

JAGUAR QUALITY

ANTIQUE & COLLECTORS FAIRS

FOR MORE INFORMATION VISIT

www.jaguarfairs.com

JAGUAR FAIRS LTD., PO BOX 158, DERBY, DE21 5ZA TEL: 01332 831404

PIOB MHOR *of* SCOTLAND

Border
FINE ARTS

SCOTTISH ANTIQUES,
GIFTS & COLLECTABLES

37–43 High Street   Blairgowrie
Perthshire PH10 6DA

Telephone +44 (0)1250 872 131
Fax +44 (0)1250 873 649

www.piobmhor-of-scotland.co.uk
www.clancol.dircon.co.uk

TITUS KENDALL

4TH FLOOR   ORMOND HOUSE
3 DUKE OF YORK STREET   LONDON SW1Y 6JP

DEALER AND AGENT IN ANTIQUE

SILVER

AND WORKS OF ART

WHETHER BUYING OR SELLING
SINGLE PIECES OR COLLECTIONS
ALL IS HANDLED WITH
THE UTMOST DISCRETION

by appointment only

TELEPHONE: 020-7839 1454
FAX: 020-7321 0685

Expert in Russian Art

Petr Vereshagin. **A View of the Kremlin in Moscow.** *Sold for 580.000 €*

If you are interested in selling Russian art and antiques we recommend you to contact our experts at Bukowski-Hörhammer. In recent years Helsinki has become an important centre for the sale of Russian art due to the success of our auctions.

Top ten Russian artworks sold in the spring 2004

Artist	Price (EUR)	Artist	Price (EUR)
1. Petr Vereshagin	580.000	6. Firs Zhuravlev	62.000
2. Konstantin Juon	175.000	7. Vladimir Muraviev	54.000
3. Nicolai Sergeyev	80.000	8. Robert Falk	54.000
4. Konstantin Makovski	76.000	9. Jossif Kratschkowski	53.000
5. Alexandr Villevalde	68.000	10. Izrael Pass	36.000

www.bukowski.fi

Telephone: +358 (0) 6689110 Fax: +358 (0) 6121266

Bukowskis HÖRHAMMER

BUKOWSKI OY AB ⦙ ISO ROOBERTINKATU 12 00120 HELSINKI, FINLAND ⦙ E-MAIL: BUKOWSKI@BUKOWSKI.FI

Beauty Past Change

Beauty Past Change

THE PIED PIPER

of Cheltenham

Why Not Invest?

in a . . . **Steiff** Limited Edition or a **Deb Canham** Miniature
or a **Merrythought Rocking Horse** for the grandchildren?

Call Georgie on 01242 251 532 or visit us anytime in Cheltenham.
Quote 'MG05' for a special 10% discount.

Jill & Nane
by Hildegard Gunzel £1,195

Pembroke Grange £220 (kitform)

Antonia by Bevern Baren £269

GREAT QUALITY BABY GIFTS
and PLAY DOLLS from GOTZ

Steiff British Collectors Bear
Limited Edition 4000 £139

Shire Rocking Horse
by Merrythought £480

Winnie-the-Pooh
New Limited Steiff £225

Jim from
Deans £75

1 Montpellier Avenue Cheltenham Gloucestershire GL50 1SA
Telephone: 01242 251 532 Email: piedpiperchelt@aol.com

Geli by
Annette Himstedt £415

Order online at www.piedpiper.uk.com or www.bearsanddolls.co.uk

Classic Ceramics

Specialist Suppliers of early Staffordshire & fine English Pottery

*Pot Lids • Pastille Burners • Measham
Staffordshire figures & animals • Toby Jugs*

Tel: 01278 425752
Email: info@classic-ceramics.com
www.classic-ceramics.com

Grays Antique Market

is home to one of the largest and most diverse collections of fine antiques, jewellery and collectables in the world. Seconds from Bond Street and Oxford Street, Grays is a focus of the London antiques trade and is home to some of its finest dealers.

The labyrinth corridors of Grays are a hive of activity with dealers and collectors alike searching through the myriad treasures hoping to find that special piece. For those who don't have the patience to wait for an auction in their field of interest, Grays and its sister markets present a splendid alternative with such a massive range of high quality items available to purchase all year round.

The market is situated in a beautiful nineteenth century terracotta building in the heart of London's West End, is second away from Sotheby's, Phillip's, Asprey's, the Royal Academy and the many other institutions which make London the unquestioned epicentre of the art and antique dealing world.

1-7 Davies Mews, 58 Davies Street, London W1K 5AB Tel: 020 7629 7034

Grays is open Monday to Friday from 10AM to 6PM

The splendid Grade 2 listed building was commissioned by John Bolding and Son, the water closet manufacturers – 'a toilet factory'. In the 19th century they vied with Thomas Crapper for supremacy, and whilst it is his name rather than theirs that has entered the dictionary they nevertheless left us a supreme legacy in the building that is now Grays. In the true spirit of the great 19th century merchants they took great pride in creating from scratch a headquarters that was just as much a thing of beauty as a functional site. It is this tradition that Bennie Gray bore in mind when he set about restoring the near-derelict glories of the former water closet showroom.

Alfies Antique Market

13-25 Church Street, Marylebone, London NW8 8DT
Tel: 020 7723 6066 www.alfiesantiques.com

Have a hunt amongst the treasure troves for bargains galore and find something special for everyone! Whether you have ten minutes or two hours, Alfies will captivate and enthral you with their vast array of wares.

Alfies is a hidden oasis to any gift seeker. Tucked away in the heart of Marylebone, Alfies is home to over 100 dealers spread across the five floors. Alfies is the perfect place to be inspired by an abundance of unique collectables, twentieth century design, antiques and vintage fashion.

If you're looking for stocking fillers or extravagant gifts for your beloved, Alfies offers presents that are unique, one-off and from the heart. Prices can range from £6 for original 1960s car badges, £70 for 1950s never-worn lingerie to £170 for silver 1950s cocktail shakers.

Alfies has it all under one roof. From pristine antique furniture and ornate wall-hangings, through to timeless vintage jewellery and fashion, art deco items and decorative interior pieces, Alfies has it all.

"Generally speaking, people looking for art and antiques want four things which hardly ever hang together - a huge selection, the genuine item, bargain prices and an enjoyable search. Alfies Antique Market is about the only place which has it all in spades." Bennie Gray, Proprietor of Alfies.

Alfies in located in a former Edwardian department store 'Jordons.' Alfies was opened by Bennie Gray in 1976 and is the sister market to Grays Antique Market in Mayfair. A careful and extensive rebuilding programme in 1988 culminated in Alfies receiving a four-storey extension. The market complex now covers 35,000 square feet over five floors. A restaurant is also located on the top floor of the building.

Many of the dealers and their goods feature regularly in the media with fashion and interior journalists often using items from Alfies for photos shoots and props. TV and film production companies also use Alfies to source items for period productions.

Dealers at Alfies profit from low overheads and are therefore able to sell at trade prices - one of the main reasons designers and collectors alike consider Alfies to be a mecca in London.

Alfies is open Tuesday to Saturday from 10AM to 6PM

SPITALFIELDS
ANTIQUE MARKET
Commercial Street, London E1
EVERY THURSDAY 7am - 3pm

COVENT GARDEN
ANTIQUE MARKET
The Jubilee Hall, Southampton St
Covent Garden WC2
EVERY MONDAY from 6am

STRATFORD-UPON-AVON
ANTIQUE CENTRE
60 Ely St, Stratford-upon-Avon
7 DAYS A WEEK 10am - 5pm

YORK
ANTIQUE CENTRE
2a Lendel, York
MON - SAT 10am - 5pm

Tel: 020 7240 7405
Sherman & Waterman Associates

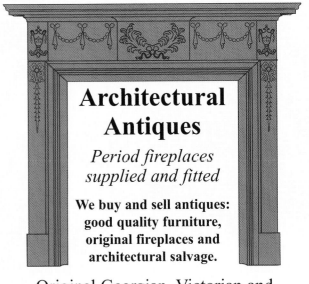

Architectural Antiques
Period fireplaces supplied and fitted

**We buy and sell antiques:
good quality furniture,
original fireplaces and
architectural salvage.**

Original Georgian, Victorian and
Edwardian fireplaces in marble, slate, cast
iron, mahogany, oak and pine.

*Please call in or telephone
Mon-Fri 12 pm-5pm, Sat 9am-5pm*

Tel: **01234 213131**
70 Pembroke Sreet, **BEDFORD**, MK40 3RQ
(Take M1: Junction 13 or A1: A428)

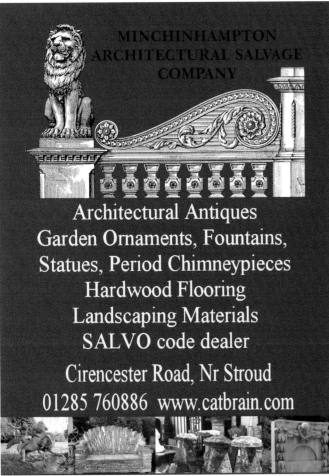

MINCHINHAMPTON ARCHITECTURAL SALVAGE COMPANY

Architectural Antiques
Garden Ornaments, Fountains,
Statues, Period Chimneypieces
Hardwood Flooring
Landscaping Materials
SALVO code dealer

Cirencester Road, Nr Stroud
01285 760886 www.catbrain.com

don't replace your bath, phone us first...

**All work done on site
for a fraction of the
replacement cost...**

- Bath resurfacing
- Chip & abrasion repairs
- Chemical cleaning, descaling and polishing
- Non-slip surface application
- Domestic, building trade and leisure industry
- Free quotations

FREEPHONE
0800 138 2202
www.renubath.co.uk
Please quote ref. F2G   Est.1965

renu bath

GROSVENOR STONE

Manufacturers of composite and natural stone pieces

Discover the beauty of stone

Manufacturers of natural & composite stone products handmade at our Chester workshops

Architectural, garden, landscaping & bespoke products

Golborne Bridge Farm, Handley, Chester CH3 9DR Telephone 01829 770 632 Fax 01829 770 642

www.grosvenorstone.co.uk

New CD Brochure available upon request

Key to photographic credits

What's It Worth? and *Antiques & Collectables* are very grateful to the following for the use of their photographs, catalogue information and hammer price or estimate.

Most are listed in our price guide by initials, some by their full name.

ACAD   Academy Auctioneers & Valuers
Tel: 020 8579 7466

AMER   Amersham Auction Rooms
Tel: 08700460606
www.amershamauctionrooms.co.uk

Antique Bathrooms of Ivybridge
Tel: 01752 698250
www.antiquebaths.com

The Antique Trader
Tel: 020 7359 2019
www.millineryworks.co.uk

Assembly Antiques
Tel: 01225 310388

www.bath.co.uk/babada/markets

BEAR   Bearne's Auctioneers & Valuers of Fine Art
Tel: 01392 207000
www.bearnes.co.uk

Bloomsbury Auctions
Tel: 020 7495 9494
www.bloomsbury-book-auct.com

BON   Bonhams, London
Tel: 020 7393 3900
www.bonhams.com

(PH BA)   Bonhams, Bath
Tel: 01225 788988
www.bonhams.com

(PH ED)   Bonhams, Edinburgh

Tel: 0131 225 2266
www.bonhams.com

(PH KN)   Bonhams, West Midlands
Tel: 01564 776151
www.bonhams.com

BOO   Boothman's
Tel: 01244 312300

BRI   Brightwells Fine Art Saleroom
Tel: 01568 611122
www.brightwells.com

BRIS AUC   Dreweatt Neate
(Bristol Auction Rooms)
Tel: 0117 973 7201
www.dnfa.com/bristol

BR AUC   Brooks Auctioneers Ltd
Tel: 020 7228 8000
www.brooks.co.uk

BK   Bruton Knowles
Tel: 012042 573904
www.bkonline.co.uk

CANT   Canterbury Auction Galleries
Tel: 01227 763337
www.thecanterburyauctiongalleries.com

Capes Dunn
Tel: 0161 273 1991

www.capesdunn.com

CHEF   Cheffins
Tel: 01223 213343
www.cheffins.co.uk

CHRIS   Christie's
Tel: 020 7839 9060
www.christies.com

CLEV   Clevedon Salerooms
Tel: 01934 830111
www.clevedon-salerooms.com

COLL   Collectoys
www.collectoys.fr

CO OW   Cooper Owen or COOP
Tel: 020 7240 4132
www.cooperowen.com

COTT   Cottees Auctioneers & Valuers
Tel: 01929 552826

www.auctionsatcottees.co.uk

CRIT   Criterion Auctioneers
Tel: 020 7359 5707
www.criterion-auctioneers.co.uk

DANDO   Andrew Dando Antiques
Tel: 01225 865444
www.andrewdando.co.uk

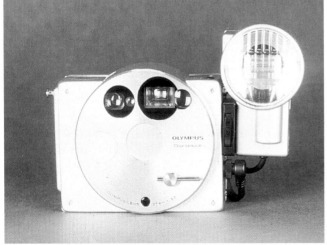

DAH — Dee Atkinson & Harrison
Tel: 01377 253151
www.dahauctions.com

DPSG — Drew Pritchard Stained Glass
Tel: 01492 874004
www.drewpritchard.co.uk

DREW — Dreweatt Neate Fine Art Auctioneers
Tel: 01635 553588
www.auctions.dreweatt-neate.co.uk

FELL — Fellows & Sons Auctioneers and Valuers
Tel: 0121 212 2131
www.fellows.co.uk

George Formby Society
www.georgeformby.co.uk

FRAS — Fraser's Autographs
Tel: 020 7836 9325
www.frasersautographs.com

GORR — Gorringes
Tel: 01273 472503
www.gorringes.co.uk

Greenslade Taylor Hunt
Tel: 01823 332525
www.gth.net

Grimes House Antiques
Tel: 01608 651029
www.grimeshouse.co.uk

HART — Andrew Hartley
Tel: 01943 816363

www.andrewhartleyfinearts.co.uk
Hallidays Fine Antiques
Tel: 01865 340028
www.hallidays.com

HAMP — Hamptons International Auctioneers & Valuers
Tel: 01483 423567
www.hamptons.co.uk/fineart

Paul Hopwell Antiques
Tel: 01788 510636
www.antiqueoak.co.uk

George Kidner
Tel: 01590 670070
www.georgekidner.co.uk

LASSCO Architectural Salvage
Tel: 020 7749 9944
www.lassco.co.uk/antiques

LAW — Law Fine Art
Tel: 01635 860033
www.lawfineart.co.uk

LW — Leaske Ward
Tel: 020 7435 9781

LOCK — Locke & England Auctioneers and Valuers
Tel: 01926 889100
www.leauction.co.uk

LOD — Loddon Auctionswww.loddonauctions.com

LTAY — Louis Taylor Fine Art Auctioneers
Tel: 01782 215283

LYTU — Lyon & Turnbull
Tel: 0131 557 8844
www.lyonandturnbull.com

MALL — Mallams
Tel: 01865 241358
www.mallams.co.uk

MILL — Miller's Collectables 2003/4
www.millers.uk.com
Publisher: Miller's
ISBN 1-84000-852-0

Minchinhampton Architectural Salvage
Tel: 01285 760886
www.cabtrain.com

Movie Market
Tel: 01935 811000
www.moviemarket.co.uk

PH — Phillips
(see Bonhams, London)

PH BA — Phillips
(see Bonhams, Bath)

PH ED — Phillips
(see Bonhams, Edinburgh)

PH KN — Phillips Knowle
(see Bonhams, West Midlands)

Nicholas S Pitcher
Tel: 020 7499 6621
www.asianart.com/pitcher

Barry Potter Auctions
Tel: 01642 767116
www.vectis.co.uk

Quintet Publishing
Tel: 020 7700 8001
www.quarto.com

RDP — Richard Dennis Publications
Tel: 01460 240044
www.richarddennispublications.com

ROSE — Rosebery's
Tel: 020 8761 2522
www.roseberys.co.uk

Royal Collections PR
Tel: 020 7839 1377

Rugby Relics
Tel: 01639 646725
www.rugbyrelics.com

SHREW — Shrewsbury Antique Centre
Tel: 01743 247704

Somervale Antiques
(now ceased trading)
www.somervaleantiques.co.uk

SOTH — Sotheby's
Tel: 020 7293 5000
www.sothebys.com

SPEC AUC — Special Auction Services
Tel: 01189 712949
www.invaluable.com/sas

SPI — Spink
Tel: 020 7563 4000
www.spink.com

TF — Taylor & Fletcher Auctions
Tel 01451 821666

RT — Rupert Toovey
Tel: 01903 891955
www.rupert-toovey.com

Lee Towersy
www.brookebondcollectables.co.uk

VEC and VECTIS — Vectis Toy Collectors
Tel: 01642 750616
www.vectis.co.uk

WA WA — Wallis & Wallis
Tel: 01273 480208
www.wallisandwallis.co.uk

WINT — Wintertons Fine Art
Tel: 01543 263256
www.wintertons.co.uk

WOWA — Woolley and Wallis Fine Art Auctioneers
Tel: 01722 424500
www.woolleyandwallis.co.uk

Index to Advertisers

Index

For ease of reference, all of the sections and their divisions are arranged alphabetically

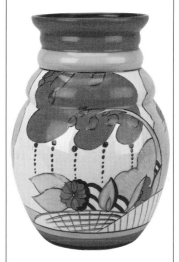

FREE FAIR TICKETS

BEST ANTIQUES • BEST FOR COLLECTORS • BRILLIANT VALUE!

October 2004 Issue 66 £2.95

Antiques & Collectables

Stylish Dresser
Best designer label

OVER £440 WORTH OF GOODIES UP FOR GRABS!

DISCOVER BRIGHTON
A city for all ages

BARE-FACED EXPERTISE

ERIC KNOWLES

WHAT'S IT WORTH? 10-PAGE BUMPER ILLUSTRATED PRICE GUIDE

MARLON BRANDO CELEBRATING THE SCREEN LEGEND

Passion for fashion
Collect vintage glamour

PLUS BOOK BINDING
• KATE GREENAWAY • FREE VALUATIONS • TOY TALK
• TRAVEL COLLECTABLES
• FAIR & AUCTION LISTINGS
• RECLAMATION • NEWS
www.antiques-collectables.co.uk

5 reasons why you should subscribe

- Three past issues of A&C free!
- FREE post
- You never miss an issue
- Protection from any price increase
- A further 12 issues of A&C delivered to your door

3 FREE back issues

WHEN YOU SUBSCRIBE

Subscribe now and get any three available back issues free! Want to know more about Wedgwood? Need to know how much your Art Deco is worth? Choose from our list on the following pages and fill in the form below – but hurry, many issues are in limited supply – 17 back issues have sold out already!

Antiques & Collectables magazine offers you great value for money. This is why we are the <u>No.1</u> antiques magazine in the UK.

CALL OUR ORDER HOTLINE TODAY ON 01225 786814
Quote code AC67 when calling

You can also subscribe online at
www.antiques-collectables.co.uk

Free back issues offer open to UK residents only. In the event of a back issue being sold out, we will offer an alternative issue. Please order early to avoid disappointment.

SUBSCRIPTION ORDER FORM

✓ **YES!** I would like to subscribe to *Antiques & Collectables!*

☐ UK 12 ISSUES **£35.40**

☐ EIRE/EUR 12 ISSUES **£57.20** ☐ REST WORLD 12 ISSUES **£82.20**

Issue **1** Qty ☐   Issue **24** Qty ☐   Issue **44** Qty ☐
Issue **4** Qty ☐   Issue **25** Qty ☐   Issue **45** Qty ☐
Issue **5** Qty ☐   Issue **26** Qty ☐   Issue **46** Qty ☐
Issue **6** Qty ☐   Issue **27** Qty ☐   Issue **48** Qty ☐
Issue **8** Qty ☐   Issue **28** Qty ☐   Issue **49** Qty ☐
Issue **9** Qty ☐   Issue **29** Qty ☐   Issue **50** Qty ☐
Issue **11** Qty ☐   Issue **30** Qty ☐   Issue **52** Qty ☐
Issue **12** Qty ☐   Issue **31** Qty ☐   Issue **53** Qty ☐
Issue **13** Qty ☐   Issue **32** Qty ☐   Issue **55** Qty ☐
Issue **14** Qty ☐   Issue **33** Qty ☐   Issue **56** Qty ☐
Issue **15** Qty ☐   Issue **34** Qty ☐   Issue **59** Qty ☐
Issue **16** Qty ☐   Issue **35** Qty ☐   Issue **61** Qty ☐
Issue **17** Qty ☐   Issue **37** Qty ☐   Issue **62** Qty ☐
Issue **18** Qty ☐   Issue **40** Qty ☐   Issue **63** Qty ☐
Issue **19** Qty ☐   Issue **41** Qty ☐   Issue **64** Qty ☐
Issue **21** Qty ☐   Issue **42** Qty ☐   Issue **65** Qty ☐
Issue **23** Qty ☐   Issue **43** Qty ☐   Issue **66** Qty ☐

☐ Please tick this box if you would prefer not to receive information on tailored offers and promotions

YOUR DETAILS (BLOCK CAPITALS PLEASE)

Full Name (Mr/Mrs/Miss/Ms) _____

Address _____

Postcode _____

Telephone _____

PAYMENT DETAILS

I enclose a cheque/postal orders for £_____ : _____ (payable to Merricks Media Ltd)

or please debit my credit/debit card to the sum of £_____ : _____

Card no.

Expiry Date   /   Issue/Valid Date   /

Card Holders Name

Signature   Date

Please return this form along with payment to:
Antiques & Collectables Subscriptions Dept., Merricks Media Ltd,
Units 3&4 Riverside Court, Lower Bristol Road, Bath BA2 3DZ, ENGLAND

WIWB01